thor photo: Sanjay Malapur

Nilanjan Mukhopadhyay embarked on a career in journalism in the early 1980s and is best known for his reportage and analysis of the rise and growth of Hindu organisations, their politics and agitations. He was among the first journalists to track the emergence of the Ram Janmabhoomi-Babri Masjid conflict from the late 1980s. He has followed, and written about, the political and electoral emergence of the BJP and its allies from that period.

He is the author of *The Demolition: India at the Crossroads* (1994), one of the first books on the Ayodhya discord and the rise of Hindutva. His biography of Narendra Modi, *Narendra Modi: The Man, the Times*, was published in early 2013, before Modi's campaign to become prime minister took off. It is widely considered the most credible and authoritative account of Modi's rise to power. His most recent book, *The Demolition and the Verdict: Ayodhya and the Project to Reconfigure India*, was published in 2021. He is a regular columnist in, and contributor to, several leading newspapers and web portals, and a well-known commentator and host on Indian television news and video channels. An unabashed college dropout, he lives in India's National Capital Region.

By the Same Author

Narendra Modi: The Man, The Times

Sikhs: The Untold Agony of 1984

THE RSS

ICONS OF THE INDIAN RIGHT

NILANJAN MUKHOPADHYAY

First published by Tranquebar, an imprint of Westland Publications Private Limited, in 2019

Published by Westland Non-Fiction, an imprint of Westland Books, a division of Nasadiya Technologies Private Limited, in 2024

No. 269/2B, First Floor, 'Irai Arul', Vimalraj Street, Nethaji Nagar, Alapakkam Main Road, Maduravoyal, Chennai 600095

ISBN: 9789395767415

10 9 8 7 6 5 4 3 2 1

Typeset by Ram Das Lal and R. Ajith Kumar
Printed at Nutech Print Services, India

For Varsha...
Often the peg where I hang my stuff.

'A must read for anyone trying to understand Narendra Modi's mind.'

TCA Srinivasa Raghavan, *The Telegraph*

'The book is an excellent preface to further reading on the Hindu Right.'

The Financial Express

'Mukhopadhyay lays bare the fascinating, unique and perhaps startling world of the Rashtriya Swayamsewak Sangh.'

The Sunday Standard

'The book covers all icons of the RSS, putting in perspective the veneration of Sangh leaders by the current dispensation, and also focuses on its political aspirations.'

News18

CONTENTS

AUTHOR'S NOTE

This book defines itself. The Indian Right-wing understandably evokes extreme reactions. This is especially true of the Rashtriya Swayamsevak Sangh (RSS), its affiliates and individuals who have at various times influenced its thought processes and actions. I was drawn to its workings from the early 1980s, thanks to encouragement from my editors who gave me the opportunity to report and analyse several episodes involving communal conflict. Later, many proceeded to indulge me in what they defined as my growing 'obsession' with the Ayodhya dispute.

Often their point being, and this group gradually included many politicians and several close friends, about my interest in subjects involving sectarian violence. There was of course scepticism about my premise and many arguments would be put forth about the 'inherent secular character of Indians'. I was told ad nauseam that this was a 'transitory phase' in the history of Indian politics and that the sangh parivar constituents had 'peaked a little too early'.

Yet, my apprehensions rang true even as India was overwhelmed by several episodes, including the Babri demolition case in 1992, and the Gujarat riots almost a decade later. Even on the eve of the 2019 elections, my concern is that whichever way the final verdict goes, it will not alter the trajectory the country is already on.

One of the most difficult things about writing on this subject was to fundamentally disagree with the premise of Hindu nationalism, yet apply reason while analysing it and its iconic leaders. Over the years, considerable literature has been added to what was previously available. In my view, most of them continue to exist in black or white, either as hagiographies or denunciations. This book not only endeavours to examine the ideologies of Right-wing leaders, but also explores the personas behind the personalities.

I am sure my readers will have several complaints, foremost being that many who may have played decisive roles in bringing the Indian Right-wing to the forefront are either absent in this book, or even if present, then not in the manner many may have imagined them to be. The initial idea of limiting these portraits to mere thumbnails, did not do justice to any of the personalities listed in the book. The worry at times was that each personality included in this edition necessitated a separate book and which may turn out to be more than one. With time, and further expansion of the Indian Right-wing, and with due indulgence from my family, readers and publishers, it may be worth its while to return to the theme, but let me not worry about it at this stage.

For a variety of reasons, this book has been a long time in the making. A significant part of its form, content and style has altered over the years, save a major part of the title. Relief often becomes the overarching emotion at the end of a creative exercise and it is no different for me.

It was Gyanesh Kudaisya who had first suggested that I write this book. This was way back in 1999–2000 when Atal Bihari Vajpayee was India's prime minister and the Rashtriya Swayamsevak Sangh and its affiliates had suddenly sprung from near obscurity to centre stage. I had even written a few chapters, but made no headway as professional engagements took me on to another path. Yet, he prodded me continuously, particularly after the 2014 elections, never once giving up hope in my ability, and patiently pointing out what was lacking after he had read one of the chapters. I hope he notices that his suggestions were taken seriously.

No words shall suffice in thanking Dilip Deodhar who held my hand and guided me through what I think is an extremely complicated world inhabited by the sangh parivar. He was aware of my basic disagreement with its ideological premise, but he never shied away from sharing information, often enlightening me, besides lavishing praise for my sense of what he thought was, fairness. Dilip Deodhar introduced me to several members of the Right-wing whose identities must remain secret, for many continue to be in the RSS.

Thanks are also due to Sanjeev Kelkar for sharing his insights and understanding of the RSS, its weaknesses and strengths.

A major part of this book was written during a professionally trying period and my family stood like a rock behind me to lighten the burden. It remains a joke amongst them that restraint is not one of my virtues, but they also acknowledge that the courage to be truthful never weakened. Over the years, Gyan Verma's understanding of the Right-wing has sharpened considerably, and every conversation with him helps me to reconsider various premises. Varsha remains my first reader and critic, who constantly debated with me and enabled me to sharpen certain arguments which helped me to recast some of my views. It shall still be several years before my granddaughters understand what I write, but now they grumble less for the time not spent with them.

This has been my third book with Sudha Sadhanand as editor and we have developed a capacity to be patient with each other. Often, it was her enthusiasm for the book which prevented me from becoming cynical. I hope that her passion for the book is shared by my readers.

I would also like to thank the several books and pamphlets and other materials that I read and re-read which helped my narrative immensely.

A last word of gratitude for Sanjay Malapur who approached me in 2018 during the Bangalore Literature Festival with a request to take my pictures. I asked him if he could also take some for this book. He agreed and did a splendid job knowing well there was no other reward than seeing the photograph in print. May success come in abundance to him.

Nilanjan Mukhopadhyay
New Delhi, February 2019

KESHAV BALIRAM HEDGEWAR

In the history of the Rashtriya Swayamsevak Sangh (RSS), which is known for the domineering presence of Konkanastha or Chitpavan Brahmins, it is probably one of the biggest quirks of fate that its founder was born into a family of migrants from a village in Telangana.

In the early decades of the nineteenth century, several landless Brahmin families who made their living as priests in Nizamabad district, were forced to flee their homes under the Mughal rule. Many chose to settle in Nagpur, a city which was ruled by Maratha Bhonsle kings, mainly because the dispensation supported Vedic learning. Keshav Baliram Hedgewar's great-great-grandfather was among those who had made the city his home. Gradually, these immigrant families from Andhra Pradesh began to assimilate, and not only did they adapt to Maharashtrian customs, but also began looking up to local historical icons as their very own.

It is also paradoxical that the RSS, which was established by Keshav Baliram Hedgewar along with a few associates (mainly Brahmins), with the avowed aim of culturally and politically organising the Hindus, should have laid great emphasis on the daily physical drill.

According to several accounts, amongst different Hindu caste groups in the nineteenth century, the Brahmins were considered to be the least inclined towards martial traditions. The fact that the RSS even today gives equal weightage to *baudhik* or the intellectual capability, and *sharirik* or the physical attributes, with designated chiefs in the organisation's command structure stems from the exposure that young Keshav had to daily exercise.

Even after five decades of shifting to Nagpur, the Hedgewar clan followed the tradition of sending its male progenies to Vedic schools. Keshav's father had faced an awkward situation when he had discovered that not only was his firstborn, Mahadev, naturally drawn towards gymnastics and bodybuilding, but he had also succeeded in influencing his siblings. Keshav, the youngest male child in the family was the first to do his bidding, and willingly took to the vigorous routine suggested by his eldest brother. It was a hectic daily schedule for the young chap, but he ran several miles, swam many laps, and worked out in the makeshift gym at home. But Keshav was also an industrious boy who regularly attended school and poured over books to complete his lessons well into the night.

In school, besides religious and spiritual texts, stories eulogising historical heroes inspired him to such an extent that very soon, the iconic Maratha ruler, Shivaji Bhonsle became Keshav's indisputable ideal. At a very young age, the boy began perceiving Shivaji as the redeemer of Hindus who had been wronged by the Mughals, and dreamt of securing 'dignity' for Chhatrapati's legacy.

In Keshav's mind, the concept of classical heroism was substituted with the idea of patriotism, and there is a telling incident of how the eight-year-old boy had once expressed it by throwing away sweets that were distributed on the occasion of Queen Victoria's sixtieth anniversary in his native Nagpur.

'Of course, I got the sweets,' he told his elder brother when asked about his empty hands, and proceeded to explain rather precociously that he had thrown them away because the British had usurped power and overthrown the Bhonsle dynasty. 'How can we participate in these imperial celebrations?'[1] he is supposed to have remarked to his elder brother with great indignation.

A few years later in 1901 after King Edward VII's coronation, there was yet another round of celebrations in Nagpur. The twelve-year-old Keshav had not only kept away from the commemorative events, but had also convinced his friends to replace the Union Jack with Shivaji's standard atop the local fort. The children had failed to achieve what was deemed to be an act of sedition, but the event had made heroes out of Keshav and his band of volunteers.

Despite his growing interest in the nascent anti-Colonial struggle and local revolutionary movements, Keshav seldom lost sight of his goals. In his early Twenties, he had enrolled to study Medicine at the *indigenous*, National Medical College in Calcutta. Yet, physical exercise or *vyayaam* remained essential to his daily routine. Soon, the young doctor-in-the-making earned the epithet of a 'man with muscles of iron and nerves of steel.'[2] He would routinely throw challenges to his classmates and fellow-revolutionaries, but no one could ever manage to knock his hand down in bouts of arm-wrestling. Keshav was also famous for his huge appetite: he ate chappatis in the multiples of five, and drank several litres of milk. But despite his physical prowess, his innate sobriety and commitment to activism earned him the reputation of a significant influencer amongst the youth, but more of which later...

Early Days

In 1902, the dreaded plague brought death and devastation to the city of Nagpur. The good priest that he was, Keshav's father considered it his duty to stay put and perform obsequies for the dead. But a few weeks later, even the Hedgewars were struck by a huge tragedy—first, Baliram and his wife were consumed by the epidemic; second, their eldest son, Mahadev tired of shouldering familial responsibilities, went to seed; Seetaram, who was next to Mahadev, left Nagpur and moved to Indore, to become a priest. But Keshav remained undeterred in his life's mission and stayed on in Nagpur.

It was around this time when a young medical doctor called Balakrishna Shivram (or, B.S.) Moonje was emerging as an inspirational figure for the young radicals in Nagpur. Although the young medico had spent several years as the King's Commissioned Officer in South Africa during the Boer War, he had become a great admirer of Bal Gangadhar Tilak and joined the Indian National Congress upon his return to India. He soon took the 'orphaned' Keshav under his tutelage.

One year before the plague had hit Nagpur, Antaji Kale, a schoolteacher in Nagpur had initiated a project called Paisa Fund which was aimed at crowd-funding—considered to be the first ever in India—indigenous industries in the region. Antaji Kale had somehow managed to convince Tilak, which in turn had motivated his followers including the young Keshav, to plunge into the fund-collection drive. The young boy began visiting his neighbourhood and would seek out every person in religious congregations and festivals to make a donation of just one paisa each. Unlike the time when he had encouraged his friends to hoist Shivaji's standard on top of the local fort, Keshav's Paisa Fund pitch was a larger initiative and was aimed at the average householder to become part of India's struggle for independence.

Even as Nagpur was buzzing with several local revolutionary movements, the spirit of the swadeshi movement was spreading like a bush fire beyond Bengal and soon reached the shores of western India. Keshav became a regular at such public gatherings and was so riveted by the electrifying speeches made by political leaders that he had resolved to learn the art of public speaking.

In 1907, on a visit to his uncle's house during the festival of Dussehra, he along with some other youngsters decided to sing Vande Mataram on the dais where the ritual destruction of Ravana, symbolising evil in the Ramayana, was to be enacted. While the elders in the family had censured him for the gross transgression, Keshav was noticed by the local Intelligence officer who was stationed at the site to keep an eye out for any untoward incident. But the young lad was nonplussed and was intent on defying the establishment. For instance, in the very next year when the Inspector of Schools visited his school, Keshav had orchestrated a plan to deride him openly. The moment the Crown's representative had stepped inside a classroom, he was greeted with a loud roar of 'Vande Mataram'. The school's principal launched an enquiry into the incident, but he was stonewalled by the students who had refused to disclose the name of the accused or the group which had planned the protest. Eventually, he was forced to expel the entire batch.

However, as several schools in the region were consumed by the patriotic fervour, the students boycotted classes for two months before a compromise was worked out. The school authorities sought a written pardon from the erring students, but when Keshav had refused to give any such undertaking, his expulsion was deemed final, and he was forced to move to Pune to pursue his studies.

It was because of this disruption that Keshav Baliram Hedgewar cleared his Matriculation examination at the age of twenty. Later when he moved to Pune to pursue his higher studies and took his school-leaving examination conducted by the National Council of Education (Bengal), he was debarred from studying in all British-affiliated institutions.

By now, the robust young man had already cemented deep relationships with local revolutionary groups and had even assisted fugitives in locating to safe havens, while raising funds for groups such as the Anushilan Samiti*. Dr Moonje, who continued to play a significant role in shaping Keshav's political ideology, gave his protégé the most valuable advice: leave Nagpur, and study Medicine at the National Medical College, Calcutta. Although Keshav was severely constrained due to his poor financial condition, he managed to raise enough money with local assistance and also from his own savings that he had accumulated from fees as a private tutor. Ramlal Vajpayee, an associate of Keshav, wrote in his autobiography that the decision to send him to Calcutta was not just to train him as a doctor, but also with the 'object of receiving training for revolutionary work'[3] under the tutelage of Pulin Behari Das, the founder of the Dhaka chapter of Anushilan Samiti.

In mid-1910, the year when Vinayak Damodar Savarkar was imprisoned in the Andaman and Nicobar Islands' Cellular Jail, Keshav landed in Calcutta with a letter of introduction from Dr Moonje. He

---

* This group of revolutionary nationalists was set up in Bengal, but its key members were often forced to hide in other provinces after committing violent acts against the British.

was on his way to becoming a medical doctor and would later acquire the moniker of 'Doctor Saheb' within the RSS.

Calcutta Days

By the time K.B. Hedgewar arrived in Calcutta, the swadeshi movement had considerably ebbed in Bengal. Even though several revolutionary groups remained active in the region, the nationalist movement was in a transitory phase. As mentioned earlier, Dr Moonje eulogised Tilak, and it was only natural that his protégé should also follow the same path and saw in Tilak a hope for India's multitudes. Furthermore, way back in 1889, Bal Gangadhar Tilak had declared that the 'common factor in Indian society is the feeling of Hindutva.' Therefore in 1908 after Tilak's arrest, Dr Moonje and Keshav Hedgewar had felt directionless and decided to forge closer ties with Bengali revolutionaries who were from long using religious symbols to further their protest movement.

Despite being drawn to local revolutionaries, K.B. Hedgewar remained an unwavering 'Tilakite' and in deference to his jailed leader, observed a monthly fast till he was released from Mandalay Jail (then Burma; now Myanmar) in 1914. Although Keshav was originally a Brahmin from Telangana, he had little trouble in securing entry into the subversive world of Bengali radicals because groups like the Jugantar or Anushilan Samiti were 'composed entirely of young Hindu men of the upper classes.'

As a student, Keshav struck a balance between academics and politics. He familiarised himself with the region's social mores, and not only did he learn to speak Bengali, but he also began to dress like a local. But despite his efforts to appear like a Bengali gent, he soon discovered that it wasn't easy to subsume his Marathi–

Telugu identity—it was proven during a procession when a British officer 'approached him and began straightaway speaking to him in Marathi.'[4] Thereafter, Keshav Hedgewar remained under strict British surveillance in Calcutta and even had an 'agent' for a roommate. He was however undeterred and soon accepted to be formally initiated into the Anushilan Samiti. As a rule, the undercover society followed a strict code of conduct under which new entrants were first expected to pledge lifelong loyalty to the organisation, and then assigned to specific *dals* or groups led by team-leaders. It was here that Keshav Baliram Hedgewar learnt his first lessons in organisation-building and delegation of work. Soon, Cocaine[5], as Keshav came to be known by his code-name in the group, was mighty impressed with the organisation's credo: to place the 'right person in charge of the right place and the right mission,' and surged forward in what had become his life's avowed mission.

Keshav's entry into the charmed circle of the Anushilan Samiti finally established him as a young revolutionary. When he went home for vacation that year, he carried books, pamphlets and most importantly, revolvers for revolutionary groups in Nagpur. He was expected to maintain a low profile, which he did rather successfully, and in fact, 'did not acquire enough importance in these activities to incur the wrath of the authorities.'[6] Curiously, none of the RSS hagiographies nor other accounts make any 'mention anywhere...of the revolutionary responsibilities which he carried out in this period, with who and who he came in contact and what lessons he drew from his experiences in this work.'[7]

Despite being a backroom boy for the Anushilan Samiti, Hedgewar had first-hand knowledge of activities that enabled mass contact and mobilisation, including assisting people during natural disasters, which later stood him in good stead. The flooding of River Damodar, also known as the 'Sorrow of Bengal' was routine, but in 1913, the situation was particularly grim in the Bardhaman district of Bengal. Initially, Keshav had joined a relief team from the Ramkrishna Mission to rescue people from the ravaging waters, and later helped victims of a cholera epidemic that had broken out in the aftermath of the deluge. Subsequently, this became an annual ritual in his life and he would join a team of medical volunteers at the Gangasagar fair every winter at the confluence of River Ganga and the Bay of Bengal. It was courtesy this exposure to the spirit of sewa or service towards humankind that Hedgewar realised how it made for an excellent 'entry point' within any community, as it helped engage with people on various socio-political issues.

Although the young man had promised to pursue Medicine seriously, for which he had borrowed money and also relocated to Calcutta, his academic performance wasn't spectacular, given that a considerable part of his time was spent in attending protest meetings. It was clear that his commitment to the chosen path was taking precedence over everything else.

In 1913, Keshav somehow managed to secure a Licentiate in Medicine and Surgery (LMS). Even as he had completed the mandatory practical training for medics, the First World War had created havoc around the world. Keshav Hedgewar had wanted to join the British Army's Medical Corps to gain experience during a war situation, but had failed to continue mainly due to two reasons: first, he was blacklisted for his involvement with revolutionary groups, and second, medical degrees from Indian institutions were not recognised by the British administration.

As a young student-activist, Keshav decided to retaliate and conceived of a unique 'movement' to secure recognition for Indian degrees. He first met the Vice Chancellor of Calcutta University, Sir Ashutosh Mukherjee and thereafter the editors of prominent newspapers and extracted promises of adequate coverage for the 'campaign'. The invincible Raj was taken aback at the natives' deviousness, but the movement created a benchmark of sorts and is acknowledged as the first disinformation campaign in history—no protest meetings were actually held, but false information was disseminated successfully by creating a smokescreen with support from the media. After causing considerable disquiet within the Colonial administration, Keshav Hedgewar organised a public meeting in the presence of senior Congress leader, Surendranath Banerjee, where a resolution was adopted demanding that the British should either recognise Indian medical degrees, or conduct another examination to certify doctors.

The government opted for the latter as a face-saving device and scheduled an examination on 3 November 1915. Turning the tables on the British yet again, Keshav refused to sit for it, arguing that he had already cleared a test under an indigenous system—the 'University has examined us and awarded its degree. Where then is the question of government recognition? It is precisely to avoid having to submit to alien dictation that we boycotted government educational institutions!'[8] Dr Keshav Baliram Hedgewar had no desire of seeking government employment, and as far as his people were concerned, no one doubted his capabilities as a medical practitioner.

In early 1916, Keshav returned to Nagpur armed with an Indian medical degree in hand, and nationalist fervour brimming in his heart. He already had a plan in place for utilising Britain's preoccupation with the First World War to further the Indian freedom struggle. Although the idea of India's liberation had taken firm root in his mind, there was something else which he wanted to share with his mentor, Dr Moonje.

The Mainstream Nationalist

In Nagpur, several groups had expectations from the 'Calcutta-returned' young doctor. Foremost amongst them was his family who wanted him to get married, set up medical practice, and provide financial stability to extricate them from a piteous existence. The return of the dreaded plague to the city had further added to their despondency. Nagpur had very few doctors those days and in the face of an epidemic, they dreamt of a lucrative career for their Keshav. But neither was the doctor in a hurry to set up practise, nor get married.

On the other hand, his old comrades were exhorting him to re-join their ranks and motivate them just as he had done earlier. After a few days, Keshav Hedgewar re-connected with his old network of revolutionaries and formed an organisation called the Kranti Dal with revolution as its main objective, and armed rebellion as the means to its end.

He devised a unique plan to raise funds for the Dal and organised fund-raising dinners and lunches, in attendance of the wealthy, albeit nationalist landlords of Nagpur. A benevolent patron provided for a gymnasium which became the recruiting ground for the Dal and also enabled Keshav to continue with his mandatory physical drill. Soon, it was time for Keshav Hedgewar to up the ante, and he decided to set up the military arm of the Kranti Dal by recruiting special teams to acquire weapons from Bengal; his past apprenticeship with the Anushilan Samiti bore fruit, for it had taught him precision while planning an armed rebellion, and he proceeded by assigning another trusted colleague with the task of servicing and repairing pistols.

Keshav Baliram Hedgewar had long sensed that the British's preoccupation with the First World War provided the nationalists with an opportunity. He was hopeful of convincing all Indian nationalists to make a simultaneous declaration: 'From today onwards Hindusthan is an independent country.'[9]

His first port of call was to his mentor, Dr B.S. Moonje, but he was quick to realise that his idea found little favour with the elderly man. However, Moonje gave his protégé a letter of recommendation for Bal Gangadhar Tilak and suggested he get an audience with him in Pune to discuss the proposal. Although Tilak was extremely cordial to Hedgewar, even he had felt that it was rather premature in the nation's narrative to initiate such a plan. Surprisingly, Hedgewar wasn't in the least disheartened by Tilak's reluctance to endorse his plan and continued to motivate his band of young revolutionaries to achieve what he considered was their ultimate goal, often narrating inspiring stories about leaders such as Mazzini and Joan of Arc to awaken their commitment to nationalism.

However, several years had now passed since a young boy had flung away sweets for an occasion he thought was an insult to the soul of India. Keshav was now in his mid-Twenties and after turning down a regular profession and the prospect of a marriage, he suddenly felt the need for a meaningful purpose, considering the revolutionary movement was also somewhat petering out. He still looked up to Dr Moonje as his political guru and the two remained dedicated Tilakites, mainly because of his firm belief in anti-Colonialism being synonymous with the resurgence of Hinduism. Therefore, when Tilak launched the Home Rule League in Belgaum in April 1916 with the dual aim of seizing the leadership of the Congress and pressurising the British to grant India Home Rule, the medical doctor's flagging spirits found flight.

Initially, Bal Gangadhar Tilak's campaign was limited to the Marathi-speaking areas in Maharashtra, Karnataka, Berar, and the Central Provinces. By 1918, he was completely focussed on the Home Rule movement and covered a distance of 2,000 miles within a fortnight and delivered thirty-five lectures which were attended by nearly three lakh people. The movement was Tilak's 'first attempt to initiate a national campaign'[10] and was a progression from the revivalist campaigns of the 1890s.

The impact of Tilak's pan-Indian movement was so overwhelming that Keshav Hedgewar began to understand the limitations of smaller protest movements spearheaded by an individual or a minuscule group. The actual realisation however came after a failed attempt at securing ammunition for the Kranti Dal. According to the plan, Hedgewar's associates were to collect the weapons from a ship in the Portuguese-controlled port of Goa. But the British had seized the ship mid-sea and put paid to the carefully laid-out plan of the young revolutionaries.

After the setback, Keshav Baliram Hedgewar decided to join a few Congress functionaries in Nagpur and established the Rashtriya Mandal in 1918 to organise political campaigns in the city. In contrast to the conservative opinion of most Congress leaders who had felt that as an independent Dominion, India could only be part of the British Empire, K.B. Hedgewar unequivocally demanded for complete independence from the Raj. The Mandal launched a Hindi journal called *Sankalp* and Keshav embarked on a tour to address the people of his region.

In the same year, Hedgewar also established the Rashtriya Utsav Mandal with the purpose of holding religio-cultural functions, such as the birth and coronation anniversary of Shivaji; Ganesh Chaturthi; Shastra (weapons) puja; Dasanavami; and Sankranti. In a way, the Mandal appropriated a tradition which had been introduced by Bal Gangadhar Tilak with the Ganesh festival—introducing religion into the public space and using it to hold large congregations for cultural assimilation. Such gatherings were often addressed by Hindu revivalists, who would specifically stress on the need for Hindu unity.

It is another matter that the Rashtriya Utsav Mandal later morphed into a rabid communal outfit and was found guilty by the Justice D.P. Madon Commission for instigating the Bhiwandi riots in 1970. During the course of a visit to the city, the noted litterateur, Bhisham Sahni was so reminded of the horrific Partition riots that he was prompted to write *Tamas,* which won him the Sahitya Akademi Award in 1975.

In 1919, post the massacre of thousands of innocents in Jallianwala Bagh, K.B. Hedgewar travelled to Amritsar for a special session of the Indian National Congress. On his return to Nagpur in 1920, he began hectic preparations to hold the next Congress session in the city and was at the forefront of a campaign to have Bal Gangadhar Tilak preside over the proceedings. The reason: his meeting with Mohandas Karamchand Gandhi, whose suggestions had deeply unsettled the young Keshav.

At this juncture, Hedgewar's discomfort with Gandhi was mainly due to the latter's open declaration at the All India Khilafat Conference of launching a non-cooperation movement unless the demands of the Muslims were met forthwith. Gandhi, along with several Indian Muslims, had rued over the decline of the Ottoman Caliphate and was worried about the looming uncertainties following the end of the First World War. The Khilafat Manifesto, published at the end of the congregation in Delhi, demanded that the British protect the Caliphate and urged the Muslims to unite for the cause.

Not only was Bal Gangadhar Tilak not in favour of Gandhi's suggestion because he believed that the Muslims must be drawn to the Congress on the issue of self-rule or swaraj and not on the basis of religion, K.B. Hedgewar had openly 'disapproved of Gandhiji's policy of launching the non-cooperation movement with Khilafat as its major plank.' He further added that the Congress backing the Khilafat agitation would, 'only breed extra-territorial religious fanaticism among the Muslims.'[11]

Although the young man was insignificant in the Congress hierarchy, his open disagreement with Gandhi was the first step towards his distancing himself from the Indian National Congress. But more of which later.

One of the peculiarities of national politics at the time was the practise of simultaneous membership in multiple organisations. For instance, both the Indian National Congress and Hindu Mahasabha boasted of several common members, including stalwarts such as, Pandit Madan Mohan Malaviya, and K.B. Hedgewar's mentor, Dr Moonje who was at ease in both parties. One of the reasons for the dual membership practise was that prior to 1920, neither the Congress nor the Hindu Mahasabha had a mass character and therefore, Keshav Hedgewar, despite his disagreements with Gandhi, saw no contradiction in organising the Nagpur Session of the Indian National Congress.

He not only became part of the Reception Committee, but focussed all his efforts in raising a 1,000–1,500-strong volunteer force to ensure that the session was managed efficiently. Unfortunately, Bal

Gangadhar Tilak's untimely demise in August 1920 threw a spanner in the works and also had several other repercussions. Firstly, there was no one of eminence who could've opposed Gandhi's proposal to launch the non-cooperation movement, and more importantly, Tilak's supporters had to now identify another Hindu revivalist leader to preside over the session. As part of the effort, Dr Hedgewar accompanied by Dr Moonje proceeded to Pondicherry to persuade Sri Aurobindo to preside over the session, but the revolutionary-sage turned down the offer.

Often, the beauty of a well-written hagiography is in its ability to successfully evolve a new paradigm of truth. In the case of K.B. Hedgewar, there was a surfeit, and full of exaggerated accounts of his role in organising the Congress' Nagpur session. For instance, the way it was presented in B.V. Deshpande and S.R. Ramaswamy's book, *Dr. Hedgewar, The Epoch Maker: A Biography* as follows:

> Doctorji's independence of thought and outlook expressed itself in the Nagpur session of the Congress. At one of the meetings, Doctorji and his friends framed a resolution to the effect, "complete Independence is our aim." They met Gandhiji and pleaded with him that Congress should endorse this resolution. Gandhiji simply said, "that meaning is implied in the word Swaraj" and dismissed the suggestion.[12]

The writers also asserted that a resolution submitted by the Reception Committee at the Congress session was at variance with K.B. Hedgewar's ideology at the time: 'It is the aim of the Congress to establish democracy in India and to strive to liberate all nations from the grip of capitalist countries.'

According to his biographer, C.P. Bhishikar, it was Keshav Hedgewar who had first mooted the resolution, which was eventually rejected. But a one-time member of the RSS, Des Raj Goyal had refuted the claim saying that until then Hedgewar, 'was not known to think either in terms of ending capitalist exploitation or internationalism.'[13] Similarly, there are no credible accounts of Hedgewar's plea to Gandhi about adopting the resolution for complete independence.

Curiously, despite his sharp disagreements with Gandhi over the intermeshing of the Khilafat and non-cooperation movements, Keshav Hedgewar had 'plunged into'[14] the movement. He campaigned in the rural areas of the Central Provinces and Bombay, along with Dr Moonje and Narayanrao Savarkar, the younger brother of V.D. Savarkar. One of the reasons for their commitment could have stemmed from the fact that the non-cooperation movement had the overwhelming support of the people, and keeping away from it could have been construed as reluctance to lend support for the initiative. In 1921, K.B. Hedgewar was arrested on the charge of sedition for participating in the movement. He decided to plead his own case and levelled charges against the British government which the judge found 'even more seditious than his original speech!'

> India belongs to Indians. We therefore demand Independence.... That the British have been carrying on their despotic rule in our beloved country is obvious to everyone. What law is there that gives one country the right to rule over another? We demand nothing short of Complete Independence. Till we achieve it we cannot be at peace.[15]

K.B. Hedgewar was found guilty and sentenced to one year's rigorous imprisonment. However, he was given the option of seeking pardon by affirming to refrain from making such subversive statements in the future, which he refused and was interned in Ajani Jail, Nagpur.

Why did he participate in the Khilafat and non-cooperation movements despite sharp disagreements with Gandhi? Why did he deliberately provoke the judge by making incendiary speeches in court? Why did he refuse to commit that he would no longer make seditious speeches? Would it be correct to surmise that despite his outward rejection of the idea, Keshav Baliram Hedgewar also believed that mass-based politics and Hindu–Muslim campaigns were the only way to vanquish the Imperial forces. G.M. Huddar, who later went on to become the first general secretary of the RSS, wrote in the *Illustrated Weekly of India* on 7 October 1979 that every decision of K.B. Hedgewar was motivated by the desire to 'demonstrate that they (he and his supporters) were as unafraid of imprisonment as any other patriot having faith in a mass movement.'

Another sympathetic viewpoint was that Hedgewar didn't seek pardon because he would 'have to hang his head in shame,' when 'thousands were going to jail.'[16]

K.B. Hedgewar was given a hero's welcome in Nagpur after his release from jail. Despite heavy rains that day, prominent citizens of the city had gathered to cheer a man who had made Nagpur proud and foremost amongst them included, Dr Moonje, L.V. Paranjpe, and N.B. Khare. The news of his incarceration, and his commitment to the cause of India's independence spread so far that Motilal Nehru felicitated him at a public meeting for his contribution. Even as he was being feted and celebrated by leaders across India, K.B. Hedgewar was planning his next crucial move and that was to sharpen his criticism against Gandhi, which eventually resulted in his severing all links with mainstream nationalism. It was only a question of time before he would do that.

The Birth of the RSS

By the time K.B. Hedgewar was released from jail, Mahatma Gandhi had suspended the non-cooperation movement in the wake of the Chauri Chaura massacre in 1922. According to some accounts, K.B. Hedgewar had felt somehow cheated at what he thought was Gandhi's unilateral decision to end a mass movement. As mentioned earlier, he was initially attracted to the idea of individualistic and violent forms of protest against the Colonial regime.

In the years immediately after Gandhi's return to India in 1915, Hedgewar, much like the revivalists, had found Gandhi acceptable because of his emphasis on *tapasya* and satyagraha, concepts which were part of ancient Hindu precepts. But when Gandhi had insisted that every form of protest must remain non-violent, Hedgewar along with several others had vociferously disagreed. They had felt that non-violent action was inadequate to counter the might of the British empire. Moreover, the adoption of ahimsa or non-violence, they felt, would further weaken the Hindus and give Muslims an opportunity to ride roughshod over the 'original dwellers' of India. The denouncement of non-violence as a tool to counter the enemy became a recurring theme of Hedgewar's theory all through his life. In 1936, more than a decade after he founded the RSS, the doctor said at a speech in Nagpur, that Hindus must understand that,

> ahimsa (non-injury) is not swa-himsa (self-injury) and that the former should not result in the latter. Further, the precept 'ahimsä paramo dharmah' (the highest code of morality is non-injury) is well rooted in the Hindu mind. It is the duty of the Hindu society to teach the same sublime principle to other

> communities as well. But if our well-meant teaching is not to be listened to respectfully by others, we should have the necessary strength. Unfortunately, our society today is weak and the predatory communities simply do not care for the weak ones. Therefore, we have first to eradicate the weakness from the Hindu society and make it invincibly strong. Strength, it should be remembered, comes only through organization. It is therefore the duty of every Hindu to do his best to consolidate the Hindu society.[17]

It may be recalled that Chhatrapati Shivaji was Hedgewar's childhood hero because he had valiantly resisted the Mughals; his deep-rooted resentment against Muslims went back several years when his great-great grandfather was forced to flee from his village in Telengana because the Mughals had neglected the region. When Gandhi launched the non-cooperation movement in support of the Khilafat and gave a call for Hindu–Muslim unity, Hedgewar seemed to ratify it initially, but had finally made up his mind and chose his original path to political salvation.

In the following account of a purported conversation between Keshav Baliram Hedgewar and M.K. Gandhi (as there are no documents to prove its veracity), the former's views on Gandhi's decision to make the anti-Colonial struggle socially inclusive is clearly manifested:

> He (Hedgewar) once met Gandhiji to explain his viewpoint. Without mincing words, Doctorji questioned Gandhiji:
>
> 'There are in India people of various religions like Hinduism, Islam, Christianity, Zoroastrianism, Judaism, etc. Why then

> do you harp upon only "Hindu-Muslim Unity" instead of promoting the unity of all the various sects?'
>
> Gandhiji replied, 'This will secure the friendly attitude of Muslims towards our country. As you are witnessing, they can be persuaded to side wholeheartedly with us in the nationalist struggle.'
>
> Doctorji said: 'Long before this slogan of Hindu-Muslim Unity came into vogue, many leading Muslims had identified themselves with our nation and worked shoulder-to-shoulder with Hindus under the leadership of Lokmanya Tilak—e.g., Barrister Jinnah, Dr. Ansari, Hakim Ajmal Khan and others. But I am afraid that this new slogan, instead of helping unity, might further aggravate the feeling of separateness among the Muslims.'
>
> 'I have no such fear,' said Gandhiji and closed the issue.[18]

It is important to mention at this juncture that communal tensions in Nagpur predated Dr Hedgewar and Moonje's emergence in public life, and there existed a past history of serious clashes between Hindus and Muslims particularly in 1903–04 and 1914. By the time Hedgewar was released from jail, the Hindu–Muslim issue had occupied centre stage in the narrative of India's struggle for freedom. This was because of the worsening communal situation in other parts of India, most severely in the Malabar region of Kerala where Muslim leaseholders and cultivators had rebelled against Hindu landholders who were backed by British forces. Called the Moplah (Muslim peasantry from the Malabar region) rebellion, the peasant uprising was termed by the followers of Tilak and other similar groups as proof of weakness in the face of a growing aggression amongst Muslims in India. Hedgewar had heard of it in jail and also learnt of Dr Moonje's visit to the Malabar region as head of a 'Commission' appointed by the 'Nagpur public.'[19] Even before the official report was finalised in 1923, Hedgewar was told by Moonje that the incident was nothing but a case of forced conversion. As a consequence, he termed the Moplah Rebellion as 'the biggest Muslim attack on the Hindus after the Muslim rule.'[20]

In the wake of Dr Moonje's report, the well-known Arya Samaj missionary, Swami Shraddhananda had initiated a shuddhi or purification/reconversion movement in the region. The Swami's deposition to the Moonje Commission, as we shall later see, helped Dr Hedgewar firm up his viewpoint and he proclaimed that the 'Hindus are not as well organised as the Muslims, and are divided among themselves. The only solution to the problem is for Hindu leaders to organise their own society.'[21]

But more than a year before the large-scale 'reconversion' of Muslims (who were 'originally' Hindus) had begun, Dr Hedgewar had initiated a campaign to reconvert orphans, who were sheltered in Christian missionary homes, to Hinduism. In time, he refurbished the argument that re-admitting Muslims and Christians into the Hindu order was just another form of asserting their original Hindu identity. In any case, he believed that,

> by changing religion, they (Hindus who converted to Islam and Christianity) do not change their nationality. On the pedestal of *Rashtra Dharma* they are bound to stand as one with other communities, though at the level of *Vyakti-dharma* they

> are free to adopt any religion....They are as much sons of the Motherland as are other communities or the Hindus are.[22]

It is precisely this idea, that all Indians irrespective of their religious faith are originally Hindus, which forms the kernel of the controversial ghar wapsi programme run by the affiliates of the RSS. This postulation also underscores the nuanced differences between Hedgewar and Savarkar—the latter's reluctance in considering non-Hindus as dwellers of the Hindu Rashtra. But more of which later.

As stated previously, Nagpur had a past history of sectarian violence—there were disputes between Hindus and Muslims in 1903–04, also a decade later in 1914 when the Muslims had protested against music being played during religious processions of Hindus, particularly when they crossed a mosque. The issue resurfaced in 1923 when K.B. Hedgewar declared that he would take 'a leading part in asserting that in Nagpur they would not go in for any kind of peace pact as was being done elsewhere but would assert the right of the Hindus by bringing out the processions with music ahead even before the mosque.'[23] For him the right to play music was not a trivial matter, but a manifestation of 'Hindu strength'. When the local administration had clamped an embargo on playing music, Dr Hedgewar had convinced local Hindu leaders to postpone the immersion of Ganesh idols that year. But a month later, when a group of Hindus had contravened the administration's order and organised a procession through the same route and were stopped by the police, several members of the community had joined in the march. In the annals of the RSS, this agitation is called the Dindi Satyagraha, referring to a group, or *dindi*, singing devotional songs.

According to a report published in an Urdu newspaper, the

processions would deliberately slow down while crossing mosques to, 'give them a full opportunity to play the music with the utmost noise.'[24] The Dindi Satyagraha was the handiwork of none other than Dr Moonje, while Hedgewar who was still his protégé, 'acted as the stormtrooper.'[25]

Incidents of such nature continued sporadically for a couple of months and finally culminated in the setting up of the Hindu Mahasabha in Nagpur. Dr Moonje was appointed its vice president, K.B. Hedgewar became its secretary, while the appointment of the former ruler of Nagpur state, Raja Lakshmanrao Bhonsle as the Mahasabha's president, sent out a strong message that the mission was spearheaded by a member of Hindu royalty. As someone who had come to be revered as the guide and mentor for the Hindus, Dr Hedgewar also took it upon himself to resolve private matters and once reassured the father of a Hindu bridegroom who was terrified about his son's marriage procession crossing a mosque. In the lore surrounding Keshav Hedgewar, the Dindi Satyagraha is hailed as his maiden 'victory'; for instance during a procession, whenever the musicians would demur, 'Doctorji himself would take over the drums and rouse the dormant manliness of the Hindus.'[26]

Clearly, 'Hedgewar the bodybuilder' was an appropriate foil for someone who was entrusted with the task of resurrecting Hindu pride. The city of Nagpur witnessed yet another clash between Hindus and Muslims in July 1924, but by then the Hindus were not only 'on the alert and prepared,'[27] but Dr Hedgewar was at the forefront of evacuating Hindus from Muslim-majority colonies.

Despite acquiring a near-cult status in his native Nagpur, Keshav Baliram Hedgewar felt that the so-called initial 'victory' in the movement needed several initiatives to reach its ultimate goal of 'refurbishing' Hindu society. Flush from the success of 1924, he first established a gymnasium called the Maharashtra Vyayamshala; a study circle called the Shiksha Prasarak Mandal; and the Rashtriya Swayamsevak Mandal, a volunteer force. He was also drawn to the Rifle Association which was formed some years ago by Dr Moonje to train Hindus in the use of arms and ammunition.

By now, Dr Hedgewar had firmly concluded that unless the theory of a Hindu Nation or Rashtra was actively propagated, the idea of Indianness or *Bharatiyata* would not find acceptance amongst the people. But he somehow felt alone in his mission because Dr Moonje, his mentor for years, was reluctant in lending credence to the idea of a monolithic India. The reason for the difference in opinion stemmed from the fact that while Moonje considered the 1924 riots in Nagpur solely as an opportunity to reenergise the Hindu Mahasabha, Dr Hedgewar's focus was on the overt belligerence displayed by local Muslims. In January 1925 at a public meeting in Pune, Dr Moonje said that although the Muslims formed only 20,000 of Nagpur's total population of 1,50,000, they were a threat to the life, property and wealth of the Hindus.[28] But while he made this claim with an eye on increasing the support base for the Mahasabha, Hedgewar was more occupied about finding a way to counter the threat.

At this stage entered Vinayak Damodar Savarkar, but in absentia, and in the form of a handwritten pre-publication copy of a pamphlet titled, *Hindutva—Who Is A Hindu?* According to Narayan Hari Palkar (the author of K.B. Hedgewar's first biography in Marathi, which was later translated into Hindi), the doctor had obtained Savarkar's manuscript after it was smuggled out of prison and delivered to one of his close friends. Hedgewar was instantly attracted to Savarkar's postulation of Hindus being a monolithic, original, superior and an inherently tolerant race, and considered his theory as an 'extremely well argued, definitive and consistent advocacy of Hindutva.'[29]

Meanwhile, V.D. Savarkar was already recognised as a national leader of repute and several Congress leaders, including Sardar Vallabhbhai Patel had demanded for his release in the Bombay Legislative Council. At a public meeting organised by the Nagpur Congress on 14 October 1923, Keshav Baliram Hedgewar had thundered in support of the leader as follows:

> The government has murdered justice...if the government is interested in washing off this blot let it forthwith release him.... If even now the government does not care to release him, it will only be one more evidence of its evil intentions towards our country.

Shortly thereafter, Hedgewar launched a daily newspaper called *Swatantra* and fiercely advocated for complete independence from the British. One would have imagined that by now, armed with the security of Savarkar's pamphlet, which was nothing short of a canon for many, K.B. Hedgewar would have come full circle from the precocious child who was forever looking for ways to unite his Hindu brethren. But far from it, for he continued to be obsessed with the question of uniting the community.

'From his youth, he had searched for a reason to explain India's inability to ward off foreign domination,'[30] argue Walter K. Andersen and Shridhar Damle in their book, *The Brotherhood in Saffron*, but he had obviously found no answers. After what seemed like a lifetime of a struggle involving quasi-philosophical and religio-cultural debates, stretches of apprenticeships under various leaders, and home-grown revolutionary movements, K.B. Hedgewar finally seemed to have identified the reason: a psychological and inherent weakness amongst Hindus which could only be overcome by creating a common emotional cause within the community; and to build a disciplined and cadre-based organisation to achieve the ultimate goal.

From early 1925 onwards, K.B. Hedgewar was firm in his decision to set up an organisation, but had also resolved to not replicate either the Hindu Mahasabha or the Congress party. In March 1925, after V.D. Savarkar was released on parole, Hedgewar travelled to Ratnagiri to discuss the idea with him. After all it was Savarkar's 'treatise' which had helped him buttress his argument in support of a pure Hindu sangathan or organisation. He began touring different cities in Maharashtra and addressed meetings along with like-minded leaders, including members of the Congress party.

Amongst other things, Hedgewar's theory of a delineation between Hindiwadi (not linguistically, but indicative of inclusive nationalism) and Hinduwadi stood out sharply at these public gatherings. He argued that the former was based on the policy of appeasing the minorities, while the Hinduwadis ensured that the Hindus' interests were protected. However within the Indian National Congress, because of leaders such as Mahatma Gandhi and Jawaharlal Nehru who were Hindiwadis, it was next to impossible to expound against the Muslims*.[31] It was also after his meeting with Savarkar and in departure from his previous position that, 'India was the nation of

* That this argument of Palkar is a latter day construct is evident, because in the mid-1920s, Jawaharlal Nehru was not exactly a Congress stalwart that he eventually went on to become. Palkar's theory however highlights the genesis of the argument put forth by leaders of the sangh parivar since the mid-1980s that while they believed in genuine secularism, their adversaries were 'pseudo-secularists'.

all people living here,' Hedgewar now insisted that, 'Hindutva was nation-ness (Rashtriyatva).'[32] According to him, no person could be defined as a true Indian or Bharatiya, unless he believed in this principle. In Keshav Baliram Hedgewar's mind, this was the point at which he made a clear differentiation between cultural nationalism and territorial nationalism.

In the biography, Narayan Hari Palkar mentions how in the months preceding the formation of the RSS, Hedgewar was convinced that the Hindus were not only capable of undertaking the Herculean task of weaving their landmass into a nation, but most importantly, had insisted that the country was rightfully theirs. In what was one of his most astounding theories, he was of the view that dishonour to the Hindu samaj or society wasn't so much because of the Muslims or the British, but was the result of the erosion of national sentiment or pride from public discourse. According to this polemic, very few Hindus considered themselves as units of the nation and were not even willing to contribute their might to strengthen and reorganise themselves as a nation. After having spent more than three decades in the national movement, albeit in marginal capacities, Keshav Baliram Hedgewar decided to dedicate his life by evoking a spirit of nationalist sentiment in Hindus and to create a cohesive sangathan for the purpose. Although he was yet to give it a name, but a basic structure of the outfit had taken shape in his mind's eye.

On 25 September 1925, when a few men had gathered in K.B. Hedgewar's house, he asked each one for their views about the nature of programmes to be pursued by the 'said' outfit. This was at variance with the accepted norm because the world over, organisations, political parties, and institutions come into being only after they are given a name, and the core principles, constitution and financial basis are firmed up. But in this case, not only were each of these aspects absent, it had taken seven long months for the men to even decide on a name for it.

Eventually in April 1926, the outfit had a name—the Rashtriya Swayamsevak Sangh or RSS*, and a little later, a saffron-coloured flag called the bhagwa dhwaj was chosen as one of the first symbols of Hindu hegemony. But it would take a good two-and-a-half decades before the RSS would adopt a constitution and only after the government had made it a precondition to lift the ban which was imposed on it in the aftermath of Mahatma Gandhi's assassination in 1948.

However, on the day of its formation, K.B. Hedgewar had declared that the sangh required its members to pledge themselves in the pursuit of physical, military and political education, while simultaneously committing to train others. There was immediate concurrence amongst the group on fulfilling Hedgewar's dream of resurrecting the Hindu Rashtra.

K.B. Hedgewar had chosen the tenth day of the Hindu festival of Navratri to form the RSS—Dussehra, which marks the victory of good over evil in the Ramayana. This was the same day when a young Keshav had earned the wrath of the British administration for singing Vande Matram at a site where Ravana was due to be ritualistically consigned to the flames. The careful selection of that particular day not only underscored that ancient Hindu values were at the core of the RSS, but also mythology which would henceforth be integral to its functioning.

---

* In the name, while the words Rashtriya and Sangh, meaning 'national' and 'association' probably selected themselves, the choice of 'swayamsevaks' or 'self-helpers', pointed towards Hedgewar's belief that there was no better strategy for Hindus than to take up their own cause.

The three-year period beginning with his release from Ajani Jail had immense significance in Keshav Baliram Hedgewar's life. With the formation of the RSS, he had discovered his life's mission, and the challenge hereafter was not only to ensure its expansion, but also to establish its relevance in Indian polity.

The Growth of the RSS

Within a month, K.B. Hedgewar had succeeded in admitting more than 1,500 volunteers into the RSS and initiated a daily and mandatory ritual of an assembly called the *shakha*. Soon thereafter, the swayamsevaks or volunteers of the RSS became a discernible lot, easily identifiable from a distance by their all-khakhi uniform—a pair of shorts, a full-sleeves shirt, and a cap. In 1930, the khakhi cap was replaced with a black one, but the first major alteration in the official attire was made in 1940 when the British banned the use of military colours and the white shirts were replaced with khakhi. The most recent change in the RSS uniform was made in October 2016 when the iconic shorts were dropped in favour of brown-coloured trousers.

After assigning the uniform, Hedgewar chose the lathi or stick as the symbol of defence for the initiates. As part of the regimentation process, each day would be heralded with a salutary ode to the bhagwa dhwaj and concluded with a customised RSS prayer, which personified the nation as a Goddess or the Motherland. The prayer had one stanza in Marathi, and another in Hindi and ended with a salutation to the seventeenth-century saint-poet Ramdas Swami, who was also the patron saint of Chhatrapati Shivaji. This prayer was however replaced by a Sanskrit hymn in 1939.

In 1927, K.B. Hedgewar introduced the Officers' Training Camps (OTCs), which were made mandatory for *pracharaks* or preachers in order to qualify for the post. Since then, the OTCs have continued to function as a barometer to evaluate the leadership qualities amongst RSS trainees. Although the annual training camps were later given the formal name of Sangh Shiksha Varg, but even today they are referred to as OTCs, the word 'officer' reflecting the importance of hierarchical systems in the RSS.

As mentioned earlier, although Hedgewar laid great emphasis on the physical drill, he also ensured that the RSS wasn't relegated to just an outdoor gymnasium facility, and introduced the concept of baudhik or intellectual discourse in shakhas whose numbers were growing rapidly. It is worthwhile mentioning here that when Hedgewar was at the forefront of the Dindi Satyagraha, several people who ran akharas, gyms or other bodybuilding clubs, were invited to participate in the campaign, despite no prior experience in politics. When Hedgewar established the RSS, he invited them yet again to steer the physical activities of the sangh. The doctor also enlisted the assistance of a retired army officer, Martandrao Jog to conduct a weekly parade for the swayamsevaks. The fact that Jog also headed the Congress Sewa Dal, didn't deter Hedgewar from involving him in the sangh's activities. It was clear that as long as the ideological control remained in his hands, he saw no harm in utilising professional expertise from elsewhere.

A major part of the RSS cadre comprised middle class youth—the emphasis being on young, able-bodied, and upper caste boys. There came a time when it was felt that the cadre needed to be classified into different age-groups in order to ensure better interaction within peer groups, and they were named after Hindu mythological characters to reflect the age of its clusters: the one dedicated to the youngest lot was called Luv and Kush, after the sons of Lord Rama, while the others were called Dhruv, Prahlad, Abhimanyu, Bheem, and Bhishma—the last one reserved exclusively for the elderly within the organisation. If there was anything that Hedgewar placed premium on irrespective of age, it was strict obedience, and carried out a thorough check on the loyalty and compliance quotient of each member. What flummoxed several political scientists and observers routinely was RSS' insistence on abstinence and a strict adherence to ancient principles, similar to that of a religious commune. But despite a punishing regimen and a life of a near-renunciate, one of the reasons for large number of youth joining the RSS was because of a feeling of self-aggrandizement—first, that they were the chosen ones in the service of the Motherland, and second, that they were indispensable for the elders within the system.

As mentioned above, the RSS continued to attract a large number of volunteers and required funds to run its various activities. Initially, several members not only lived with Hedgewar in his home, but were also supported by him. Although it is not known if the doctor made any money from his practice, he had once taken strong objection after he had discovered that some of his closest aides were handing over money to his sister-in-law for the upkeep of his family home. Thereafter, in an effort to help Hedgewar's growing band of volunteers, a few friends had floated an insurance company and arranged a retainership for him, but the plan had failed to take off. Therefore, it once again fell upon Hedgewar to find a permanent solution to keep the RSS running and he went back to the ancient concept of guru dakshina or offering made to a guru in return for knowledge imparted in ashrams of yore. But in place of a human being officiating as the guru, Hedgewar decided that the bhagwa dhwaj would be the object of reverence because it, 'symbolizes that timeless principle...brings before our mind's eye the entire history, the glorious culture and tradition of our land; inspiration wells up in our mind.'[33]

Even after four years of its formation, the RSS continued to function without a formal command structure. Since it had no governing council or a decision-making body, K.B. Hedgewar 'called senior RSS figures to Nagpur in November 1929, to evaluate its work and consider ways to link together the expanding network of shakhas.'[34] It was decided at the meeting that the RSS should be presided over by one supreme leader with absolute powers, and he who assumes the position should have an appropriate title to reflect his pre-eminence. The nomenclature of *sarsanghchalak* was found suitable for the position and Keshav Baliram Hedgewar was unanimously declared as the first supreme leader of the RSS.

It was also firmed up that the principle of *ek chalak anuvartitva* or follow one leader, would be the principal code for the RSS. This command structure was similar to the Hindu joint family system where the karta or patriarch is the undisputed head and expects life-long obedience and adherence to an unwritten code within the family. In his book on the RSS, Des Raj Goyal argues that this terminology is 'rather difficult to distinguish' from what is often called the 'Fuehrer principle followed by the Fascists in Italy and Nazis in Germany.'[35]

Meanwhile, Keshav Baliram Hedgewar also held a special fascination for linguistic purity. He deliberately chose to 'mystify' the organisation's structure by choosing archaic titles for office-bearers: *sarkaryavah* for a general secretary, *sah sarkaryavah* for a joint general secretary and *sarsenapati* (originally, a military title used by the Maratha empire) for the chief trainer. He opted for such epithets to not only delineate the RSS from other organisations, but to also enhance its stature by creating a classical aura around it.

The RSS was presented with its maiden opportunity for demonstrating its commitment towards 'protecting' the interests of Hindus in September 1927 during the outbreak of communal riots in Nagpur. Hindu–Muslim conflagrations had reared its ugly head across the country in the months preceding the Nagpur riots, following the murder of the much-revered Arya Samaj leader, Swami Shraddhanand in December 1926, who it may be recalled had spearheaded the reconversion or shuddhi programme for Hindus in Kerala.

By this time, the RSS had already imparted training to a few swayamsevaks in the art of using sword, javelin and dagger[36]—obviously weapons for fighting fellow-citizens, and not the Colonial regime, indicating that the prime targets were Muslim groups. The Nagpur riots also gave Hedgewar the opportunity to test if the organisation was capable of facing an 'emergency' situation, and asked one of his close aides to raise sixteen squads of swayamsevaks to spread out to areas where the Hindus were in small numbers. That the operation was a grand success became evident when leaders of the Hindu Mahasabha asked Hedgewar to send a team of RSS volunteers in full gear to its annual session in Ahmedabad in December 1927. While addressing the session, Dr Moonje had praised K.B. Hedgewar publicly[37]:

> I come from the province where the Hindus have fought back Muslim aggression. This miracle of eradicating the lowly and submissive nature of our society has been achieved by the organization which has been created under the leadership of Dr. Keshav Baliram Hedgewar.

No Direct Politics

Keshav Baliram Hedgewar's primary objective in establishing the RSS was not only to awaken and harness the Hindu consciousness, but also to convert the community into a cohesive group. His lengthy monologues were often directed exclusively towards the Hindus, for he believed that public engagement must be populist with adequate emphasis on the cultural aspects. In his mind's eye, the RSS was not a political 'party' in the tradition of either the Congress or the Hindu Mahasabha.

As mentioned earlier in this chapter, dual membership in political organisations was a norm in the 1920s and despite being the RSS chief, Hedgewar had retained his membership of the Congress as well as the Hindu Mahasabha (he was also its secretary between 1926–31). In 1928, as member of the Congress Working Committee (Central Provinces), he had travelled to Calcutta for the annual session and met with Subhash Chandra Bose who was then Mayor of the city, to seek support for the RSS. Bose had heard him out patiently, but had politely turned down his request citing other commitments. Hedgewar's choice to continue as member of the Indian National Congress and seek an audience with a stalwart of a party that was anathema to his nationalistic brand of politics, was somewhat duplicitous, as he had precluded active politics from the ambit of the organisation he had created—for instance, the participation of swayamsevaks in the annual session of the Hindu Mahasabha in 1927 was merely symbolic, and their role was restricted to being protectors of public order.

Three years after the birth of the Rashtriya Swayamsevak Sangh and despite Hedgewar's firm relsove to keep out of anti-Colonial agitations and work exclusively for Hindu consolidation, the British administration kept a vigil over it. This was not only because of Hedgewar's past links with revolutionary groups in Nagpur and Bengal, but the Home Department of Central Provinces had a strong suspicion that the RSS had the potential of transforming into a revolutionary outfit. However, the Imperial government's worries were rather unfounded, because Hedgewar's decision to stay aloof from the freedom struggle was not in the least appreciated amongst several of his own peers and 'brought consternation, criticism and disappointment from many Hindu partisans.'[38]

There was no gainsaying the fact that K.B. Hedgewar insisted on retaining the RSS' basic character of a socio-cultural outfit which was devoted to reinforcing Hindu society. But to define it as completely apolitical was erroneous, because it actively promoted prejudice against religious minorities (except the Sikhs, Jains and Buddhists). For Hedgewar politics at the time was mainly defined by the stance taken by any organisation towards the Colonial regime, and the RSS had chosen ambivalence on this issue. Narayan Subbarao Hardikar, a member of the Congress Sewa Dal, who'd worked with Hedgewar during the Nagpur session, denounced this very aspect of the RSS in a scathing speech. Hedgewar however ignored every criticism and was unwavering in his standpoint, until it drew the harshest denouncement from a person who had inspired him to establish the RSS in the first place.

In 1937, V.D. Savarkar almost rubbished Hedgewar's obsession with character-building and organising the Hindus: 'The epitaph for the RSS volunteer will be that he was born, he joined the RSS and died without accomplishing anything.' Although it was a different matter that Savarkar himself displayed little interest in joining the national movement, his disagreement with Hedgewar was about prioritising organisation-building as against direct confrontation.

V.D. Savarkar's severe indictment was obviously the final denunciation, but as mentioned earlier, even Hedgewar's closest associates were critical of his stance. Anna Sohoni, who had conceived the routine of physical exercises for the initiates quit after failing to convince Hedgewar to be more aggressive and take the *enemy* head-on by marching in front of mosques; Hedgewar insisted that offence was the last resort and for it to even manifest after a provocation, required a paradigm shift in the Hindu mind-set through a sustained campaign. Additionally, such acts could also draw the ire of the British and was best avoided, he had submitted. Yet another leader of significance, G.M. Huddar, the first sarkaryavah of the RSS also quit because K.B. Hedgewar had disapproved of his involvement in an armed robbery in 1931 to raise funds for an anti-British agitation.

No Disobedience

Never before was the RSS' carefully-constructed, albeit peripheral relationship with the Congress more evident than at a watershed moment in India's pre-Independence history—the Lahore Resolution of 1929 seeking purna swaraj or complete freedom from the British. Hedgewar's duplicity couldn't have been more apparent in the way he responded to this significant development, followed by symbolically observing India's 'independence' day in January 1930, more than seventeen years before the actual Transfer of Power.

As mentioned earlier, from 1920 onwards, Hedgewar had been repeatedly pleading that complete independence should be the Congress' objective and as reported by his band of admirers, he had even sparred with Gandhi on the issue. However, when the Congress made a formal demand for purna swaraj, the RSS found itself in a quandary.

On the one hand, Hedgewar had publicly refused to ratify the Lahore Resolution because he feared being viewed as an appendage of the Congress. However, as there was a general concurrence amongst the people over the issue, the RSS couldn't have afforded to remain aloof. Consequently, Hedgewar issued a press release, expressing both his pleasure and predicament as follows:

> That the Indian National Congress too has adopted 'our goal' (*sic*) of Independence naturally gives us immense joy. It is our duty to cooperate with any organisation working for the cause... on the evening of 26-1-1930 all the shakhas of the Rashtriya Swayamsevak Sangh should hold rallies at their respective places and worship the national flag, that is, the Bhagwa Jhanda.

The directive to worship the RSS flag on Purna Swaraj Day and not the Tricolour as adopted by the Congress, established Hedgewar's stand on the Lahore Resolution. The press release indicated Keshav Hedgewar's innermost desire—that the 'occasion was to be utilised for propagation of the sangh ideology and not the ideas that inspired the Lahore Resolution.'[39]

In the history of the freedom struggle, the grand hoisting of the Tricolour on 26 January 1930 seemed like mere symbolism when compared to an event which was to unify the entire country two months later. That the Dandi March and later the Salt Satyagraha launched by Mahatma Gandhi in March 1930 would elevate the national movement to another level was not expected initially, but when a seemingly innocuous act had succeeded in shaking the foundations of the invincible British Raj, the RSS and its chief were caught in a cleft stick, yet again:

> Many workers of the Sangh sought permission to participate in the movement. But Doctorji had undertaken the enduring and basic task of national rejuvenation through the Sangh. That long-term work had to go on unhindered and grow stronger whatever the external conditions. Doctorji wrote to all the Shakha Pramukhs: "...The Sangh as such has so far not resolved to participate in this movement. However, those who would like to participate in their personal capacity are free to do so after obtaining permission from their Sanghachalaks."

Hedgewar's raison d'être was that the Salt Satyagraha and other anti-British stirs were irrelevant when seen through the prism of rearming Hindu society. Yet, he felt that the RSS' participation was mandatory for it to be in sync with the short-term political aspirations of the people, and to also ensure that they were viewed as patriots in the struggle for India's independence. It may be recalled that Hedgewar had displayed similar behaviour almost a decade ago during the Khilafat and non-cooperation movements. The contradiction in his claims is best evidenced in a statement attributed to him as follows:

> I would undertake any means in order to achieve Independence... if need be, take to polishing the boots of the English or take out his boot and crush his head with the same...have no prejudice against any method...have only one supreme goal before me—driving out the British.[40]

However, all the bombast about forcing the English out was a façade, as the RSS' activities remained centred on strengthening the Hindus against Muslims. Hedgewar's emphasis was on reinforcing the RSS, and marking its participation by allowing the swayamsevaks to join the Civil Disobedience movement in their individual capacities. But when it came to a formal association, the doctor was careful about maintaining a degree of separation between the two. For instance, 'a contingent of swayamsevaks, trained in providing medical care was instructed to attend to the injured salt satyagrahis in their uniforms and (they) wore the Swastika symbol on their shoulder.'[41]

By allowing individual participation, Hedgewar had deftly stymied any rumbles of a discord within the RSS; he was also well aware that in order to protect his reputation as chief of the sangh, he shouldn't be seen to be distancing himself from the movement. Consequently, he planned his participation meticulously—first, he chose not to break the salt law as it was not only closely identified with the Congress, but with Gandhi's epochal protest movement which had shaken the British empire. Instead, he joined the Jungle Satyagraha in the Central Provinces which was one of the sub-regional protest movements. Second, he appointed L.V. Paranjpe as the interim sarsanghchalak to manage RSS' internal affairs during the period of his anticipated detention.

Before joining the Jungle Satyagraha, Hedgewar addressed his volunteers as follows:

> Going to jail is today considered a sign of true patriotism. However, a person who would willingly court a two-year prison term hesitates when he is asked to come out of his house and work for organising the freedom movement. Why should this be so? Is six months or a year enough to secure the country's Independence? However, the people are not yet prepared to realize the simple truth that organised work for several years

> alone can take us to our cherished goal. The present fate of the country cannot be changed unless lakhs of young men dedicate their entire lifetime for that cause. To mould the minds of our youth towards that end is the supreme aim of the Sangh.[42]

Although Hedgewar had made every attempt to distance the RSS from Gandhi's Civil Disobedience movement, it did not dampen his cadre's enthusiasm. They joined the Salt Satyagraha in droves, but in their eagerness to ensure that the action did not invite their chief's ire, they turned out in RSS uniform! K.B. Hedgewar was livid because satyagrahis in RSS uniform denoted official participation, whereas the medical care squad which was treating the injured was part of the RSS' sewa programmes. He censured his cadre severely, and said:

> Have you realized the full implications of offering Satyagraha in uniform? It will mean that Sangh itself has officially joined the agitation. But, as you are aware, that is not our policy....[43]

Meanwhile on 21 July 1930, thousands of protestors had gathered in the Yavatmal district of Maharashtra to raise their voice against British forest laws. K.B. Hedgewar was arrested the moment he had stepped into the prohibited area with other satyagrahis. In what was widely seen as his commitment to the freedom struggle, resulting in a mild punishment of six months of rigorous imprisonment and another three months of routine incarceration, Keshav Baliram Hedgewar had 'absolved' himself in the eyes of his cadre and the nation.

After his release from jail in February 1931, Hedgewar resumed charge as sarsanghchalak and embarked on a series of tours to expand the RSS' network. After a short visit to Bombay, he had proceeded to

Varanasi in March 1931, where he met with several important leaders including, Pandit Madan Mohan Malaviya and established two shakhas in the city. But most importantly, his first trip to a city considered to be the abode of Lord Shiva gained immense significance for he met a future comrade-in-arms, a young man who was counted amongst the brightest of RSS' luminaries—Madhav Sadashiv Golwalkar, popularly known as 'Guruji'. However, it would take another year before the two men would not only forge a close personal relationship, but lend a decisive thrust to the RSS.

Amongst others who were impressed with the RSS' reach and K.B. Hedgewar's unmatched dynamism, was a young man called Ganesh Damodar Savarkar aka Babarao, the brother of V.D. Savarkar who had organised the Hindu youth from 1922 onwards under the banner of Tarun Hindu Mahasabha—the unofficial youth wing of the Hindu Mahasabha. From the 1920s, several militant Hindu groups were established in the country, such as the Mahavir Dal and Agni Dal in UP and the Punjab; the Hindu Rashtra Dal in Pune; the Hindu Rashtra Sena in Bhopal; and the Mukteshwar Dal and Rashtriya Swayamsevak Mandal in the Central Provinces. There was no doubt that each of these outfits had mushroomed with great speed only in response to the imagined fear of a Muslim domination.

In 1931, Babarao Savarkar merged the Tarun Hindu Mahasabha with the RSS. Other organisations followed suit, most notably the Mukteshwar Dal, headed by a well-known figure in militant Hindu circles, Swami Pachlegaonkar. The Hindu Mahasabha, of which K.B. Hedgewar was still a member, helped him set up shakhas and secure support at several strategic locations. In time, several Mahasabha leaders began considering the RSS as a youth wing of their organisation, which benefitted Hedgewar in establishing his network in the Vidarbha and Chhattisgarh regions.

In May 1932, Bhai Parmanand, a leader of the reformist Arya Samaj movement held an all-India Hindu Youth Conference in Karachi and used Babarao Savarkar's influence to invite Hedgewar. The Karachi Conference was a great success for it had overtly endorsed RSS' activities. On his return, Babarao assisted Doctor Saheb in establishing shakhas in Delhi, and invited him to travel to Bombay and other regions in Maharashtra. It was during this leg of the journey that the doctor was accompanied by a young man who was to earn severe notoriety more than a decade-and-a-half later. His name was: Nathuram Godse.

Gradually, K.B. Hedgewar's sustained campaigns resulted in a significant growth for the RSS. According to several reports, between 1931 and 1933, the number of shakhas had doubled to 125 and the membership had increased to an impressive 12,000. The rising trend continued through the 1930s and at the time of Hedgewar's death in June 1940, the RSS had more than 60,000 members. The British government took note of this burgeoning trend and concluded that the RSS was 'undoubtedly of a communal nature' and that 'its participation in political movements is increasing.' But despite all the objections, the government chose not to proscribe the RSS, and only put an embargo on government employees joining the outfit. Hedgewar countered the government's step by launching a formal protest forcing the British to quietly withdraw the order.

Meanwhile, even as the Indian National Congress had begun drawing up plans to determine the future plan for the country after independence, some of its leaders were worried about the RSS exerting influence over its members. As a first step towards curtailing its growing impact, the Congress deputed the industrialist-turned-philanthropist Jamnalal Bajaj to seek certain clarifications from the RSS and Hindu Mahasabha. A detailed questionnaire was sent to K.B. Hedgewar and Dr B.S. Moonje on a wide-ranging issues—untouchability; Khadi; and the organisational links between the two outfits. Hedgewar took this as an affront and refused to answer the questionnaire, and asked Jamnalal Bajaj to meet him in person. When Bajaj met Hedgewar in Nagpur in January 1934, he was told categorically that the RSS was not involved in politics and that there was no question of a personal animosity towards Gandhi or his campaigns to promote Khadi and denounce untouchability. However, the meeting had failed to allay Congress' fears and in June 1934, it passed a resolution prohibiting its members from associating themselves with the Hindu Mahasabha, RSS, and the Muslim League. Finally, Hedgewar's favourite child, the RSS had been deemed communal and dangerous by both the British and the Congress party, although the former later withdrew the charge.

For historians of different hues, Mahatma Gandhi's December 1934 visit to a RSS camp in Wardha and his subsequent meeting with K.B. Hedgewar continues to generate interest. By all accounts, it was a meeting amongst equals and Gandhi's 'attitude towards the RSS in 1934 may have been somewhat noncommittal.'[44] However, more than a decade later, when Mahatma Gandhi was asked about RSS' role in the deteriorating communal situation in 1946, he was unequivocal in his denunciation. When several leaders within the Congress had praised the RSS for its discipline and dedication in assisting refugees at transit camps during Partition, Gandhi had reminded them of similar traits displayed by the Nazis and Mussolini's followers and remarked sarcastically that the way to independence did not 'lie through akhadas.'[45]

The RSS considered Gandhi to be the fountainhead of pseudo-secularism and even if we were to take his comments to be biased for a moment, there is incontrovertible evidence that besides Hedgewar's reluctance in taking the British head-on, he displayed a keen interest in European fascism as a significant ideological tool in countering liberal and democratic thought. In this endeavour, it was once again his one-time mentor, Dr Moonje who provided the lead; he was the first Hindu nationalist to interact with Italian fascists, including Benito Mussolini. In 1931, en route to the First Round Table Conference in England, Dr Moonje had made a long stopover in Italy. In the *Economic and Political Weekly* dated 22 January 2000, Marzia Casolari mentions that amongst the various institutions that he visited, two 'were the keystone of the fascist system of indoctrination.' For instance, Dr Moonje was taken aback at the sight of Opera Nazionale Balilla and Avanguardista, and one of the entries in his diary read as follows[46]:

> India and particularly Hindu India need some such institution for the military regeneration of the Hindus: so that the artificial distinction so much emphasised by the British of martial and non-martial classes amongst the Hindus may disappear. Our institution of Rashtriya Swayamsewak Sangh of Nagpur under Dr Hedgewar is of this kind...

Dr Moonje's return from Europe coincided with Dr Hedgewar's massive territorial expansion of the RSS' network which included his renewed campaigns for militarising Hindus. It may be recalled that this was amongst the three objectives that he had set out for the RSS in 1925. Dr Moonje was mighty impressed with his protégé's zeal, and spearheaded a Hindu Mahasabha resolution in September 1932 which openly praised Hedgewar for his success in building a strong Hindu organisation. In late January 1934, Hedgewar presided over a seminar on fascism, while Dr Moonje delivered the concluding speech. In a private meeting a few months later, the two further discussed the rearming of Hindus. Yet another jotting in Dr Moonje's diary reveals the duo's thought process as follows, 'This ideal (organising Hindus) cannot be brought to effect unless we have our own swaraj with a Hindu as a dictator like Shivaji of old or Mussolini or Hitler.'[47]

The British were alarmed at the sudden admiration among top Hindu leaders for Mussolini and fascism, and an Intelligence report dated 1933 stated that 'perhaps (it is) no exaggeration to assert that the Sangh hopes to be in future India what the "Fascisti" are to Italy and the "Nazis" to Germany.'[48] The two Maharashtrian medical doctors may have held their own when it came to disagreeing on the nuanced differences between the RSS and the Mahasabha, but they were united in their admiration for European fascists and the need to militarise Hindus. Dr Moonje came up with a proposal to establish a national militia to guard against the 'enemy within'. Although this plan had eventually fallen through, he did succeed in setting up the Bhonsala Military School in Nashik under the aegis of the Central Hindu Military Education Society, with Hedgewar as a board member.

Eventually, the school came to be recognised as the nursery of Hindu terror in the early years of the twenty-first century after allegations of several Hindu group's involvement had surfaced in terror strikes. As it turned out later, in more ways than one and despite the fact that he had depended on his mentor for an insight into the workings of European fascism, K.B. Hedgewar emerged as the true upholder of its tradition. It may be recalled that the principle of ek chalak anuvartitva had strong similarities with the fascist idea of 'obedience to one leader'.

But all was still not well between the guru and his pupil. For instance, one of the most contentious issues between the two was Hedgewar's insistence to stay away from anti-Colonial protests. In 1938–39, he had disappointed his mentor yet again by refusing to lend support to a Civil Disobedience movement launched by the Mahasabha against the princely state of Hyderabad. By this time, Savarkar was out of jail and had little interest in strengthening the Hindu sangathan or the RSS. Instead he took charge of the Mahasabha and along with Dr Moonje formed several military wings and groups—the Hindu Swayam Sevak Dal and Hindu Women's Protection Corps were set up in 1937; while the Ram Sena was launched in March 1940.

It is often said that a good player must play to his strength. Hedgewar was aware of his limitations—while he may have reached out for assistance in formulating his political theories, his skills in organisation-building and networking was unchallenged even within his own fraternity. The only instance when he had gone against his core beliefs for the benefit of the organisation was in his decision to involve women in the RSS, but in a roundabout way.

While M.S. Golwalkar (see chapter, Madhav Sadashiv Golwalkar, p. 98) is credited with developing a network of allied organisations which gave rise to the concept of the sangh parivar, it was in fact K.B. Hedgewar who had initiated the process. But in order to do so, he had to go against his own principles. Early in life, in a letter to his uncle explaining his resolve to stay single, Hedgewar had said that since he had chosen to work for the country, it won't be 'good to risk the life of any girl.' On the one hand, if the statement expresses his concern for a woman who may find herself neglected owing to his preoccupation, it also indicates how Hedgewar precluded women from playing a role in the service of the nation. This notion was mandated upon pracharaks who were sworn to celibacy as Hedgewar did not want to risk their 'purity' by admitting women into the RSS. However, following several requests, Hedgewar finally agreed in 1936 to the setting up of the Rashtra Sevika Samiti as a separate, albeit cohesive entity of the RSS.

The Samiti, which was also established on Dussehra, affirmed its allegiance to all RSS principles and articles of faith. The choice of its founder Laxmibai Kelkar, a widow and mother of a young swayamsevak, and therefore presumed to be 'asexual', was apt. The women's group was allowed to draw up drills, which were symbolic of masculinity, only because the leadership was in the hands of older women, mothers and sisters of swayamsevaks, and not single women who could potentially 'entice' single male volunteers.

The Last Years

Around 1937–38, Keshav Baliram Hedgewar's health began deteriorating. The quintessential organisational man that he was, he took it upon himself to expand the RSS from a Maharashtra-centric outfit to one with a pan-Indian entity—several shakhas came up in Lahore, Sialkot and Rawalpindi in the Punjab; as also in Delhi, Lucknow, and Patna. In the east, he took the RSS to Calcutta and in the south to Madras (now Chennai), and Karnataka. Significantly, the RSS' expansion was most notable in places where the Hindu–Muslim equation had worsened and the swayamsevaks sensing an opportunity had formed defence squads in violence-prone areas. In each of these cities and towns, Hedgewar's Nagpur plan was replicated and needless to say, the benefits were impressively much the same.

Yet, Hedgewar's refusal to convert the RSS into a political front and contest elections after the 1935 constitutional reforms had left several of his supporters disappointed. However even his detractors had acknowledged in private that the RSS was indeed handicapped in the absence of a mass leader to steer its future. Furthermore, V.D. Savarkar's release from jail had weakened Hedgewar's authority over his cadre who were hugely drawn to the former's magnificent oratory.

In 1939, owing to his failing health, Hedgewar announced the first chintan baithak or brainstorming session at Sindi, near Nagpur. Although the grand old man was not suffering from a terminal disease, but his cadre was worried about the sudden summons. Gradually, it became clear to them that the meeting was to determine Hedgewar's succession plan and identify leaders who could take the RSS' mission into the future. Amongst those invited to the deliberations were, M.S. Golwalkar and Balasaheb Deoras, and several others. The Sindi chintan baithak is recalled as a unique phenomenon in the annals of the RSS, because it was the only instance when three men who had presided over the RSS for almost seven decades (from 1925 to 1994) were huddled together for several days to deliberate on its past, present, and the future.

There was no doubt that the rapid expansion of the RSS (in 1938, there were approximately 400 shakhas with nearly 40,000 swayamsevaks, and the number rose to 76,000 in 1943) in the years preceding the Sindi baithak had significantly boosted the RSS' clout, but it had also created certain practical problems for it. For instance, because the RSS at its inception happened to be Maharashtra-centric, the Marathi language as a natural corollary became its lingua franca. Not only was the language used for inter-personal communication, but the part eulogising the Motherland in the RSS hymn was also sung in Marathi. In contrast, the stanza in Hindi which was an invocation to Ramdas Swami did not have as many followers in other parts of India; the prayer sought refuge in the saint and pleaded recognition as a Rampanthi. Most importantly, even instructions during the daily drill to the cadre were given in Marathi.

When language became a barrier for reciting the prayer, the shakha heads in different states requested that the first stanza be translated into the local language. There were also questions about the relevance of Ramdas Swami in regions where he was unknown and finally permission was granted that every region invoke seers who had a following and commanded respect in the area.

Historically in north India, the RSS had always piggybacked on the Arya Samaj movement, as a result of which its tradition of adhering to 'idolatrous rituals and rites'[49] was opposed by reformists. For instance, Lord Hanuman was invoked with great reverence in RSS ceremonies, but in several parts of India, the Monkey God was not even part of the main pantheon.

Finally, K.B. Hedgewar came up with a solution for tackling cultural and linguistic differences and his proposal to change the prayer was endorsed at the Sindi chintan baithak. Even today, the Sanskrit prayer, *Namaste sada vatsale* is recited every day in shakhas across the country. It however ends with a salutation to the nation—Bharat Mata Ki Jai.

The construct of a nation as Motherland or Fatherland is undoubtedly a universal tradition, but in India the deification of the nation as a Hindu goddess was a twentieth-century phenomenon. It is to the credit of the RSS which lent it a political dimension by associating it to an image which was first depicted by Abanindranath Tagore in 1905.

For fourteen long years since its inception, the RSS leadership had braved frequent pressure from its cadre to join the anti-Colonial or anti-State protests. The 1938 satyagraha against the despotic Nizam's regime in Hyderabad had acquired communal undertones and there was a growing demand within the RSS to join the protest, especially since anti-Imperialism had come to be synonymous with anti-Muslims. When Bhaiyaji Dani, a trusted Hedgewar aide and general secretary of the RSS, had lent support to the anti-Nizam movement, he was not only pulled up by the doctor, but excluded from the crucial Sindi baithak. That was possibly the strongest message Hedgewar had sent out to those who desired direct involvement in both political movements and public protests.

Yet, in order to ensure that the decision of not extending an invite to someone of Dani's seniority wasn't viewed as a personal whim, Hedgewar had opened up the subject for discussion saying that after Savarkar had donned the top mantle of the Hindu Mahasabha, several swayamsevaks had been attracted to his programmes and electoral politics. He also anticipated a growing support for electoral politics and spoke about how the RSS would counter the influence of V.D. Savarkar, while keeping its core values intact. Eventually, the RSS chose not to be part of electoral politics but allowed swayamsevaks to engage with other affiliated organisations, including political parties. However, several senior functionaries of the RSS were not only barred from participating in such engagements, but were also asked to encourage volunteers to continue attending the daily shakha. Although the move had enabled the cadre to become members of other organisations, this later became a matter of great controversy (for instance in 1977–80, when the Janata Party split on the issue of 'dual-membership') as many saw this as a tactic on the part of the RSS to influence decision-making in other parties.

The Sindi chintan baithak happened to be Hedgewar's last engagement with his cadre. On 21 June 1940, Keshav Baliram Hedgewar died in Nagpur after a protracted illness. He was cremated in Reshimbagh, the twenty-one acre plot that he had helped acquire to establish the RSS campus in Nagpur where a memorial called the Smriti Mandir was built in his honour in 1962. Unlike the memorial, which was left for later generations of RSS leaders to complete, in life, K.B. Hedgewar was undoubtedly the architect who had not only built the organisation, but had identified a team of custodians to take charge of it in the coming decades. Just as every individual with frailties, he too had many. But unlike many others, he played to his strengths. He built a strong edifice for an organisation that continues to play a significant role in Indian politics.

After taking over as prime minister, Narendra Modi had strategically chosen to widen the 'soft component' of India's foreign policy by focusing on yoga, ayurveda and Buddhism. He had personally lobbied with the United Nations to recognise 21 June as International Yoga Day. The date and day has great significance not only because it is summer solstice in the northern hemisphere, but it is also Keshav Baliram Hedgewar's birth anniversary. The prime minister's move may continue to draw flak for years to come, but by linking the RSS founder's birth anniversary with a UN celebration, it was almost as if Narendra Modi had offered the most unusual guru dakshina to an iconic leader.

VINAYAK DAMODAR SAVARKAR

On a cold October evening in 1906, barely three months after his arrival in London in July, a city across the proverbial 'seven seas', the Maharashtrian Brahmin who eventually emerged as one of the most polarising figures in India, in life and in death, sautéed prawns in his room in India House. He would be playing host to a vegetarian Vaishya Gujarati—also destined to acquire, in life and in death, a revered demigod status—who had docked a few days ago at Southampton, on 20 October to be precise. The Gujarati guest was in England as part of a two-member deputation of the British Indian Association of the Transvaal, South Africa, the other being Hadje Ojeer Ally, Chairman, Hamidiya Islamic Society, to lobby against the humiliating and discriminating Asiatic Law Amendment Ordinance signed into law in the Transvaal in August 1906. The host had arrived from India to train as a barrister at Gray's Inn, one of the historic societies that educate barristers in England and Wales.

Although a Brahmin who had travelled to England on a scholarship from Shyamji Krishnavarma, the former Dewan of Ratlam, Udaipur and Junagadh (also a nationalist and consistent supporter of other

Indian patriots) the host of this unpublicised and chance interaction between the two did not adhere to the caste system or vegetarianism. The Gujarati, however, despite being from the caste that comprised mainly traders, was firmly vegetarian. This odd setting for the meeting was significant for two reasons. For one, it was a perfect example of the dichotomy which existed, and still does, between the personal lives and political ideologies of Indian politicians. For example, Mohammed Ali Jinnah's political conviction was totally at odds with his fondness for Scotch and ham sandwiches. Closer to our time, Shiv Sena chief Bal Thackeray was known for his 'indulgences', which included warm beer and Cuban cigars, despite being a champion of regional and national chauvinism and culture. Secondly, events of that evening acted as a precursor to the manner in which these two men would engage with each other—fervently disagreeing on almost everything, all through their lives. The pattern of future behaviour was also apparent from their first interaction, one of them the more patient and the other more impetuous.

The twenty-three-year-old Vinayak Damodar Savarkar, student of Law in England, interrupted Mohandas Karamchand Gandhi, the Indian lawyer who was readying to launch a satyagraha in Johannesburg, mid-sentence. Gandhi was explaining to Savarkar why his strategy against the British was far too aggressive, almost bordering on militancy. Instead of listening to the contention of his polite visitor, Savarkar asked him to join for dinner. When Gandhi declined, explaining he ate no meat or fish, Savarkar ridiculed him. How can anyone challenge the might of the British without consuming animal protein, he is said to have asked Gandhi.[1] At this point, three months had elapsed since Savarkar's arrival in London and it was also almost three months since 20 July, the day when

Gandhi took the vow of celibacy for life. There is no mention in any known records of Savarkar being in the know about this. It thus remains a matter of speculation whether he would have commented on this choice of Gandhi's too, arguing that celibacy was a sign of effeminacy and would come in the way of Gandhi's efforts to fight the colonialists. Sexuality was a recurring theme in Savarkar's life, especially of the violent kind, but more on this later.

Like their dietary choices, their political paths were at sharp variance too. Gandhi, who was eventually revered as the Mahatma, followed a non-violent or pacifist course which drew strength from India's diversity and culture of co-existence in the fight against imperialism. In contrast, Savarkar chose aggression, which he used mainly against the 'enemy within', a euphemism for Muslims. Both wanted to revive India's glorious past—Gandhi's idea of a Ram Rajya was at the other end of the spectrum when compared to Savarkar's idea of a Hindu empire that he dreamt of resurrecting someday. In Gandhi's construct of an ideal and inclusive state, justice was ensured for the meek. Savarkar believed nationality and citizenship were predicated on religious identity. History was central to the political ideology of both men. But while Savarkar's idea of history was intrinsically linked to violence and Hindutva, Gandhi's search was for a non-violent and shared heritage that could be used to motivate individuals to pursue a path of non-violent and inclusive nationalism.

That cold evening, Gandhi left Savarkar's apartment with an empty stomach and without having secured support for his impending satyagraha. He would not have gone hungry, however, thanks to Shyamji Krishnavarma, who ran India House for all Indian students and nationalists regardless of their religious identity. Gandhi and Ally would have stayed in India House for the entire duration of their visit, only moving to the expensive Hotel Cecil because they often had to meet important people.

The meeting between Gandhi and Savarkar was the beginning of an intensely complicated relationship between the two men. The two had no love lost for one another for the major part of period of forty-two years till the former's assassination by the latter's disciple. Yet, when the situation demanded magnanimity from Gandhi, like in 1920, when Savarkar was jailed in the Cellular Jail, Andamans Islands and Gandhi's advice was sought on the issue of seeking pardon from the colonial administration, the Mahatma acted true to his moniker. This trait of Gandhi was not negatively impacted despite sharp disagreements with Savarkar over the efficacy of violence and revolutionary methods to secure India's liberation from the British. In fact, during his short stay at India House in 1906, Gandhi also had long conversations with Krishnavarma and discovered that his views were similar to Savarkar's. Yet, Gandhi kept his opinion to himself and it was not until his third visit to London in 1909, but the first after 1906, that he decided to voice his differences with 'the so-called extremists who may be better described as the party of violence'.[2] Gandhi did not specifically name Savarkar in the cited missive to a senior British official. But there was no ambiguity that he was among the Indians of 'every shade of opinion' that Gandhi met in London.[3]

This second meeting with Savarkar disturbed Gandhi immensely, so much so that he wrote to Gopal Krishna Gokhale sharing his regret, especially about Savarkar's viewpoint of adopting violence as a legitimate political tool to overthrow the British. The meeting between them, took place in public, in the midst of a large gathering. Gandhi had returned to England on 10 July 1909 for his third visit to the country, this time to canvas for the education of Indians across the British Empire and also lobby for resident rights for south Asians in South Africa. What brought him and Savarkar together, although in disagreement again, was an assassination—Savarkar's sanction of violence and assassinations for political objectives and Gandhi's denunciation of these methods formed the foundation of their differences.

On 1 July 1909, Madan Lal Dhingra, a member of the Abhinav Bharat Society, an organisation that Savarkar had founded, shot dead Curzon Wyllie, who he suspected was working for police intelligence, at a function of the National Indian Association. A guest at the function, Dr Cawas Lalcaca, was also accidentally killed in the shooting, a tragedy for which Dhingra expressed regret later. The murders shocked nationalist Indians and on 5 July, a meeting was held to condemn it. It was attended by several prominent Indians in London, including Surendranath Banerjea, Bipin Chandra Pal, the Aga Khan and Savarkar. Speaker after speaker condemned the assassination and a resolution was adopted, seemingly unanimously.

This, however, was contested by Savarkar, whose statement was published as a letter by *The Times* (London). In it, he argued that the proper procedure for voting was not adopted at the meeting. He added that since the matter had become sub-judice, the resolution breached the privilege of the court. Savarkar also wanted Dhingra to be treated fairly. This public defence of Dhingra resulted in Savarkar getting a fair amount of media coverage for the first time, when he was just twenty-six. The website 'savarkar.org', stated to be the product of the 'combined efforts of several individuals and organisations', acknowledges the support of Swatantryaveer Savarkar Rashtriya Smarak, Mumbai, Abhinav Bharat Mandir Trust, Nashik, Deccan Education Society, Pune, Hindu Mahasabha Bhavan, New

Delhi, among others. Significantly, it claims Savarkar 'gifted Dhingra with a Belgian-make Browning pistol and took his leave with great affection. Dhingra was overcome with emotion. Savarkar said, "Do not show me your face again if you fail this time." Dhingra reassured him that this would not happen.'

Dhingra's trial was held on 19 July and after being pronounced guilty, he was swiftly executed on 17 August. The Abhinav Bharat Society published a postcard to commemorate Dhingra's execution and termed him a revolutionary. In the postcard, parts of Dhingra's defence statement, in which he asserted that the assassination had been the right thing to do, were published. Savarkar's public celebration of Dhingra's act was in contrast to Gandhi's reaction.

For Gandhi, the two assassinations were 'a terrible thing' and he asked 'every Indian' to 'reflect thoughtfully on this murder. It has done India much harm; the deputation's efforts have also received a setback'. In Gandhi's view, Dhingra's act was that of a 'coward' and his defence was 'inadmissible'. Gandhi could only 'pity the man. He was egged on to do this act by ill-digested reading of worthless writings'.[4]

Savarkar was, in Gandhi's mind, the agent provocateur. Gandhi wrote that, in his opinion, 'Mr. Dhingra himself is innocent. The murder was committed in a state of intoxication. It is not merely wine or bhang that makes one drunk; a mad idea also can do so.' Without doubt, Gandhi was of the opinion that Dhingra was not the only one guilty of the crime. The person who planted the idea of assassinating Wyllie was equally to blame, if not more.

More than two months after Dhingra's execution, Gandhi and Savarkar came face to face in perhaps the only public meeting of their lives. This was on 24 October 1909 in London. Gandhi was the guest of honour at a contributory dinner to celebrate Vijayadashami and the audience comprised about sixty to seventy Indians. The magazine *Indian Opinion*, in its issue dated 27 November 1909, included in the *Complete Works of Mahatma Gandhi*, Volume 10, wrote that in his speech, Gandhi pointed out that 'as a historical personage Shri Ramachandra could be honoured by every Indian. Everyone, whether Hindu, Muslim or Parsi, should be proud of belonging to a country which produced a man like Shri Ramachandra. To the extent that he was a great Indian, he should be honoured by every Indian.' The same report states that Savarkar 'delivered a spirited speech on the great excellence of the Ramayana and said that every Indian should realize the significance of the fact that Vijaya Dashami is preceded by Navratri'.

Vinayak Chaturvedi, in his 2022 book *Hindutva and Violence: V.D. Savarkar and the Politics of History*, presents a detailed account of this public encounter between the two men. He quotes a CID report of the meeting according to which Gandhi unequivocally stated that 'he belonged to a different school of thought from Savarkar. He said he considered Savarkar's teaching injurious to the well-being of the country, and that the real oppressor—the ten headed monster [Ravana]—was within them'. Gandhi has referred to more detailed discussions with Savarkar and also with Shyamji Krishnavarma, who clearly shared Savarkar's opinion. He wrote, 'When I was in London, I had talks with many revolutionaries. Shyamji Krishnavarma, Savarkar and others used to tell me that the Gita and the Ramayana taught quite the opposite of what I said they did.'[5] According to Chaturvedi, the primary divergence between Gandhi and Savarkar was over the former interpreting the violence in the Ramayan and Mahabharat 'as allegories for the internal conflict in all humans. For Savarkar, the necessity of violence in both texts was meant to be interpreted literally, as an essence of the human condition. Moreover, he argued that violence was a central feature of all human history. Their divergent interpretations of violence set them apart from this moment forward'. Gandhi returned to South Africa a few days after this meeting and began writing one of his most definitive works, *Hind Swaraj*, which he wrote in the form of a dialogue with an unnamed revolutionary, considered by many scholars, including Chaturvedi, as one of his more articulated responses to Savarkar's views on the two epics and on the use of violence.

For instance, in *Hind Swaraj*, the revolutionary claims, 'At first, we will assassinate a few Englishmen and strike terror; then, a few men who will have been armed will fight openly.' To this the 'editor', or Gandhi for all purposes, retorts, 'Do you not tremble to think of freeing India by assassination? What we need to do is to kill ourselves. It is a cowardly thought, that of killing others. Whom do you suppose to free by assassination? The millions of India do not desire it.'

It is evident that Gandhi and Savarkar differed over not just the violence in the epics—whether they were allegorical and intended to depict inner turmoil or if they were literal, as in Savarkar's understanding. The two also disagreed over the use of assassination as a nationalistic tool. It is not a paradox but only natural then that Savarkar should have remained connected with Dhingra and other assassins, including the one to whose bullets Gandhi eventually fell on 30 January 1948.

On 5 February 1948, the sixth day after Mahatma Gandhi's assassination, Savarkar was arrested in Bombay (as the city was then known; now, Mumbai), on the charge of being a co-conspirator. Although he was acquitted a year later in February 1949, the J.L. Kapur Commission of Inquiry, which had concluded its investigations two decades later, stated that the 'facts (unearthed or established by the Commission) taken together were destructive of any theory other than the conspiracy to murder by Savarkar and his group'.[6] Savarkar had passed by then, well before the last word could be written about his involvement in murdering India's apostle of peace.

* * *

Circa 2014: the 131st birth anniversary of Vinayak Damodar Savarkar was being celebrated on 28 May. Within two days of assuming office after a hard-fought victory, Prime Minister Narendra Damodardas Modi paid obeisance to the leader at an official function in Parliament. Several Bharatiya Janata Party (BJP) MPs and other allies had joined him in the dome-shaped Central Hall. But, much like the past decade and more, the Congress party and several others belonging to the Opposition boycotted the commemoration. They had stayed away from this annual ceremony since 2003 when the late Prime Minister Atal Bihari Vajpayee had unveiled Savarkar's portrait in Parliament.* It is another example of how polarising a figure Savarkar has remained even several decades after his death in 1966.

It is ironic that even though Savarkar was not a member of BJP's erstwhile political avatar, the Jana Sangh or the Rashtriya Swayamsevak Sangh (RSS), leaders of the Sangh Parivar, including

* The portrait unveiling ceremony by President A.P.J. Abdul Kalam on 26 February 2003 was particularly controversial. The Opposition, with the exception of former Prime Minister Chandrashekhar, boycotted the function. The Deputy Speaker of Lok Sabha, P.M. Sayeed, too, was a notable absentee. In 2000, Vajpayee had proposed to the then President K.R. Narayanan that India's highest civilian award, the Bharat Ratna, be conferred on Savarkar. But it wasn't approved.

Modi, have always held him in great reverence. He was undeniably an iconic figure, despite his sharp ideological divergences with several leaders of the RSS, because his legacy was readily co-opted as part of BJP's history and heritage. Several important BJP leaders, including party president Amit Shah, prefer being photographed with Savarkar's portrait in the backdrop over pictures of other leaders. Many in the saffron fraternity have openly admitted to being more influenced by Savarkar than either K.B. Hedgewar or even M.S. Golwalkar, also known as Guruji.[7]

The reason for Savarkar's indisputable pre-eminence among saffron icons is because of his 'first full articulation'[8] of a Hindu nationalist manifesto in the form of his seminal 'prison' treatise, 'Essentials of Hindutva'. But more on this later.

Early Nationalism

Greatness was neither acquired nor bestowed upon him; it was bequeathed to him by destiny, believed Vinayak's followers. His biographer, Dhananjay Keer, averred that Vinayak Damodar Savarkar, who was born seventy-five days after Karl Marx's death and sixty-two days after Benito Mussolini's birth, was in no way lesser than the two Europeans.[9] Providence may not have determined his life, but John Milton's famous words: 'The childhood shows the man, as morning shows the day' rang true for Savarkar.

When Vinayak was a boy of ten in 1893, riots between Hindus and Muslims erupted in Azamgarh, United Provinces (Uttar Pradesh), and a few months later, spread to Bombay as well. Even in the days when sophisticated methods of communication were next to non-existent, several versions of the riots were widely circulated, and in the tiny village of Nashik, little Vinayak began believing in the stories of injustices perpetrated on Hindus.

The young boy decided to act and 'led a batch of selected schoolmates in a march upon the village mosque'.[10] After pelting stones and breaking a few windowpanes in the building, the group claimed victory. The attack didn't go unchallenged and in retaliation, local Muslim schoolboys 'gave battle to Vinayak, the Hindu Generalissimo'.[11]

That this wasn't just a flash in the pan, or an act by a precocious child was proven when Vinayak organised marching drills for his classmates, involving callisthenic exercises and mock war games. This childhood obsession with militarising and his view of Muslims as the devious 'enemy within' became the foundation of his fervent opposition to Gandhi's choice of non-violence for combating anti-Imperialistic campaigns.

One of the most important reasons for Savarkar's early indoctrination was his exposure to Hindu revivalism that had begun with a reassertion of Hinduism in the 1890s. Bal Gangadhar Tilak was one of the leading lights of the movement which was sweeping across western India and was credited with bringing ritualistic religious practices into the public domain. Tilak began the practice of holding the Ganapati (another name for Lord Ganesha) festival in civic venues in an effort to unite Hindus across the spectrum on a common religio-cultural platform. Community celebrations of a religious festival hitherto performed in homes also worked as a counter-balance to the Muslim festival of Muharram, a festival that occurs in public spaces during which Muslims participate in processions on the streets.

Julian Anthony Lynch, while pursuing his PhD in Ethnomusicology and Anthropology at the University of Wisconsin–Madison where his research focused on issues of conflict in musical practices in colonial and contemporary India, wrote about Tilak more or less single-handedly reinventing the Ganapati festival in Maharashtra. [12]

The celebration of the Ganesh festival hereafter became 'a public spectacle with strong political motivations'. Tilak would have been unsuccessful in skirting past restrictions imposed by the colonial regime on overtly political programmes. He had no such difficulty with the administration when the celebration was religious in nature and the anti-colonial narrative was merely latent. In 1893, when the festival was celebrated for the first time, its dates coincided with the observance of Muharram. Previously, Hindus used to join the public procession and other rituals connected with the festival, but not after 1893: 'Tilak called upon Hindus to boycott the festival that year, offering Ganapati as a new, and divisive, alternative. The festival, therefore, was also an attack on syncretic religious practices that previously had flourished in India.' (Lynch, ibid)

The decision to pitchfork Lord Ganesha into the forefront of Hindu religiosity in the form of an annual public festival was a well-calculated move, as the elephant-headed god was neither part of the Holy Trinity—Brahma, Vishnu and Shiva—nor the main deity of any particular community in Maharashtra. The festival was, therefore, one of the first attempts to create a pan-Hindu identity, countering divergences between different sects and philosophical schools within Hinduism and, more importantly, among various castes. The open display of religious fervour induced a sense of collectiveness, and became an occasion for Hindus to not only pray, but also celebrate with gusto.

Buoyed by the success of the festival, Tilak launched the Shivaji festival to arouse nationalistic sentiment amongst Marathi youth. On a lighter note, one can speculate that young Savarkar was attracted to Tilak's initiative perhaps because of his first name, Vinayak, which is one of the many names for Lord Ganesha! But what is certain is that the ten-year-old boy was a ready convert to Tilak's initiative of creating a Hindu collective around a benign god.

As mentioned earlier, Vinayak Savarkar had already earned the moniker of a child 'Generalissimo', and it was not surprising that in the late 1890s, he became an active member of Mitra Mela, a secret society for young revolutionaries. Later, he engineered the transformation of this miniscule initiative into the more expansive Abhinav Bharat Society, or Young India Society, a title inspired by Giuseppe Mazzini's 'Young Italy'. In the early twentieth century, Savarkar 'officially' became part of the Indian freedom struggle and played a decisive role in dovetailing Abhinav Bharat Society with Bengal's most formidable revolutionary organisation of the time, the Anushilan Samiti.

Despite the latent anti-Muslim sentiment in Maharashtra during this period, Hindus were coming out in large numbers to fight the colonial rule and the 'firangee'. Among other things, the Abhinav Bharat Society fanned aversion for foreign rule, which later transmogrified into a sentiment against the 'traitors within', i.e., the Muslims and Christians, by portraying them also as outsiders or 'foreign'. Eventually, Savarkar became the organisation's chief theoretician.

In 1902, at the age of nineteen, Vinayak enrolled in Fergusson College, Pune, and continued with his revolutionary activities. The young man from Nashik was fast becoming a cause célèbre—the first Indian to be expelled from college for his radical views. He found support in Tilak, who condemned the college administration for its action against a promising student. While this did not persuade the college administration to revoke the expulsion order, money and sympathy poured in for Savarkar, enabling him to pursue higher studies in Bombay.

The young Vinayak impressed Tilak to such an extent that he recommended his case to a wealthy nationalist, Shyamji Krishnavarma, who had founded India House in London. In a letter, Tilak wrote that the student was a 'spirited young man very enthusiastic in the swadeshi cause'. This powerful endorsement coupled with Savarkar's opening sentence in his application letter, which read: 'Independence and Liberty I look upon as the pulse and breath of the nation' clinched a scholarship for him (named after the Maratha ruler, Shivaji), to study law in England.

On 9 June 1906, Vinayak Damodar Savarkar set sail after bidding goodbye to his wife, Yamunabai and their one-year-old son, Prabhakar. Unfortunately, he never saw his son again as the baby died after contracting smallpox in 1909, while Savarkar was studying and inspiring violent nationalists in London.

At the time of Savarkar's arrival in London, the idea of Hindu nationalism was yet to take root in its soil, despite a strong sense of unity among resident Hindus, and a cloaked but fierce anti-Muslim sentiment. As academics was not his sole motivation to be in London, Savarkar joined a group of revolutionaries in their mission to liberate India through an armed rebellion. He set up the Abhinav Bharat Society in London, and also began attending the Sunday meetings called by Free India Society, which was founded by the feisty Madame Bhikhaiji Cama. Much like his mentor, Tilak, Savarkar introduced Hindu festivals in London and began commemorating heroic figures from India's ancient past. Within months of his arrival, he translated select essays from Mazzini's *Collected Works* in 1907 into Marathi with an introduction to his writings, and followed it up with a book titled *The Indian War of Independence of 1857* in 1909 to mark the golden jubilee of the First War of Independence.

Alas, for the young revolutionary-turned-author, the book ran into trouble when a few chapters of the Marathi manuscript fell into the hands of Scotland Yard. An English translation was eventually published a year later, in 1909, in Holland. It did not carry Savarkar's name as the author, crediting instead 'An Indian Nationalist'. The book was banned in India until 1946, and it was the Congress government in Bombay which had finally rescinded the proscription. However, despite being unavailable in India for almost four decades, several youngsters continued to read it surreptitiously. For instance, L.K. Advani once wrote how as a schoolboy in Sindh, he had bought a copy of the book at a princely sum of twenty-eight rupees![13] According to Vinayak Chaturvedi, Savarkar exposure to Mazzini had a 'transformative impact' on him and he incorporated key ideas of the Italian into his book on events in 1857 and even later Mazzini's works influenced Savarkar's works on Hindutva. [14]

By the time Savarkar devoted himself to taking Mazzini to the Marathi reader, it was already several decades after a wide range of Indians had begun discovering the Italian revolutionary. By this time, prominent nationalists like Surendranath Banerjea, Bipin Chandra Pal, Gandhi and even Lala Lajpat Rai were already in London. Some of them were drawn to Mazzini's writings because of his thesis on the interconnection between religion and politics while for some, the interest was spawned by Mazzini's narratives of secret societies and guerrilla strategies which justified the use of violence. There were others too for whom Mazzini was of significant interest because of his ideas of democracy and nationalism. There were some like

Banerjea who disagreed with some of Mazzini's views (like universal franchise) while Gandhi, through an essay in 1905, 'Joseph Mazzini: A Remarkable Career', inverted the common interpretation of Mazzini being committed to the use of violence in his political strategies. Gandhi also considered that Mazzini 'could be regarded a citizen of every country,'[15] and was a person who 'gave up his books out of patriotism and undertook the study of law, and began using his legal knowledge gratuitously to help the poor'. Italian scholar, Fabrizio de Donno, has argued that Gandhi in his early years countered the Indian liberalism that was 'imbued with Mazzinian ideas'. In the process, Gandhi conceptualised a 'Gandhian Mazzini' in contrast to the Savarkarite viewpoint that Mazzini's democratic nationalism had insurrectionary elements that could inspire the revolutionary actions of Indian nationalists.

Soon, India House became the hub of revolutionary activity in London and Savarkar came to play a significant role in furthering its cause. He began writing newsletters for a Marathi paper and took the lead in publishing leaflets, including one in Gurmukhi prodding the Sikhs to revolt against the British and, in 1908, even organised celebrations to mark the birth anniversary of Guru Gobind Singh.

Meanwhile, the London branch of the Abhinav Bharat Society produced copies of a bomb manual for revolutionaries back in India. Savarkar also despatched pistols back home, one of which was used to assassinate a British magistrate who had sentenced Vinayak's eldest brother, Ganesh (popularly known as Babarao), to six years' imprisonment for writing patriotic songs that were deemed seditious by the imperial government.

In London as well, the British administration queered the pitch for Savarkar. This was a fallout of what happened on 1 July 1909, when Madan Lal Dhingra, one of the regulars at India House and a 'young man inspired by Savarkar,'[16] assassinated Curzon Wyllie, aide-de-camp to the Secretary of State for India. Although the British government had failed to establish Savarkar's direct culpability in Wyllie's assassination, they were not only aware of his close friendship with Dhingra, but also that his 'ringing defence of the killing had been drafted by Savarkar'.[17] Shortly thereafter, India House shut down and Savarkar was forced to shift to a non-descript inn, strictly meant for Indians, in a London borough. On 23 July 1909, upon being produced in front of the magistrate at the Old Bailey, Madan Lal Dhingra (who had chosen to defend himself) was debarred from reading out his statement. It was V.D. Savarkar who had it published in a London newspaper with assistance from an aspiring British journalist, although it had little impact on Dhingra's trial.

Furthermore, in the aftermath of the British officer's assassination in Nashik, life became tougher for Vinayak Savarkar. In a much-publicised case which came to be called the Nashik Conspiracy case, his elder brother, Ganesh (Babarao) Savarkar, was exiled and sent to the Cellular Jail in the Andaman and Nicobar Islands. Initially, the British knew of Vinayak's association with the assassin but had little evidence to establish his firm connection with the conspiracy. However, the British administrators got lucky when the man who had couriered the pistols to India changed sides and became the King's witness.

In anticipation of an impending arrest, Savarkar's associates advised him to take refuge in Paris in the hope that the matter would soon die down. But the hunt for Savarkar continued, and when he returned to London in March 1910, he was arrested the moment he stepped out of Victoria Station. At first, the British deliberated over whether he should be prosecuted in London or India since the actual crime was committed in Nashik during the time Savarkar had been residing in England. Moreover, the only charge he could be tried under was incitement to murder and, if convicted, would have only been given a maximum sentence of two to three years.

Eventually, authorities in India recovered speeches which he had delivered while visiting the country to examine if they served as sufficient evidence to prosecute him. British authorities finally concluded that although the speeches were fairly innocuous at the time they were made, they could now be termed subversive.

Upon being alerted of his imminent arrest, Savarkar plotted to escape jail. However, after he learnt that the British had got wind of his plans, particularly of his pre-emptive escape bid, he told David Garnett, his British 'admirer' who had helped him hatch the original escape plan that it 'does not matter whether one wins or is defeated, whether one succeeds or fails. Care nothing about the result so long as you fight. The only thing that matters is the spirit'.

On 8 July 1910, as the ship which was bringing him back to India docked in Marseilles, Vinayak slipped out through a porthole inside the bathroom. The dramatic escape would have been successful but for the alertness of a brigadier of the French maritime gendarmerie who detained Savarkar and handed him back to the British. After the British ship left French waters, the arrest of Savarkar from the territory of France was considered improper and the matter reached the Arbitral Tribunal at The Hague. On 24 February 1911, the Tribunal ruled that 'while admitting that an irregularity was committed by the arrest of Savarkar, and by his being handed over to the British Police, there is no rule of International Law imposing, in circumstances such as those which have been set out above, any obligation on the Power which has in its custody a prisoner, to restore him because of a mistake committed by the foreign agent who delivered him up to that Power.' As a result, the Tribunal formally decreed that 'the Government of His Britannic Majesty is not required to restore the said Vinayak Damodar Savarkar to the Government of the French Republic.' By that time, Savarkar had already been convicted and sentenced to imprisonment for life.

The episode nonetheless pitchforked the twenty-seven-year-old Savarkar into fame and he was celebrated as a national hero. He became an international symbol of British repression—several articles in the press condemned the British; the Italian parliament and the Republican Party of Italy demanded his release; in August 1910, a Savarkar Release Committee was established in England; many diplomatic efforts were made to petition the imperial government for his release. At home, stories about his dramatic escape were embellished till it acquired a status of mythical folklore and anecdotes eulogising his patriotic fervour came to be highly circulated, presenting him as a figure comprising the stuff of legends.

The books he had authored, including those that were banned, returned to circulation and readers and scholars began devouring them with renewed vigour. What merits mention here is that Savarkar was among those rare revolutionary nationalists who supplemented his activism with propaganda literature. At that particular stage of his life, Savarkar's idea of nationalism had not yet integrated with his childhood ambition of restoring Hindu dignity by raising the spectre of 'cultural' Hindus. The codification of Hindu nationalism, which was arguably Savarkar's true contribution to Indian political thought, occurred at a later stage in his life. However, a careful reading of *The Indian War of Independence, 1857* provides enough indication of his future postulations because he had clearly focused on Hindu and Maratha exclusivity and didn't celebrate 'a unified and composite past, present, and future Indian nation.'[18]

Significantly, Savarkar challenged contemporary historiography when it came to the analyses of 1857. In particular, he questioned the propensity to emphasise specific incidents as being the principal causes for the war. According to him, the justification behind the First War of Independence was far more serious than the use of animal tallow to grease cartridges or the poor administrative skills of the British.

Although by no stretch was he advancing the compositeness of the Indian nation state, he highlighted the 'revolutionary principles of swadharma (acting according to one's nature) and swaraj (self-rule) as being shared by Hindus and Muslims, who fought as Hindi brethren against British rule'.[19] He was indisputably evolving as a political thinker and often lapsed into 'epic and magisterial explication of battles and strategies, alliances and betrayals, victories and defeats'[20] that had the capacity 'of inciting passion for revenge'. Moreover, he presented a manual for organising a revolution in a chapter titled, 'Secret Organisation',[21] in which he delineated the 'strategies to prepare for and engage in revolutionary warfare'.

On the one hand, Savarkar believed that Indians of different faiths needed to unite against the imperial forces. Yet, he also articulated that the 'feeling of hatred against the Mahomedans was just and necessary in the times of Shivaji.' Suffice it to say that there were inconsistencies in his postulations that were evident in his writing:

> Though the ruling prince of Oudh was a Mahomedan, most of the big land-owners under him were Hindus. Jahgirs and Talukdari rights had continued from father to son in the families

> of these Zemindars for generations. Hundreds of villages were administered under the single authority of each of these proprietors. They possessed forts and had small armies under them to protect these Jahgirs. No wonder, then, that these Zemindars very soon incurred the displeasure of the Company.[22]

Similar self-contradictory assertions came to the fore yet again in the book when he analysed the reasons for installing the Mughal Emperor Bahadur Shah Zafar for a brief period in May 1857. On the one hand, Savarkar theorised that the 'restoration of the deposed Emperor was apparently not a retrograde action' and on the other, he propounded that the act was,

> ... no restoration at all. For, the Mogul dynasty of old was not chosen by the people of the land. It was thrust upon India by sheer force, dignified by the name of conquest, and upheld by a powerful pack of alien adventures and native self-seekers ... such thrones are conquered and not received ...[23]

Savarkar's limited acceptance of Emperor was because the 'old venerable Bahadur Shah was not the old Mogul succeeding to the throne of Akbar or Aurangzeb—for that throne had already been smashed to pieces by the hammer of the Mahrattas'.[24]

The Hindu Nationalist

Vinayak Damodar Savarkar's political life can be neatly divided into three phases—first, when he struck a balance between revolutionary nationalism and Hindu nationalism which ended when he was sentenced to life imprisonment. His acts of bravado coupled with conviction earned him the label of the 'brave freedom fighter' or 'swatantra Veer Savarkar'. But the heroism associated with the likes of Mahatma Gandhi, Jawaharlal Nehru and even Tilak wasn't what he desired. Rather, Savarkar wanted to go down in history as the 'organiser' of Hindus—to adopt a larger-than-life mantle than merely a soldier sworn to the freedom of the country. In his several articles, books and essays written during the first phase, the idea of Hindu nationalism was still an ideology in the making.

The second phase of his life began in 1911 with his confinement in the Cellular Jail and continued till 1937. He spent the first decade of the next twenty-six years in the Andaman Islands after which he was lodged in Yerawada Jail, Pune, and finally in Ratnagiri. It was during this phase when he wrote his seminal work, *Essentials of Hindutva*, later given the title of *Hindutva! Who is a Hindu?* with the second phrase as a sub-title in the 1928 reprint, following which he became a revered ideologue for future generations of Hindutva votaries. Further, from January 1924 till May 1937, Savarkar was allowed to live with his family, but within the periphery of his hometown, Ratnagiri. During this time, he pretended to distance himself from all kinds of political activity and the British authorities took little notice of a campaign that the ex-convict was planning in his village within two weeks of his arrival. It was a seemingly noble, innocuous social reform campaign to eliminate untouchability but cleverly dovetailed into his ultimate political goal of uniting Hindus across caste lines. The British were also hoodwinked because campaigns to end social ostracisation had been repeatedly conducted in the past by the votaries of Hindutva. It was also during this part of his life that Savarkar guided Keshav Baliram Hedgewar in establishing an organisation to 'supply the Hindu society with power and pillars'.[25]

The final phase was the least significant of Savarkar's life, in terms of gains made. It started out after all the restrictions on him were lifted and he became the president of the Hindu Mahasabha in 1937. He led the Mahasabha to its moment of glory—recognition from British administrators as the sole representative of India's Hindus and also as a coalition partner of the Bengal government. This was also the phase when Nathuram Godse, a Savarkar acolyte, assassinated Gandhi, ringing curtains for the turbulent relationship between him and Savarkar. Yet, even deceased, Gandhi caused major setback to Savarkar and the Hindu Mahasabha from which neither could recover entirely.

In the final phase, after the initial flourish, Savarkar was unable to stem the Mahasabha's growing decline. He had failed to comprehend that, in the fast-changing political landscape of India, the Mahasabha's ideology was proving to be self-limiting. Eventually, Savarkar and his organisation came to be viewed with distrust because it remained suspect of having hatched the conspiracy to kill Mahatma Gandhi.

* * *

Savarkar was certainly not the first to expound the idea of Hindu nationalism, but he was indeed the first to codify it and provide coherence to the idea. In the last decades of the nineteenth century, a rudimentary form of Hindu nationalism had emerged, mainly as a reaction to the British response to home-grown social reform movements. As mentioned earlier, apart from Tilak's Hindu revivalist programmes, there were several others which were aimed at 'reforming' the Hindus from 'within' and opposed the introduction of certain laws which threatened to regulate Hindu society.

The All-India Muslim League was formed in December 1906 and catalysed the formation of the Hindu Mahasabha in the same year in undivided Punjab. However, despite the involvement of senior Congress leaders like Lala Lajpat Rai and the founder of the Banaras Hindu University (BHU), Pandit Madan Mohan Malaviya, who was its first president, the Mahasabha conclaves were restricted to being annual jamborees and lacked the political raison d'être. It was to the credit of Vinayak Damodar Savarkar that he eventually provided its framework and established the process of creating a separate and structured channel for Hindu nationalism. Instead of the token alternative presented by revivalists within the Indian National Congress, Savarkar helped create an alternate outfit to the existing nationalist mainstream, in idea as well as structure. The best example of this phenomenon was represented by none other than Keshav Baliram Hedgewar who abandoned the Congress and founded the Rashtriya Swayamsevak Sangh which in time evolved into one of the most ideologically-driven organisations in India.

Meanwhile, Savarkar had an epiphany during his solitary confinement in Cellular Jail—something which had been churning in his mind since childhood all through his rebellious youth and, finally, as a young revolutionary nationalist, it began taking shape. It was in jail that Savarkar was convinced that the Hindus were being outnumbered by Muslims.[26] He noticed how large numbers of untouchables were converting to Islam because Hindu prisoners were prone to ostracise their low caste brethren. Once when Savarkar learnt that an untouchable boy was being converted, he decided to engage with him and earned the terrible epithet of 'Savarkar Bhangi Babu' (meaning, someone who took the low castes under his wing). This was obviously a slur, but Savarkar soldiered on and prevented the boy's conversion.

Emboldened by his first success, Savarkar began the process of 'reverse conversion' by performing the shuddhi ceremony on several others and although this move was initially met with stiff resistance, it demonstrated that Hindus who had converted to either Islam or Christianity could be brought back into the fold. Soon it was time for census enumeration in the country, and Savarkar campaigned vigorously amongst the Arya Samajis and Sikhs in jail to register their religion as 'at least Hindu, with the words Arya and Sikh in the bracket'.[27]

As mentioned, the idea for *Essentials of Hindutva* germinated in the island jail in which he defined a Hindu as 'a person who regards this land of Bharatvarsh from the Indus to the Seas as his Fatherland as well as his Holy Land, that is the cradle of his religion'. Savarkar distinguished between punyabhoomi (holy land) and pitribhoomi or matribhoomi (fatherland or motherland) which when extrapolated meant that 'non-Hindus' couldn't call India their nation. Yet, as we shall see subsequently, Savarkar contradicted his postulation on several occasions.*

It must be mentioned here that the concept of punyabhoomi was first posited by Swami Vivekananda in 1897 as a land where, 'all souls aspiring towards a spiritual quest must attain their last home.'[28]

* Often Savarkar's use of the word 'pitrubhumi' has been cited to depict commonality with European fascist ideology. A more 'sympathetic' view would be to believe the word denotes 'land of ancestors', drawn from the period of pitripaksh or pitrupaksha. During this fortnight before the Navaratri festival period and prior to Dussehra and Durga Puja, Hindus are mandated to make offerings in the name of the deceased in their families. It is done to 'express' gratitude to ancestors for their role in bringing current generations to their current position.

Much like Vivekananda, Savarkar also saw India as a seamless and 'eternal civilisation', but his concept of a nation was different—he saw it as being far more exclusive because he considered the people whose sacred lands were in other countries (Muslims, Christians, Jews and Zoroastrians) as not entitled to refer to India or Bharatvarsh as their own nation.[29] Savarkar's efforts in linking religion and culture with national identity was the genesis of cultural nationalism which eventually became the cornerstone of the virulent phase of Hindutva from the late 1980s. In Savarkar's understanding, Hinduism was not just a religion, but a culture or a way of life—the word 'Hindutva', as a political construct, did not predate Savarkar's dissertation although it was in use in limited circles and in the early 1920s, the idea blazed like a meteor across the nationalistic horizon. For the first time, a new hypothesis or political theory was presented to disentangle the complexities of Indian society. Episodes of conflict and confrontation that occurred between various religious communities were theorised about and Savarkar provided a framework for Hindu communalists to justify their actions.[30] Several Hindu nationalists who had hitherto been unable to articulate their thoughts and forced to withdraw from the public sphere found reasons to step beyond the nationalistic mainstream after Savarkar's treatise.

On his part, Savarkar remained self-contradictory, as we have seen earlier. After his argument on who could consider Bharatvarsh as their own land, his formal definition of Hindutva was conspicuous for its exclusivity:

> Hindutva is not a word but a history. Not only the spiritual or religious history of our people as at times it is mistaken to be by being confounded with the other cognate term Hinduism,

> but a history in full. Hinduism is only a derivative, a fraction, a part of Hindutva. Unless it is made clear what is meant by the latter, the first remains unintelligible and vague. Failure to distinguish between these two terms has given rise to much misunderstanding and mutual suspicion between some of those sister communities that have inherited this inestimable and common treasure of our Hindu civilization ... Hindutva is not identical with what is vaguely indicated by the term Hinduism ... Had not linguistic usage stood in our way then 'Hinduness' (elsewhere, he also used the word 'Hindudom') would have certainly been a better word ... Hindutva embraces all the departments of thought and activity of the whole Being of our Hindu race. Therefore, to understand the significance of this term Hindutva, we must first understand the essential meaning of the word Hindu ...

Savarkar elaborated on his basic premise about other religionists, most importantly, the followers of Islam. His postulation clearly indicated that he precluded them and the other three from his idea of who can claim to be Indian:

> ... although the root-meaning of the word Hindu like the sister epithet Hindi, may mean only an Indian, yet as it is, we would be straining the usage of words too much—we fear, to the point of breaking, if we were to call a Mohammedan a Hindu because of his being a resident of India. It may be that at some future time the word Hindu may come to indicate a citizen of Hindusthan and nothing else; that day can only rise when all cultural and religious bigotry has disbanded its forces pledged to aggressive egoism ...

Savarkar further elaborated on that thought as follows:

> An American may become a citizen of India. He would certainly be entitled, if bona fide, to be treated as our Bharatiya or Hindi, a countryman and a fellow citizen of ours. But as long as in addition to our country, he has not adopted our culture and our history, inherited our blood and has come to look upon our land not only as the land of his love but even of his worship, he cannot get himself incorporated into the Hindu fold ... Hindus are not merely the citizens of the Indian state because they are united not only by the bonds of the love they bear to a common motherland but also by the bonds of a common blood. They are not only a Nation but also a race—jati ... All Hindus claim to have in their veins the blood of the mighty race incorporated with and descended from the Vedic fathers, the Sindhus.

He left no room for ambiguity on what, according to him, should be the future of Muslims, even those who accepted that their forefathers had converted to Islam from Hinduism:

> The majority of the Indian Mohammedans may, if free from the prejudices born of ignorance, come to love our land as their fatherland, as the patriotic and noble-minded amongst them have always been doing. The story of their conversions, forcible in millions of cases, is too recent to make them forget, even if they like to do so, that they inherit Hindu blood in their veins. But can we, who here are concerned with investigating into facts as they are and not as they should be, recognize these Mohammedans as Hindus?

Savarkar's book not only romanticised the idea of being a Hindu, but also instilled a sense of victimhood among Hindus. There was also this accompanying awe-inspiring story about the method of his writing. According to his biographer, because he was in solitary confinement with no access to either pen or paper, Savarkar had scribbled his initial thoughts on the bare walls of his cell with pebbles. Thereafter, he learnt every word on the walls by rote, and when he was discharged from Cellular Jail and sent to Yerawada in Pune, he continued writing on loose sheets which were either smuggled out or memorised by his followers who further recorded for him. Eventually, *Essentials of Hindutva* was first published in 1923 under the pseudonym of 'A Maratha' (as prisoners were not allowed to publish any work), and immediately became a manual on Hindutva and Hindu nationalism. The book created a sensation because Savarkar steered clear of the 'chaos and confusion created by nearly fifty definitions of the word Hindu including the one made by Tilak.'[31] His choice of words left no scope for any doubt:

> (You), who by race, by blood, by culture, by nationality possess almost all the essentials of Hindutva and had been forcibly snatched out of our ancestral home by the hand of violence—ye, have only to render wholehearted love to our common Mother and recognize her not only as Fatherland (Pitribhu) but even as a Holy Land (Punyabhu); and ye would be most welcome to the Hindu fold. This is a choice which our countrymen and our old kith and kin (sic), the Bohras, Khojas, Memons and other Mohammedan and Christian communities are free to make—a choice again which must be a choice of love. But as long as they are not minded thus, so long they cannot be recognized as Hindus.[32]

The above definition does little but confuse when juxtaposed with Savarkar's contradictory views on the same subject (as cited previously). However, Hindu nationalists of different hues who emerged in the post-Savarkar era continued to revere him despite the fact that he was never part of any organisation. They readily identified with him not only because he represented a similar socio-religious conundrum, but also because they found several aspects of his argument closest to their beliefs.

*   *   *

V.D. Savarkar would have remained one amongst thousands of freedom fighters had he not written *Essentials of Hindutva*. What also made its publication possible was the benevolence shown by the British, partly due to his constant assurances to them that he would abide by strictures and not participate in any anti-colonial protests. Within months of his deportation to the Andaman and Nicobar Islands in July 1911, Savarkar submitted a mercy petition to the government which mysteriously vanished from the official records, but its reference was later found in another plea submitted in November 1913. In the letter, Savarkar had pledged to serve the 'Government in any capacity' and asked with utmost seriousness, 'Where else can the prodigal son return but to the parental doors of the Government?'[33] The Home Member of Bombay, Sir Reginald Craddock, recorded in an official note that he had met Savarkar in October 1913 during which the 'swatantra veer' (*sic*) had submitted a mercy plea.[27]

In retrospect, these clemency petitions put Savarkar's commitment to the nascent nationalist movement under a cloud. He submitted two other pleas in 1914 and 1917, in which he offered his 'services to

Government during the war in any capacity.' A Savarkarite member of the Imperial Legislative Council, G.S. Khorpade, asked in the House if it was not true that the jailed leader had pledged that once the proposed administrative reforms (later called Montagu–Chelmsford reforms or the Government of India Act, 1919) were enacted, he would 'try to make the Act a success and would stand by law and order'. This was neither the first nor the last time when Savarkar attempted to secure his liberty by offering to further the interests of the Imperial government. He made similar offers even after Independence. While in detention in Cellular Jail, Andaman Islands, Savarkar was truly prolific when it came to writing petitions, seeking the mercy of the authorities in 1911, 1912, 1913, 1914, 1916, 1918 and, finally, twice in 1920.

Phrases like, (I) 'am ready to serve the Government in any capacity', (where else) 'can the prodigal son return but to the parental doors of the Government', (seeking) 'a last chance' to submit his case 'before it is too late' and (his) 'firm intention to abide by the constitution and stand by it,' are strewn across his letters between 1911–1920 seeking leniency from the British government. However, Vinayak Chaturvedi, in a video conversation with me, stated that Savarkar used the language of the time and that there were far worse 'crimes' that Savarkar committed for which he must be held accountable.[34]

Peculiarly, in October 2021, the Union Home Minister, Rajnath Singh, justified the mercy petitions Savarkar wrote by claiming that he had sought clemency from the British in 1920 on the advice of Gandhi, as if this would absolve the Hindu nationalist codifier for cosying up to British authorities.[35] Before getting into the circumstances in which this 'advice' was given by Gandhi, it is necessary to recall that he was yet to return to India from South Africa when Savarkar wrote at least the first four of his petitions.[36] Even on his homecoming in January 1915, Gandhi had no occasion to engage immediately with Savarkar and in any case, it is highly unlikely that Gandhi would have been over-enthusiastic about seeing him again because of the bitter memory of their first meeting in London in 1909. He also would have undeniably been aware that Savarkar considered violence an essential aspect of political strategy, while Gandhi was of the view that depiction of violence in epics and legends are metaphors for internal conflict within humans and those engaging in violence are unable to control the phantoms within. It is important to recreate the situation in India and the sequence of events just prior to when Gandhi 'advised' Savarkar in January 1920. By that time, the nation had been plunged into turmoil following the uncalled-for enactment in March 1919 of the Rowlatt Act, indefinitely extending the government's repressive emergency powers. One development led to another: the Jalianwala Bagh massacre, the subsequent apology of an enquiry commission, Gandhi preparing for the first-ever mass movement in the course of the freedom struggle and the backing to the Khilafat movement—all a sequence of events that were part of a composite strategy that Gandhi was evolving to counter colonial repression. At that time, when he was also trying to gain control over the Congress, Gandhi would have consciously felt the need to widen the platform and form strategic alliances with different groups and communities.

Against this backdrop, Gandhi received a letter from Narayan D. Savarkar, the younger brother of the two jailed siblings. Although Gandhi was frank in writing back that it was 'difficult to advise you', he nonetheless suggested 'framing a brief petition setting forth the facts of the case bringing out in clear relief the fact that the offence committed by your brother was purely political'. It is often missed amid the din over Savarkar's petitions that Narayan D. Savarkar pleaded with the British regime for 'at least a change to some Indian jail of better climate'.

Gandhi's next intervened in easing Savarkar's situation in May 1920 in the form of an article in *Young India*. Articulate lawyer that he undoubtedly was, Gandhi first quoted the Royal Proclamation dated December 1919, which provided clemency for 'political offenders' who broke laws previously but would henceforth pledge to 'respect it in the future'. Gandhi pointed out that political prisoners included the 'Savarkar brothers' and that they remained in jail although 'five months have gone by after the publication of the Proclamation'. Writing of V.D. Savarkar and his elder brother, Ganesh, Gandhi wrote: 'Both these brothers have declared their political opinions and both have stated that they do not entertain any revolutionary ideas and that if they were set free, they would like to work under the Reforms Act, for they consider that the Reforms enable one to work thereunder so as to achieve political responsibility for India.'

Gandhi was unequivocal in his understanding that the brothers 'feel that India's destiny can be best worked out in association with the British'. Gandhi's commitment to non-violence is evident in his claim that 'the cult of violence has, at the present moment, no following in India'. Viewed from Gandhi's perspective, his call for clemency for the Savarkar brothers was a 'victory' because from being a guru of Dhingra, the younger (V.D.) Savarkar was committing to a path of non-violence.

By writing to Narayan D. Savarkar or in his journal, Gandhi did not condone previous mercy petitions—he, in fact, glossed over them because of his political motivations in collecting nationalists of all hues on a non-violent platform prior to the launch of the first mass agitation against the British in September 1920. This episode, in fact, demonstrates Gandhi's large-heartedness and political inclusivity, for he set no conditions to make a plea publicly on behalf of Savarkar and his elder sibling. In return, on being moved from the Cellular Jail to prisons in Maharashtra, Savarkar exhibited no sympathy for Gandhian ways and strategies and remained single-mindedly focused on emphasising the primacy of Hindus in the country. In jail, he gave final shape to what eventually became the seminal text of the Hindutva ideology, *Essentials of Hindutva*. This essay stood in complete opposition to the inclusive nationalism Gandhi was pursuing. Savarkar's belief in violence as a strategy to secure concessions from the British remained unshakeable. He saw himself primarily as a guru to this school of thought.

Indeed, while under 'detention' in Ratnagiri, although he was not lodged in jail, Savarkar wrote copiously. And since he was not permitted to write on politics, he camouflaged his polemical works with thinly veiled fictionalised narratives. Much of this was extremely vehement in nature—violence, vendetta and vindictiveness formed major themes of his writings. In contrast to Gandhi's emphasis on non-violence in his political thoughts and action, Savarkar insisted that violence was an integral element of 'Hindu civility'.

In an act that was symptomatic of Savarkar's ungratefulness, he was soon criticising Gandhi and his worldview once again. He dismissed the Mahatma rather unflatteringly and commented about his 'queer definitions of non-violence and truth'[37] while denouncing the non-cooperation and Khilafat movements, claiming that the latter 'would prove to be an aafat—a calamity.' His disagreements with the Congress and Gandhi on administrative reforms were also public: while Gandhi wanted to boycott the Imperial Council, Savarkar was 'sure that many a revolutionist would, like me, cry halt under the circumstances and try to meet England under an honourable truce, even in a half-way house'. Despite the bitter criticism, Gandhi made a distinction between Savarkar's detention and his political stance. His article in *Young India* was evidence of fair play. Unsurprisingly, Savarkar's anti-Gandhi posturing stood him in good stead. When his jail term came up for a review, the British government's leniency, combined with a campaign by non-Congress members of the Central Legislative Assembly, resulted in Savarkar being shifted in 1921 from Cellular Jail to a prison in Ratnagiri, and later to Yerawada Jail for a total of two years and eight months, until he was released from prison in January 1924 and permitted to stay with his family within the boundaries of Ratnagiri district. The clincher for the British was when Savarkar promised to 'not engage publicly or privately in any manner of political activities without the consent (sic) of Government for a period of five years'.

Savarkar's release was mainly due to the unwavering support of a man called Jamnadas Mehta, a Tilakite and member of the Interim government of Bombay. It was Mehta who had campaigned relentlessly for his release and formed the Savarkar Release Committee. He had also supported his campaign by writing a pamphlet titled 'Why Savarkar Should Be Released' and had organised a meeting in Bombay with Vithalbhai Patel in the chair. What may come as a surprise to many within the Hindu Right-wing today is that Savarkar's release was also courtesy the Indian National Congress which had adopted a resolution for his release in its Coconada (now Kakinada) session in 1923.[38]

Over the years, Savarkar's hostility towards Muslims was amplified while he was in Cellular Jail, but became overt and acquired a virulent dimension after he shifted first to Yerawada Jail and later to Ratnagiri. (The Moplah Uprising of 1921 was one of the main reasons for his antagonism. His antipathy towards Muslims was at par with his loathing for 'weak' Hindus. Once out of jail and at home in Ratnagiri, Savarkar wrote his next book in 1925 titled *Hindu Pad-Padashahi* in which he presented the Maratha Empire as the eventual avenger of Hindu honour. He wrote that the 'successful struggle of a military race against the powerful Moghul Empire' was 'a noble and inspiring ideal ... (for) the establishment of an independent Hindu Empire'. In the foreword of the book, Savarkar warned the Hindus as follows:

> Before you make out a case for unity (between Hindus and Muslims), you must make out a case for survival as a national or a social human unit. It was this fierce test that the Hindus were called upon to pass in their deadly struggle with the Muhammadan power. There could not be an honourable unity between a slave and his master.[39]

Savarkar was often subsumed by the thought of Indians' proclivity to be dominated by foreigners, and by the time he was released from jail, he concluded that the primary reason for Hindus' repeated subjugation was a deep-seated psychological shortcoming. He believed that this anomaly could only be rectified by unifying Hindus under the aegis of a sangathan or organisation, an opinion that played a decisive role in Hedgewar's eventual decision to establish the RSS.

At the core of Savarkar's argument was the postulation that Aryan settlers chose India and organically adapted to the superior Hindu religion, while the other communities who retained their original religion, or agreed to be converted to Islam or Christianity, remained foreigners.[40] Even while campaigning amongst Sikhs in the Cellular Jail to enlist as Hindus, he had submitted that Hindutva was not identical to Hinduism and that followers of other faiths could also be termed as Hindus (later named as Indian Religionists or IRs). He further convinced his fellow-inmates that Sikhism, Jainism and Buddhism could be treated as IRs because their sacred places (punyabhoomi) lay within the geographical boundaries of India.

Interestingly, as Savarkar was debarred from participating in any kind of political activity during his stay in Ratnagiri, he opted to write fiction—a kind of veneer to conceal its political content from law enforcers. His readers lost no time in inferring the real intent of their favourite author, but the British authorities took the book at face value and did little else. In January 1927, he also launched a weekly titled *Shraddhanand* and began writing about socio-political issues. The following extract from an article that he wrote on 27 January 1927 was cited in the judgement in the case filed in Bombay High Court by Gopal Godse, the brother of Gandhi's assassin, Nathuram Godse, against an order of forfeiture of his book titled *Gandhi Hatya Ani Mee* (Gandhi's Assassination And I):

> The truth is that the majority of Muslims do not consider India as their own country and the existence of Hindus therein pricks them like a thorn. This feeling is at the root of the conflict. Except for some sensible Muslims, the others appear to be anxious that like Turkey, Iran and Afghanistan, Hindustan should also become an Islam nation and if that happens, they would love the country as their own.[41]

The British did not act despite the obvious incendiary content of the book. His 1926 novel titled *What Do I Care* or *The Revolt of the Moplahs* gave graphic details of Muslims attacking Hindus, including the 'defilement of Hindu women.'[42] Savarkar also took a shot at writing plays—for instance, *Sangeet Unshraap* (1927), which was a sharp, critical social commentary around the issues of untouchability, conversion and sexual violence against Hindu women. In one particular scene, a character called Bangash Khan delivers a monologue as follows:

> The more I abduct Hindu girls and include them in my zenana, the more my respect among Muslims enhances ... enjoyment of temporal pleasures clears the way to other worldly benefits. I have corrupted so many Hindu girls and made them my mistresses that hundreds of Muslims consider me a true missionary and preacher of Islam; this is because I have produced progeny through these women who are Muslims ... [43]

On closer inspection, it becomes evident that most of Savarkar's fictional work was focused on examining three kinds of relationships: between Hindu men and Muslim men, between Hindu women and Muslim men and, finally, between Muslim men and Muslim women. He also alluded to the relationship between Hindu men and Hindu women, presented as equal, but with women being the progenitors and carers of men. In Savarkar's representation, the relationship between Muslim men and Hindu women was based on sexual violence against the latter, presented as 'fields' to wage a demographic battle. Finally, the relationship between Muslim men and Muslim women was seen as one where men were polygamous and exerted unquestionable authority over their women.

Savarkar's use of sexual violence in his fictional works displayed a deep-seated misogyny coupled with communal hatred. It may be recalled that projecting Muslim men as sexual marauders, with the objective of siring Muslim children from Hindu wombs and reversing the population ratio, was the motivating spirit behind the Sangh Parivar's 'love jihad' campaign from 2013-2014 onward. The theory that Muslim men are polygamous and treat women unfairly is also the basis of the campaign against triple talaaq and nikah halala.*

For a man who was viewed as the votary of reinstating Hindu dignity, his long confinement within a district was a matter of great concern for his followers. For them, his seclusion from political activity was no better than a jail term and they, therefore, began yet another campaign to end his confinement which was extended periodically by the British. In January 1935, when a review date had loomed ahead, Savarkar was advised to not protest and appeal for release. In November 1934, this one-time revolutionary who was sworn to his motherland promised that 'he would be on the right side of law and constitution even if he took to politics'.[44] However, the government concluded that allowing Savarkar to travel and speak publicly was inadvisable, and his internment was extended for two more years.

At the end of the stipulated period, Savarkar petitioned the British yet again and this time, he was advised to route his application

---

* In the aftermath of the Muzaffarnagar riots in 2013-14, a propaganda was started claiming that Muslims were waging a systemic campaign under which young Muslim males were befriending Hindu girls and marrying them after converting them to Islam. The campaign added to the prevailing stereotypes of the typical Muslim youth as someone who marries more than one woman and discriminates against them. For additional background, read: https://scroll.in/article/877483/)

through the local administration. By then, a new Savarkar Restrictions Removal Committee had been formed and included former acolytes of Tilak and other social reformers. A signature campaign was initiated which pleaded for removing restrictions on Savarkar. Mahatma Gandhi was also approached to sign the petition, which he refused to do, contending that it would be below his dignity to plead with the British while fighting for India's independence. 'You do not beseech adversaries,' the Mahatma is said to have stated emphatically. Jamnadas Mehta played a vital role in Savarkar's release yet again who, it may be recalled, lobbied for his release from prison in 1924. Mehta bargained with the British over the issue when they approached him to help convince the Congress party to join the provincial governments which had to be mandatorily formed after elections following the agreement on the Government of India Act, 1935. Mehta agreed to plead for the British but set a precondition: release V.D. Savarkar.

Release and Thereafter

On 10 May 1937, all restrictions on V.D. Savarkar were finally lifted and he was free after twenty-seven years of confinement. The town of Ratnagiri erupted with several celebratory functions—Savarkar was invited for each as the guest of honour—which were also attended by local Congress leaders. Very early after his release, Savarkar, in a meeting with a group of journalists, stated that he remained committed to the belief that 'independence could only be achieved through an armed revolution.' His speeches and statements during this phase elucidate his activities, but not necessarily in any chronological order; it was more like pages from a book about his life.[45]

For instance, at one of the functions, Savarkar turned emotional and recalled his agitation against untouchability which he said pitted one Hindu against the other. He explained that although the movement was met with stiff resistance, he had focused on it, considering it to be in the 'best interest of the Country, God, and Man'.[46]

At another public gathering, Savarkar declared that his ultimate goal was the independence of India and spelt out a three-pronged strategy to achieve it: resistance, alliance and pressure. However, unlike Mahatma Gandhi or other leaders of the freedom movement, he dwelt little on how to go about achieving these. During the early days of his life out of jail, Savarkar spoke at length about a democratic India which should follow 'one man, one vote,' which was interpreted by some Muslims (when separate electorates existed for the community) as a ploy to establish a government for and by the Hindus. He also called for all citizens of the state that he hoped Hindu Mahasabha would preside over to 'be treated according to their individual worth irrespective of religious or racial percentage in the general population' without accounting for the fact that heritage, upbringing and family status played a crucial role in people's individual value or capacity.

A few months after settling into life as a free person, Savarkar embarked on an extensive tour of Maharashtra and went to Pandharpur, Kolhapur, Pune and eventually, Bombay. In Pune, Savarkar reached out to a group of untouchables who were considering conversion to Islam or Christianity as an escape from caste-based discrimination. He counselled them against converting to other religions and suggested that they join forces with social reformers to fight the malaise from within. Even as he went about participating in inter-caste dinners, a long tradition in western India, Savarkar urged the youth to learn to use guns, arguing that drama and poetry were fine hobbies, but not when the 'mother was on her death bed'—a clear allegorical reference to the nation. In one public meeting after another, Savarkar kept reiterating his ultimate political mission, which was to establish a free nation 'on the bedrock of the Hindus, the national majority'. His objective, he said, was to ensure that this 'paper majority' realised its capacity and 'the fact that they were the bedrock and mainspring of the national life and the State'.[47]

By 1937, Savarkar had undoubtedly emerged as the greatest icon of the Indian Right-wing or Hindu nationalist politics. The period of his imprisonment had made him doughtier; this despite his cosying up to the British and relegating the cause of India's freedom to the backburner in the face of his campaign to build a strong and unified Hindu India, which was viewed by many of his followers as an act of great sacrifice. Two months after restrictions on his movement were lifted, Savarkar joined the Democratic Swaraj Party formed in 1933 to propagate the political ideals of Bal Gangadhar Tilak. Within a short period of time, however, he concluded that it did not have the potential to evolve into a pan-Indian party and left it.

The next logical step for him would have been to join the RSS and he visited a branch in Wardha at the request of Hedgewar, but surprisingly engaged no further with it. There were two reasons for his reluctance. First, despite its subsequent significance in Indian politics, the RSS was a minor organisation when compared with the larger-than-life image of Savarkar. In fact, the RSS would have benefitted greatly from its association with the man, and not vice versa. Second, after years of his confinement, Savarkar desired a larger political role for himself; mainly to act as a counter to the Congress party and its politics of social inclusion.

On the other hand, both Hedgewar and M.S. Golwalkar harboured no such ambitions and were solely devoted to the RSS for which (or so they felt) falling foul of either the British or Congress would be counter-productive. The dissonance between Savarkar and senior RSS leaders came as a surprise to many because the RSS owed its genesis to Savarkar, albeit in absentia, as an inspirational figure. Despite Savarkar's publicly stated reservations about the RSS, Hedgewar remained the archetypal dyed-in-the-wool Hindu leader—someone who believed that it was enjoined in the ancient Hindu precepts to show respect towards an elder and that it was also politically prudent to keep a line of communication open with Savarkar, no matter what. Consequently, although he treated Savarkar with utmost reverence while remaining conscious of RSS's independent identity, Hedgewar feared that the young cadre may be swept away by Savarkar's political romanticism and his charismatic personality.

Interestingly, an attempt was made from an unusual quarter to plead for RSS's case with Savarkar, to convince him that its trajectory was promising and he should extend his full support and join it forthwith. The man was none other than Nathuram Godse who, in a letter to Savarkar dated July 1938, wrote:

> The only organisation in Maharashtra as well as in all Hindustan that is capable of uniting the Hindus is the Rashtriya Swayamsevak Sangh ... There is only one leader who is your equal and peer, and that is Dr. Hedgewar.[48]

But Savarkar paid no heed to such entreaties and, seven months after being allowed to travel freely and speak without restrictions, had already accepted the post of the president of the Hindu Mahasabha in December 1937 at its nineteenth annual session in Ahmedabad, and remained at its helm till 1942. Yet, Savarkar did not break ties with the RSS and there are several instances of either his participation in RSS functions or of swayamsevaks organising Savarkar's meetings and even raising funds for him and the Mahasabha. As president of the Mahasabha from 1937–1942, Savarkar delivered six presidential lectures which form part of what is considered to be a major repository of his political thought and ideology. Titled *Hindu Rashtra Darshan*, the Savarkar lectures examine the twin ideas of the Hindu nation and swaraj (self-governance), a term which was used extensively by nationalists such as Gandhi, Tilak and Sri Aurobindo. But Savarkar's definition of swaraj was different from the others, in that it did not imply freedom from colonial rule; independence for him meant, 'as far as the Hindu Nation is concerned, the political independence of the Hindus, the freedom which would enable them to grow to their full height.'[49]

He argued that the Hindus would be denied freedom if they were governed by non-Hindus whether from within or without and, therefore, both political and territorial control must rest in their hands. He further recommended 'Sanskritized Hindi' as the lingua franca for the natural inhabitants of such a land and exhorted them to eschew the usage of 'spoken Hindustani', an amalgamation of Hindi–Urdu (or what is referred to in north Indian literature as the Ganga–Jamunitehzeeb) which he termed as a 'linguistic monstrosity' which must be 'ruthlessly suppressed'. In his interactions, he always called for the militarisation of Hindus and Hinduisation of politics at all levels.

His lectures were focused more conspicuously than before on the increased propagation of armed violence and the rejection of the Gandhian principle of non-violence, which he dismissed as a futile weapon in India's struggle for independence. Barely months after taking over as Hindu Mahasabha president, Savarkar spoke glowingly of Benito Mussolini and claimed he had armed even children with rifles, an assertion that suggested that he wanted Hindus to do the same. In the years immediately following his release and prior to the outbreak of the Second World War, Savarkar was favourably inclined towards the Axis powers. In August 1938, he asserted that Germany had every right to follow Nazism just as Italy was free to embrace fascism. He was of the view that every country ought to follow the political system that was best suited for it, indicating that he did not believe in the idea of universal political ethos. He was also critical of Nehru for his stance on the Axis Powers:

'Surely Hitler knows better than Pandit Nehru does what suits Germany best. The very fact that Germany or Italy has so wonderfully recovered and grown so powerful as never before at the touch of Nazi or Fascist magical wand is enough to prove that those political "isms" were the most congenial tonics their health demanded.'[50]

To highlight his differences with Congress over the Axis powers, he further added that 'Hindu Sanghatanists in India, whom neither Pandit Nehru (sic) nor the Congress represents, cherish no ill-will towards Germany or Italy or Japan'. Even on the highly polarising German imperial expansion into Sudetenland, Savarkar stated that 'Hindu Sanghatanists in India hold that Germany was perfectly justified in uniting the Austrian and Sudeten Germans under the German Flag'.[51]

With war clouds gathering over Europe and several other parts of the world, Savarkar was unequivocal in asserting that 'any nation who helps India, or is friendly towards her struggle for freedom is our friend'. These statements secured for Savarkar an appreciative comment in the German newspaper, *Volkischer Beobachter*. There was little doubt that Savarkar's reference to the issue of German minorities in Czechoslovakia was his way of drawing attention to what, in Savarkar's understanding, was the Indian 'situation'. In his statements through 1937-38, it is evident that he strongly desired the complete separation of Hindus and Muslims. Savarkar, at that time, also found Bose an able associate in endorsing the racial discrimination underway in Germany, although the latter did not probably support such eventuality in India in the future.

Marzia Casolari asserts that barely weeks after the coordinated wave of anti-Semitic violence or, Night of Broken Glass, on 9 November 1938, 'pro-Hindu Mahasabha journals published articles in favour of German anti-Semitism. This stance brought the Hindu Mahasabha into conflict with the Congress which, on 12th December, made a statement containing clear references to recent European events. Within the Congress, only Bose opposed the party stance. A few months later, in April 1939, he refused to support the party motion that Jews might find refuge in India. Savarkar and the Hindu Mahasabha had a similar opinion.' There was little ambiguity that Savarkar was of the view that to resolve its 'Muslim problem', India must follow the same strategy employed by Germany. Actually, Savarkar and the Mahasabha shared Bose's viewpoint that the Congress resolution to allow European Jewish refugees into India must be opposed. Savarkar explicitly stated his position in a public meeting in Malegaon at that time. He wanted India to follow Germany while approaching its Muslim 'problem': 'A Nation is formed by a majority living therein. What did the Jews do in Germany? They being in minority were driven out from Germany.' Despite opposing Gandhi's view that '... Palestine belongs to the Arabs in the same sense that England belongs to the English or France to the French' Bose was not successful in preventing passage of the aforesaid resolution. In response, Savarkar stated, in the presence of RSS swayamsevaks in Thane: 'In Germany, the movement of the Germans is the national movement but that of the Jews is a communal one.'[52] Savarkar had been more unequivocal earlier when he stated in Poona that, 'Nationality did not depend so much on a common geographical area as on unity of thought, religion, language and culture. For this reason, the Germans and the Jews could not be regarded as a nation.' Not just the comparison between Jews and Muslims and the situation in India with the German 'realities', the Indian government's response to the developments in West Asia in the fall of 2023 can be traced to Savarkar's views expressed in 1938.

By March 1938, if not earlier, Savarkar also established a thriving communication with Rash Behari Bose who had by then lived for close to two decades in Japan, a considerable period of which was spent associating with the Japanese right-wing. They agreed in principle for Rash Behari to open an office of Hindu Mahasabha in Japan to act as 'an authorised international mouth piece of the Hindu Mahasabha and Hindudom as such in Eastern foreign countries.'[53] As the Second World War neared and Germany became noted for its anti-British posture, Savarkar, Subhas Chandra Bose and several other Hindu nationalists began viewing Germany as a potential ally against Britain. Very significantly, Savarkar, in a cable to the American President Franklin D. Roosevelt in April 1939 (in response to his message to Hitler and Mussolini), requested him to 'ask Britain too to withdraw her armed domination over Hindustan and let her have free and self-determined Constitution.' (Casolari)

Cunningly, however, Savarkar adopted a duplicitous stance. While admiring the German leadership and supporting Nazism, he did not close the option of furthering relations with the colonial administration. In its Working Committee meeting in September

1939, the Mahasabha, with Savarkar at its helm, adopted the stance that it did not 'believe in the claims of any Power among the belligerent Nations engaged in the present War in Europe'. The resolution termed each nation locked in the war as 'imperialistic in character and outlook, to the effect that it has been actuated solely by moral and altruistic considerations apart from its own national self-interest'. The Mahasabha was actually condemning the British for entering the war but, at the same time, was willing to collaborate with the colonialists. Committed to raising the Hindu National Militia, Savarkar saw the possibility of British support for this Mahasabha project if the colonial power could be guaranteed backing in its war campaign. Moonje wrote a formal circular to Mahasabha members intimating them about the proposal to raise a Hindu Militia and mentioned that it would be named Rama Sena.

Shortly thereafter, in October 1939, Lord Linlithgow extended separate invitations to several leaders from different political outfits to discuss their views on the war. The leaders included Savarkar who met the Viceroy on 9 October. The Mahasabha president seized this chance to discuss militarising Hindus—Savarkar emphasised 'the importance of military training for Hindus' alongside 'compulsory military training for the educated youth of the Hindu community'. Savarkar also stated 'frontier tribes' (Muslims) must be chastised 'with Hindu troops, the only troops on which we could rely'. Taking this exchange forward, during the Second World War, Savarkar even demanded that Hindus enlist in the war effort, viewing it as an opportunity to militarise them in preparation for future conflicts with other communities.[54]

It was evident that Savarkar viewed an able-bodied and armed Hindu as the answer to the 'growing danger from the designs of the awakened Muslim mind'.[55] He had already stated previously during a session of the Hindu Mahasabha in 1938 that 'if [we] Hindus in India grow stronger in time, these Moslem friends of the League type will have to play the part of German-Jews'.[56]

In fact, it was a year after this declaration that Savarkar was approached by the British viceroy for assistance in the war effort of the Allied powers. In their urgency to secure support locally, the British overlooked Savarkar's endorsement of Hitler and Nazism. Savarkar launched an intensive Mahasabha campaign to recruit Hindus and suggested that Sikh and Gorkha battalions be deployed on the north-western borders of British India. He addressed several public meetings and visited schools, colleges and literary conferences to convince young Hindu men to enlist in the British army. He further argued that in order to defend India from the Muslims, there was a need to curtail the presence of 'Muslims in military, police, and public service and to exclude Muslims from owning or working in munitions factories.'[57]

Besides expanding the political framework of the Mahasabha, Savarkar also travelled far and wide in India to get more people to sign up as members. There was no doubt that in many places, he was treated like a cult figure, but the high point of his tour was when he had met and convinced the iconic Syama Prasad Mookerjee to join the Mahasabha.

After his release from detention, Savarkar may have been every bit a demagogue while addressing public meetings to draw people into the Hindu Mahasabha, but he quietly put the spirit of revolutionary nationalism behind him. This obvious change in his strategy was quite simply the result of the loss of freedom he had faced over two-and-a-half decades and at no cost did he wish to repeat it. Moreover, his political stance had altered dramatically over the years, and anti-Colonialism was no longer central to it. He did not state this categorically but it nevertheless became evident in the most unusual fashion.

After Gandhi's Quit India movement in 1942 when the Congress had asked its ministers to resign from the provincial government, Mohammed Ali Jinnah saw it as an opportunity to form coalition governments in the Muslim-majority provinces. Meanwhile, Savarkar had already instructed his ministers in the provincial government to remain in office, arguing that if they quit, Muslim ministers and the British bureaucracy would ride roughshod over them.

In the summer of 1943, Jinnah invited Savarkar to explore the possibility of forming a government in Muslim-majority provinces, obviously with assistance from the Hindu Mahasabha. Savarkar responded that he was willing to discuss any plan provided it had nothing to do with the idea of Pakistan. He also declined to visit Jinnah's residence for the meeting, stating that any interaction on the matter should happen only at a venue of his choice. This was unacceptable to Jinnah, and after several deliberations, the two decided to break the stalemate and meet at a neutral venue. Unfortunately, even that plan had fizzled out because Savarkar had initially dilly-dallied and, subsequently, as the news of the proposed meeting made it to the press, Savarkar 'outdid Jinnah in resorting to delaying tactics and egoistic gestures'.[58]

The extremists within Muslim organisations were severely critical of Jinnah's plan to collaborate with the Mahasabha and in accepting Savarkar's demand that his party be allowed to voice its criticism about the idea of Pakistan. In a shocking retaliatory move, a member of the Khaksar Movement, Rafiq Sabir, physically assaulted Jinnah.

In his new avatar as a pan-Indian political leader, Savarkar issued a statement which was once again contrary to his past beliefs and actions: 'Such internecine, unprovoked murderous assault—even if the motive be political (sic) or fanatical—constituted a stain on public and civic life and should be strongly condemned.'[59]

No Great Leader

Despite deploying unrelenting resolve and fabulous oratorical skills in the mobilisation of large numbers of Hindus across India, V.D. Savarkar was unable to convert the Mahasabha into a mass organisation. The reasons: his antipathy towards Muslims, considered by many as a narrow sectarian agenda in the face of the larger goal of India's independence; the deceitful support to the British in the Second World War while backing the Axis powers at heart; the Mahasabha's decision to not vacate office in Bengal after the Quit India call in 1942 and, finally, Savarkar's deteriorating health. A year prior to India's independence, Savarkar had suffered a massive heart attack in January 1946.

After convincing Syama Prasad Mookerjee to join the Hindu Mahasabha, Savarkar also persuaded him to join the coalition government in Bengal in 1940. But unfortunately for Syama Prasad, the Hindu Mahasabha was floundering even as India was inching closer towards freedom. In the provincial elections of 1946, the Muslim League swept almost all seats for Muslims, while the Congress won the majority of Hindu seats, leaving the Mahasabha holding little beyond a rump. It may be safe to presume that the political narrative had moved beyond the discourse of the late 1930s and early 1940s. Although a feeling of religious sectarianism was on the rise amongst Muslims because of Jinnah's tenacity and Congress's failure in preventing them from flocking to the Muslim League, large number of Hindus were opposed to communalism because the Congress had retained its following amongst them.

The Mahasabha was seen to be practising negative politics and contributing little to the cause of Indian independence at a time it appeared imminent. When patriotic fervour was peaking across the country, the Mahasabha was found canvassing for a divisive cause and this eroded its credibility amongst people. That alone was instrumental for its poor electoral performance in the 1946 elections as well as for its eventual decline.

As president of the Hindu Mahasabha, Savarkar displayed poor temperament not befitting a leader of his stature—he came across as autocratic, erratic, given to mood swings and often failed to conduct negotiations either with his party colleagues or other parties. Stricken by a heart ailment, he used it as an emotional ploy and threatened to quit thrice in the 1940s, mainly as a strategy to have his way. Eventually, his resignation was accepted and Syama Prasad Mookerjee took over as president of the Mahasabha.

Curiously though, Savarkar had thrown a spanner in Mookerjee's presidency on an earlier occasion. In December 1944, the 'Lion of Bengal', as Syama Prasad was referred to by his followers, was to chair his first Mahasabha session in Bilaspur (then in Central India). Without consulting his party colleagues, Savarkar convened a gathering at the same venue to demand a rollback on the ban (ordered by the Sindh government) of a book called *Satyarth Prakash* written by the founder of the Arya Samaj, Dayanand Saraswati. It was strange that Savarkar should have chosen to address the meeting just outside of where Mookerjee was still presiding over the Mahasabha session.

Since the crowds were drawn to hear the mesmerising Savarkar speak, Mookerjee's show ended with a whimper. Yet, throughout his presidency, not once did the Bengali leader show any retaliatory disrespect towards his colleague although the incident revealed Savarkar's eagerness to attain personal glory. He may have stepped down as president of the Mahasabha but Savarkar remained its de facto chief and every crucial decision was run past him. This included Syama Prasad Mookerjee's decision to accept Nehru's offer to join his ministry after independence.

Nathuram Godse was one amongst several individuals whose path crossed Savarkar's at crucial junctures of his life. Beginning from the time when a young Godse would spend several evenings at Savarkar's home in Ratnagiri after his release, the two kept meeting thereafter. In 1944, after Savarkar's resignation as president of the Mahasabha, Godse started a newspaper with Savarkar's picture on the masthead. Although the broadsheet was launched as an in-house journal of the Mahasabha, it remained a 'Savarkarite' pamphlet. Earlier, Savarkar had lost no time in assigning one of his favourite disciples a crucial task—in the agitation against the Nizam's rule in Hyderabad, Godse was put at the head of the first brigade of protestors.

The extent of information that Savarkar had regarding Godse's plan to assassinate Gandhi and his own involvement in the conspiracy remains open to speculation but it is worth noting that unlike Nathuram Godse, Savarkar pled not guilty. He clearly had no intention of being in the dock and did not want his image of an intellectual and political thinker sullied. Preaching or acquiescing to violence was one matter, but being seen as a violent person—that too in the said incident—was another. That he did not wish to be identified alongside the other accused was evident from the protest he lodged for being photographed with them. Yet, so great was the reverence for him that at the Red Fort trial when the judge acquitted him and pronounced Godse and Narayan Apte guilty to be hanged to death, some of the other co-conspirators had fallen at Savarkar's feet in the dock and 'raised shouts of "Akhand Hindustan Amar Rahe; Hindu-Hindi-Hindustan, Kabhi Na Hoga Pakistan."'[60]

On his release in February 1949, Savarkar remained the votary of Hindu Rashtra, as he always had been. There was no deviation from one of his statements made to a Marathi journal, prior to his arrest in February 1948, in which he had said:

> Muslims in India should be given the same kind of treatment as Pakistan gave to the Hindus in Pakistan. Frankly, the Indian Union was a Hindu State as every nation was called after the name of its national majority. However, the Hindu Raj was not to be a theocratic state; it was not to be based on religious tenets. If the Muslims in India gave up hating the Hindus and were emotionally and loyally prepared for national integration, a state without distinctions of caste and creed could be established. In such a state, society would be reconstructed on economic basis and Hindu socialism would do the work. The tenets of Hindutva were consistent with democracy ... [61]

Decades later, the same sentiments reverberated in India after the BJP government assumed office in 2014 and people became unabashed about their endorsement of majoritarianism.

A few months after his release, Savarkar sent a cable to Rajendra Prasad who was then president of the Constituent Assembly. It read: 'I am voicing the sense and sentiment of millions of our countrymen when I beseech the Constituent Assembly to adopt Bharat as the name of our nation, Hindi as national language and Nagari as the national script.*

The Hindu Mahasabha had been in disarray after Mahatma Gandhi's assassination and the death of two senior leaders, Bhai Parmanand and B.S. Moonje. Syama Prasad Mookerjee had even suggested that the Mahasabha be converted into a religio-cultural organisation, but it was obviously overturned. After the Mahasabha was revived in November 1949, Savarkar presided over its session. Yet again, it became evident that he wasn't sure where he belonged—he was in politics, but made a distinction by saying that it wasn't 'active politics'.

In April 1950, two years after Mahatma Gandhi's assassination, the government placed Savarkar under detention. This was done as a precautionary measure to maintain peace in the run-up to the visit of the then Pakistani Premier, Liaquat Ali, who was scheduled to meet Prime Minister Nehru. A campaign for Savarkar's release was mounted yet again, but the government stated categorically that he would only be discharged from prison if he took a pledge to not participate in any kind of politics till the first general elections. Despite all the histrionics surrounding the order, Savarkar acquiesced, as he had done on previous occasions in his political life.

During this period, Savarkar busied himself with lecturing on social issues and campaigned on the need to end the social scourge of untouchability. But he also spoke in favour of what were obviously retrograde ideas—how women must not look at household chores and motherhood as a curse—which clearly reflected his patriarchal outlook.

---

* As a practise those days, the Persian script was often used for Hindi alongside Urdu.

Eventually, the government allowed him to participate in politics shortly before the first general elections in 1952 and he began seeking votes for the Mahasabha. It, however, did little to influence voters and the Hindu Mahasabha performed poorly, winning just three seats in parliament. After the elections, S.P. Mookerjee, who was now the leader of the Bharatiya Jana Sangh, met Savarkar and requested him to join the new party. Not only did Savarkar refuse, but also forewarned Mookerjee that his party was following in the Congress' footsteps: 'The tragedy of the Congress would overcome the Jan Sangh also, for Muslims would remain Muslims first and Indians never.'[62] On his part, Mookerjee pointed out to his comrade that in his state of West Bengal, the two communities lived in perfect harmony even after the brutalities of the Partition, as they had in the preceding years. Savarkar rejected Mookerjee's claims, and nearly shamed him for forgetting the Calcutta killings.

It was clear that Savarkar was now disillusioned with politics and after failing to find many who would give him their ear, returned to delivering public lectures on history and culture, if only for a short duration. Soon thereafter, he went back to focusing on issues that were part of his larger mission.

As part of his campaign to propagate the idea of Hindu Rashtra, Savarkar mounted a public and scathing criticism of Christian missionaries in November 1953, accusing them of converting Hindus. He repeated what he had been saying for years—the ultimate objective of proselytisation was to undermine Hindu nationality. In October 1956, Hindu society was faced with a major challenge when Dr B.R. Ambedkar led thousands of his supporters in converting to Buddhism. Savarkar's response to the act was guarded and he commented that the decision did not symbolise a desertion on their part from Hindu ranks, but merely reflected the tardy pace of reforms within Hindu society. Savarkar claimed that despite his 'conversion', Dr Ambedkar remained a Hindu because he had 'embraced a non-Vedic but Indian religious system within the orbit of Hindutva' and this was not a 'change of faith'. This was a response consistent with his lifelong definition of nationalism—whose pitribhoomi and punyabhoomi were within the territorial boundaries of India, they were Hindus.

Meanwhile, in 1956, preparations were also afoot to celebrate the centenary year of India's First War of Independence. An organising committee was established to steer the celebrations and Savarkar was asked to be a speaker at the event because of his book. Prime Minister Nehru was requested to participate as well, but had turned down the request after learning that Savarkar had been extended an invitation. Nehru made his objections on the issue rather clear when he said:

> Savarkar is a brave man, a hero, a great man. When I was a student in England, we were inspired by his book on 1857. It is a great book which has inspired many Indians. But it is hardly history. We have differed on several problems and it would be embarrassing to him if I were to speak in a different tone … speaking on the same platform would be unjust for both of us.[63]

As he neared his eighties, Savarkar was grappling with ill health and progressive senility. In many ways, Savarkar's increasing political isolation after he stepped down from the presidentship of the Mahasabha stemmed from his seclusion during his incarceration in the Cellular Jail. For thirteen long years, he had become used to being companionless, and after Independence when he realised that his brand of politics had no place in Indian polity, was once again reconciled to his own company.

He lived a quiet life with his wife and son. Ironically, for all his frugality, Savarkar was known to have fine taste and savoured chocolates, Jintan, snuff and a shot of whiskey, especially when he was past seventy. His tirade against Christian missionaries notwithstanding, the Bible had been one of his constant companions in jail; the other two being the Sedition Committee Report of 1918 and Patanjali's *Yoga Sutra*. He was known to be very particular about his physical appearance—a black umbrella was an indispensable accoutrement of his persona and as a devoted biographer mentioned, perfume was his 'abiding luxury'.

On 27 May 1962, on the eve of the eightieth year of his life, Savarkar issued a statement requesting his admirers and well-wishers to not visit him to offer him birthday greetings. The next morning, on his eightieth birthday, Savarkar fractured his thigh bone and was bedridden for a few months. Even as he managed to barely walk around, his wife Yamunabai fell critically ill and was moved to a hospital. From her hospital bed, when Yamunabai pleaded to bid goodbye to her husband, fearing her imminent death, Savarkar turned down her request and never visited her thereafter. When she died in November 1963, he issued instructions to cremate her at an electric crematorium without performing the necessary obsequies as mandated in Hinduism. Despite several pleas from other members of the family, Savarkar refused to relent and disallowed the body to be brought home. L.G. Thatte, a young, emotional Hindu Mahasabha member at the time (one who later became a general secretary of the party), was among those who protested against Savarkar's decision. He offered satyagraha at Savarkar's house and was subsequently arrested for the offence. In his book, Dhananjay Keer referred to a 'poor widow'[64] who had also attempted to persuade Savarkar to perform his wife's last rites, but to no avail. Eventually his son Vishwas performed his mother's funeral rights, and it is still contested whether he had his father's permission to do so.

It can be speculated that for a man like Vinayak Damodar Savarkar, it was imperative that he be recognised as a modernist for whom religion did not mean adhering to rituals, but rather an aspect which defined his nationality, politics and culture.

For the significant part of the forty years that Vinayak and Yamunabai lived together after his jail term, the man spent most of it fulfilling his life's mission. He had little time for his wife, and hardly made any effort to help her come into her own. For all practical purposes, Yamunabai was the mother of Savarkar's three children and, at best, his caregiver. This was a woman who had just been eleven when she had married the eighteen-year-old Vinayak after an undertaking that her father would pay for his university education.

After his release from detention, Savarkar completely 'excluded his wife from public life,' but 'attracted women followers to the cause of militant Hindu nationalism.'[65] In his role as a social reformer, Savarkar had campaigned relentlessly to secure the right for women to participate in religious ceremonies publicly but once the right was granted, his wife never had the chance to visit a temple.

There is no doubt that Savarkar fought for women's rights but also believed that they should have limited power. He supported women's education, just not the kind that men pursued in universities. He was clear that women's education must be restricted to spheres that enabled them to perform their role as carers of the home, hearth and, of course, their man. He placed restrictions on their behaviour although he remained silent about their adulation for him. According to him, beauty was an important element of feminine charm but the possession of this attribute should enforce a responsibility upon the women to remain within the boundaries of morality.

During India's struggle for independence, Savarkar had campaigned for women to propagate the swadeshi spirit while emphasising that public action shouldn't be the ultimate goal for them. They had to be adept only in cooking and rearing children. 'A woman's greatest pleasure did not lie in material, political or social accomplishment but in suckling a child.'[66]

He wanted women to tell their sons stories eulogising Hindu warriors so that they grew up with the desire to annihilate the enemies of the sacred motherland. On the one hand, he praised women like Rani Lakshmibai because of her valour and indomitable spirit. Yet, he blamed her and other women who participated in the First War of Independence for acting prematurely in the aftermath of events in Meerut, resulting in the failure of 1857.

At the ripe old age of eighty, it was far too late for Savarkar to come to terms with such deep contradictions between his public posturing and personal life, even if he had felt the need to do so. Till his death in February 1966, Savarkar often remained confined to bed. The last two decades of his life were years of political isolation and public dishonour. The Hindu Mahasabha had failed to resurrect itself as a credible political force while the RSS had emerged as the principal organisation advocating Hindu nationalism.

In conclusion, V.D. Savarkar was certainly the creator of an insidious ideology but had lacked in giving his organisation a clear direction. There was no doubt that he could create and bring ideas to fruition. However, in so far as managing people, devising political strategies and delegating responsibilities was concerned, he was found severely wanting. According to some accounts, his long stretches in solitary confinement spanning a decade-and-a-half had made Savarkar withdraw into a shell and become less socially amiable.

Till his death, the man believed that India would eventually embrace a party that reflected his version of nationalism—exclusively Hindu—while making space for others who were willing to genuflect to its ancient precepts and philosophies; a nation whose natural inhabitants were Hindus and whose dignity could only be restored by relegating the dangerous 'enemy' within to the backburner. For him, Hindutva was history but not, as Chaturvedi argued, simply 'history' or 'the history'. Instead, it is 'a history', or more specifically 'a history in full'.

Owing to deteriorating health and a possible realisation deep within himself about failing to ignite a sustained political process and an institution that would realise his dream of Hindu supremacy, sometime in the early 1960s, Savarkar wrote an essay in Marathi whose title was translated by Chaturvedi as 'How Hindu organisers should read and write their national history'. Targeted at political leaders, journalists and members of the intelligentsia—those he thought would have the capacity to pursue his ideas and thoughts after his passing—Savarkar had intended to write this piece for long but had put off penning it till the very end. There was little new Savarkar had to say, but he chose to be precise in framing directives that were to hold the key to his legacy or his oeuvre: Hindus, he reminded the readers, live amid a perennial war to protect the Hindu nation and in this act of protection, history, Hindu history to be exact, has to be a major tool (Chaturvedi chose not to translate 'itihaas' as history while writing on this essay). For Savarkar, history had to hold the 'truth' and this in turn was necessarily founded on Hindutva.

Much like Savarkar's essay that contained little that he had not said or written at various stages of life, RSS Sarsanghchalak Mohan Bhagwat's interview to the organisation's official organs, *Panchjanya* and *The Organiser* in January 2023, also had little that he had not already stated from 2014 onward. He, however, was not so unambiguous in following a Savarkarite thesis: that Hindus are engaged in a perennial war. Bhagwat's assertion stated: 'Hindu society has been at war for over 1,000 years—this fight has been going on against foreign aggressions, foreign influences and foreign conspiracies.' He implicitly suggested that due to the Sangh Parivar's campaign over decades, 'Hindu society has awakened' and that 'it is but natural for those at war to be aggressive'. This viewpoint was also forcefully reiterated by Modi, first at the globally important US Congress, where during his visit to the country on a bilateral visit, he referred to India's medieval era as a period of 'foreign rule'. He repeated that assertion on Indian soil during his speech on the occasion of Independence Day in 2023.

Days after the interview, quite like Savarkar and Bhagwat's ad nauseam assertions regarding Hindu society and war, Union Home Minister Amit Shah repeated his call for writing the 'truth' that is history or the 'correct' history. Shah called for weeding out 'angreziyat' from the discipline to ensure that the 'right message of history' could be conveyed, exactly as Savarkar would have wanted his followers to do. Simultaneously, various bespoke writers and new historians began arguing that freedom from British had been delivered not just on the shoulders of a non-violent national movement led by the likes of Gandhi, Nehru and Patel and that the honours should be equally shared by revolutionary nationalists who engaged in individual acts of violence, directly or by instigation, as Savarkar did. The Indian Council of Historical Research also announced some weeks prior to this its project for a new (Hindu) history of India. In May 2014, within two days of taking oath for the first time as India's Prime Minister, Narendra Modi, on 28 May, paid floral tributes to Savarkar's portrait contentiously installed inside Parliament by the Vajpayee government. The process of fulfilling the directives of Savarkar, penned in the aforementioned essay, started with this act on his 131st birth anniversary. Few, however, had realised the symbolism in the new prime minister's performance.

MADHAV SADASHIV GOLWALKAR

On 9 September 1947, around 3:00 p.m., two Sindhi men were blown to smithereens while making crude bombs in a house in Shikarpur Colony, Karachi. They were later identified as members of the Rashtriya Swayamsevak Sangh.

From early 1946 onwards, a constant refrain amongst the RSS cadre in Karachi was: 'Pakistan will definitely happen. Then, we will take over Sindh's police stations, airports, railway stations.' Pribhdas Butani did not live to see if his bluster bore fruit, as he was amongst the two who had died in the mishap.*

The previous day, on 8 September, a bomb had exploded in a crowded Karachi market killing five Muslims. The attack pointed towards a macabre plot in a series of counter-offensives across the newly-created Indo–Pak border. If Muslims were targeted in Delhi,

---

* There is a discrepancy regarding the date of the blast in the Shikarpur Colony house. In *The Making Of Exile: Sindhi Hindus and The Partition Of India*, Nandita Bhavnani mentions the date as 10 September, while L.K. Advani in *My Country My Life*, mentions it as 9 September. This chapter follows dates mentioned by L.K. Advani as he was a key eyewitness to the events.

Hindus were attacked in Karachi and other cities of Pakistan.

However, what stood out in the Karachi market bombing case was that it seemed carefully orchestrated, and wasn't the usual spontaneous venting of anger in a communal tinder box. The killing of Muslims added fuel to the prevailing anti-Hindu sentiment. Most locals believed that the attack was the handiwork of militant Hindu groups. Although it was said to be in retaliation for the attack on Hindus[1] by mohajirs (refugees) near the Drigh Road railway station in Karachi, the Muslims were persuaded to cool off mainly because of lack of evidence.

However a day later, a firm connection was established between the attack in the market and the explosion inside the Shikarpur Colony house.[2] It turned out that the house, or rather bungalow, where the two men were killed while manufacturing a bomb, belonged to a Hindu businessman who had packed off his family to India amidst winding up his businesses in Karachi. Before leaving, he had handed over the house keys to a twenty-two-year-old RSS worker, who was not only his friend's son, but the personal aide of its chief, Madhav Sadashiv Golwalkar, popularly known as 'Guruji'. Fortunately, the young man, Nand Badlani was not in the makeshift factory that day, but was arrested later when the police had discovered a 'list' of RSS activists from the site.[3] While the list included the name of Khanchand Gopaldas (or K.G.) Mansukhani, the regional sanghchalak of RSS who was sent to jail, several others fearing arrest, planned their escape to India.

Four days later, on 12 September 1947, a twenty-year-old man had boarded a British Overseas Airways Corporation (BOAC) plane in Karachi. It was Lal Krishna Advani's maiden flight, obviously not under pleasant circumstances, for he was a fugitive; not only was his name listed as an accused, he was identified as a front-ranking member of the RSS' youth brigade. His recent activities included organising a swayamsevaks' march in Karachi, prior to a public meeting by M.S. Golwalkar, barely ten days before Partition.[4] In the rally, which was the last public gathering of Hindus in Pakistan, Golwalkar had said, 'Sindh, through which flows the sacred Sindhu River, is being severed from India.'[5]

After the police investigation, thirty-odd RSS activists were rounded up and charged with conspiracy for waging a war against the 'state of Pakistan'. K.G. Mansukhani and Nand Badlani were sentenced to life which included ten years of rigorous punishment. However, three months later in November 1947, Mansukhani and several other RSS workers were exchanged for Muslim prisoners in Indian prisons under an informal pact between the two governments.

Despite a vehement opposition for the move, the 'exchange of prisoners' pointed towards the RSS' political clout in India. Such was M.S. Golwalkar's influence that he could directly reach out to Deputy Prime Minister Sardar Vallabhbhai Patel when some RSS workers were found missing from a batch of prisoners from Sindh.[6] In fact after the Partition, even the Mahatma had met Golwalkar to discuss RSS' role in running refugee camps.

The occasion for the dialogue had come up during Gandhi's address to a gathering of RSS volunteers a few days after the Shikarpur Colony blast, in a Delhi colony. He later spoke with Golwalkar who said that the organisation had no intention of fomenting trouble and added that 'the policy of the Sangh was purely service of the Hindus and Hinduism and that too not at the cost of anyone else. The Sangh did not believe in aggression. It did not believe in ahimsa. It taught the art of self-defence. It never taught retaliation.'[7] It remains unsubstantiated if Gandhi 'believed these assertions,'[8] a fact borne out by the not-so-subtle messages that he sent out to the RSS regarding its worldview. In his address to the swayamsevaks, Gandhi affirmed that:

> Hinduism had absorbed the best of all the faiths... (consequently) could have no quarrel with Islam or its followers as unfortunately was the case today...if the Hindus felt that in India there was no place for anyone else except the Hindus and if non-Hindus, especially Muslims, wished to live here, they had to live as the slaves of the Hindus, they would kill Hinduism.[9]

Significantly, and particularly for those who continued to argue that Gandhi was soft towards the Muslims, he had said in the same speech,

> if Pakistan believed that in Pakistan only the Muslims had a rightful place and the non-Muslims had to live there on sufferance and as their slaves, it would be the death-knell of Islam in India.

Gandhi's views drew criticism from Karachi's leading newspaper, *Dawn* which while reporting on his interaction with the swayamsevaks emphasised on his assertion about a possible conflict between India and Pakistan. The report was grossly inaccurate, for it had omitted to mention that Gandhi had preached the same lesson to both countries—to be accommodative towards religious minorities. But the newspaper had selectively picked and extrapolated on his statement, 'if Pakistan persisted in wrongdoing, there was bound to be a war between India and Pakistan.' In fact Gandhi had questioned the leaders of the newly-created Pakistan as to why they did not 'plead with the Hindus and the Sikhs and ask them not to leave their homes and ensure their safety in every way?'[10] In no way was Gandhi alluding to a possible Indo–Pak conflict, but was merely hinting at how the two countries should provide space for religious minorities.[11]

Meanwhile, M.S. Golwalkar's timely intervention with the Indian government yielded results and nineteen RSS volunteers were released from prison and arrived in India. The transfer was carried out across the border in Ferozepur (Punjab), and a welcome reception was held in Delhi in the presence of several leading lights, including L K. Advani, despite his fugitive status in Pakistan. In February 2002, when India and Pakistan were locked in an eyeball to eyeball conflict, Islamabad had reopened the Shikarpur Colony case and labelled Advani 'an absconder.'[12]

In the final analysis, it seemed as if the chief of the RSS had achieved the near impossible—his ability to influence the government, particularly a few months prior to his imprisonment on the charge of conspiring to assassinate the Father of the Nation.

At the time of his arrest in February 1948, M.S. Golwalkar had held the top post in the RSS for eight long years, and he held on to it for another quarter of a century.

In the pantheon of RSS sarsanghchalaks, Golwalkar continues to be a revered figure—his long hair, a flowing beard, and the moniker of Guruji worked as perfect symbols in projecting him as the true inheritor of Swami Vivekananda's spiritual legacy. Yet, initially, this wasn't what he had wanted....

The Growing Up Years

Madhav Sadashiv Golwalkar was born in 1906 in Ramtek near Nagpur in Maharashtra. Much like V.D. Savarkar, K.B. Hedgewar, and later, Nathuram Godse, he was also born into a Brahmin family. However, unlike Hedgewar's ancestors who were priests, his father, Sadashivrao Golwalkar was a civil servant in the Post and Telegraph department. The family was poor, but what was more unfortunate was that it was struck by a string of tragedies–in what seemed like a mysterious and incurable disease, the Golwalkar family lost three infant boys and five girls in quick succession.

In 1909, when Madhav was three years old, his father quit the civil services and took up a schoolteacher's job in Chhattisgarh. Subsequently, his job took him to different parts of Central India, and Madhav went to different schools in Raipur, Durg, and Khandwa.

Sadashivrao Golwalkar wished his son to take up Medicine, and in 1922, Madhav enrolled in Fergusson College, Pune. Unfortunately, owing to certain regulations which forbade the migration of students to institutions away from their place of domicile, he was forced to return to Nagpur from where he earned a degree in Science in his Intermediate. In 1926, he secured a BSc from the Banares Hindu University (BHU), and continued in the same university to pursue his MSc in Zoology.

In college, although the young man displayed little interest in active politics, he had a deep understanding of the subject. For instance, in a letter of January 1929 to a close friend, Baburao Telang, Madhav made a reference to Bhagat Singh and his comrades who had carried out the assassination of John Saunders, and wrote that the incident was a 'matter of satisfaction' because the 'insult meted out to the nation by the power-crazy foreign rulers was avenged.'[13] Yet, this was in contrast to his previous stance when he had 'denounced violence, hatred, the attitude of revenge etc...'[14]

It wasn't as if he was deliberately glossing over his principles vis-a-vis the use of violence for a political end. In the same letter, he had confessed that he was facing inner turmoil: 'On the one side there is the desire to take revenge and the impulse of youth, and on the other the serene but immutable Vedic thought.'[15] Although he was yet to manifest his mission of propagating Hinduism as a means to a political end, his inclination towards spiritualism was propelling him to become a 'social,' and subsequently, a 'political Hindu'. At this juncture of his life, Golwalkar saw no dispute between the conflicting viewpoints, and said that the 'real relationship between Hindus and Muslims will have to be made known to all,' and further added that the 'Brahmin-non Brahmin controversy will have to be ended.'[16]

Golwalkar's observations regarding caste during the early years of his life establishes what Hindu nationalists have always held as a social reality—the schism between upper and lower caste Hindus as the primary impediment in the final consolidation of the community. Even prior to his formal indoctrination, Golwalkar had firmly concluded that the so-called unequal relationship between Muslims and Hindus, wherein the latter were purportedly subjugated by the invading Muslims, could not be successfully contested until the inner contradictions within Hindu society were eradicated. His biographer, C.P. Bhishikar made an illuminating comment in this regard as follows:

> Golwalkar had thus, independently, decided about his direction even before he came into contact with the Rashtriya Swayamsevak Sangh. It is really God's grace that such a clear

> realisation of his duty had dawned on a young man who was selfless, scholarly, pure of mind, spiritually inclined, possessed of a comparative knowledge of modern and ancient learning absorbed from hundreds of books, and had just crossed the threshold of the university. No wonder, nearly eleven years later this young man accepted the responsibility of the mission of national awakening launched by Dr. Hedgewar and guided it with exceptional ability for 33 long years.[17]

In the decade or more since his letter to the friend, and before he had assumed the leadership of the RSS, his life's trajectory was anything but linear, and at one point, he had almost veered away from the path he had chalked out in Banaras. But before his mid-career 'blues' hit, and a few years after earning his Masters, Golwalkar had headed towards Madras (now Chennai) for pursuing a doctorate in marine life, which he had to unfortunately abandon, because by then his father had retired, and was unable to fund his doctoral thesis.

Consequently, Madhav returned to Banaras and took up a job as a lecturer in 1930. He taught there for three years after which he returned to Nagpur where among other things, he also studied Law and soon began his legal practise.

In was during his three-year stay in Banaras when he first met with his mentor, K.B. Hedgewar. In the year 1931, the two men knew of each other's existence, but it would take another year before they actually met in person. It may be recalled that Keshav Baliram Hedgewar had embarked on a nationwide tour and travelled to Banaras to widen his cadre base in the holy city, and it was here that he was instantly struck and 'attracted to the ascetic twenty-five-year-old teacher.'[18] Although the two men were seventeen years apart in age, they developed an abiding relationship, which at one point became so contentious that it almost threatened to split the organisation that the two had so carefully built.

An Internal Conflict

As mentioned earlier, unlike other RSS leaders, M.S. Golwalkar had no formal initiation into politics. As a young man, he was naturally drawn towards spiritualism and it would be rather simplistic to attribute this solely to his Brahminical upbringing. At the young age of twenty-three, Golwalkar had said that he had 'no desire to attune (myself) to a mundane human life.'[19] Like most young men, although he may have wrestled with several existentialist questions, he was certain that the life of a *grihast* or householder, was not for him. According to him, happiness was attainable if one followed the path of Shuka (the son of Vyasa, also the compiler and narrator of the Vedas) who was said to have triumphed over Rambha's (the celestial nymph) advances to 'attain *Brahmapad* (the ultimate abode of the Supreme) while a Vishwamitra, treading the same path, succumbs to Menaka and bites the dust.'[20]

In his resolve to remain celibate, Golwalkar considered 'breaking all its (mundane matters) bonds and straight away go to the Himalayas.'[21] Yet, an inexplicable force had restrained him, and he'd held back because, as he asked, 'how can you leave everybody to his fate and go away seeking your own happiness?'[22] Eventually, he overcame the conundrum and confessed to his friend, Baburao Telang that he has,

> already accepted initiation into Sanyas, but it is not yet complete. Perhaps my original idea of going to the Himalayas was faulty....

> Now I shall not go to the Himalayas, rather Himalayas shall come to me—its serene silence will dwell within me.

Along with a deep and abiding faith in spirituality, M.S. Golwalkar was a master in mallakhambh (gymnastics performed on an upright pole); an 'expert in war; had used his hands in the Nagpur Hindu-Muslim riots.'[23]; and a 'votary of Hindu pride.' The contrasting aspects in his personality, of a hermit-warrior, made him an ideal candidate for an organisation which laid great emphasis on both the physical and spiritual aspects of its cadre, and by the late 1920s, Madhav was enlisted as a teacher in the RSS and was soon considered the 'patron and chief of the University Shakha.'[24]

During the course of his teaching assignment in Banares, Madhav Sadashiv developed a close relationship with Prabhakar Balwant Dani aka Bhaiyaji Dani (a swayamsevak from Nagpur, who was appointed the organiser of the local shakha by K.B. Hedgewar), and while Golwalkar helped Dani to complete his education, the latter reciprocated by 'popularising Madhavrao's name as Guruji in the Sangh.'[25] Even before his formal ascent in the sangh hierarchy, the honorific lent a hallowed image to the young teacher who had begun shaping the minds of young RSS volunteers.

It was also during this phase when he had met with one of Congress party's tallest leaders in Banaras, Dr Madan Mohan Malaviya who provided space for the RSS to open a small office in the precincts of the BHU. Sometime later, K.B. Hedgewar invited the young man to Nagpur for the annual Vijaydashami (also the RSS' foundation day) function. The visit to his hometown was a turning point in Golwalkar's life. On his return to Banaras, he discovered that his lectureship had come to an end, and he returned to Nagpur to seek another job.

Engagement with the RSS

After setting up legal practise in Nagpur, M.S. Golwalkar began teaching on the side in his uncle's college to manage the upkeep of his family which included his ageing parents. However, even as his engagement with the RSS continued alongside, it was his inclination towards spiritualism which became a cause for an 'extraordinary tussle'[26] between him and his mentor—two men who steered the RSS for almost five decades. The fact of the matter was that despite all his industriousness, Golwalkar was the quintessential maverick, who didn't give in easily to blind obedience.

For instance, although he was sent to Bombay to widen the RSS' network and was appointed the sarvadhikari (chief) of the training camp in Akola in 1935, his inner calling distracted him from work. It wasn't as if he had abandoned the RSS, but he was beginning to spend more time at the Ramakrishna Mission Ashram in Nagpur. This worried Hedgewar no end who said that,

> while on the one hand the nation was faced with the challenge of achieving freedom and deliver it from the degradation of slavery, on the other a gifted young man...was merely striving for liberation for himself.[27]

He was also cautioned by his mentor about the dangers of intolerance as an impediment in organisation-building.

In the 1930s therefore, M.S. Golwalkar was an inward-looking, reticent young man, when compared to the outgoing and extroverted, Hedgewar. He came across as a reluctant initiate, and Hedgewar feared that he would eventually take flight and become a sanyasi.[28]

Three years later, it actually happened when M.S. Golwalkar

perfunctorily abandoned his legal practise, left the RSS, his home, and headed for Murshidabad district in undivided Bengal to join the Sargachhi Ashram of Swami Akhandananda who was a disciple of Ramkrishna Paramahansa, and a guru bhai of Swami Vivekananda. He had learnt about the ashram from another sanyasi called Swami Amoortananda aka Amitabh Maharaj, who later played an important role in retaining him in the sangh's fold.

Golwalkar had also left a letter with a friend requesting that it be delivered to his mother after his departure. What was strange was that while Madhav had walked away from his mother towards monkhood, after her death in 1962, he had desired complete severance from all worldly pursuits as if in penance for his absence during his mother's last moments. This was when he had been RSS sarsanghchalak for twenty-two years.

Meanwhile after his sojourn in the ashram, it was Amitabh Maharaj who had advised him that the, 'Sangh's work is still incomplete. For its sake you will have to go back.... Your sadhana should take place not in the lap of the Himalayas but *in that room*[29]' (meaning the RSS office; *emphasis mine*).

But in 1936 when he had headed for the Sargachhi Ashram, Golwalkar had no intentions of retracing his steps. One major reason for his resolve to become a monk was Swami Akhandananda, whose deep influence on his pupil is evident from an apocryphal story.

As was the practise in most monastic Orders, the disciples of Swami Akhandananda took complete care of him, including performing 'chores like washing his clothes, bathing him, serving him tea, looking after his meals, making his bed and so on.'[30] Golwalkar also followed the strictures of the ashram and soon formed a strong bond with his master. Swami Akhandananda was not only old, but also ailing and the young, devoted Madhav would often spend nights sitting next to his bedside. At the time of joining the ashram, Golwalkar already had long hair, but it was here that he began growing a beard as well. One day, the master stroked his disciple's head in an avuncular fashion and said, 'Looks good for (*sic*) you. Don't ever cut it.'[31] And henceforth, Madhav, who was already sworn to a life of sanyas, actually began looking like one.

Despite a lifelong ambition of abstaining from the routine life of a householder, destiny had other plans for Madhav Sadashiv Golwalkar. His guru died within a month of his initiation and thereafter, Madhav found little peace at the ashram. Meanwhile, Amitabh Maharaj had got wind of Madhav's inner turmoil and took him to Belur Math, the headquarters of the Ramakrishna Order, on the outskirts of Calcutta. At long last, Madhav seemed to have found equanimity and was perhaps sufficiently distanced from a past that had been one of the most turbulent phases of his life. He immediately expressed his desire to permanently stay at the ashram, when he was informed by Amitabh Maharaj that prior to his death, Swami Akhandananda had wished Golwalkar to return to Nagpur.

Finally in March 1937, the two returned to Nagpur where after spending a few days at the local Ramakrishna Mission, Golwalkar went to meet Keshav Baliram Hedgewar.

Going Up the Ladder

Although there are several accounts of the master's happiness at the return of the prodigal son, there are also a few references of the discomfort that the former had felt over the latter's self-confession of being 'a rather blunt and short-tempered young man.'[32] In Narayan

Hari Palkar's biography of K.B. Hedgewar, M.S. Golwalkar is quoted as saying that, 'there developed around me a thick intellectual sheath through which the Doctor's words could not penetrate.'[33]

Golwalkar had a seemingly brusque manner, which not only worked against him, but also impacted the RSS when it was banned in the aftermath of Mahatma Gandhi's assassination. The mediator who was engaged by the government to strike a bargain with the RSS for rescinding the ban, had commented that Golwalkar was a 'blunt man innocent of the etiquette required in a correspondence with Government. The soft word that turneth away wrath is not among his gifts.'[34]

On his part, K.B. Hedgewar continued guiding his young pupil and advised him yet again that, 'a person should not lose himself in the pursuit of personal happiness but should pledge all his powers to the cause of national regeneration.'[35] But Golwalkar was still undecided and vacillated between the RSS, Ramakrishna Mission, his large circle of friends, and even playing the flute.

In a surprise move, despite Golwalkar's obvious shortcomings, Hedgewar placed him in charge of the annual Officers' Training Camp (OTC) for three consecutive years. One of the reasons for giving the young man an important assignment could have been because of Hedgewar's failing health, and the need to have someone as sharp and young as Madhav to manage the camp. All this was clearly pointing in a particular direction and finally in 1939, Madhav Sadashiv Golwalkar was appointed general secretary of the RSS, the second most important position in the organisation's pecking order.

One of the reasons that Golwalkar's elevation was accepted without any demur was because of his image of an ideologue-thinker. Apart from his ascetic-like appearance and various sojourns to ashrams,

Golwalkar had taken upon himself to translate G.D. (aka Babarao) Savarkar's book in Marathi titled, *Rashtra Mimansa* into English, which was published in March 1939 as *We or Our Nationhood Defined*.

Although this proved to be a significant milestone in his career, for some strange reason, Golwalkar denied the authorship to Savarkar and instead claimed the book to be his 'maiden attempt' in the Preface of the first edition. He however did acknowledge *Rashtra Mimansa* as amongst his 'chief sources of inspiration and help' and further explained in the Preface that he wrote it, despite it being 'superfluous.'[36]

The original Marathi version was published in 1934, but when Golwalkar began translating it, copies of the book were withdrawn and hence unavailable to readers. For a period spanning quarter of a century, Golwalkar had supposedly concealed the fact that the book was not his original work.[37] Yet another observation was that the book often lapsed 'into intemperate language here and there,' and when a second edition was published a few years later, it had been 'somewhat cleansed of these excesses of language.'[38]

The book went into three reprints, the last in 1947, but it took more than a decade and a half before a public statement was made in 1963 attributing the original authorship of *We or Our Nationhood Defined* to G.D. Savarkar. Finally, Golwalkar declared that his was an abridged version of *Rashtra Mimansa* and that he had handed over the Hindi translation to someone, and put to rest the mystery surrounding the book.

Despite Golwalkar's proclamation, the story of two authors claiming authorship of the same book did not create any ripples in the local press. Amongst other reasons, it was because the RSS was still a marginal political force at the time; second, as the declaration was made during the eightieth birthday celebrations of V.D. Savarkar, who was still suspected to be involved in Gandhi's assassination, the controversy was given short shrift and continued to be under wraps for the next four decades. For the people at large, Madhav Sadashiv Golwalkar was the author of *We or Our Nationhood Defined* and the book is still regarded as a seminal work by the RSS.

Eventually, a booklet titled, *Sri Guruji and Indian Muslims* released by the RSS in February 2006 (written by Prof. Rakesh Sinha, an RSS-leaning academic who was nominated to the Rajya Sabha in 2018) made two critical points in this regard: first, that the book 'neither represents the views of the Guruji nor of the RSS,' and second, that this was an abridged version of G.D. Savarkar's work which was previously mentioned by Dhananjay Keer in his autobiography of K.B. Hedgewar and was accepted by the RSS.

But what was most intriguing and given Golwalkar's scholarship, was that if he did take recourse to such a route, then why did he do so in the first place? Was it to ride roughshod over the RSS leadership and gear up to combat any opposition to his appointment as general secretary, and eventually sarsanghchalak? Moreover, the basic premise of G.D. Savarkar's *Rashtra Mimansa* was already treated as a sacred principle by the entire sangh:

> I have throughout the work scrupulously stuck to one idea "Nation" and except where it was unavoidable have given no consideration to the allied concept, the "State." "Nation" being a cultural unit, and "State" a political one, the two concepts are clearly distinguishable, although there is certainly a good deal of mutual overlapping....In applying the Nation Concept to our present day conditions, there is a discussion of the relations

> of the various communities to the Hindu Nation—but not from the political point of view...All passing remarks to the relations between the "Nation" and the "Minority Communities" as appearing in this work are to be understood in this light, without confusing the question of the Minorities' political status with that of their inclusion or otherwise into the body of the Nation.

At no point did Golwalkar disagree with G.D. Savarkar's postulations. Since then, the RSS has somehow failed to ward off claims that as an organisation, it ratifies Golwalkar's version of the original book. This charge has been repeatedly used by the Opposition and even as recently as November 2015 when at a special commemorative session of parliament, Sitaram Yechury, the general secretary of the Communist Party of India (Marxist), quoted from the book to argue that the RSS admired the way German 'managed the Jews'.

> Germany has also shown how well-nigh impossible it is for races and cultures, having differences going to the root, to be assimilated into one united whole, a good lesson for us in Hindustan to learn and profit by....[39]

This viewpoint was however not repudiated by Golwalkar, and remains the 'official line' of the RSS and its affiliated organisations.

In September 2018, there was a concerted effort by the RSS to debunk parts of Golwalkar's contentious political arguments. At a three-day lecture series, the RSS' sarsanghchalak, Mohan Bhagwat had asserted that many of Golwalkar's views had outlived their purpose, because they were made in a particular historical context. This was however not the first time when Golwalkar's theories were rejected by the RSS. The organisation had expressed its discomfort over *Bunch of Thoughts*, a compilation of Golwalkar's speeches and articles, published in 1966. The book contained a chapter titled, "Internal Threats", with sub-sections on Muslims, Christians, and Communists. The section on Muslims argued that the community had adopted a two-fold strategy after Partition—'direct aggression', and 'swelling numbers', and that the problem was a 'time-bomb' for they had neither forgotten nor learnt anything and were working towards creating 'miniature Pakistans.'

In the chapter, Golwalkar had claimed that not all 'pro-Pakistan elements' had gone away and in fact the 'Muslim menace has increased a hundredfold.' In 2004, the RSS released a twelve-volume compendium titled, *Sri Guruji Samagra* or the Collected Works of Sri Guruji.

However, a year later, the organisation felt the need for a 'diluted' version of Golwalkar's political views and published *Sri Guruji: Drishti aur Darshan* (or, Sri Guruji: Vision and Mission). In his speech, Bhagwat argued that the views contained in this particular book were more representative of Golwalkar's thoughts.

Although the RSS continues to grapple with certain aspects of its past, in so far as Madhav Sadashiv Golwalkar is concerned, the cadre continues to revere him as he was projected in its annals.

Storm Over the Appointment

As witnessed in the history of the RSS, M.S. Golwalkar was the only one to have made a lateral entry into the organisation and unlike others, he did not rise through the ranks. In the 1920s when the core group had codified matters relating to the functioning of the RSS, they hadn't obviously specified any procedures nor laid down any rules for a succession plan. As the RSS expanded its base and came to occupy a significant position in post-Independent India, this had led to considerable confusion in its ranks, lasting several years.

In February 1939, Hedgewar had convened a meeting of his select aides to discuss certain important issues as a result of his failing health. It was a decade since the RSS had adopted the principle of ek chalak anuvartitva—the supremacy of one leader—and therefore there was complete concurrence when Hedgewar had nominated Golwalkar as the organisation's sarkaryavah or general secretary, the second most powerful position in the RSS. Appaji Joshi, 'considered Doctorji's right hand man at that time,'[40] and thought to be among the chief's most likely successors, had also conceded in deference to the chief. When an ailing Hedgewar had asked Joshi about his opinion of Golwalkar as 'the future Sarsanghachalak,' he had replied promptly, 'Excellent! A most proper choice.'[41] It wasn't only Joshi who may have had the feeling of being superseded in preference to someone who hadn't risen from the ranks. Madhukar Dattatreya Deoras (see chapter, Balasaheb Deoras, p. 247), popularly known as Balasaheb, was yet another hopeful, for many considered him to be Hedgewar's 'heir apparent'[42], but he was sent to Bengal on work and there the matter had ended.

On 21 June 1940, K.B. Hedgewar died at the home of the Nagpur sanghchalak, Babasaheb Ghatate, leaving the RSS in a quandary over the succession issue. In his last days, besides his personal physician, he only spoke with either Ghatate or Golwalkar[43] and which meant that no one knew what had transpired between the three men. His death put the RSS in an unprecedented situation, because the only time Hedgewar had not been at the helm of affairs was when he had courted arrest during the Civil Disobedience movement, but even then he had formally handed over charge to a loyal aide.

An unpublished dissertation submitted to the Agra University in 1959 claimed that a day before his death, Hedgewar had 'handed over to him (Golwalkar) a slip of paper on which was written: Before giving this body finally in the hands of doctors, I wanted to tell you that hereafter you look after the organization and shoulder the whole responsibility.'[44]

Meanwhile after the mandatory thirteen-day mourning period was over, the top brass of the RSS met in Nagpur on 3 July which included, Dr B.S. Moonje, L.V. Paranjpe, Golwalkar and Balasaheb Deoras, to deliberate over their collective future. At the end of the meeting when a formal announcement was made about M.S. Golwalkar's elevation, it 'stunned many RSS members, who had expected that Hedgewar would choose an older, more experienced person.'[45] The nomination issue had so impacted the cadre that in a memorial issue of the *Organiser* published after Golwalkar's death, Balasaheb Deoras, who had succeeded him, was quoted as saying:

> Possibly some of us may have thought at that time that Guruji Golwalkar was new to the Sangh, and not experienced enough. So we might have been doubtful about how he would discharge his responsibility. Those who were outside the Sangh, but had love for it were also apprehensive about the Sangh after Doctor Saheb.[46]

Amongst several other factors which may have tilted the balance in Golwalkar's favour, his knowledge of the English[47] language was in all likelihood one the reasons for his appointment. But the scepticism over his elevation, as also mentioned by Deoras, was partly because of his lack of experience and also due to a lack of transparency in the entire nomination process. Although Hedgewar had discussed Golwalkar's nomination in a private conversation with Appaji Joshi, it wasn't taken to be his final decision. There was 'considerable speculation both within and outside the RSS over whether Golwalkar was, in fact, Hedgewar's choice for the position.'[48] Moreover, Ghatate's role in the entire process was also questioned as many in the RSS had felt that he,

> might well have fabricated Hedgewar's choice or planted the idea in the dying man's mind. It is impossible to verify the rumour...Joshi did not believe the announcement; moreover, he did not think Golwalkar had the requisite political sophistication to lead the RSS.[49]

Yet, the loyal soldier of the sangh that he was, Joshi 'defended Golwalkar against those who charged that Golwalkar had abandoned the objectives laid out by Hedgewar.'[50]

The Initial Success

After the controversy over his nomination had died down, Madhav Sadashiv Golwalkar's elevation helped the RSS to retain its distinct identity, and not be subsumed by the Hindu Mahasabha which was led by none other than the charismatic V.D. Savarkar, whose firm hold over the cadre was legendary.

After his release from the Cellular Jail, Savarkar had frequent run-ins with K.B. Hedgewar over the latter's refusal to engage with politics. As mentioned in many accounts, the Hindu Mahasabha leader was often exasperated with the RSS for limiting its role to either character-building of its cadre or fortifying the edifice of their Hindu brethren. With Golwalkar at the helm of affairs, it became doubly difficult for Savarkar to influence the RSS, because he was now faced with a man who was not only loathe to engaging in active politics, but was known to be inclined towards spiritualism.

With the formation of the provincial governments in 1937 and the outbreak of the Second World War in 1939, while V.D. Savarkar initiated the idea of militarising Hindus and recommended that the country's youth enlist in the British army for tactical reasons, Golwalkar not only ordered the closure of the RSS' military wing, but ensured that it 'refused to assist the various militarization and paramilitary schemes advocated by other Hindu nationalists.'[51]

Golwalkar's attempts at deviating from the trodden path was strongly resisted by several members of the Mahasabha, the most prominent being the founder of the Hindu Rashtra Dal, Nathuram Godse.[52] Yet, Golwalkar stood his ground and the imminent threat to his leadership passed without any 'large scale defections'[53] owing to Balasaheb Deoras' intervention who 'did everything to establish the leadership of Golwalkar in the RSS.'[54]

Much like K.B. Hedgewar, who had opted for political conservatism during the Civil Disobedience movement, Golwalkar also kept his cadre insulated from activities that had the potential of inviting the wrath of the British and kept out of the Quit India movement (more of which later).

As the sarsanghchalak, Golwalkar's first major step in firming up the RSS' ideology was to establish a pathological dislike for Communism—'Not socialism but Hinduism'[55] was a slogan he popularised which was a progression from Hedgewar's catchphrase, 'Hinduism is Nationalism.' This was viewed as a significant expansion of the RSS' basic ideology: from an organisation which'd raised the spectre of being subsumed by minorities, it was now positioning itself as staunchly anti-Marxist. In time, this evolved into a theory within the sangh parivar and other

Hindu nationalist groups that pandering to Muslims, Christians, and communist ideology were major impediments in consolidating the Hindu community.

In post-Independent India, the theory of secularism being synonymous with Marxism became one of the most significant maxims for the sangh parivar. This was strongly manifest in the Eighties after the Ram Janmabhoomi agitation had gathered storm. It may be recalled that in 1989, even as the Bharatiya Janata Party was readying itself to launch the famous Ayodhya to Somnath rath yatra with L.K. Advani at the forefront, senior functionaries of the RSS had recommended that the ultimate path in gaining credence across India lay in waging an ideological struggle, and not just a programmatic agitation to secure its place in Indian politics. Consequently, both Leftist and liberal thought became the BJP's primary targets—mainly intellectuals ranging from artists, filmmakers, writers, activists, and academicians. A most telling instance of this selective targeting was the hounding out of one of India's best known artists, Maqbool Fida Hussain, who was forced to spend his last years in exile.

In the recent past, one of the most aggressive campaigns by Hindu groups has been to 'reinstate' India's history, which it believes was taken over by Leftist historians who had deliberately eclipsed relevant portions eulogising Hindus' achievements in the past. It was none other than M. S. Golwalkar who had influenced subsequent generations of the RSS and its affiliated organisations to adopt this thought as its core principle.[56]

A Difficult Leader

In 1939 when M.S. Golwalkar had assumed office, the RSS' founding sarsanghchalak was dead and the cadre needed a leader who would continue to inspire them. Golwalkar straightaway decided to assert his authority and declared that he was a legitimate appointee and anyone who had objections should tell him 'now. If someone does it tomorrow, I will throw him out of (the) RSS like a stone in rice, just as Mahatma Gandhi did to N.B. Khare.'[57]

Besides the feeling of insecurity under a new leader, many found Golwalkar's aversion to politics extremely problematic. While Golwalkar believed that his primary duty was to keep the RSS 'pure', reinforce the strength of Hindus through his cadre who needed to be kept away from the corrupting influence of 'immoral' politics, several felt that in order to alter the nature of the political discourse, it was imperative to participate in India's struggle for independence.

Curiously, even as Golwalkar and his core group were opposed to assuming political power, they also wanted credit for it. For instance, he wished that the 'assets from the political work' carried out by members of the RSS accrue to the organisation, but wanted to avoid the 'liabilities of the hard work to deliver the goods.'[58] However, both privately and publicly, he made it known that active politics was not central to the life of a nation.

This resulted in a dichotomy—after the formation of the Rashtra Sevika Samiti, other affiliated organisations that were set up from the 1940s onwards, like the Akhil Bharatiya Vidyarthi Parishad (ABVP), Bharatiya Mazdoor Sangh (BMS), Jana Sangh, and the publications division, Bharat Prakashan Trust, had a greater political orientation. In July 1949, the Trust began publishing a weekly newspaper in English called *Organiser*, and a few months later, *Panchjanya* and *Rashtra Dharma* in Hindi. Although all such efforts enabled the RSS to retain its influence and were ably managed by swayamsevaks, Golwalkar neither 'recognised' any 'good' work done by them nor 'own up' to the work. In fact, it has been pointed out that despite the growth of a significantly large network of similar organisations during his tenure, Golwalkar personally maintained that,

> the only work that needs to be done is to unite and organize fragmented Hindu society into a large corporate entity through the daily work of the RSS. He had no interest in any other type of work, except for that of the Vishwa Hindu Parishad.[59]

Yet another peculiarity in Golwalkar's character was that while he didn't encourage frequent interactions with the Hindu Mahasabha, he routinely had regional Congress leaders preside over RSS' programmes.[60] The reason for this stark contradiction in a man who was known for his bitter criticism of the Congress party, could have stemmed from the fact that he wanted the RSS, and not the Hindu Mahasabha, to appropriate the space for shepherding the Hindus and moreover, his antipathy towards the Congress had not yet developed into an ideological hatred.

* * *

As mentioned elsewhere in the book, during the early 1940s when Golwalkar was the RSS sarsanghchalak, a great debate had ensued amongst political parties regarding India's role in the Second World War. On the one hand, if the Indian National Congress and the Communists considered it to be an 'Imperialistic' war, Golwalkar remained neutral over the issue. He was also anxious that people may turn against the RSS if it supported the war effort like its doppelganger, the Mahasabha.[61]

Amongst other things, the early 1940s witnessed three significant developments in the history of national politics—the first was led by the Congress post the Quit India movement, finally culminating in independence; the second was led by leaders like Subhash Chandra Bose, who were even willing to collaborate with the Axis powers to secure freedom; and thirdly, forces like the Hindu Mahasabha and the Muslim League, who were pushing their own agendas.

While the first two political forces had opted out of political negotiations except on how and when independence was to be granted (Bose in any case, never entered into parleys with the British and his followers, barring naval mutineers, had had no interactions with the Colonialists); the Mahasabha and Muslim League had petitioned the British in return for favours. As a matter of fact, the RSS was largely absent from the national discourse during this period[62], barring the Muslim League's Direct Action Call of 1946 and its aftermath, and made little efforts to influence it, focussed as it was on expanding its network across the country. Jawaharlal Nehru had in fact made a mention apropos the contradictory stance of not only the Congress party, but also that of 'religious-communal organisations.'[63]

In the first four years of Golwalkar's tenure as sarsanghchalak, the RSS grew at a sluggish pace and according to official estimates, only 76,000 swayamsevaks attended the daily shakhas. While fifty per cent of the shakhas were located in the Central Provinces, in close proximity to Nagpur, the others were evenly distributed in Bombay and Punjab. However, in 1945–1948 while the Hindu Mahasabha, which was committed to active politics, failed to benefit electorally, the RSS grew exponentially in north India—Punjab, Sindh, Delhi and the United Provinces—regions which were also facing intense communal strife.

By now it was safe to surmise that the RSS had a pan-Indian presence, although its leadership continued to be predominantly Maharashtrian Brahmins. Unlike Maharashtra, where the majority of its members were middle class working professionals, in other regions like north India, they were mainly from the mercantile community, which later made the RSS appear like the protector of Hindu business interests, as the group was one of the primary targets during post-Partition riots. Yet, Golwalkar did little to either alter the RSS' image or its leadership.

In what is viewed as a contentious claim, Sanjeev Kelkar mentions in his book that Golwalkar was intrinsically anti-intellectual and that 'his popular outward image was that he did not even read newspapers.'[64] As a result, both knowledge and information trickled down from the top, strictly in the form of instructions or regulations. The leaders provided the 'light of eternal principles[65]' and the cadre was instructed to 'work out the details.'[66]

Although there were similar issues regarding strictures even during Hedgewar's tenure, under Golwalkar, 'there was no discussion, no spark of scholarship on any problem that beset the nation at the ground level...RSS was enshrined in converse of scholarship—it upheld and praised mediocrity.'[67]

As mentioned earlier in the chapter and a trait that was noticed by many of his peers, the added impediment to Golwalkar's acceptance within the sangh was his abrasive personality—'His words used to be sharp and cutting. Sometimes it would even hurt. He could not suffer incompetence or laxity...'[68] Gradually, once he realised that it had become incumbent upon him to project a more pliable self, Golwalkar chose to widen the shakha network which despite growing steadily to about 500 shakhas with approximately 60,000 swayamsevaks at the time of Hedgewar's death, was mainly concentrated in Maharashtra. As a result, intense efforts were made in establishing the RSS in distant provinces like Sindh and the Madras Presidency. Consequently, by early 1940s, the number of swayamsevaks had gone up to one lakh despite the RSS' 'apparent retreat from activism.'[69] According to the Intelligence Bureau, the number of volunteers who joined the RSS every day had doubled in five years between 1938 and 1943[70] and this was primarily due to Golwalkar who had succeeded in retaining the principal core of the RSS network. He was aware that the pull to be a part of the RSS among youth, an age-group 'favourable for the enrolment into a movement of this kind,' worked best when it was dovetailed to the image of an 'ideal man', or rather the 'model man, that is the pracharak.' An account by a former swayamsevak from Punjab, as quoted by Christophe Jaffrelot, highlights how his devotion to the RSS was mainly due to his 'deep attachment,' to the pracharak who had inducted him. Furthermore, between 1945–48, a period which had witnessed sharp polarisation between Hindus and Muslims, 'the RSS membership (had) surged.' In the context of the growth of the RSS, the correlation between the two arguments cannot be perhaps negated.

This was also the period when Golwalkar had decided to 'Indianise the external format of the Shakha,' by replacing its instructions in English with Sanskrit, and had also changed the names of its units to *Gana*, *Vahini*, *Anikini*, while renaming the RSS band as, *Ghosh*.

As part of an effort to build a strong network of loyal, state-level leaders, Golwalkar would travel twice a year to every corner of the country to evaluate the progress of the organisation. Although Gowalkar was ably assisted by his lieutenant, Balasaheb Deoras in consolidating his hold over the RSS machinery, it came back to haunt him after he became the sarsanghchalak. The men who were promoted by Golwalkar 'did not always accept him (Deoras) and his thoughts the way they did Golwalkar.'[71]

Political Choices

With the Congress launching the Quit India movement in August 1942, M.S. Golwalkar was forced to make a strategic choice—whether to join or stay away, like his mentor had done during the Civil Disobedience movement in the 1930s. He is supposed to have weighed in his options against the backdrop of,

> the meagre strength of the Sangh, the lack of planning by those conducting the movement, the lack of a clear direction, and the possibility of a national struggle not continuing for long for lack of a single command for the movement.[72]

Finally, the RSS chief stayed away from the movement but did not prevent his swayamsevaks from participating in their personal capacities. Dattopant Thengadi, who later established the trade union for the RSS, explained the predicament of the swayamsevaks as follows:

> The 1942 movement had created turmoil in the minds of many Swayamsevaks and even Pracharaks. The question troubling them was—if the Sangh was to do nothing even at such a crucial juncture what was the use of all its strength built up so far?

M.S. Golwalkar had expected Mahatma Gandhi to invite him for consultations, but when no such thing had happened, he had fulminated over the fact that,

> the leaders of the agitation have not consulted any of the other organisations who strive for the nation's freedom. There is no effort to distribute work and responsibility to each other according to their capacity and liking.[73]

Golwalkar's decision to dissociate from the Quit India movement was also to avoid any confrontation with the Imperial government. In the wake of a British crackdown on leaders of the national movement, Golwalkar discontinued the RSS' military drills and directed swayamsevaks, pracharaks, and senior functionaries to stop wearing the uniform. He explained in an internal circular dated 29 April 1943[74] that he desired to 'keep our work clearly within the bounds of law.'[75]

The British reciprocated to this gesture when the Home Department noted in an official report that the RSS could not be construed to be posing a threat to the law and order situation in the country. It also observed that the RSS had kept itself completely distanced from anti-government agitations in the wake of the Quit India movement.

But internally, there were differences—between Golwalkar's pacifist line and the viewpoint of others like Deoras who recommended plunging headlong into the agitation and use it as a political launch pad. However, the RSS chief tided over such irritants and directed his energy towards strengthening the organisation which soon proved to be beneficial as the 'Sangh Shakhas spread out rapidly from province to province. Workers were mobilised to move from place to place. Swayamsevaks could be seen flooding in Shakhas all over.'[76]

By 1945, 10,000 swayamsevaks had registered their presence at the Officers' Training Camp in various parts of India.

This was also the year when Golwalkar had decided to build the RSS headquarters in Nagpur. The foundation stone for Hedgewar Bhawan was laid formally and work on it began in all earnest. For Golwalkar, the impressive growth rate of the RSS may have been a victory of sorts, but his distance from the Quit India movement, became the proverbial albatross around his neck.

This was mainly due to Golwalkar's view that all politics was immoral, which included every form of protest. According to him, agitations impeded constructive work. He labelled agitational activity as *rajasik* or valorous which inherently attracted people, but if the RSS adopted this path, Golwalkar feared that it would 'deviate from the *satvik*, the "saintly" path it had chosen for itself.'[77] Furthermore, the sarsanghchalak was of the view that since the RSS' principal objectives were 'man-making and the achievement of the goal of Hindu Rashtra'[78], this could be achieved without any 'external stimuli.'[79]

Golwalkar justified the decision to stay away from the Quit India movement by citing Hedgewar's stance during the Civil Disobedience and used the term 'certain constraints'[80] which the founder chose to impose on the sangh. But Golwalkar was silent on why he had not followed in his predecessor's footsteps in joining the movement after temporarily handing over charge to a loyal aide. Moreover, while Golwalkar was of the opinion that self-imposed limitations that Hedgewar had talked about 'can be kept aside at a critical time like this if by doing so it would help the attainment of freedom,'[81] he was also resentful of the fact that neither the Congress, nor Gandhi had consulted him before starting the agitation. Golwalkar paid little heed to the fact that compared to the Congress, the RSS had a marginal presence in India.

Preparing for Partition

With the possibility of Partition looming large, Golwalkar took the lead in campaigning against it. Starting from the mid-Forties, the RSS chief beseeched the Indians to stay united and repeatedly evoked the popular symbols of Hindu valour and sacrifice. The leitmotif was none other than the iconic, Chattrapati Shivaji, whose 'supreme devotion to our Hindu way of life coupled with his unparalleled organisational acumen which gave it a practical dynamic form, that made him a force which changed the entire course of our history.' In speeches after speeches, Golwalkar's constant refrain was that 'only the idea of Akhand Bharat would solve the problems of Muslims in this country.'[82]

The centrality of the idea of Akhand Bharat remained within the parivar. It was based on the belief that 'Bharatiya nationalism was based on the concept of one people, one country, one culture.'[83] After India became independent, 'all the local branches of the RSS, on August 14 every year, began to hold a function called Akhand Bharat Sankalp Diwas for the formation of a reunited India.'[84]

For the affiliates of the RSS, this was an article of faith as well. On 15 August 1953, the Jana Sangh had resolved that the party 'will always keep this ideal before itself and will work for Akhand Bharat.' Yet another resolution of the party in 1965 during the war with Pakistan had affirmed that as 'long as partition exists, there shall be no peace between India and Pakistan.'[85] As recently as December 2015, the general secretary of the BJP, Ram Madhav had declared in the course of a television programme that the 'RSS still believes that one day these parts (India, Pakistan and Bangladesh)...will again, through popular goodwill, come together and Akhand Bharat will be created.'[86]

In the 1940s, M.S. Golwalkar drew large crowds at meetings and although he thundered against dividing the country, in its defence, he presented an idea which created a further rift between Hindus and Muslims. In August 1946, the Muslim League's call for Direct Action in Calcutta provided an ideal opportunity for the RSS to 'finally prove, through provocative as well as retaliatory actions, that Hindus and Muslims could not live together.'[87]

Several prominent leaders of the RSS openly planted diabolical stories of 'Muslim plans to stage a coup and establish Muslim raj in India.'[88] In his collection of speeches titled, *Bunch of Thoughts*, Golwalkar made several references to Partition. In one such exposition, he had asserted that:

> If that spirit (fiery and heroic aspect of devotion to our motherland) had been there in our leaders and in our common folk, could Partition have taken place? Would they not have risen uncompromisingly, heroically as one man against all such machinations of the British and the Muslim, prepared to shed their last drop of blood for maintaining the sacred integrity of the motherland? Alas, that did not happen. On the contrary, people, led by the leaders, were busy in celebrations on the advent of so-called independence!

Even after independence, Golwalkar did not seek a political role for the RSS and sat out of the Interim government, as well as during negotiations with the British. The reason being that he believed that India would forever remain a British colony. This was evident during an Officers' Training Camp in Phagwara, Punjab. When asked by a participant about the RSS' role in free India, Golwalkar had quipped:

> Do you believe that the British will quit? The nincompoops in whose hands they are giving the reins of government will not be able to hold on even for two months. They will go crawling on their knees to the British and ask them to kindly return. The RSS will have to continue its work as in the past.

Post Partition

Madhav Sadashiv Golwalkar may have kept the RSS 'pure' by excluding it from politics in a newly-created nation, but he ensured that it earned goodwill for its humanitarian role—running relief camps for Hindu and Sikh refugees from across the border; the setting up of Hindu paramilitary groups to protect Hindus fleeing from Pakistan. In what was one of the most terrible and largest forced migration of people in the world, there was unprecedented violence, loot and rape witnessed on both sides of the border. The RSS which is still recalled for its stellar work during the period, had however come under fire because not every activity of it was directed at peacefully providing relief to refugees. A former swayamsevak has been quoted as saying that 'swayamsevaks were assigned to guard Hindu homes; they collected weapons to use during anticipated Muslim attacks; and they manufactured hand grenades.'[89] This was the reason why the RSS was described by some as, 'probably the best organised of the paramilitary groups' when 'few hands were clean.'[90]

On 16 September 1947, Mahatma Gandhi requested swayamsevaks to let the government manage the deteriorating law and order situation, and not resort to retaliatory attacks on Muslim colonies or camps. In defense of his cadre, Golwalkar had responded that 'the RSS was purely defensive, though he could not vouch for the actions of every swayamsevak.'[91]

Despite Gandhi's open disagreement with Golwalkar, Sardar Patel had sought his assistance in convincing the Hindu Maharaja of Kashmir to merge his kingdom with India under the Instrument of Accession. Golwalkar met Maharaja Hari Singh in October 1947 and Kashmir became a part of the Indian Union.

In recognition for his contribution, when Indian troops were sent to Kashmir, RSS volunteers and members of the National Conference led by Sheikh Abdullah were provided arms by the government.

That Golwalkar and the RSS' role in Kashmir was valued by Patel was evident when the Iron Man had accepted[92] recommendations to appoint the RSS chief of Punjab, Rai Bahadur Dewan Badri Das, as the acting governor of Eastern Punjab, and handing over the entire responsibility of managing refugee camps to the Punjab Relief Committee 'which was virtually a signboard for the RSS.'[93] In the same period, the military commander of the Delhi region had enlisted the support of Golwalkar to depute swayamsevaks for maintaining law and order in the capital.

At a time when people went around looking for the bodies of their family members; when several women were raped or killed by lumpens on both sides; when a nation had been cleaved into two bloody halves, the RSS' relief work amongst Hindu refugees was widely acknowledged as exemplary in the absence of a 'working' government in Delhi. There are several accounts of how Hindu refugees had warmed up to the organisation; the RSS had also started a drive to enlist members from the community. Gradually, as these uprooted Hindus-turned-swayamsevaks began rebuilding their lives, a majority of them took to trading and started small businesses and eventually it was this class which became the primary support base for the RSS and its affiliated organisations. This explains why first the Jana Sangh, and later the BJP is referred to as a 'traders' party'.

On 12 January 1948, Mahatma Gandhi went on a fast protesting against the attacks on Muslims in Delhi and demanded that the Indian government releases the pending fifty-five crores to Pakistan without further delay. Five days later, on 18 January 1948, the Mahatma ended his fast after Hindu and Sikh representatives agreed to his six conditions, and Hans Raj Gupta, the RSS sanghchalak had given him an assurance of securing Muslim properties and shrines.

That Gandhi was obdurate in his ways was a given, but for several people, 'his stand on Muslims and Pakistan had become a tipping point.'[94] On 20 January 1948, Gandhi escaped a bomb attack, but the assassins got their target ten days later on 30 January. Nathuram Godse had not only spent several years in the RSS but also had a close association with Savarkar after he had parted ways with his parent organisation. Given the past association of the RSS with the assassin, on 1 February 1948, Golwalkar was arrested along with leaders of the Hindu Mahasabha and on 4 February 1948, the RSS was banned by the Indian government.

In the months following Golwalkar's arrest, an estimated 20,000 swayamsevaks and leaders were also taken into custody. But the RSS was kept alive, albeit stealthily by a few who had refused to give up.

Coping with the Ban

Prior to Gandhi's assassination, the organisation had come under the scanner during the Chief Ministers' Conference in Delhi in November 1947. There was a loud clamour to proscribe the RSS, but it was eventually decided to initiate action on a case by case basis against certain swayamsevaks, in case of complaints against them. Several people had spoken against the RSS at the Meerut Congress session in November, including Pandit Nehru at a public meeting in Amritsar even a day before Gandhi's murder. He returned to the Indian capital a couple of hours before Gandhi's assassination and later spoke to an estimated two lakh angry mourners who had assembled at the Birla House, the place where their beloved Mahatma had fallen to the bullets of Nathuram Godse. On 31 January 1948, *The Hindu* had reported that Godse 'was beaten by the crowd and was slightly injured.'

Madhav Sadashiv Golwalkar was in Madras when he received news of the assassination. In a dramatic recap of the moment, C.P. Bhishikar mentions in his book how Golwalkar was holding a cup of tea in his hands, when someone had conveyed the news to him. After putting the cup down, the RSS chief had lapsed into a long silence, before uttering: 'What a misfortune for the country!'

Thereafter, Golwalkar had cancelled the rest of his tour, and after wiring condolence messages to Pandit Nehru and Vallabhbhai Patel, he flew back to Nagpur. As is the practise amongst Hindus, he had immediately issued instructions to suspend all shakha activities for thirteen days as a mark of respect for the deceased.

On the morning of 31 January 1948, angry mobs began gathering outside M.S. Golwalkar's house. An equal number of swayamsevaks were summoned to defend their chief, but they could do little in warding off stone pelters from the opposite side. Golwalkar issued a press statement through the Associated Press (AP) and while he appealed for peace and unity in the country, he asked the swayamsevaks to,

> keep calm under any kind of situation and behave with amity and affection, and understand that the trouble, given by people who had fallen prey to misunderstanding, was also an index

of the great love and respect that our countrymen felt for the great man who had brought glory to our motherland in the eyes of the whole world.

On the midnight of 1 February 1948, the Nagpur police swooped down on M.S. Golwalkar and arrested him for conspiring to murder Mahatma Gandhi. While walking towards the police jeep, he told his supporters that the, 'clouds of suspicion will soon be dispelled and we shall come out without a blemish.' Bhaiyaji Dani, the man who had rechristened Madhav as Guruji, sent telegrams to all the shakhas—*Guruji interned, be calm at all costs.*

The next day, the government promulgated an ordinance banning the Rashtriya Swayamsevak Sangh. The legislation stated that it 'considered it its duty to put down such a fanatic manifestation of violence, and so, as a first step, the RSS was being declared illegal.' The ordinance charged the RSS of not adhering 'to their professed ideals (fostering feelings of brotherhood, love and service among Hindus)', and said that there was evidence that the organisation was 'circulating leaflets exhorting people to resort to terrorist methods, to collect firearms, to create disaffection against the government and suborn the police and the military. These activities have been carried on under a cloak of secrecy…'

The ruling was made public on 4 February 1948 and close to thirty thousand swayamsevaks were thrown into jails. M.S. Golwalkar's worst fears had come true, but not one to give up, he had made yet another valiant attempt to salvage the situation. On 5 February, when Dattopant Deshpande, his lawyer and friend had come visiting him in jail, Golwalkar had handed him a statement which read as follows:

> It has always been the policy of the RSS to be law-abiding and carry on its activities within the bounds of law. Therefore, since the Government has declared the RSS an unlawful body it is thought advisable to disband the RSS till the ban is there, at the same time denying all the charges levelled against the organisation.

Dattopant's visit brought good tidings for his comrade and within a day or two, Golwalkar was rid of the serious charge of conspiring to assassinate Mahatma Gandhi and was instead held under the National Security Act, meaning preventive detention. Six months later, on 6 August 1948, Golwalkar was released from prison, but with a caveat: to stay within the municipal limits of Nagpur and not engage in any kind of political activity, including addressing public meetings, writing articles or issuing statements. As there was no embargo on writing letters, Golwalkar used the opportunity and wrote to Prime Minister Nehru and Sardar Patel separately on 11 August 1948. In his letter to Nehru, he had raised a question about why he had been denied a,

> chance to clear my position and to convince you of my feelings and readiness to cooperate with the Government in these crucial times. Even now I hope our rapprochement is not afar.

With no reply forthcoming for six weeks, Golwalkar wrote to them yet again on 24 September. In his missive, he had pleaded with both the prime minister and deputy prime minister that the ban on the RSS be lifted, and offered assistance in countering the threat of Communism in the country. He said that as the Communists 'considered the RSS as their main obstacle and had tried to denounce and vilify it,' the government should 'help create an atmosphere in which the RSS will be able to work honourably and help the Government fight the menace, on its own cultural lines.' The threat from the Communists, argued Golwalkar, was because 'intelligent youth are rapidly falling into the snares of Communism. With the alarming happenings in Burma, Indo-China, Java and other neighbouring states, we can envisage the nature of the menace.' While specifically addressing Sardar Patel, the chief of RSS reminded him that, 'I and all my co-workers have been striving from the very start to cooperate with you to bring the situation under control and make our Motherland invincible.'

Both the men replied back, and although Vallabhbhai Patel in his letter dated 11 September 1948 acknowledged the work done by the RSS in protecting the women and children who had arrived as refugees from across the border after Partition, he also sent out a strong message that the,

> objectionable part arose when they, burning with revenge, began attacking Mussalmans. Organising the Hindus and helping them is one thing but going in for revenge for its sufferings on innocent and helpless men, women and children is quite another thing.

In the same letter, Patel had touched upon a sensitive issue and said that he was 'convinced that the RSS men can carry on their patriotic endeavour only by joining the Congress and not by keeping separate (identity) or by opposing.' Opening the doors for swayamsevaks barely a few days after Gandhi's assassination and without prior discussion with members of the Congress, was not appreciated within certain sections of the party, including the prime minister. In a way, Patel's letter to Golwalkar had brought into sharp focus the divergent views held by two Congress stalwarts with regard to the RSS.

A few days later, an officer in the Prime Minister's Office or PMO, A.V. Pai, wrote to Golwalkar that the RSS, 'was engaged in activities which were anti-national, prejudicial from the point of view of public good.'[95] Nehru also said that the objectives of the RSS were,

> completely opposed to the decisions of the Indian Parliament and the provisions of the proposed Constitution of India. The activities (of the RSS), according to our information, are anti-national and often subversive and violent.

One wonders if it was the beauty of democracy and therefore the respect accorded to a stalwart of a leader like Patel, but in October 1948, Madhav Sadashiv Golwalkar was allowed to travel to Delhi to discuss the lifting of the ban. He first met Patel, after Nehru had declined to meet him as the prime minister had felt that it would not 'serve any useful purpose.' Unfortunately, Golwalkar's meetings (he had had two by now) with Patel too came to naught and the RSS remained on the proscribed list. Patel also asked his office to issue instructions to Golwalkar to 'make immediate arrangements to return to Nagpur,' as restrictions on his travel which had been kept in abeyance, were now re-imposed.

The official order from the government of India stated that M.S. Golwalkar had committed to the RSS' agreement, 'entirely in the conception of a Secular State for India and that it accepts the National Flag of the country,' which however did not suffice to end the ban because Golwalkar's commitment was 'inconsistent with the practice of his followers.'

Golwalkar was extremely disappointed with Sardar Patel's response and in a letter dated 5 November 1948, he openly expressed his bitterness as follows:

> I tried my utmost to see that between the Congress and the Rashtriya Swayamsevak Sangh...there be no bad blood, there be only everlasting mutual love, one supplementing and complementing the other, both meeting in a sacred confluence. I extended my hand of cooperation. With utmost regrets I have to say that you have chosen to ignore my best intentions. My heart's desire to see the converging of both the streams has remained unfulfilled.

However, his impassioned plea proved to be futile and after his subsequent requests to meet Patel were turned down, Golwalkar decided to defy the order, and stayed put in Delhi. There was a midnight knock on the door of a RSS functionary for the second time that year, the difference being that this time around, the posse of police had landed up at Delhi's RSS chief and industrialist, Lala Hansraj Gupta's bungalow on Barakhamba Road. Golwalkar was spared the ignominy of an arrest, but was put on the earliest flight to Nagpur. It was obvious that the door had been slammed shut on the RSS at Nehru's insistence. Patel's proposal of merging the RSS with the Congress was not only rejected by the prime minister, but also by the sarsanghchalak, who wanted the RSS to henceforth dedicate itself towards establishing Hindu hegemony in the country. He was also doubtful about Patel exerting his influence over the prime minister, and after virtually being hounded out of Delhi, Golwalkar had little option but to revive the spirit of his cadre.

He began by writing an open letter to the swayamsevaks contending that the ban was 'an insult to the honour of the citizens of free Bharat,' and suggested that shakhas be made operational despite the governmental order. In many ways, the letter was symbolic of Golwalkar's assertiveness in independent India, and the stage was readied for a head-on confrontation with the government.

It was rather ironical that in December 1948, eleven months after Gandhi's assassination, the RSS launched its first mass agitation using the Mahatma's principles of non-violence and non-cooperation, demanding the lifting of the ban. A massive all-India signature campaign was launched for the cause and amongst the nine lakh signatories, there were also several Congress leaders like Acharya Kripalani who had been Gandhi's inmate at the Sabarmati Ashram.

Although M. S. Golwalkar was lodged in Seoni Jail (in what is now Madhya Pradesh) where he was confined in anticipation of the agitation, the protest was a great success—an estimated eighty to sixty thousand[96] supporters were put into jail for violating prohibitory orders. The 'satyagraha' had succeeded in rejuvenating the sagging spirits of the swayamsevaks and there was an all-round condemnation of police action against hapless citizens in a newly independent India.

The government swung into action to quell the rebellion and decided to resume its dialogue with the RSS. The process had already been initiated, albeit secretly, during the RSS' 'satyagraha', when the mediators had convinced Golwalkar to withdraw the agitation.

As Golwalkar was in prison, D.P. Mishra, then Home minister of the Central Provinces (father of the late Brajesh Mishra, who was National Security Adviser under Prime Minister Atal Bihari Vajpayee) had acted as an interlocutor between him and Sardar Patel in yet another effort to rescind the ban after the failed bid made between August–November 1948.

While Sardar Patel acquiesced to Mishra's suggestion about finding a legitimate method to lift the ban on the RSS, Mishra convinced Golwalkar of the need to suspend the satyagraha. Yet another man who had played a crucial role in aiding Golwalkar to adopt a reconciliatory posture was G.V. Ketkar, editor of the Marathi newspaper, *Kesari* which was started by his illustrious grandfather, Bal Gangadhar Tilak. A few weeks after Golwalkar suspended the 'satyagraha', a new interlocutor arrived on the scene—T.R. Venkatarama Sastri, the former Advocate General of Madras and a leader of the Liberal Party, who had past experience of mediating between Mahatma Gandhi and the British.

On 13 February 1949, Sastri met Golwalkar at Seoni Jail and discussed several issues, including steps to rescind the ban. Although the Tamil leader had discharged his duties, he found Golwalkar 'a blunt man, innocent of the etiquette required in a correspondence with Government. The soft word that turneth away wrath is not among his gifts,' and that 'Golwalkar's reply is said to have been such as to give offence to the Government of India. I can well believe it.'[97]

According to a report by a member of the jail staff, Golwalkar had given Sastri a 'blank cheque to make any decision they like and assured them that he would honour the decision they arrive at.'[98] During the meeting, it was also decided that the RSS adopts a draft constitution, and the task was delegated to two experienced hands, Bhaiyaji Dani and Balasaheb Deoras.

Over the next few months, several letters were exchanged between Golwalkar and representatives of the government (compiled later as *Justice on Trial: Historic Document of Guruji-Govt Correspondence*). Despite what was essentially seen to be an effort to accommodate the RSS to function within the ambit of the Constitution, the dialogue had run into several problems, First, Home Secretary, H.V.R. Iyengar informed Golwalkar that despite all the pledges to abide by the rule of law, including being peaceful and legitimate, this was 'in practice been systematically violated by your followers.'[99] Second, the government sought a specific declaration of allegiance from the RSS to both the Constitution of India and the Tricolour. And finally, the government ordered a close scrutiny of RSS' account books; an end to the practise of functionaries being 'nominated from above,'[100]; and that the RSS should 'unequivocally recognise and act upon the democratic elective principle. The government was particularly wary of the functions of the head (sarsanghchalak) which had not been defined with any degree of precision and wanted that all vestiges of a dictatorial character should be removed.'[101]

As was expected, the government reached an impasse; Golwalkar accused the government of misinterpreting the clauses in the draft constitution and applying different yardsticks to the RSS, in comparison to other 'cultural' organisations. The stalemate continued for a while before the government sought the assistance of one Mauli Chandra Sharma, a former Congress leader-turned-president of the Jana Sangh. He along with Deendayal Upadhyaya reworked the draft and amongst several other things, emphasised on two crucial points—the first was to acknowledge the organisation as democratic, and second, that while Keshav Baliram Hedgewar had nominated Madhav Sadashiv Golwalkar as his successor, the latter would choose the next chief with the consent of the kendriya karyakarini mandal. On the other issue, which had been brought up during Sastri's intervention regarding the entry of minors into the fold, the reworked draft mentioned that while admissions would remain open for fourteen-year-old boys, but if the parents or guardians had any objections, the child could leave the RSS at any given time. On 11 July 1949, Home Minister Sardar Patel ordered the ban on the RSS to be lifted forthwith.

Despite the month-long negotiations that had necessitated several compromises, Golwalkar claimed that the RSS had 'given up nothing.' In his address to a gathering in Nagpur, he declared, 'There was no compromise. There was no undertaking of any kind given to the Government.' At another meeting in Madras, he clarified that he did not 'want any of them (new members) to bring politics into the Sangh,' before he was asked the inevitable question by a reporter: Was Nathuram Godse a member of the RSS? Golwalkar accepted that the assassin was a member years ago, but had since left, and even had major disagreements with the RSS. He was also asked another pointed question—did the RSS subscribe to secularism? Henceforth, it was this reply by the iconic chief of the RSS that would be adopted by several Right-wing leaders to obfuscate the crucial question of secularism vis-a-vis the organisation, which Golwalkar articulated as follows, 'To a Hindu, the state is always secular.'

Much like securing the safe passage for his comrades after Partition, M.S. Golwalkar had not only succeeded in getting the ban lifted, but ensured that the RSS retained its distinct identity in the rough and tumble of Indian politics. Barring his commitment to a written constitution in which he had agreed to be open about the conduct of the RSS—eschewing violence; according respect to the symbols of the Indian State; adopting apolitical and cultural role, Golwalkar had firmly established a new construct of a nation and nationhood. For instance, he had fought tooth and nail against the portrayal of RSS as a fascist organisation and in the battle of the nerves, the government negotiators were forced to retreat because they had learnt of Golwalkar's plan to start another mass movement.[102]

In time, large number of Indians began viewing Golwalkar as a victorious leader, and he embarked on a celebratory tour of India.

Political Activism

During its seventeen-month-long ban, some members of the RSS had articulated the need to establish a political party in order to further their cultural and ideological premise. As mentioned earlier (also mentioned in the chapter, Syama Prasad Mookerjee, p. 164), M.S. Golwalkar hadn't warmed up to the idea and to quote the well-known author Christophe Jafrrelot[103], the man was perhaps content to be the king's guru and not the king.

Meanwhile during the ban, several swayamsevaks had 'operated largely on their own' which gave them, 'a relatively freehand to experiment' because of the 'unprecedented independence…during the eighteen months ban.'[104]

Most importantly, they were faced with the emerging new political realities in an independent India and found themselves in an 'ideological vacuum' in a parliamentary democracy supported by a strong constitution.[105]

After the ban was lifted, M.S. Golwalkar became aware of the latent disgruntlement amongst his cadre, and worried that there may soon be a coup d' etat, undermining the authority of senior members of the RSS. In order to regain control, he made certain crucial changes in his team of office-bearers, both at the national and provincial levels. Although Golwalkar was unable to prevent some members of the RSS from getting involved in the formation of the Bharatiya Jana Sangh in 1950, he made yet another attempt to rein in his cadre at a conference of district organisers in March 1954, and mooted the idea of 'positive

Hinduism'—emphasising on the spirit of service. It didn't require deep analysis to understand that by using the word 'positive' strategically, Golwalkar was pointing towards certain 'western' anomalies that had crept into the sangh's core principles.

While 'positive Hinduism' was presented as a truism, Golwalkar argued that western philosophy emphasised on materialism. In contrast, Hinduism according to him was based on the philosophy of *vaisudhaiva kutumbakam* or the world is one family. While propounding that one could reach God by service to other human beings, he initiated the setting up of vastuhara sahayata samitis which began by assisting refugees from West Punjab and survivors of the Assam earthquake in August 1950.

Character-building and being the moral custodian of the 'king and his aides' was the sort of role Golwalkar had in mind when he had initiated a series of parleys with Patel and other Congress leaders.[106] RSS leaders had been gripped with this sentiment from late 1947, well before Gandhi's assassination and the subsequent ban on the RSS. As part of this effort, Golwalkar attempted to convince Nehru and met him on four occasions between 1947–49. While the first meeting in 1947 was to inform him about his visit to Kashmir, which was arranged by the government to meet Maharaja Hari Singh, the second was held almost immediately after the ban on the RSS was lifted. Two other meetings had also taken place in September and November 1949 and while these were projected by the RSS and its various mouthpieces as a successful breakthrough,[107] Nehru did not appear to have changed his position on the RSS. An account of these interactions highlighted that while Golwalkar had expressed his views quite candidly on subjects like culture and nationalism; the place of non-Hindus in the national mainstream; the form and objective of Sangh work; religious tolerance, non-violence etc., and had answered

Nehru's doubts and queries[108], the prime minister continued to denounce the RSS as 'fascist and communal.'[109]

In fact, it was Nehru's intervention which got the Congress to rollback on a Congress Working Committee resolution passed in October 1949 when Nehru had embarked on a tour of the United States of America. This resolution, which had the blessings of Patel, allowed RSS members to be part of the Congress.[110] On his return, Nehru had not only ensured that the resolution was rescinded within a month, but added a rider that members of the RSS could be part of the Congress but only after ending their association with the parent body. For writers who were sympathetic to both the RSS and Golwalkar, the subsequent resolution essentially meant that although the 'Sangh's constitution might have given the Swayamsevaks the freedom to join any political party, but the Congress insisted that if they wanted to join the Congress they would have to give up their connections with the sangh. Thus the doors of the Congress were closed for the Sangh.'[111]

Despite his intense dislike for power politics, and the pressing need to be vigilant against accusations such as of having violated Article 4 (B) of the RSS' constitution which stated that the organisation 'had no politics and is devoted to social work,' at times Golwalkar came precariously close to striking a political posture. In early 1950, he issued a statement saying that the government must 'act fearlessly, without getting mired in a senseless discussion of communalism etc. and to do the needful, whether it is police action or exchange of Hindus and Muslims. A plan for a proportional exchange of Hindus and Muslims left over in Bharat should be put into action immediately...'

Golwalkar's explicit statement regarding 'Muslims left over in Bharat', was clearly against the principles enshrined in the Indian

Constitution. The Congress did not present a counter to this statement which reflected its ambivalence regarding the RSS despite Nehru's forceful rejection of the Patel-backed proposal for alllowing cooperation between the two organisations.

The Birth of the Jana Sangh

In what was considered to be a gross violation in a disciplined, cadre-based organisation, there came a time when the demand for political participation was being articulated even on public platforms. In its first issue post the ban in August 1949, the *Organiser* made a strong pitch for deeper political engagement in an article headlined, "The RSS and Politics". Yet another piece articulating a similar viewpoint was written by Balraj Madhok, who later became president of the Jana Sangh in the late 1960s, in which he had argued that the RSS must 'give lead to the country in regard to the political and economic problems' because 'any organisation of the people which fails to guide its component parts about vital questions influencing their lives is bound to lose the force...'

It is interesting to note how Golwalkar dealt with the issue of RSS' alignment with the Bharatiya Jana Sangh and its founding president, Dr Syama Prasad Mookerjee, who was also the Minister for Industry and Supplies in Prime Minister Nehru's Cabinet. In 1949–50, M.S. Golwalkar had met with Dr Mookerjee several times in Nagpur to seek assurances that his views were not at variance with the RSS. Golwalkar made his intent clear and stressed on two principal issues—first, that the Jana Sangh should have no structural ties with the RSS, and second, that it should adhere to the RSS' idea of cultural nationalism, and its definition of nation and nationhood. Dr Mookerjee readily agreed to both, yet Golwalkar vacillated when it came to lending support to the Jana Sangh. On the other hand, when Dr Mookerjee's differences with Nehru became public, several senior RSS leaders in Delhi drew him into a dialogue, offering support in case he chose to leave the government.

Eventually, when Dr Syama Prasad Mookerjee resigned from his ministerial position in April 1950, he was accorded a public reception in Delhi. However, throughout all the backroom discussions and parleys with Mookerjee, Golwalkar kept a careful distance because he was wary of a political party making his organisation irrelevant. He had already said on record that people 'have forgotten that politics is only a part and parcel of comprehensive life. Life is higher and wider than politics,' and to 'regard politics as all-comprehensive is to abandon the soul of Bharat.' There was no gainsaying the fact that Golwalkar had a solid narrative to back his ideology of perpetuating a Hindu nation which would be governed by the ancient principles enshrined in its scriptures and philosophical treatises, but he was also undoubtedly naïve to not recognise the dreams and aspirations of a newly independent India which had a socialist-leaning prime minister at the helm of affairs.

As mentioned earlier, after the ban on the RSS, M.S. Golwalkar had hoped that the Indian National Congress would open its doors for swayamsevaks. However, with Sardar Patel's death in December 1950, any semblance of hope was also cast aside and finally, Golwalkar deputed a few of his associates to work with Dr Mookerjee for forming a new political party. Purushottam Das Tandon's election as Congress president three months after Patel's death may have given rise to Golwalkar's aspiration of associating with the party, but Nehru had established his dominance in the Congress by resigning from the Working Committee in August 1951 as a tactic to pressurise Tandon.

In the event, Tandon had quit in a month and Nehru became Congress president and with that the last flicker of a hope for an association between the RSS and Congress was extinguished. But yet again, what was missing was a sense of urgency amongst the RSS cadre and with the impending elections post 26 January 1950, Dr Mookerjee wanted to accelerate the process.

In early 1951, Golwalkar decided that as a prelude to the formation of a pan-Indian political outfit, regional units should be established in Delhi and Punjab. A draft constitution of the proposed party along with a note was circulated which stated that because the RSS was 'disinclined to contest in the coming elections,' Golwalkar must be 'persuaded to lend support of the organisation to the new party.' Even as Dr Mookerjee went about setting up a unit in Bengal, and later in Punjab, Golwalkar remained non-committal. But it was only a matter of time before M.S. Golwalkar was presented with a fait accompli and he had to face up to the reality of a political outfit affiliated to the RSS.

On 21 October 1951, Dr Syama Prasad Mookerjee was formally nominated as the president of the Jana Sangh at its inaugural convention. M.S. Golwalkar initiated the process of 'dual membership', when he appointed an important RSS functionary, Bhai Mahavir, as general secretary of Jana Sangh. It may be recalled that Golwalkar had extracted a promise from Dr Mookerjee that the political party would be a separate entity, yet by placing important RSS functionaries in pivotal positions, Golwalkar ensured that he kept a hold on the Jana Sangh, a tradition which continues till today in the BJP.

Four days after the Jana Sangh's first convention, came the historic moment of the first general elections in the country.[112] Golwalkar's conduct during this hectic electioneering period was rather peculiar—

he suddenly felt the need to awaken his inner spiritual core and proceeded on a twenty-five-day-long retreat in December 1952 to Lokmanya Tilak's residence at Sinhagarh, a short distance away from Pune in Maharashtra. After staging an escape of sorts from the electoral din, Golwalkar's aide and general secretary of the RSS, Bhaiyaji Dani issued an aseptic directive to the cadre: 'Vote only for that party which works for the good of the country as a whole.' Clearly, he along with Golwalkar feared Nehru's wrath and avoided making any statement that could have been construed as political.

However, in the next five years, all his anxiety about making political comments in public were put to rest when on the eve of the second general elections in 1957, the RSS chief issued the most political statement of his entire career.

In a signed article, which sounded more like a lengthy sermon, Golwalkar exhorted the people to 'resolutely vote for men and parties dedicated to the Hindu people and Hindu Cause.' Soon, several viewpoints articulated in the article began to resonate in the manifesto of the Jana Sangh, and later even the BJP's. For instance, Golwalkar pointed out that elections did not provide the people with the right to recall representatives because, 'everything is fair (in love and war), and elections are fought as "war" against all other parties and candidates,' and 'the greatest genius for this campaign of lies is likely to pool the greatest number of votes and seize power.' This reality, argued Golwalkar, placed a 'heavy' responsibility on voters because once they cast their vote, they had 'no means of remedying' the decision.

Golwalkar also commented on the contradictory approaches of senior leaders within the same political party. He argued in the article that while Nehru was 'calling upon the people to ignore the person, the character and qualities of the individual candidates and pay attention only to the party,' C. Rajagopalachari was advocating a different view, which was to 'ignore the party and examine the individual candidate and study his character...which in the last analysis is of utmost importance in the conduct of State business within and without legislatures.'[113]

After years of emphasising on strengthening the character of any organisation as the crucial instrument in nation-building, Golwalkar finally conceded that a political party was also an integral part of the process. He however postulated that to focus either on an individual or a party was erroneous because, 'Both these views ...have to be taken together,' and said that a party without good people would be 'like a body with paralysed limbs useless and even harmful.'

In the same article, Golwalkar expressed his aversion towards the State controlling the wealth and power of people, which he said made the life of an 'individual human being a lifeless, joyless existence.' Golwalkar's stance obviously stemmed from his lifelong opposition to Socialism and Communism, which according to him were, 'perverse off springs of the same reactionary process of thought seeking to concentrate all power of the state and of wealth.'

He felt that the additional danger from both sets of ideologies was also because the Communists and Socialists 'pride themselves on being non-Hindu.' All political parties with Left-wing ideologies (including the Congress), he felt, interfered with the 'Hindu way of life' and targeted tradition by their 'disinclination to respect the Hindu sentiments in relation to the cow, and their partial treatment of Muslims, their pro-Muslim communal outlook in reservation of seats out of their candidates by the Congress.' Unless Hindu voters acted on the basis of their religious interests, 'all they cherish and hold in reverence stand in danger of being wholly obliterated if the reins of power are entrusted in the hands of such un-Hindu-often anti-Hindu-elements,' declared the RSS chief and rounded it off by a clarion call: vote as Hindus and for the Hindus.

Focus on Hindu Causes

Despite striking dramatically different postures in the first and second general elections, M.S. Golwalkar failed to garner votes for the Jana Sangh. In the first Lok Sabha polls, the Congress party won 364 of the 489 seats; the Jana Sangh put up 94 candidates, but won only three of which two were from West Bengal. The party had an alliance with the Hindu Mahasabha which won four seats, out of which one was yet again from Bengal. Therefore, both the parties had barely polled four per cent of the total votes. During the second general elections, the Jana Sangh's performance was unimpressive—it won four seats, and even its vote share remained at a meagre six per cent. The Hindu Mahasabha's tally slipped to just one seat, but more importantly, both parties also drew a blank in West Bengal.

After the failure of the Jana Sangh in the first general elections, Golwalkar did not wish the RSS to stay confined to the social sphere, and steered it to take up issues that required the support of Hindus in projecting the nationalist orientation of the organisation. The Akhil Bharatiya Pratinidhi Sabha met in September 1952 and evolved a two-pronged strategy—the first was to revive the spirit of swadeshi. Golwalkar challenged the earlier and original idea mooted by Mahatma Gandhi and declared that 'Love for Swadeshi did not have the positive content,' as it was viewed only as a form of protest against the British. Instead, he recommended that 'love for Swadeshi should be the constant, guiding spirit of the nation.'

The RSS exhorted people to adopt the swadeshi way of life; Golwalkar went back to one of his earlier premises arguing that adapting Western attitudes had become the norm in post-Independent India and must be rejected. He strongly criticised ostentatious Hindu marriage ceremonies and receptions, especially those where 'the bride and the groom were dressed in Western style.' He also condemned beauty pageants, which began to be held in the early 1950s, and remarked caustically, 'We really miss India in this whole affair.'[114]

While the swadeshi campaign provided the mandatory nationalistic thrust to Golwalkar's overall vision for the RSS in independent India, the Hindu course was flagged off by a resolution seeking a complete ban on cow slaughter as promised in the Directive Principles of the Constitution. A nationwide signature campaign was launched in which more than 50,000 swayamsevaks fanned out to 85,000 cities, towns, and villages to collect what the RSS claimed were two crore signatures. These petitions were loaded on to bullock carts and presented to President Dr S. Radhakrishnan in Delhi. The campaign succeeded in bringing the RSS closer to both Hindu religious leaders and organisations and was an unambiguous attempt at 'ethno-religious mobilisation.'[115]

Eventually, the movement recommending a Central law to ban cow slaughter became a principal rallying point for the Hindutva cause. The demand was clearly aimed at protecting the religious sentiments of a section of Hindus, while denying the right of dietary choice to millions of Indians, including several Hindus, and particularly, Muslims.

While discussing the impact of 'reactionary Hinduism', Golwalkar wrote in *Bunch of Thoughts* as follows:

> Some are Hindus, not out of conviction, but out of reaction. To give an example, our workers once approached a prominent Hindu leader during the signature collection campaign demanding ban on the slaughter of cows. But they were greatly shocked to hear him saying, 'What is the use of preventing the slaughter of useless cattle? Let them die. What does it matter? After all, one animal is as good as the other. But, since the Muslims are bent upon cow-slaughter, we should make this an issue. And so, I give you my signature.' What does this show? We are to protect the cow not because the cow has been for ages an emblem of Hindu devotion but because the Muslims kill it! This is Hinduism born out of reaction, a kind of 'negative Hinduism'.

In so far as eating beef was concerned, Golwalkar was circumspect while holding forth on the issue and justified this as a practise forced by ignorance and necessity. He wrote about the Bhils (tribals inhabiting parts of central India who were beef-eaters) and asserted that the Hindus should express sympathy for the community. 'Has anyone gone to them and taught them devotion to cow?' he asked, adding that the choice was forced,

> out of sheer necessity, they have taken to beef eating. It is not out of flair or fashion. Here too, the lapse is ours. It is up to us, the rest of the Hindus, to make amends by going to them, educating them, and elevating their living conditions and also their cultural standards (*sic*).

The issue of cow protection gave the RSS a major boost to harness greater support even after the signature campaign of the 1950s had petered out. In August 1964, Golwalkar inaugurated a RSS conference in Delhi called Bharat Gosevak Samaj to revive the demand for a Central legislation to ban cow slaughter. There was now an element of greater synergy between different wings of the sangh parivar, as evidenced in Deendayal Upadhyaya's forceful advocacy of the demand in the conference.

After the Indo–Pak war in 1965, and the sudden and tragic death of Prime Minister Lal Bahadur Shastri in January 1966, the cow protection movement was revived yet again by establishing the Sarvadaliya Goraksha Mahaabhiyaan Samiti (SGMS) in September 1966. The agitation was initiated weeks before India's fourth general elections, making it amply evident that the RSS was focussed on reaping political mileage at a time when the Congress was facing an inner-party upheaval. Golwalkar became a member of the SGMS' steering committee, proving that he had moved a considerable distance away from the time when he abhorred political activism.

A violent protest by the SGMS on 7 November 1966 at the gate of the Parliament House resulted in the death of eight people, including a policeman, and the then Prime Minister Indira Gandhi in a bid to demonstrate her secular credentials had sacked Home Minister Gulzarilal Nanda, long considered to be an advocate of soft Hindutva. In retaliation, Golwalkar began a hunger strike accompanied by several well-known religious leaders associated with the SGMS, including the Shankaracharya of Puri. Delhi was simmering and came to the boil when a fasting sadhu had died on its streets. Meanwhile, several other religious leaders decided to continue with the fast and a few days later, a small group announced its intention of establishing a political party with a single point manifesto on cow protection.

Alarmed at the new development and eager to 'avoid the exploitation by another party of this increasingly tense situation,'[116]

M.S. Golwalkar and Deendayal Upadhyaya initiated back channel talks with the Hindu clergy and averted the formation of a new party. Finally, the fast was called off after the government agreed to form a committee to re-examine the various facets of the cow protection issue. The Shankaracharya of Puri was nominated to the committee as was Golwalkar who had immediately written to the government expressing his inability to attend any meetings for the next three months. In close succession came the Shankaracharya's resignation, and the government's lofty plans to tackle the issue came to naught.

In the course of almost three years starting August 1964, Golwalkar had undoubtedly succeeded in harnessing the political potential of Hindu seers, but he had also realised that they could not be controlled at will. This made him, and the RSS wary of allowing religious leaders to seize control of an agitation and the lesson stood the organisation in good stead in the Eighties during the Ram Janmabhoomi agitation, when the idea of cultural nationalism became more acceptable than ever before.

Towards a Global Hindu Samaj

It was actually a meeting with Simboonath Capildeo, son of an immigrant from Uttar Pradesh in Trinidad and Tobago, which gave birth to one of the most potent RSS affiliates of the 1980s, catapulting the BJP to centre stage. According to Daurius Figueira, Capildeo's biographer, the Trinidadian politician who went by the moniker of 'Lion of the Legislative Council', was the 'progenitor of Hindu nationalist discourse in Trinidad and Tobago.' Capildeo was the maternal uncle of the renowned author, the late V.S. Naipaul, and during one of his trips to India had rued over the fact that 'Bhaaratvanshis living for over 150 years in his country and other countries in West Indies were losing touch' with their ancient culture. He later met with Golwalkar and impressed the RSS chief to such an extent that the two decided to set up a global Hindu organisation.

Golwalkar deputed a senior RSS functionary called Shankar Shivaram (Dadasaheb) Apte to sound out religious leaders, scholars, social and cultural activists, and finally but most importantly, industrialists and businessmen for financial support.

In Golwalkar's mind, the main intent of forming a global body for Hindus was to reactivate the 'majoritarian inferiority complex,'[117] and he was ably assisted in this endeavour by Swami Chinmayananda, a Keralite journalist-turned-guru who was later touted to be the first 'exporter' of yoga to the West. Finally, the idea of a global Hindu outfit came to fruition in August 1964, two months after Nehru's death, which had left the Congress party and his political legacy in a state of uncertainty. In order to avoid any unnecessary controversy, Golwalkar instructed Apte to exclude every political party, including the Hindu Mahasabha and Jana Sangh from the ambit of the proposed organisation.

As the chief of RSS, Golwalkar had a decisive say in the matter of selecting a name for the organisation. While the word, Vishwa (world) was considered most befitting, there were several suggestions that the word dharma or righteousness be included in the name. It was once again Golwalkar who settled the matter and said, 'We have to promote comprehensive thinking on all four Purusharthas—Dharma, Artha, Kama, Moksha. Our desire is to strengthen Hindu Social life from all points of view and infuse Hindu ideals of life in it. So let us not use Dharma in the name of the organisation. Similarly the term Sammelan does not give a clear idea of the work. I think Parishad would be proper.'

In an attempt to broaden the religio-cultural base of the proposed global outfit, Golwalkar invited the senior Akali Dal leader, Master Tara Singh, who declared, 'Sikhs and Hindus are not two separate communities. Prosperity of Sikhs is possible only so long as the Hindu Dharma is alive.' Although Capildeo did not attend the meeting, he had sent a representative to preside over the proceedings. It however took another two years before the inaugural assembly of the Vishwa Hindu Parishad (VHP) or World Hindu Conference was held during the kumbh mela in Allahabad (now, Prayagraj).

In his speech, Golwalkar said that the VHP must not be reduced to an assembly, but should have a programmatic orientation. However, what stood out in his speech during the VHP convention was the way in which he had highlighted the 'lack of self-confidence' amongst Hindus and proceeded to define the premise as follows:

> Sanatana Dharma implied principled human conduct, applicable to all human beings of all claims and times. It embodies all the various persuasions like Buddhism, Sikhism etc., born out of the same Dharmic traditions. An eminent Jain Muni has truly said, "How can he who does not call himself a Hindu also be a Jain?" All our different sects in fact, share the same holy traditions and values of life. It is our duty to evolve harmonious accord among all of them...

While the VHP was set up to rejuvenate and involve vast numbers of Indian settlers abroad, it also precluded communities which were not viewed as the original dwellers of a Hindu India. For instance, at one of the VHP meetings in 1970 at Jorhat, Golwalkar said, 'Muslims give inflated figures. We must be on guard against this. Every Hindu should register himself as a Hindu. Tribals, followers of any special sect, or hill tribes should register themselves as Hindus only not by the name of their tribes.' In the same year, the VHP established a branch in London and continued to propagate the superiority of Hinduism.

Golwalkar had felt the need for international outreach even earlier and the opportunity came in September 1960 when Atal Bihari Vajpayee, then a first term member of the Lok Sabha, was invited to visit the United States when John F. Kennedy and Richard Nixon were locked in a historic presidential contest. When Vajpayee informed Golwalkar about his visit, the latter asked him to carry a message to the American people. Vajpayee delivered his speech in Washington on 28 September 1960, which not only revealed his worldview, but also read out Golwalkar's message which highlighted the RSS chief's ambition to be recognised internationally as a modern political thinker:

> The world is torn into two sections...conflict is not of Democracy versus Communism as it appears to superficial observers. It is the age-old struggle between gross materialism and Dharma. Communism stands for the former and tries to manifest itself as a Universal ideology. It can be countered not by sectarian religious dogmas but only by Universal Religion (Sanatana Dharma)...

Golwalkar's tirade against Communism was a modification of his assertion eleven years ago during a lecture in Bangalore in November 1949 in which he had reasoned that, 'communism came up as a reaction against the new tyranny of capitalism.' For the Washington audience however, Golwalkar left out his criticism of capitalism, suggesting he did not wish to target the economic and political system of another country. It also revealed that in the event of a clash between these two 'isms', he viewed Communism as a greater threat to the Hindu political order because it undermined the religious foundations of the society.

A Personal Tragedy

For a man as deeply involved as Madhav Sadashiv Golwalkar in his life's mission of establishing a Hindu nation, he was also a devoted son and took extremely good care of his parents. In July 1954, his father had passed away at the age of eighty-two. Golwalkar was then travelling and left instructions with his associates to go ahead with the cremation, while he had hurried back. After fulfilling the mandatory funeral rites and spending a few days with his mother, he resumed his duties in the RSS within a fortnight.

But eight years later, when his mother died in August 1962, Golwalkar's emotional distress was insurmountable. Tai, as Laxmibai was fondly called by her son and other swayamsevaks, had suffered a paralytic stroke, and was confined to bed for some time prior to her passing. Golwalkar tended to her needs with utmost care and would dutifully seek her permission before embarking on every tour, and in his absence, a senior RSS leader, Krishnarao Mohrir kept Golwalkar informed about her health. There were occasions when her condition would deteriorate suddenly and her son, Madhu (as she lovingly called him), would stay put by her bedside.

It was therefore no wonder that Laxmibai's death had left him inconsolable, and his desire to escape the material world and retreat to the mountains resurfaced. Swami Amoortananda, or Amitabh Maharaj who it may be recalled, had played a crucial role in Golwalkar's youth, ensured that he overcame his grief and plunged into the activities of the RSS once again. Golwalkar's feeling of remorse at continuing with life after a period of mourning was also alleviated by a letter that he had received from the Shankaracharya of Kanchi Kamakoti Peetham. In his letter, the seer wrote that although his mother was no more with him, he could continue to take care of Bharat Mata or Mother India as the nation needed sons like him.

The 1960s was the most decisive decade in the history of the RSS. Madhav Golwalkar had shed his reluctance for direct engagement with politics, and consequently widened the canvas of the organisation to reach out to new sections. He allowed the general secretary of the RSS, and his successor, Balasaheb Deoras, the privilege of addressing the Jana Sangh's session in 1965, and personally advised party leaders against forming an alliance with Communists for the 1967 general elections. He also travelled abroad and addressed Hindus in Burma (now Myanmar) and Kathmandu, where he met the King and invited him to a RSS function in Nagpur. When Nepal's monarch accepted the offer, it had created a bit of a diplomatic embarrassment because for a Head of State—and that too of an avowedly Hindu kingdom—to attend a RSS function would have been politically sensitive for the government. Eventually, Mahendra Bikram Shah was advised by New Delhi to stay away from the function and he had communicated his inability to Golwalkar.

The strategies deployed by Golwalkar contributed greatly to the RSS and its affiliates finding support from new sections of society and in the 1967 election, the Jana Sangh won 35 seats, which was its best performance so far. It also partnered with non-Congress parties in several states to form governments, albeit for a short duration.

The growth of the sangh parivar in the 1950s and 1960s required the grant of functional autonomy for affiliated organisations and Golwalkar evolved the process of unstructured command mechanism where consultations on a one-to-one level was the norm as against any high command formally endorsing decisions made by the affiliates.

In the late 1960s, the Jana Sangh was hit by internal squabbles with Balraj Madhok and a few other conservative leaders contesting the decisions taken by younger leaders led by Vajpayee and L.K. Advani. When Advani had questioned Madhok's actions and pushed for disciplinary action against him, the latter had demanded that the dispute be referred to Golwalkar. Advani had refused, displaying immense confidence because 'on a matter as important as this, Advani very likely had already conferred with Golwalkar before writing to Madhok,' pointing to his indiscipline.

Golwalkar was in complete control of his organisation and had the quiet satisfaction of seeing its influence spread slowly, but steadily. He was probably preparing for the next round of expansion but alas, he was diagnosed with cancer in 1969 and he spent the next four years in excruciating pain. Yet he did not leave the RSS in a state of uncertainty, and passed on the baton to Deoras in a transparent manner unlike what was done during his nomination by Hedgewar.

After Golwalkar's death on 5 June 1973, his secretary, Pandurang Kshirsagar opened three letters that the chief of RSS had written to him two months earlier.

The first of these, read by the chief of the Maharashtra unit of RSS, Babarao Bhide, over a microphone at the RSS headquarters in Nagpur, mentioned the nomination of Balasaheb Deoras as the next sarsanghchalak. Among those assembled at the RSS headquarters that day was also Advani, who had recently been elected the president of the Jana Sangh and had travelled 500 kilometres from Delhi to join thousands of mourners. The other letters were read out by Deoras and one of them contained the instruction that no memorial was to be built for him.

The gathering of mourners heard out the last words of a man who strode over the RSS like a colossus for thirty-three long years.

Many of his followers found Golwalkar's leadership oppressive at times, and were often dismayed by his disinterest to evolve. But in the end, Golwalkar could be credited for 'knitting the organisation while also expanding it.'[118]

Indira Gandhi had never met Madhav Sadashiv Golwalkar, but it was well known that much like her father, she was strongly opposed to the RSS. Yet at his death, she accepted that he had 'held a respected position in national life by force of his personality and the intensity of his conviction, even though many of us could not agree with him.'

SYAMA PRASAD MOOKERJEE

On 23 June 1953, Prime Minister Jawaharlal Nehru was in Geneva, en route to Cairo, after attending the coronation of Queen Elizabeth II, when he was brought the news of a bereavement from India. He had immediately despatched a condolence letter through the diplomatic post to Lady Jogmaya Mookerjee, in which he had stated: 'Though we may have differed in politics, I respected him and had great affection for him.' However for the mother, who believed her son had died a mysterious death in faraway Srinagar, the prime minister's commiseration was inadequate. In her reply, Lady Mookerjee demanded 'justice', and condemned the condolence message as being of little value because 'it comes from people who themselves should stand a trial.' She had further concluded:

> A fearless son of free India has met his death while in detention without trial under most tragic and mysterious circumstances. I...demand an absolutely impartial and open enquiry...

The anguish of a mother notwithstanding, it was against contemporary wisdom that the woman in question had 'Lady' prefixed to her name, while her son—the fifty-two-year-old Syama Prasad Mookerjee—had died defending the principles of a Hindu nation in the cold confines of a jail, thousands of miles away from his native West Bengal.

By a strange quirk of fate, it was another prisoner lodged in the same Srinagar jail, a separatist leader called Masarat Alam, who had brought back the focus on the departed leader. On 9 March 2015, Prime Minister Narendra Modi spoke in parliament in defence of his coalition partner* in Jammu & Kashmir, the People's Democratic Party (PDP), which had ordered the release of Alam, the dreaded militant. The Opposition had accused the ruling BJP government of giving militants safe passage, while the prime minister had firmly reiterated that his party would 'not compromise with the unity and integrity' of India. But the Opposition benches were relentless, and when the prime minister was charged with obfuscation, he had responded firmly, 'There is no reason for us to remain silent,' and added after a pause, 'We are the ones who sacrificed Syama Prasad Mookerjee. We don't need lessons in patriotism....don't teach us patriotism....'

Narendra Modi was well within his rights for having invoked Syama Prasad Mookerjee, because the man had left an invaluable 'Kashmir legacy', first for the Bharatiya Jana Sangh and later for the BJP. In the context of Prime Minister Modi's reference to 'sacrifice', an oft-repeated slogan which was routinely raised by many in the memory of the iconic leader, would have been more apt:

* The Bharatiya Janata Party withdrew from the coalition in June 2018 bringing the curtain down on an uneasy political partnership.

Jahan hue balidaan Mookerjee,
woh Kashmir hamara hai[1]

(The Kashmir where Mookerjee laid down his life, is ours)

Equally, whenever the perennially contentious and unresolved issue of Kashmir's special status was brought into focus, Mookerjee was recalled for his famous slogan:

Ek desh mein do vidhan
Ek desh mein do nishan
Ek desh mein do pradhan
Nahin chalenge, nahin chalenge[2]

(In a nation which is one entity, there can be no room for two constitutions, two heads, nor two flags)

A fortnight after his death, the Jana Sangh's Central Working Committee had passed a resolution stating how India was 'stunned by the mysterious circumstances' of Syama Prasad Mookerjee's passing, and alleged 'criminal medical negligence.'

Ever since its formation in 1951, first the Jana Sangh's, and later the BJP's stand on Kashmir hinged on two basic premises: first, that the Hindu-majority region of Jammu was neglected in preference for the Muslim-majority Kashmir Valley; and second, the integration of the state with the rest of India was impossible until Article 370 of the Constitution (which grants a special autonomous status to the state) was not abrogated. It was none other than Syama Prasad Mookerjee who had made significant contributions in firming up the two postulations.

In 1998, when the BJP was at the helm of a coalition government at the Centre, it could do little in solving the Kashmir conundrum, also as an alliance partner with the PDP led by Mehbooba Mufti from 2015–2018. In April 2017, Kashmir was burning yet again with students marching the streets shouting *azaadi* (freedom) slogans eulogising the death of an alleged militant, Burhan Wani. The nation had watched helplessly even as Chief Minister Mehbooba Mufti had gone up and down the corridors of Delhi to meet Prime Minister Modi to help resolve the crisis.

From the very onset however, it was more than evident that the coalition partners would eventually part, the only speculation being on the timing of the severance. Eventually, when one of BJP's general secretaries had announced that his party had chosen to go its way, no one was surprised.

Therefore, that day in parliament when Narendra Modi had reminded the Opposition benches of his party's commitment to Kashmir, it was the late Syama Prasad Mookerjee who had come to his rescue, as he had done for more than six decades since his death in 1953.

Meanwhile, after returning to India, Prime Minister Nehru rose up in parliament to pay homage to the departed leader:

> In any event, his passing away would have been sad and a great blow to this House and the country, but in the peculiar circumstances in which it took place, naturally this added to our sorrow.

In order to understand the 'peculiar circumstances' of Syama Prasad Mookerjee's death, one needs to go back to early twentieth century, when the man in question lived in the lap of luxury, and no one could have imagined that his death would become a subject of criminal scrutiny.

The Young Master: *Choto Karta*

The Chowringhee Road in Kolkata has different names for different stretches. At one particular point, it metamorphoses into Ashutosh Mukherjee Road, named after one of the legendary sons of the city. Further ahead, the road is called S.P. Mukherjee Road. For first-time visitors to the city, it may appear strange that two stretches of the same road are named after a father-son duo, and both illustrious in their own way.

Ashutosh Mukherjee*, popularly known as *Banglar Bagh* or the Tiger of Bengal, was born into an elite Brahmin family and as a young man, followed the usual trajectory reserved for Bengali boys from genteel backgrounds, which was to join the freedom movement.

The year was 1883 and students in Bengal were protesting against the arrest of Rashtraguru Sir Surendranath Banerjee[3]. Much like his peers, Ashutosh Mukherjee also came under the scanner, albeit for a different reason: he was pronounced guilty for contempt of court for writing an incendiary editorial in his paper, *Bengalee*, in which he had questioned the wisdom of an English judge who had disputed the antiquity of a particular Hindu idol, despite evidence to the contrary.

Soon, Ashutosh Mukherjee emerged as a man who stood out amongst the band of young Bengali revolutionaries in twentieth century Calcutta. Amongst several other things, he was a brilliant

* The father and son spelt their surnames differently. Syama Prasad's second name was registered as Mookerjee when he went to study at Lincoln's Inn, London.

academician and pursued simultaneous careers as a mathematician, lawyer, judge and educationist. In his last avatar, he was Vice Chancellor of Calcutta University; presided over the inaugural session of the Indian Science Congress; and was member of the Sadler Commission, which was set up to conduct an inquiry into the state of education in India. In 1911 at the age of forty-seven, Ashutosh Mukherjee was knighted by the Imperial government in recognition for his stellar achievements.

Although Sir Mukherjee had gradually drifted away from the national movement, but when it came to sending his son to school, he had opted for Mitra Institution which was well known for instilling Indian values amongst its students. In July 1906, the five-year-old Syama Prasad started school and rode in style in a horse-drawn carriage. One of his teachers later recalled that the boy was markedly humble and did not ever belittle his fellow students, some of whom were from far lesser affluent families.[4]

At sixteen years of age, Syama Prasad cleared his Matriculation examination and in 1921, graduated with Honours in English from the prestigious Presidency College, Calcutta. When it was time for him to pursue his Masters, he chose Bengali instead of English, in deference to his father, who as Vice Chancellor of Calcutta University had introduced the language as a subject in 1906.

As a twenty-year-old man in 1921, Syama Prasad wasn't even half as politically aware as his father was at that age. According to Tathagata Roy in the *The Life and Times of Shyama Prasad Mookerjee*,

> very probably he had designs, following his father's footsteps, to become an educationist and a lawyer....His philosophy of life seemed to be contained in the oft-quoted Sanskrit saying, *Chattranam Adhyanam Tapah,* for a student, study is worship.[5]

Much like scions of renowned Bengali families of the time, Syama Prasad was also expected to fulfil certain mandatory familial duties, and in 1922 he was married off to Sudha Devi. However, when his father had died two years later in May 1924, the twenty-four-year-old Syama Prasad had found himself saddled with responsibilities and felt that his life had 'changed its course... all the mirth and joy disappeared from my life. A new chapter had begun....'[6]

At the time of his death, the sixty-year-old Sir Ashutosh Mukherjee had quit as Vice Chancellor of Calcutta University as a result of a 'heated controversy' with the Governor of Bengal, Lord Lytton over the funding of the institute.[7] Prior to his stint with the University, he had retired as judge of the Calcutta High Court and was regarded as one of the most deserving candidates for a career in public life.

A few months after his father's death, Syama Prasad Mookerjee was nominated to the Senate and Syndicate of the university; in 1934, he was appointed as Vice Chancellor of Calcutta University; and at thirty-three, he became the youngest in the history of the institute to preside over its affairs.

Despite all the outstanding achievements at a young age, he decided in the interim to firm up a career path that he felt was most suitable for him. According to several accounts, he was initially disinclined to be a fulltime career educationist, and consequently set sail for England in 1926 to mainly study Law at Lincoln's Inn, and also to represent Calcutta University at a Conference of Universities. A year later, the young barrister returned home, but instead of pursuing a legal career, he entered a field which was thought to be tailor-made for his late father: politics. In 1929, Syama Prasad was elected to the Bengal Legislative Council from the Calcutta University constituency as a member of the Indian National Congress*.

Regardless of what was obviously a conscious political choice, Syama Prasad was beginning to feel constrained in the Congress party, most importantly, with what was its most potent weapon against the British: Mahatma Gandhi's mass mobilisation movements, particularly the Dandi or Salt March which he had undertaken in 1930. Ironically, it was Gandhi who had eventually come to his rescue when at his insistence, all the Indian members of Legislative Councils were instructed to give up their seats throughout British India, facilitating Syama Prasad Mookerjee to resign from the Congress 'because he was opposed to the (Civil Disobedience) movement.'[8]

In retrospect, several writers have justified Mookerjee's decision to quit the Congress, propelled as he was, according to them, by a greater political insight than even Gandhi. But the fact of the matter was that apart from his discomfort with Gandhi, Syama Prasad strongly believed that mass agitations and resignations gave space for 'toadies, to play mischief. He felt it necessary that the interests of the university be safeguarded in the legislatures, particularly because education had become a transferred subject under the Montagu-Chelmsford Reforms of 1921.'[9]

In the aftermath of the mass resignations, although the legislative bodies were left with little or no credibility, Mookerjee decided to fight the impending elections from the same university constituency,

* Indians were granted limited franchise under Colonial rule and constituencies were divided—at the first level—between nominated and elective seats. The latter were split between general seats—reserved separately for Muslims and non-Muslims—and special constituencies, divided between Europeans, Bengal Chamber of Commerce, big landowners, Indian Jute Mills Association, Indian Tea Association, Indian Mining Association, the Marwari Association, Calcutta Traders Association, and Calcutta University.

but as an independent candidate. At a time when India was in ferment over the arrest of top Congress leaders, Mookerjee consciously shunned political campaigns and plunged head long into the job at hand by becoming an assistant to Hassan Suhrawardy, the Vice Chancellor of Calcutta University.

There was no doubt that Syama Prasad was an efficient administrator, but his vision for the university was no different from that of the British. On the one hand, if his parting with the Congress party in 1930 had given rise to his two decades-long opposition to its policies, it had also enabled his rise in the pecking order of the university. In 1934, he became the youngest Vice Chancellor of Calcutta University, a position which handed him 'the right to talk on just a little less than equal terms to the governor.'[10]

As a well known votary of Lord Macaulay, Vice Chancellor Syama Prasad Mookerjee was insistent on producing a class of English-speaking 'brown sahibs' in the university. In his presidential address to the All India Educational Conference in Nagpur in 1935, he said that educational institutions should be geared towards producing 'students who are capable of providing leadership to our self-governing institutions, such as municipal corporations, provincial and central legislatures.' In other words, what he meant was that the core purpose of a university education was to produce officers and junior officials for serving the Colonial regime.

In 1937, the poet-litterateur Rabindranath Tagore arrived in Calcutta University to deliver the annual convocation lecture and it was his endorsement of the institution under Syama Prasad's baton—introducing Bengali medium for several subjects; compilation of technical terms in Bengali; and most significantly, standardising Bengali spellings—which had catapulted him from being the son of

Banglar Bagh to an eminent educationist in his own right. A year later in 1938, the thirty-seven-year-old Syama Prasad Mookerjee retired as Vice Chancellor of Calcutta University and three months later in recognition for his achievements, Viceroy Lord Brabourne conferred an Honorary Doctorate of Law upon him. In his address, the Viceroy said:

> Nobody can say that Syama Prasad Mookerjee is being honoured by this Honorary Degree because he is the son of a great father. It is because he is himself. He has earned every bit of it.

Choto Karta or the young master, as he was respectfully addressed at home, was now his own master and was raring to go in the next decade, and even further.

Politics is My Destiny

Unlike Sir Ashutosh who did not cross the seven seas (considered taboo amongst several Indian communities at the time), in deference to his mother, Syama Prasad had set sail for England in 1926 to study for Bar-at-Law. Although several students' groups were politically active in London at the time, Mookerjee steered clear of them. In the two years that he spent in London, he 'pursued his studies single-mindedly' and had no time for 'soapbox oratory at Hyde Park'[11]. a fine tradition in the city since the 1870s when people gathered to hear speeches on religion, politics etc. The platform was also used by young Indian Communists and Congress supporters to protest against the British, but Mookerjee had little interest in such pursuits. Instead, he pursued quaint hobbies, which included metaphysical exercises and planchette with the likes of Sir Arthur Conan Doyle, and experimented with 'spirit photography' with an Indian student.

It may be recalled that when he had set sail for England, Syama Prasad Mookerjee was already a Senate member of the prestigious Calcutta University and therefore, it seems logical to infer that his intention was less to acquire 'legal distinction' than to obtain knowledge about the workings of English and French universities. According to his roommate, Surendra Nath Sen, Syama Prasad was 'anxious to do the Bar Examination as quickly as possible' so that he could spend the rest of his time studying Western systems of education.

Within a few weeks of his arrival, he had to sit for the preliminary Bar exams in which his performance was anything but noteworthy. 'Under ordinary circumstances the result could be considered satisfactory if not creditable,' wrote Surendra Nath Sen and further added, 'but the tongue of calumny soon got busy.' The news of his average performance eventually travelled to India and was discussed at great length and with great delight by his detractors, including the then Vice Chancellor of Calcutta University, the renowned historian, Sir Jadunath Sarkar.

One of the other reasons for Syama Prasad's deliberate distance from politics in England was because of his father who had set predetermined career paths for his children. Amongst his sons, Sir Ashutosh considered the elder two, Rama Prasad and Syama Prasad as most suited for the British system. While Rama Prasad was considered suitable for a role in the judiciary, Syama Prasad was trained for 'stepping into his shoes in Calcutta University.' He soon concluded that he had made the correct decision and wrote to Pat Lovett, editor of the *Capital* that the young man had the 'makings of a man.' By all accounts, it was a wizened man who had set sail for home from England, resolute about giving a clear direction to Calcutta University by overhauling the educational system in Bengal. Within a year, as an elected member of the Bengal Legislative Council, Syama Prasad Mookerjee found the perfect platform to realise his dreams.

From August 1932 onwards, there was a palpable change in Bengal politics, and despite the anti-Imperialistic fervour across the region, religious identities were slowly beginning to occupy centre stage. For instance, the Colonial administration had introduced a separate electorate for Muslims under the Morley–Minto Reforms in 1909; in Bengal there were forty-six Hindu seats to thirty-nine Muslim seats and after the Communal Award of 1932, the Bengal Council had eighty seats for Hindus, while the number of Muslim seats had gone up to 117. Considering a large number of Hindu seats were allocated to the Depressed Classes (as the Dalits were then known) under the September1932 Poona Pact signed between Mahatma Gandhi and Dr B. R. Ambedkar, this had further angered the upper caste Bengali elite.

Syama Prasad Mookerjee as part of a 'stunning array of Bengalis'[12] or bhadraloks (genteel, elite Bengalis), including Rabindranath Tagore, Sarat Chandra Chattopadhyay, Brajendra Nath Seal, and Dr P.C. Ray, petitioned the government claiming that the 'Hindus of Bengal though numerically a minority, are overwhelmingly superior culturally' because of which they were objecting to the 'unfair and unprecedented provision to protect a majority community.' Although the group of erudite Bengali men exhorted people to hold meetings and pass resolutions protesting against the Award, the movement had failed to take off, because the arguments put forth by the petitioners were deemed 'too technical to draw the sympathy of newly enfranchised individuals' in rural Bengal.[13]

Although Syama Prasad Mookerjee cut his teeth in politics by opposing the contentious Communal Award, albeit in a limited fashion, the kernel of the protest stayed with him ever since and later shaped his brand of politics.

Times of Exploration

Following his protest against the Communal Award, Syama Prasad began pursuing legislative activism, but soon realised the limitation of such interventions. He therefore shifted focus and became an understudy to his predecessor, Hassan Suhrawardy, who was the first Muslim Vice Chancellor of Calcutta University.

In 1934, as Vice Chancellor of Calcutta University, Syama Prasad was presented with his maiden opportunity to engage in student politics when a few of his students began to involve themselves with European fascist leaders. He encouraged the young academics and assured them of forging a 'close relationship' between the Italian Institute for the Middle and Far East and Calcutta University.[14] Benito Mussolini was already at the helm of affairs in Italy and although Mookerjee did not have any direct links with him (unlike several other Indian leaders like Subhash Chandra Bose, or even B.S. Moonje), his reaching out to an Italian fascist institute established that he was engaging with a political ideology which the Congress considered as inimical to the interests of the nation.

For a major part of the 1930s, Mookerjee's experiments with politics revealed a deep-seated desire to involve with non-Congress political groups. However, owing to his limited understanding of politics, save antagonism towards the Congress party, Syama Prasad committed blunders that he would come to regret later. For instance in August 1936, the students of Calcutta University had invited Mohammed Ali Jinnah to address a meeting which was presided over by the Vice Chancellor. While introducing Jinnah, Syama Prasad had referred to him as 'an Indian nationalist...one of those fighters who knows how to fight stubbornly for the attainment of the ideal which they have made their own.' In response, Jinnah, who at the time was keen to showcase his nationalist credentials, overtly pleased with the endorsement had thanked Mookerjee profusely.[15]

The event at the university was held barely a few months prior to the 1936–37 elections to the Provincial Assemblies. Jinnah had arrived in Calcutta after addressing a series of meetings in several cities as part of his electoral campaign, and the captive students' community was just what he had needed to kick-start his campaign in Bengal.

In the impending elections to the Bengal Legislative Council, none of the political parties secured an absolute majority, because of 113 members who happened to be independents. The Congress was indeed the largest party, but with an unimpressive tally of just fifty-four seats, followed by the Muslim League with thirty-seven seats, and the Krishak Praja Party (KPP) with one seat less at thirty-six. However, despite the lowest number of seats in the Council, the fledgling KPP stood out amongst the rest because it was headed by a distinguished lawyer and an extremely astute man called Abul Kasem Fazlul Huq, popularly known as Sher-e-Bangla (Tiger of Bengal). It may be recalled that Huq and Sir Ashutosh Mukherjee's monikers were the same, save that while Banglar Bagh was in Bengali, Sher-e-Bangla was more Hindustani. This so-called 'appropriate' reference in the language was however incongruous, given that Huq, or even his colleagues in his party, were Bengalis first and Muslims later, but even this small detail was indicative of the latent communal divide in Bengal where even languages were segregated based on religious identities.

Meanwhile the British were aware of Huq's facility for politics. The Governor of Bengal, Sir John Anderson wrote to Viceroy Lord Linlithgow about the man most succinctly as, 'the most certain quantity in Muslim politics, completely devoid of principle and trust of nobody.'[16]

In April 1937, at the head of a fractious coalition, backed by the Muslim League, a few Europeans and members from the Depressed Classes, Fazlul Huq was sworn in as the Premier of Bengal. Despite the British's mistrust of him, the primary reason for his ascendance was the common objective of keeping the Congress out of the government, and in their collective pursuit, not only did they allow the Muslim League to become part of the ruling coalition, but allotted four ministerial berths to its members.

With Huq becoming Bengal's Premier, Syama Prasad Mookerjee began exploring other political avenues, and was gradually drawn to the Hindu Mahasabha. Surprisingly, he wasn't the only one to politically realign with another party, even Premier Huq was moving closer to joining the Muslim League. In fact in 1940, Huq had moved the controversial Lahore or Pakistan Resolution which demanded the creation of a separate state from the Muslim-majority areas in India. Syama Prasad was quick to respond to what he viewed as a major transgression and declared that the Premier was essentially anti-Hindu. He quoted the Bengal Secondary Education Bill and the University Bill in the context, which he felt had jeopardised the 'existence of Hindus as equal and self-respecting sons of the soil,'[17] because it undermined an educational system which was designed by the Mookerjees 'mainly with the cooperation and help of Hindu philanthropists.' His objections to the twin bills stemmed from the fact that they proposed to shift secondary education from Calcutta University (which was dominated by upper caste Bengali bhadraloks) to a Board of Secondary Education comprising fifty members drawn from Hindus, Muslims, Europeans, as also members of the government. In 1939, at the annual conference of All Bengal Teachers Association, Syama Prasad Mookerjee declared that if such a Board was ever established, 'we shall sever all connections with such an anti-educational board and shall, if necessary, seek affiliation for our schools with an outside university.' He found ready support from several Hindus for what was perceived as a bold move and even as Huq was forced to relegate the proposal to the back burner, it was Mookerjee's first major political victory against the Muslims.

Additionally, Syama Prasad was also opposed to the Calcutta Corporation Bill which proposed a separate electorate for Muslim in local body polls; as also reservation in jobs for Muslim youth. During several debates in the legislature, he argued that Muslims students were given preference in secondary education over Hindus, which once resulted in a barney between him and Huq. The former had declared, 'If you fight, we will also fight for our lives, our rights and our liberties.' In response, Huq had thundered that Mookerjee had 'challenged to a mortal combat not merely the Muslim members of the coalition party (Huq's party; *emphasis mine*) but practically the 30 million Muslims of Bengal...he has earned the reputation of being one of the most communally-minded men in Bengal.'[18]

In August 1938, Syama Prasad's resignation as Vice Chancellor of Calcutta University coincided with a No-Confidence motion against Fazlul Huq's government, which was eventually overcome but not before eroding the Bengal Premier's reputation both inside and outside the legislature.

The Hindu Leader

In the midst of a severely polarised Bengal, made worse by a tottering Legislative Council, Syama Prasad Mookerjee met Vinayak Damodar Savarkar (see chapter, Vinayak Damodar Savarkar, p. 53) in early 1939. The two men met in Calcutta in the course of Savarkar's 'whirlwind tour'[19] of India, which he had commenced in 1938 after his release from the Cellular Jail in the Andaman and Nicobar Islands. To borrow Balraj Madhok's phrase, V.D. Savarkar had 'raised a hornet's nest'[20] by joining the Hindu Mahasabha instead of the RSS.

During his conversation with several members of the Bengali elite, Savarkar espoused 'his gospel of unalloyed nationalism as the only effective antidote to Muslim separatism and divide-and-rule policy of the alien rulers.'[21] Mookerjee was already a convert, considering he had raised the anti-Hindu bogey against Fazlul Huq, and by the end of Savarkar's visit, he had become a devout loyalist. In his biography of V.D. Savarkar, Dhananjay Keer wrote, 'Indeed, Dr. Mookerjee was a discovery of Savarkar's tour of Bengal.'[22]

On 9 October 1939, Lord Linlithgow invited Savarkar and some of his associates for a meeting to discuss Indians enlisting in the Second World War as part of the Imperial army. Prior to the meeting, Savarkar had conferred with Syama Prasad Mookerjee and informed the British that he was, 'prepared to cooperate in the policy of militarisation.'[23] In turn, Linlithgow impressed upon Secretary of State for India, Lord Zetland that the British 'must now turn to the Hindus and work with their support' and although the Colonial administration and Hindus had 'had a good deal of difficulty with one another in the past,' their 'interests were now the same and we must therefore work together.'[24]

In December 1939, Savarkar's 'find' played a stellar role in organising the annual convention of the All India Hindu Mahasabha in Calcutta and was rewarded with the post of Vice President. At the convention, the Mahasabha's main thrust was on addressing the insecurities faced by upper caste Hindus and it even passed a resolution to this end which claimed that the Hindus' 'situation as a community is deteriorating day by day,' and how 'Hindu women are oppressed, Hindu boys and girls are kidnapped...Hindu temples are polluted and Hindu idols are destroyed.'

The Viceroy happened to be in Calcutta that day and in his report to the government, he described the convention as a 'monster meeting from which has emerged a series of resolutions highly communal in character and condemnatory of the Congress.' Linlithgow further added that it wouldn't surprise him if the Mahasabha stole 'a certain amount of the Congress thunder.'[25]

Within a few months of the convention, Syama Prasad Mookerjee was elevated as the Hindu Mahasabha's acting president primarily because of V.D. Savarkar's failing health. Finally, three years later in 1944, Syama Prasad became the president of the Hindu Mahasabha.

Apart from the common ideological plank that he shared with the Hindu Mahasabha, Mookerjee's decision to join the outfit in 1939 was clearly part of a carefully-orchestrated plan. He had ably elicited the support of several members of Calcutta society, including influential Marwari businessmen (the list of donors for the Calcutta convention included the Birlas, Goenkas, Jalans, Kanodias, and the Khaitans), and even members of the Congress party.

It was more than evident that Syama Prasad had joined the Mahasabha with a definite objective and which was to 'make it an effective instrument for checkmating the anti-national policies of the

Muslim League and the cowardly passivity of the Congress.'[26] Within months, Mookerjee not only began to target M.A. Jinnah, whom he had once described as a 'nationalist', but also sharpened his criticism against Fazlul Huq's regime.

The Premier of Bengal was already combating the sudden and large exodus of ministers from his government, including his Finance Minister Nalini Ranjan Sarkar who was one of the founding members of the Krishak Praja Party. A prominent Hindu leader, Nalini Ranjan was inducted into the Huq Cabinet with an aim to soften the anti-Hindu rhetoric, which obviously came to naught after he quit the party. The impact of his resignation was such that no Hindu legislator thereafter considered joining the Huq government until the jinx was broken by Syama Prasad Mookerjee in 1941, but more of which later.

In 1940, during the local body elections in Bengal, Syama Prasad Mookerjee led the Hindu Mahasabha in forging an alliance with Subhash Chandra Bose. Although the two men were bitterly opposed to each other's ideologies, Bose and Mookerjee decided that a three-way split between the Congress, Hindu Mahasabha and Muslim League would ultimately benefit the latter. The Muslim League on its part was clearly intent on playing the communal card and shortly before the polls, passed the Lahore Resolution demanding a separate country for Muslims. As a man who had mooted the resolution in the first place, Fazlul Huq now unequivocally asserted that he was a 'Muslim first and Bengalee afterwards.'[27]

Despite gaining support amongst his community, Fazlul Huq was losing his grip over Bengal with each passing day. In contrast, Syama Prasad Mookerjee had succeeded in gaining credence and won the trust of upper caste Hindus. In early 1940, he was invited by the RSS to attend a meeting in Lahore and said that, 'the one silver lining in the cloudy sky of India,' was none other than the Rashtriya Swayamsevak Sangh.

Political Options

As was evident, Mookerjee and Huq had sharp public differences, but Bengal's political demography was such that it compelled them to work together. The reason: since Hindus made up for almost forty-four per cent of the total population of the province, 'no Muslim ruler could feel secure without some Hindu support.'[28]

The wily administrator that he was, Fazlul Huq was cognisant of the fact that getting the Hindus to support his endeavours would become an impossibility if he remained associated with the Muslim League, and he therefore parted ways with M.A. Jinnah. On 17 December 1941, Syama Prasad achieved the near-impossible and began a new phase in his political career as Finance minister in the Fazlul Huq-led Progressive Coalition government. This classic case of a politically convenient marriage required no analysis—while Mookerjee's political ambition took flight, Huq described himself to be 'the best defender of Hindu interests and Mookerjee (of)...Muslim interests.'[29]

By 1941, Bengal had plunged deep into a communal abyss. Syama Prasad was somehow completely oblivious of its portent and was guided by the belief that by joining the Huq ministry, he would succeed in keeping the 'Muslim League's communalism, British's divisive policies and the Congress's browbeating at bay.'[30] In one of his interviews to a local newspaper, Mookerjee had quoted the Secretary of State for India, Leo Amery that despite several differences, Bengal could 'combine for the good of the country.'

With the passing of Rabindranath Tagore in August 1941, it was left to the other cultural icon of Bengal, the poet Qazi Nazrul Islam to hail the Huq–Mookerjee partnership as a big step in forging Hindu–Muslim unity. The poet's association with the warring duo-turned-allies rekindled hope in the people of Bengal that together they would overcome the communal fault lines. The endorsement by an eminence grise of the Bengali literary world was based on the enthusiasm manifest in the initial days of the alliance when not 'a single instance of communal rioting' was reported, and the generous allocation of one lakh rupees by Finance Minister Mookerjee for promoting communal harmony in the state.

It has been proven universally that a decline in communal conflagrations in society cannot be taken as a parameter for evaluating either the absence or presence of divisive elements in the community. In the Bengal of the early Forties, while there was a dip in sectarian violence, at a subaltern level, the Hindu-Muslim divide was deeply entrenched in certain sections of the society. One of the reasons for this was due to the Muslim League's sustained campaign against Fazlul Huq for 'betraying' Muslim interests. Finance Minister Syama Prasad had immediately sprung to Premier's Huq's defense and voiced his protest against the 'dirty calumny' spread by leaders of the League, mainly M.A. Jinnah. But in actual terms, despite the camaraderie, neither could Mookerjee aid Huq's cause amongst his Muslim brethren, nor secure support for himself amongst Hindus. In his book, Rajmohan Gandhi argues how the experiment had failed in bridging the gap between the Hindus and Muslims of Bengal:

> Though apparently successful, the bud was four years too late. Hindu and Muslim legislators should have been combined in 1937. The opportune moment was missed by Bose and others

in the Congress. The November 1941 exercise did not bring Hindus and Muslims together. Haq's exercise was seen by Bengal's Muslims as a Hindu manoeuvre.

As mentioned earlier, after the initial euphoria of having joined hands with Fazlul Huq, Finance Minister Mookerjee swiftly began losing support amongst his constituency. His credibility was further eroded after the Congress launched the Quit India movement in August 1942. Even as leaders such as, Subhash Chandra Bose were escalating the anti-Imperialist struggle in the face of repressive measures, the Hindu Mahasabha, Muslim League and the Communists opposed the Quit India movement, albeit for different reasons. In popular perception however, they were clubbed together as 'British collaborators'.

In more ways than one, the Hindu Mahasabha and Muslim League were different sides of the same coin. In their preoccupation with the 'enemy other' community, their involvement in the freedom struggle took a major beating. Gradually, the Hindu Mahasabha was perceived as an irrelevant third force and a party which had lost support even amongst its core constituency of Hindus. On the other hand, the Muslim League did marginally better, as it had already espoused for a separate nation for Muslims.

Unlike Congress ministers in other provinces who had resigned in protest against the oppressive measures of the British in the aftermath of the Quit India movement, Syama Prasad Mookerjee was faced with a difficult choice—'to defend Congress's rebellion during a war would invite dismissal, but to defend the Raj's repression when India's freedom movement was at its climax would invite the public's censure.'[31] At a time when there existed no middle path, Mookerjee attempted to find one. The Governor of Bengal asked Mookerjee and other ministers to either resign or endorse British policies. In response, Mookerjee appealed to the Viceroy to declare India independent and initiate steps to form a transitional government. He further added that if the demand was overturned, and the administration allowed the 'present impasse to continue, I must regretfully ask my governor to relieve me of my duties as a minister so that I may have the full freedom to help mobilise public opinion.'[32]

The Viceroy deigned to not reply, and Syama Prasad bought time and postponed his resignation. Yet, he was well aware of the rising tide of opposition against the British, and in order to regain lost ground, he used the ruse of inadequate relief measures in cyclone-struck Midnapore as the reason for his quitting. His resignation letter of 16 November 1942 listed two main reasons—first, in a classic instance of doublespeak, he expressed his opposition to the coercive steps taken by the British administration after the Quit India call, and secondly, the Governor's bid to convert the principle of 'provincial autonomy into a meaningless farce.' Mookerjee and Huq parted, but not as bitter rivals, for they remained cordial even after Partition when the latter became a leader of some significance in East Pakistan.

The British government on its part suppressed Syama Prasad Mookerjee's resignation letter, as a result of which he paraphrased it in a speech to the Bengal assembly in February 1943. This was indeed a clever ploy, as the Defence of India rules were not applicable to disclosures in legislatures! With that one single tactical act of defiance, Mookerjee had succeeded in proving his patriotic credentials. He explained why he had become part of Fazlul's ministry in the first place and as mentioned earlier, said that 'this way he would be able to keep Muslim League's communalism, British divisive policies and

Congress's browbeating at bay.'[33] But it was indeed doubtful if he had managed to accomplish any of these objectives.

The Reinvention

After his resignation as Finance Minister, Syama Prasad Mookerjee set about the task of re-positioning himself as an effectual Opposition leader in the Bengal Council under the newly-installed Muslim League dispensation. It may be recalled that he had also bolstered his image by playing a pivotal role in the Bengal Relief Committee, which was set up in response to British apathy towards the famine. During a debate in the Legislative Council in July 1943, Mookerjee said that the 'government was fiddling while the villagers in Bengal were crying for a morsel....They (British) want to first provide for their troops... forgetting their responsibilities to the people.'[34] Meanwhile, he also campaigned against the Secondary Education Bill introduced by the Muslim League government, terming it anti-Hindu. In response, the Muslim League declared that the Bill was 'for the Muslims, and that was why it was being attacked by Hindus.'[35] Finally in May 1944 when it was felt that there shall not be any let-up in the barrage of provocative statements from both sides, Mookerjee demanded the setting up of a non-communal and autonomous board for secondary education.

The controversy over the secondary educational board had not even subsided, when the Hindu Mahasabha picked up yet another issue to agitate about: the revival of the Chakravarti Rajagopalachari Formula, popularly known as the C.R. Formula. The idea was first mooted by the Congress stalwart in 1941 and was widely denounced, for it had ratified the idea of Pakistan. Three years later in September 1944, Mahatma Gandhi and Jinnah met to discuss the issue yet again.

The Mahasabha led by V.D. Savarkar criticised the meeting in strong words and claimed that it was the beginning of a 'downward course of Gandhi's monopoly of power as a leader.'[36]

However, Syama Prasad disagreed with Savarkar's postulation, and proceeded to meet Gandhi who reiterated that while there was no room for abandoning a dialogue on the issue, he also gave Mookerjee an assurance that he would reject the idea of Partition. Thereafter, Gandhi met Jinnah yet again and turned down the proposal of partitioning the country. The second meeting between Gandhi and Jinnah provided Mookerjee an opportunity to raise the 'irrelevant' issue of Partition and he was catapulted to the centre stage yet again.

As mentioned earlier, Savarkar was ailing by the time Syama Prasad became president of the Hindu Mahasabha and more importantly, Mookerjee's perceived success in getting Gandhi to reject the idea of partition had further weakened his grasp on the party. Finally in 1944, V.D. Savarkar bowed out and made way for Syama Prasad to take complete control of the Hindu Mahasabha.

Syama Prasad Mookerjee got down to work immediately and 'initiated a campaign to reorient the Hindu Mahasabha[37], from a class-based organisation to one for the masses.' He further ensured that it maintained sufficient distance from the Imperial government and forged closer ties with the Indian National Congress 'in the fight against the *Raj* and Pakistan.'

But all his strategies, mostly overtly political, to win back the support of Hindus failed as was proven in the elections to the Bengal Legislative Assembly in March 1946. The Hindu Mahasabha was decimated and while Mookerjee won the party's lone seat, it was only the non-elective special seat in the University.

The setback notwithstanding, there was a pending political task which required Syama Prasad's attention after the British government sent the Cabinet Mission in March 1946 to begin negotiations for the setting up of an Interim government. As head of the Mahasabha delegation, he demanded that 'the integrity and indivisibility of the country should be maintained...and that Partition would be economically unsound, disastrous, politically unwise and suicidal.'[38] He also refused to 'agree to any suggestion that Hindus and Muslims should be represented in the central government on the basis of equality.' In his deliberations with the Cabinet Mission, Mookerjee reiterated what he had once discussed with Jinnah—that Hindu and Muslim representatives should meet to discuss issues on which they required protection from each other. In so far as granting complete protection to minorities in respect of language, religion and customs was concerned, Mookerjee was willing to acquiesce, but he was unwilling to grant them equal rights.

In June 1946, the Cabinet Mission returned to England after failing to make any headway in the negotiations. Within a span of two months, Jinnah called for Direct Action Day (also known as the Great Calcutta Killings) on 16 August 1946 and with that, the partition of the subcontinent became an inevitable reality. The initial leg-work on cleaving parts of the nation had begun, except Bengal, for it was still undecided whether it would go the Punjab way and be partitioned, or merge with Pakistan, because of its Muslim-majority population.

After the horrific killings in his native city, Syama Prasad Mookerjee proclaimed during a debate in the Legislative Assembly that the deliberations were essentially over a 'no-confidence motion against the Ministry under circumstances, which perhaps, has no parallel in the deliberations of any legislature in any part of the civilised world. What happened in Calcutta was without a parallel in modern history.' In the aftermath of the Great Calcutta Killings and the riots in Noakhali in October–November 1946, the Hindu Mahasabha witnessed an exponential growth in its base numbers. In 1943–44 for instance, the Mahasabha had just about ten branches in Noakhali district, but in a period of three years, this number rose dramatically to one hundred and forty-three. The deteriorating communal situation in the country had 'brought the Mahasabha, which went into political hibernation after its electoral defeat, back on the political scene.'[39]

On 20 October 1946, precisely twenty days after the Noakhali riots, Mookerjee formed the Hindu National Guards; in order to forge unity amongst Hindus, irrespective of caste, he also set up the Hindu Society Board; in addition, he also established the Hindu Sangathan Society. From here on, he was not only 'heard' in the Bengal legislature, but was seen to be acting with great alacrity in restoring the dignity of his Hindu brethren.

* * *

Syama Prasad Mookerjee's stance on Partition has undoubtedly been one of the most significant aspects of his political career. It is interesting to note that he disagreed with most of the Mahasabha leaders on the issue, especially his mentor, V.D. Savarkar.

According to Dhananjay Keer, 'On the eve of the Viceroy's departure (to London on 18 May 1947), Dr. Mookerjee had put his demand for a separate Hindu Province in the West of Bengal.'[40] However in less than a year, political pragmatism had forced a change in Mookerjee's standpoint on this vital issue. Yet, within days of

Mookerjee's volte-face, Savarkar launched a fresh campaign for India's unity. On 27 May 1947, he made a 'fervent and forlorn appeal' to Congress leaders 'not to betray the electorates and India by agreeing to a scheme involving vivisection of the Motherland.'[41] This stark divergence in thought between the two Mahasabha stalwarts indicated that while Syama Prasad Mookerjee had come to terms with the inevitability of Partition, V.D. Savarkar was relentless in his pursuit of keeping the nation united.

Several academics, including the ex-President of India, Pranab Mukherjee has maintained that Syama Prasad Mookerjee had indeed supported India's partition.[42] Then there were others like the writer, Subrata Mukherjee who argued that his 'most important achievement was the creation of West Bengal.'[43] According to Subrata, the Hindu Mahasabha leader had come to the realisation that a united Bengal would limit the role of the Hindu community, and hence proposed that the state be partitioned into a Hindu-majority West Bengal, and a Muslim-dominated East Bengal (later East Pakistan). The ex-President however was more forthright—in August 2009 when Pranab Mukherjee was Finance minister, he was reported to have stated that the man with whom he shared a surname but little else, was 'one of the main architects of the Partition of India' who 'not only supported Partition of the country, but insisted on Partition of Bengal and Punjab on the basis of Hindu-Muslim and Hindu-Sikh-Muslim majority districts.'[44]

Even Prime Minister Nehru didn't spare Syama Prasad for endorsing the division of the country and said as much during a debate in the Lok Sabha. In response to the prime minister, Syama Prasad had retorted as follows: 'You have divided India, I have divided Pakistan.'[45]

Minister Mookerjee

Despite strong ideological differences between the two men, Prime Minister Nehru invited Syama Prasad Mookerjee to join independent India's first Cabinet. In retrospect, it would be safe to surmise that his government, which was formed after the terrible Partition, was most ideologically balanced—on the one side were conservatives like Morarji Desai, K.M. Munshi and S.K. Patil who clearly did not share Nehru's enthusiasm for Socialism. On the other was an assorted group of non-Congress leaders—Syama Prasad Mookerjee, B.R. Ambedkar, John Mathai, and C.D. Deshmukh.[46]

One of the primary reasons for Syama Prasad Mookerjee's inclusion in Nehru's Cabinet over several other leaders from Bengal was because he was backed by none other than Sardar Vallabhbhai Patel who had proposed his name after he had demanded 'Bengal's partition in March 1947 and (refused) to join an abortive bid for a united and independent Bengal that Sarat Bose and Suhrawardy made in April and May (1947).'[47] Several academics have argued that Mookerjee's decision was a strategic ploy and back it with the theory that he as well as other Mahasabha leaders were 'unsure about what their role should be. In particular, they were uncertain how to react to the Congress at the centre...some of them. Dr Mookerjee prominent among them, thought they would do best by joining the national government as partners of the Congress,' but hadn't risked initiating the process.[48] Although they had differed with each other on the issue of Partition barely three months ago in August 1947 when Jawaharlal Nehru had requested Syama Prasad Mookerjee to join his Cabinet, V.D. Savarkar had endorsed the proposal.

In his book, Balraj Madhok provides a wonderful insight into the

Mahasabha leaders' duplicity—how they launched a public broadside against the Congress in public, yet remained sympathetic in private. According to him, Mookerjee's colleagues 'had always stood for responsive cooperation...and, wanted to give the Congress leaders a fair chance to show their worth (and) advised him to accept the invitation.'[49] Despite the oath of secrecy, there was no corroboration of the fact if Mookerjee had discussed the issues relating to Nehru's policies with Savarkar.

In September 1947, Prime Minister Nehru forwarded an internal report to his Cabinet colleagues which said that his Minister of Industry and Supplies, Syama Prasad flew the Mahasabha flag at his official residence instead of the Tricolour. Mookerjee responded to the prime minister saying that although he hoisted the Indian flag regularly, he also flew the Mahasabha's flag on a few occasions. In another instance, in response to a letter which criticised some of Mahasabha's policies, Mookerjee asked his party's General Secretary, Ashutosh Lahiry to write back demanding the expulsion of Muslims from India because 'now that they have got their long-cherished dream, the Muslims now staying in Hindusthan must be made to leave....(for they) will certainly prove to be traitors, saboteurs and fifth-columnists...'[50]

Evidently, even after becoming a Central minister, Mookerjee continued to confer with the Mahasabha leaders on several political and policy matters. Mahatma Gandhi's secretary, Pyarelal reported one such instance as follows—shortly before his assassination, Gandhi had sent his secretary to meet with Syama Prasad to register his protest against the virulent rhetoric adopted by some his party associates, including incitement to assassinate a few Congress leaders. According to British author, Keith Meadowcroft 'when informed on

Mookerjee's "halting and unsatisfactory" reply, the Mahatma's brow darkened.'[51]

It was clear that Syama Prasad was caught in a cleft stick between his commitment to the Hindu Mahasabha, and his duties as a minister in Nehru's Cabinet. As he had accepted to Nehru, while he hoisted the Mahasabha flag reiterating his allegiance to the party, he also tried convincing his mentor, V.D. Savarkar that the Mahasabha must restrict its political character and metamorphose into a social, cultural and religious organisation.

In so far as the Congress party was concerned, despite the inclusion of a Hindu Mahasabha member as a minister in the government, the antagonistic views apropos Hindu nationalists persisted amongst most of its members. However one group led by Sardar Patel in the Congress wished closer ties with the Mahasabha, even suggesting a merger with the party for it felt that it was Syama Prasad Mookerjee who was instrumental in making the Mahasabha 'less aggressive than the (Muslim) League and less irresponsible.'[52] But Jawaharlal Nehru, much like several times before, opposed the move and in a letter to Mookerjee dated 28 January 1948 (exactly two days prior to Gandhi's assassination) wrote that the Mahasabha was the 'main opposition' to both the Congress and his government. The prime minister also wrote to the Director of Intelligence Bureau (IB) and drew his attention to the 'increasingly aggressive and offensive activities' of the Mahasabha.

Considering Syama Prasad Mookerjee's stature, which preceded even his Hindu Mahasabha phase, there was speculation over why Prime Minister Nehru had allocated the ministry of Industry and Supplies to him, which of course came with his Home Minister's strong recommendation of his candidature. It was rather well known that if he had had his way, Mookerjee would have 'personally preferred education which had been his special field since his early youth,' for he could have then 'laid a sound foundation for a truly national education policy.'[53] However, Nehru was well aware of the fact that a man who led an organisation like the Hindu Mahasabha, should be precluded from any decision-making involving social policies and hence put him in charge of a suitable portfolio.

The brouhaha over his portfolio notwithstanding, it must be mentioned that Syama Prasad Mookerjee was an efficient minister. Nearly five decades later, President R. Venkataraman while unveiling Syama Prasad Mookerjee's bust at a function in Kolkata on 23 February 2001 had remarked how he had 'handled the portfolio of Industries with a rare felicity,' and laid the foundation for a mixed economy in the country. 'Despite being an ardent believer in the private sector,' the former President added that Mookerjee had 'established outstanding public sector undertakings.... Pragmatism and not dogmatism informed his industrial policy.'

Saving Savarkar

As Industry and Supplies Minister, although Syama Prasad had few disagreements with Prime Minister Nehru, there were several other issues apart from ideological principles that the two bitterly disagreed on. For instance, in the aftermath of the Partition, the extent to which India could exert pressure on Pakistan to protect the rights of Hindus in East Pakistan which was, diplomatically speaking, an internal matter of India's new neighbour.

While Prime Minister Nehru was committed to running his government based on constitutional propriety and not succumb to majoritarianism, Mookerjee was of the view that India must intervene in Pakistan and provide succour to Hindus who were seeking refuge in the country. The prime minister refused to budge and repeatedly insisted that 'protection in Pakistan can be given only by Pakistan. We cannot give protection in Pakistan.'[54]

The other contentious issue between the men was Kashmir, and Mookerjee was severely critical of Nehru's handling of the state's integration with the Union of India. If viewed from the prism of contemporary politics, and particularly in the Seventies when Indira Gandhi ran her Cabinet with an iron fist, such impertinence from a minister would have meant the end of his political career.

Meanwhile, in the aftermath of Mahatma Gandhi's assassination on 30 January 1948, the RSS was banned and some of its top leaders were arrested. Although the Hindu Mahasabha wasn't proscribed, V.D. Savarkar was taken into custody days after the murder. As a senior member of the Hindu Mahasabha, Syama Prasad could have on a matter of principle resigned from Nehru's Cabinet, but he chose to stay on and cleverly strategised to secure a reprieve for his party. At an extraordinary meeting of the Mahasabha convened a day after Savarkar's arrest, Mookerjee reasoned with its members that the party either ceases 'its political activities and limits itself to social, cultural and religious problem,' or abandons 'its communalist composition (...) and opens its doors to every citizen, regardless of religion.'[55]

On 15 February 1948, the proposal was discussed in Hindu Mahasabha's Working Committee and it was decided to go with the first option in order to avoid censure from the government. Even in a moment of great crisis, when their iconic leader was thrown into jail, the traditionalists within the Mahasabha had stuck to their stand of not admitting non-Hindus into their fold. In the first place, the reason for Mookerjee's suggestion stemmed from his strong conviction that the 'Muslim problem...could be solved in free India' permanently, provided 'their outlook on cultural, social and political problems of the country was Hinduised or nationalised while leaving them free, in keeping with the Hindu tradition of absolute tolerance, to carry on their religion and way of worship as they pleased.'[56] His position on this issue was similar to the RSS' theory that the Muslims were originally Hindus and could be brought back into the 'nationalist' mainstream.

Meanwhile, the traditionalists within the Mahasabha had no intentions of ceasing political activism. Three months after agreeing to put a halt on every kind of political activity, the Mahasabha conservatives succeeded in convincing the Working Committee to reverse its decision. Syama Prasad did not take well to this rebellion and on 23 November 1948, he resigned from the Hindu Mahasabha. For a man who was at the forefront of consolidating its position and had worked tirelessly for its expansion even as a Cabinet minister, his resignation from the Hindu Mahasabha had raised several questions and foremost being if it would survive thereafter.

But Syama Prasad Mookerjee was resolute in his belief that the Mahasabha had run its course, and needed an overhauling as an expansive Hindu nationalist party. While recommending that Muslims be made part of the organisation, Mookerjee had not only encouraged a form of assimilation, but had also taken cognisance of the fact that after Partition, barring the state of Jammu & Kashmir, their numbers had come down drastically across the country. As expected, the Mahasabha thought otherwise, which gave rise to questions about the political path that he would henceforth follow and those he would eventually partner with.

Mookerjee's so-called political conundrum was not impossible to comprehend because as a national leader, he lacked both party and a cause, and there seemed little chance of his finding a place in West Bengal. For instance, after his move to Delhi in the late Forties, he was also quick to recognise that Dr. B.C. Roy was well ensconced as chief minister of West Bengal and would brook no threat to his political pre-eminence either within the Congress or from the Right.

Differences with Nehru

Unlike the norm in contemporary politics, when seldom does a leader of repute sit out of the system for long, Syama Prasad Mookerjee kept his counsel after resigning from the Hindu Mahasabha and did not jump into any other Right-wing bandwagon. It should be mentioned here that this was also a time when the nation had been spliced into two, and as a votary of Hindutva, he could have used his political clout to push the Muslims deep into the abyss.

There is no gainsaying the fact that it was also him who had mooted the idea of assimilating them by offering them membership in the Mahasabha—but according to several critics, that was more of a political ploy to detract attention from the accusation that his party faced of being the nurturer of conspirators who had killed the Father of the Nation. Be that as it may, it may also be recalled that his animosity towards the Muslims was a reality and was overtly manifest even before he had joined the Hindu Mahasabha in 1939.

This was a belief that he typically shared with several bhadralok Bengalis, that as a community they were superior to the Muslims. The 'privilege' of their caste notwithstanding, this feeling was mainly a result of the viewpoint that the 'Bengali Muslims were, by and large, "a set of converts" from the dregs of Hindu society.'[57] Even as Union minister, however much he tried couching it, considering he was part of a Congress government, Syama Prasad was primarily guided by this very premise which later became the basis of his irreconcilable differences with the prime minister.

As mentioned earlier, Mookerjee and Nehru had severe differences over the extent of India's intervention in Pakistan to protect the rights of Hindus. The differences were not only limited to the magnitude and form of exerting pressure on Pakistan, but on adherence to the basic principles of democracy. Syama Prasad Mookerjee considered his standpoint as more logical, according to which, it was obligatory on India's part to intervene and rescue Hindus from being persecuted in East Pakistan.[58]

Gradually, the growing dissent between the two spilled over to two Inter-Dominion Agreements signed with Pakistan in 1948 which addressed the problems faced by Hindus in West and East Pakistan. Despite Mookerjee's relentless campaign, and the steady stream of Hindu refugees into West Bengal, Nehru refused to go past the diplomatic route.

In April 1950, the Liaquat–Nehru Pact (also known as the Delhi Pact) to secure the safety of life and property of minorities was readied to be inked. Exactly a week before the Pact was to be formalised, Syama Prasad Mookerjee resigned from the government on 1 April 1950. A few days later, on 19 April 1950, he delivered what many consider to be 'one of the greatest political speeches in the annals of independent India.'[59] While highlighting the attacks on Hindus in Pakistan, he said:

> We saw the gradual extermination of Hindus from North Western Frontier Province and Baluchistan and latterly from

> Sind as well. In East Bengal about 13 million of Hindus were squeezed out of East Bengal. There were no major incidents as such; but circumstance so shaped themselves that they got no protection from the Government of Pakistan and were forced to come away to West Bengal for shelter...In the course of 1949 we witnessed a further deterioration of conditions in East Bengal and an exodus of a far larger number of helpless people...When about 15,000 refugees came to West Bengal in January 1950, stories of brutal atrocities and persecutions came to light...

Just a year before he quit the government, Syama Prasad had also raised the issue of police atrocities on Hindus in Khulna district of East Pakistan. However, it also needs to be highlighted that there was yet another significant issue involving the rights of Hindus about which Syama Prasad Mookerjee had vacillated for a considerable period of time. Since 1941, the question of codifying and modernising Hindu legal tradition would surface periodically and eventually, the Constituent Assembly formulated a Draft Code Bill in 1944. However, the deliberations on the Bill had led to a virtual split in the Congress party between the conservatives, led by India's first President Rajendra Prasad, and the modernists or reformists led by Jawaharlal Nehru.

During the period when the Bill was being evaluated by both groups, Syama Prasad Mookerjee had chosen to be on the side of the conservatives in the Congress and had opposed the codification of Hindu laws. But after joining Nehru's Cabinet, he had preferred to remain silent during debates. The veteran journalist, Inder Malhotra had commented about Mookerjee's studied silence in *The Indian Express* dated 1 May 2009, and wrote that the Industries Minister, hadn't said a word against the Hindu Code while he was a member of Jawaharlal Nehru's cabinet, (he) thundered in 1951 that the Bill would 'shatter the magnificent architecture of the Hindu culture'.

> ...we should never tolerate any criticism from any quarter, especially from a foreign quarter when they say that Hindu civilisation or Hindu culture has been of a static nature or of stagnant nature or of decadent nature.

This was also the same speech during which Mookerjee was at his vituperative best in criticising Nehru's government and said how the 'government did not dare to touch the Muslim community.'

A New Innings

After breaking all ties with the Hindu Mahasabha, and virtually stepping out of V.D. Savarkar's shadow, Syama Prasad was now on the lookout for a credible platform to further his political mission.

Meanwhile, the ban on the RSS was lifted in July 1949 and its leaders felt an 'urgent need for a political organisation which could reflect the ideology and ideas of the RSS in the political sphere.'[60] In the December 1949 issue of the *Organiser*, its then editor, K.R. Malkani wrote that the RSS must have a political presence,

> not only to protect itself...but to stop the un-Bharatiya and anti-Bharatiya policies of the government and to advance and expedite the cause of Bharatiya through state machinery.

Syama Prasad Mookerjee was well 'aware of this stream of thought in the RSS circles,'[61] and made several trips to Nagpur between November 1949 and early 1950 to meet the RSS sarsanghchalak, Madhav Sadashiv Golwalkar (also known as Guruji). The RSS chief 'made sure that Mookerjee was in full agreement with the ideals of the Hindu Rashtra,' before agreeing to collaborate with him.[62] Although Syama Prasad had in the past endorsed RSS for its commitment to nationalism, he knew little about its internal dynamics, but after giving the idea some thought, he was somehow convinced that he could be its potential leader in the absence of a 'logical political mentor,' as the organisation was in need of 'an ideological shepherd.'[63]

While exploring the prospect of joining the RSS, Mookerjee had firmed up his mind that his engagement with it should have political ramifications in the history of Indian politics. Meanwhile, even as he held his final plan close to his chest, he decided to reach out to his former Mahasabha colleagues. In early 1949, he met its then president, N.B. Khare and invited him to be part of the plan, but to no avail. However, a few well-known businessmen who had in the past backed the Hindu Mahasabha chose to support Mookerjee, which proved that despite the ignominy faced in the aftermath of the Mahatma's assassination, his brand of politics still held good amongst certain sections of society.

However, it would be grossly erroneous in presuming that Syama Prasad Mookerjee was the only leader to have recommended that the RSS assumes a political avatar. As mentioned earlier, on 7 October 1949, in a shocking development, the Congress Working Committee had given permission to RSS workers to join the party as primary members. What was even more shocking was that the decision was taken in the absence of Prime Minister Nehru who was travelling at the time. Although on his return, the move was reversed forthwith, it pointed towards the fact that the RSS was not a pariah even for the Congress party, and this was just one year after the killing of Mahatma Gandhi.

Even as Syama Prasad went about finalising his plans,

> the RSS found an ally in him (Mookerjee), and over the next few months, the details of the Jana Sangh were worked out between Mookerjee and the RSS leadership. The decision of the RSS to allow Mookerjee to be the leader of the new political formation was an extension of Golwalkar's well-known view that the interests of the RSS would be best served if it could utilise either existing organisations, or well known leaders to propagate their views.[64]

The arrangement suited both parties: the RSS had a cause and an organisational network, but no leader, whereas Mookerjee was looking for a cause and a base to bring his plans to fruition. Despite a common ideological plank, both sides treaded with utmost caution—Mookerjee kept an eye on the ongoing power struggle within the Congress party, while the top brass of the RSS was busy evaluating the pros and cons of the arrangement. After Sardar Patel's death in December 1950, Mookerjee realised that the doors of the Congress party were permanently shut for him, as it was for any other Right-wing leader.

In what was construed as presenting Messrs Golwalkar and company with a fait accompli, while on a tour to Punjab, Syama Prasad announced the birth of a new party called the Bharatiya Jana Sangh, which was way in advance of its formal launch in October 1951. The move to hasten the decision was a direct fall out of the first general elections which had kicked off on 25 October 1951 in the Chini and Pangi assembly constituencies in Himachal Pradesh where voting had to be mandatorily completed before snowfall. In his book, Balraj Madhok wrote:

> The RSS leadership with its greater stress on organisational working and its keen desire to have the real control of the new party in its own hands wanted to take its time to usher it into existence. The delay irritated Dr. Mookerjee who, at one stage, even thought of going alone*. His impatience was understandable.[65]

It soon became apparent that the marriage between the RSS and Jana Sangh was fraught with trouble. Syama Prasad was aware that Deendayal Upadhyaya (then an RSS pracharak who is considered iconic in the annals of the RSS) who was deputed as general secretary of the Jana Sangh was part of Nagpur's strategy to keep a close eye on the functioning of the newly-established party. Although Upadhyaya had been 'loaned' as a temporary source to the new party, this soon became a routine practise over a period of time, and many pracharaks were regularly sent on deputation to the Jana Sangh. This resulted in periodic conflicts, and according to Mauli Chandra Sharma, Mookerjee was,

> often seriously perturbed by the demands of the RSS leaders for a decisive say in matters like appointment of office-bearers, nomination of candidates for elections and matters of policy.[66]

For all his talk about establishing a Right-wing party with a difference, at the time of the first general elections in 1952, Mookerjee informed

* In fact, in West Bengal the party was called People's Party of India and it had later merged with the Jana Sangh.

the campaign committee that the party should be projected as being 'open to all citizens who owed unalloyed allegiance to India and her great culture and heritage which is essentially Hindu in character.'[67] However, not only had his strategy backfired, even his projections were grossly exaggerated. The Jana Sangh managed to win only three seats, although Mookerjee himself did well and was elected from Calcutta, while the Congress had performed spectacularly by winning 364 of the 489 seats. It wasn't as if there was a strong Opposition in parliament either; the Communists with sixteen members were the largest 'non-Congress' party.

Despite the poor show of numbers, Syama Prasad converted the moment of adversity into an opportunity and cobbled together a parliamentary forum called the National Democratic Front comprising thirty-two Lok Sabha members. The real intent behind the initiative was already manifest in Mookerjee's speech at the Jana Sangh's inaugural convention in Delhi on 21 October 1951, in which he had said, 'One of the chief reasons for the manifestation of dictatorship in Congress rule is the absence of well-organised opposition parties which alone can act as a healthy check.'[68] He had succeeded in convincing other political parties that in the absence of requisite numbers, they could act as a united front against the Congress party in the Lok Sabha.

Although he was not accorded the formal status of Leader of Opposition, Mookerjee strode the floor like a colossus, obviously because of his stature and knowledge of parliamentary affairs. He soon earned the epithet of 'Lion of Parliament' and was respected across party lines for his speeches and informed interventions.

The seasoned parliamentarian that he was, Mookerjee used every opportunity to attack Nehru's government and went back to the same issues that had driven a wedge between him and the prime minister in the past—the government's policy on Hindu settlers from Pakistan; the Kashmir issue; and the Hindu Code Bills. But Mookerjee was at his acerbic best when it came to trading personal charges with Nehru. In 1953, he alleged that he 'saw with my own eyes how government resources can be made to operate for the purpose of winning the elections. I can tell the Prime Minister some time later. He does not know that money and wine played their part in many a sphere.' Nehru was furious at the allegation, because he had heard Mookerjee declare openly that the Congress party had used 'wine and women' to win elections.

Yet, getting the better of Nehru in parliament was no solace for Mookerjee for he wished for a greater and deeper political involvement at the juncture. During the campaign for the first general elections, Mookerjee had claimed that he could 'set this man (Nehru) right if I can take even ten members of Parliament with me.' But this was easier said than done.

However, the wheel of fortune soon turned in his favour and the Jana Sangh bagged four seats in the by-elections to the Delhi assembly. The reason: his party's campaign in the capital, which was then swarming with refugees, had cleverly highlighted the government's alleged indecision on Kashmir's integration with the Union.

The Kashmir Conundrum

Syama Prasad Mookerjee was a member of the Nehru Cabinet when on 17 October 1949, the Constituent Assembly had adopted the resolution to provide special status to the state of Jammu & Kashmir. When N. Gopalaswami Ayyangar, a ministerial colleague and member of the drafting committee, in a reply to a query from Maulana Hasrat

Mohani, the Urdu poet and member of the House, had stated that Article 370 in the Constitution was being inserted 'due to the special conditions of Kashmir. That particular State is not yet ripe for this kind of integration. It is the hope of everybody here that in due course even Jammu and Kashmir will become ripe for the same sort of integration as has taken place in the case of other States,' Syama Prasad Mookerjee had acquiesced to the formulation.

Yet, within a year, his party's election manifesto had proclaimed ambitiously that it would 'end the uncertainty about Kashmir's future, it should be integrated with Bharat like other acceding states and not be given special position.'[69]

It was hereafter crystal-clear that Kashmir, especially 'the problem of (its) relationship[70]' with the 'rest of India,' and the Hindus of Jammu, had come to occupy central space in Mookerjee's politics. This was indeed paradoxical because Mookerjee's interest in the Kashmir problem only 'grew casually[71]', and although he was consulted by the state leaders on the issue from the time of India's independence, Kashmir was hitherto not the kernel of his larger political mission. In February 1952, Mookerjee criticised the government for having mismanaged the state's integration under the Instrument of Accession and committing India to plebiscite. He had also protested against the state's Constituent Assembly's decision to adopt a separate flag, and it is in this context that he had raised the iconic slogan which later became a clarion call for several Right-wing parties in the country:

Ek desh mein do vidhan
Ek desh mein do nishan
Ek desh mein do pradhan
Nahin chalenge, nahin chalenge

In his maiden speech in Lok Sabha as President of the Jana Sangh in May1952, Syama Prasad Mookerjee had posed a sharp question to Prime Minister Nehru: 'Are Kashmiris Indians first and Kashmiris next, or are they Kashmiris first and Indian next, or are they Kashmiris first, second, and third and not Indians at all?'[72] As a veteran and respected parliamentarian, he was well aware that parliamentary decorum did not require the prime minister to give an immediate reply, but Syama Prasad was relentless in his assertion and resorted to a barb that underscored his deep dislike for the prime minister, 'Nehru claims to have discovered India. But he has yet to discover his mind.'[73]

Meanwhile in the Hindu-majority Jammu, the RSS had discovered a great opportunity for mobilising the community, and at the behest of Balraj Madhok, they chose to back a well-known local leader called Prem Nath Dogra to form a party called the Jammu Praja Parishad in November 1947. When a few members of the fledgling party were subjected to police atrocities during a protest march, it was Syama Prasad Mookerjee who had come to their rescue and suggested that they storm their way into the Constituent Assembly of Jammu and Kashmir.

Mookerjee's continuing pursuit of Hindu-centric politics raised the hackles of the prime minister yet again and he accused both the Jana Sangh and the Praja Parishad of pursuing communal politics. In response, Mookerjee said that he was, 'getting quite sick of this charge which is unfounded, if we want to consider whether communalism exists in the country or whether it is openly advocated as a plank by any political organisation, let us fix a date for debate and let us discuss the matter. Let government bring forward its charges. Let us have a chance of replying.'

Despite such rhetoric and overt posturing, by the end of 1952,

Mookerjee decided to firm up his party's position on Kashmir and adopted a resolution to this effect. At its All India Session in Kanpur in December 1952, the Jana Sangh demanded a round table conference between the representatives of Praja Parishad, the Sheikh Abdullah government, and a few 'recognised leaders of India'. Mookerjee was also instrumental in the Jana Sangh's decison to partner with other Hindu organisations like the Hindu Mahasabha, RSS and the Jammu Praja Parishad in launching an 'agitation from Jammu into the Punjab and up to Delhi and beyond, on the three issues of Kashmir, refugees from East Bengal and the banning of cow-slaughter.'[74] The resolution authorised the party's Working Committee (Mookerjee was re-elected as president at the first plenary session) to 'prepare whatever is necessary for an all-India agitation for the complete integration of the State of Jammu and Kashmir.'[75]

After the drubbing that the Jana Sangh received in the first general elections, Mookerjee set his eyes on the next which was scheduled in 1957 and after planning to calibrate mass agitations, he arrived in Kashmir in 1952–53. He 'took up cudgels. Insisting on his right to travel anywhere in India, he strode across the state border without a permit—and was promptly jailed.'[76] Unlike Mahatma Gandhi, Mookerjee had little or no expertise in launching and managing mass movements and felt severely hamstrung.

On 8 May 1953, a passenger train steamed out of Delhi station en route to Punjab. Syama Prasad Mookerjee was on board along with several young party colleagues, including the late Atal Bihari Vajpayee and Balraj Madhok. Like most trains of that era, and some even today, it proceeded slowly and stopped at almost every big and small junction. On 11 May, Mookerjee reached Pathankot—the border town between Punjab and Jammu, after having undertaken part of the journey by road. The Chief Minister of Jammu & Kashmir, Sheikh Abdullah had already let Mookerjee know that he was unwelcome in the state. The moment Mookerjee entered Jammu, he was detained and taken to Srinagar.

In the annals of the Indian Right, the last forty-odd days of Mookerjee's life are eulogised—reminiscent of tragic stories of leaders who faced grave injustices at the hands of a cruel dispensation, and ended up as martyrs. But often the other view is also of failed manoeuvres by a politically naïve man.

Syama Prasad Mookerjee's death at fifty-two, along with a *cause* leading up to his end hung like the proverbial albatross around the BJP's neck, preceded by the discomfort felt by the Jana Sangh. It required the political gumption of a man, whose credentials within the party remains unchallenged, to take a step which appeared as if he wanted to emerge out of Syama Prasad's shadows. This leader, Narendra Modi, began by compromising with Mookerjee's memory by forming a coalition with the PDP. Several eyebrows had gone up in utter disbelief because the state government stood for everything that the founder of Jana Sangh had denounced during his life-time. But in 2018, Modi had returned to Mookerjee's Kashmir plan by stepping out of the partnership and eventually dissolving the state assembly.

There is no doubt that Syama Prasad Mookerjee is a martyr for the BJP and its affiliated organisations. In Prime Minister Modi's mind, Lady Jogmaya's demand for justice wasn't just in honour of her dead son's soul; justice for Syama Prasad Mookerjee will be done only when Kashmir's 'complete integration' is achieved with the rest of India. Implausible as that may sound, this is what the BJP's intends as its final salute to one of its icons.

DEENDAYAL UPADHYAYA

His life was a short octave, each key announcing death's premature arrival time and time again. He had lost his father at the age of three; when he turned eight, his mother bade him goodbye. The maternal grandfather, in whose care he was left after being orphaned, was gone too, when he turned ten. At fifteen, the aunt who cared for him decided that the boy needed to find another guardian. Life was just about stabilising at eighteen, when his younger brother had succumbed to the dreaded smallpox. As a young man of twenty-four, it was the turn of a female cousin, who was almost like a soulmate, to die.

Finally, the last key had sounded the harshest timbre—he died at fifty-two in 1968. Although his various trysts with death were undoubtedly premature, his own was by far the worst—violent, cruel, and mysterious.

* * *

That Wednesday was no ordinary day in the life of Narendra Modi. On

25 September 2013, he had been declared the Bharatiya Janata Party's (BJP's) prime ministerial candidate, after tiding over his differences with party veteran, Lal Krishna Advani. Eventually, the one-time strongman and senior leader of the party was persuaded to join Narendra Modi in Bhopal to address a public rally at noon. After the trio of Advani, Rajnath Singh (Minister of Home Affairs), and Shivraj Singh Chouhan (former chief minister of Madhya Pradesh) had finished with their speeches, Modi took centre stage to address a delirious audience.

After going past a major part of his speech, Modi reminded people of what Syama Prasad Mookerjee, the founding president of the Bharatiya Jana Sangh had once said about his colleague, 'Give me two Deendayals, and I will completely change the face of the nation.'[1] Modi had then added prophetically, 'When the country shall celebrate Deendayal Upadhyaya ji's birth centenary in 2015–16, the BJP will rule in most states in the country.' Modi's assertion was indeed prophetic—in the first round of assembly elections in November–December 2014, the BJP won in Maharashtra, Haryana, Jharkhand, and Jammu. By the autumn of 2018, and just before the assembly elections in five states, the BJP was in office, either on its own or as coalition partners, in more than two-third states, home to approximately seventy per cent of Indians.

On 20 May 2014, the day BJP had formalised Narendra Modi's elevation as prime minister, he had once again invoked Deendayal Upadhyaya, and said, 'Antyodaya, the service of the downtrodden, was Pandit Deendayal Upadhyaya's mission. That is why I say our government is for the poor and the deprived. The coming year is important for us all. It will be his centenary year...we have to strive to fulfil his dreams. The party and government must decide how to celebrate the event.'

Even before assuming office as India's prime minister, Narendra Modi had made his intent clear—Deendayal Upadhyaya had to be restored to his rightful place in the annals of Indian history.

* * *

Deendayal Upadhyaya was born in 1916 in a lower middle class family in north India. His father worked as an assistant station master in the Indian Railways and was posted in Jalesar, the United Provinces (now Uttar Pradesh). The frequent occurrences of tragedies in young Deendayal's life had impacted his academic life to such an extent that he was forced to change several schools, from Gangapur to Kota in Rajasthan; attend different colleges in Pilani, Agra, Kanpur and Allahabad, from where the twenty-five-year-old had finally earned a degree in Bachelor of Education, and later took a Masters in English literature. Although he was expected to sit for the civil services considering he was a promising student, he had rejected the idea.

It was in college that he was first exposed to politics, motivated by some of his peers, including, Nanaji Deshmukh, Sundar Singh Bhandari, and Babasaheb Apte, who had convinced him to attend the Officers Training Camp (OTC) in 1939 and 1942, respectively.

It is significant to note here that even as Deendayal was beginning to get involved in politics, the Muslim League had espoused the idea of Two-Nation Theory; the country was witnessing one of the worst episodes of Hindu–Muslim riots; and the Hindu Mahasabha was given an overhaul under the able leadership of none other than V.D. Savarkar.

Deendayal was convinced of his future, and even though his extended family wanted to see him married, it was relegated to the backburner, particularly after his meeting with K.B. Hedgewar in Kanpur.

By now, it was abundantly clear that Deendayal had chosen politics over the life of a householder. In his reply to a letter from a cousin who had requested him to return to the family fold, the young pracharak had written sensitively:

> I am torn between affection (for you and the family) and duty (towards the nation)....I have been assigned to work in a district to awaken the slumbering Hindu society and raise a volunteer corps...I will (not) be allowed to take up a stable job. The society and the country are the first priority for an RSS worker. His individual duties come later...You are apprehensive because you do not know much about the Sangh. It is no way associated with the Congress (Gandhi had already announced the Quit India movement leading to its repression; *emphasis mine*). Nor is it part of any political organisation. It is not involved in politics. RSS does not resort to satyagraha, or going to jail...[2]

Gradually, his political views began to take firm shape and were sharpened over the next few years. It was evidenced in a letter he wrote to the same cousin as follows:

> The Muslim hooligans can insult (any great man) in a matter of minutes. They can themselves become great, but they are members of a society that is weak and degenerated, devoid of all strength...That is why the Muslims often kidnap and abduct our mothers and sisters...Why is it so? Do Hindus lack strong men...?[3]

The Initiation

Although Deendayal Upadhyaya was a contemporary of Balasaheb Deoras, he joined the RSS more than a decade after his colleague, because it was yet to be established in the United Provinces. It finally happened a little after 1937 when the then sarsanghchalak, K.B. Hedgewar had deputed ten associates, students, and pracharaks, to work in Punjab, Delhi, Uttar Pradesh, and Central India.

In 1940, Deendayal Upadhyaya began his stint as an RSS pracharak in Lakhimpur under the guidance of prant pracharak Bhaurao Deoras, who was the younger brother of Balasaheb Deoras. In 1945, Upadhyaya was promoted and took over as his mentor's deputy, or sah-prant pracharak. Bhaurao Deoras was so impressed with his apprentice's performance that he wrote him a letter of appreciation lauding his perseverance despite the fact that his 'path was strewn with thorns,' and when 'no one was familiar with the Sangh activities,' how he willingly 'took over the onerous responsibility.' Deendayal was particularly praised because the RSS' presence, according to Bhaurao Deoras, 'in the province is the result of your hard work and sense of duty. Many of our swayamsevaks have been inspired by the example you set.'[4] It was during this period spanning 1945–1951 when Deendayal was recognised by the leadership as a man with extraordinary organisational prowess coupled with intellectual competence who could be vested with important responsibilities in the future.

It may be recalled that in the aftermath of Mahatma Gandhi's assassination in 1948, the government had banned the RSS alleging that contrary to its avowed principles, it was not only indulging in violent activities, but also exhorting people to violence. Deendayal was entrusted with certain special tasks during this turbulent phase in RSS' history; although he was recognised for his stellar work in the United Provinces, he was yet to be recognised as someone high up in the organisation's pecking order.

Interestingly, Upadhyaya's trajectory was very similar to the RSS' at the time—the organisation was yet to plunge into mass-based politics either like the Congress or the Hindu Mahasabha, or even the Muslim League. Neither was Deendayal aiming to be a people's leader, as he was more inclined towards understanding the ideological underpinning of the outfit. He was often seen in the company of students and scholars in universities, and later began indoctrinating them into the sangh's philosophy.

Once he had settled into his job as sah-prant pracharak in 1945, Upadhyaya took the lead in establishing the education cell for the RSS in UP, which was a crucial arm for the organisation for communicating its ideology and programmes amongst families of its volunteers. In time, Deendayal's initiative on education was taken forward and the activities by these multiple cells were consolidated by Balasaheb Deoras under the umbrella of a new affiliate, Vidya Bharti[5] (see chapter, Balasaheb Deoras, p. 247).

He also set up a publishing house in Lucknow called the Rashtra Dharam Prakashan which brought out books and other literature to propagate the RSS' ideology. But of all his endeavours, Deendayal's most significant contribution was the setting up of the *Panchjanya* magazine in 1945, which is since acknowledged as the official mouthpiece of the RSS, and a platform for furthering its ideology. (It must be mentioned here that the magazine was later re-launched with much fanfare on 14 January 1948, with the late Atal Bihari Vajpayee as its first editor.)

Meanwhile, it was Deendayal Upadhyaya's engagement with the written word which came in handy in 1949 during the drafting of the RSS' constitution. As was obvious, Deendayal's initial years in the RSS were spent more on intellectual pursuits than furthering his career prospects, and it was his proclivity towards academics and pedagogy which later made it difficult for him to be a hard-nosed political animal, but more of which later.

Meanwhile in April 1946, Bhaurao Deoras decided to put Deendayal's literary talent to better use and requested him to write historical fiction for children. The larger intent of the project was based on the premise that not only was there a dearth of suitable literature for the young minds, but a version of history that was biased when viewed from the prism of ancient Indian precepts. In 1946, Deendayal wrote a novella titled, *Samrat Chandragupta* on the life of a king who was said to have unified the country. In what was ostensibly a children's book, Deendayal inserted a bit of polemic in its Preface, acknowledging that the events in the book 'are true despite the concerted efforts of European scholars and their blind followers among Indian historians (*sic*), to distort them to serve their own purpose and vested interests.'[6]

The sangh parivar's objections to the distortion of Indian history, particularly by Left-leaning historians is well documented. However, the first red flag in the context was raised by Deendayal Upadhyaya who had perceptively blurred the lines between folklore and history, and wrote in *Samrat Chandragupta* that the, 'readers of this book need not (*sic*) be told everything about the maze of historical facts.'[7]

After the great success of his maiden book, Deendayal Upadhyaya took on a more challenging subject in 1947 and began writing about Adi Shankaracharya, the saint-philosopher from Kerala who is revered amongst other things for lending a definitive form to Hinduism. Titled eponymously as *Jagat Guru: Adi Shankaracharya*, Deendayal perhaps intended his readers to go beyond the philosophical contents of the book and said that his 'objective was to inspire the youth to look back to the country's glorious past, take pride in it and dedicate their lives to the revival of the ancient glory.'[8] This idea of invoking India's 'glorious' past and exhorting the youth to 'revive' it as part of their duty to the nation is what the RSS and its political affiliates have held on to for years.

That Upadhyaya idolised Adi Shankaracharya was not in doubt, and it was manifest in the book that the author drew inspiration from the saint-philosopher's attempt at countering the spread of Buddhism. It was therefore not surprising when it was argued that the 'methodology adopted by Shankaracharya to counter the Buddhist threat resembled to a large extent the methodology of the RSS and its thinking.'[9]

Although *Jagat Guru* was a novel in Hindi, it's still considered authentic 'history' within the sangh parivar and treated as an important treatise on one of Hinduism's greatest thinkers. Meanwhile, the book had had such an impact on its author that Deendayal was guided by the belief that 'action does not lie in mere sermonising, but in truly inspiring and motivating one's emotions; it must appeal to the heart and not to the barren intellect.'[10] It was perhaps from here on that he began rejecting everything which had an association with the materialistic world, and was drawn more towards character-building of the RSS and its cadre.

Widening the Horizons

In the mid-Forties, the idea of independence and with it the partition of the subcontinent, was fast becoming a reality. Despite its apolitical underpinning, the RSS was bitterly opposed to the cleaving of the nation, which was best explained by Deendayal Upadhyaya who said that an,

> undivided India is not only a symbol of geographical oneness, but it manifests the oneness of Indian life....Undivided India is not just a political slogan...it is the basis of our life.[11]

The premise formed part of a booklet that he wrote five years after Partition, titled *Akhand Bharat Kyon?* or 'Why Undivided India?' His essential argument being that India was more a cultural entity than a geo-political unit, and that Muslims and Christians were essentially part of this 'oneness' that was unequivocally Hindu in nature. Most importantly, Upadhyaya analysed the very idea of India's freedom that was obtained after a long struggle on 15 August 1947, and bemoaned the fact that,

> independence was announced by unfurling the tricolour from the ramparts of Red Fort, but Ravi (the river), at whose banks we had adopted a resolution of complete freedom, had been snatched away from us.[12]

In a bitter indictment of the Two-Nation theory, which had unfolded at the time of his political initiation, Upadhyaya wrote in the booklet that,

> by calling the Khilafat movement a nationalist movement, we not only put a blot on our nationalism, we also generated a feeling in the Muslims that they need not give up (*sic*) following the external forces for continuing to remain Indian nationals.[13]

Akhand Bharat Kyon? is considered to be the first comprehensive analysis of inter-community relations by the sangh in post-Independent India. 'Hindu–Muslim problem remains what it was,' wrote Upadhyaya in the booklet, and how,

> political parties have adopted the mixed culture and heritage as the basis of their operations and separatism and secessionism are on the rise, providing justification for the creation of Pakistan.

Upadhyaya was of the view that adherence to a unitary concept of the nation could have prevented Partition, and 'if the Congress leaders had stood their ground and helped the awakening among the rank and file of Indians.' He criticised the Indian National Congress for its lack of resolve when presented with the partition plan, 'British could have been forced to leave behind an undivided India by handing power to the Congress.'[14]

He was also unsparing in his denunciation of the Muslims in their insistence of maintaining a distinct identity:

> War (with Pakistan) is not a means to bring about an undivided India. War can only bring about geographic oneness, not national integration....We have to work for an undivided India...Muslims who are backward as compared to our national parameters will associate themselves with us (*sic*) if we give up this policy of compromise and appeasement...If we want unity, we must adopt the yardstick of Indian nationalism, which is Hindu nationalism, and Indian culture, which is Hindu culture. Let us allow all other streams to merge with this mainstream Bhagirathi. Yamuna will merge with it. So will Ganga, shedding all its pollution. And one continuous Bhagirathi will flow throughout India.

What is particularly telling in the above passage is the usage of the 'rivers' analogy as a tool for cultural integration, and how 'Ganga', invoked as the holiest river in India, shall shed 'all its pollution' to transform into a single national stream.

The overt politicisation of the sangh ideology as evidenced in his writings had occurred after the RSS was proscribed following Mahatma Gandhi's assassination in January 1948. As mentioned previously, Deendayal was Bhaurao Deoras' 'discovery', and after setting up a unit in the United Provinces, he had become part of a group of pracharaks which advocated mass contact programmes to ensure that the RSS remained relevant even during the ban. Yet, unlike Balasaheb Deoras, Upadhyaya didn't conform to the view that the RSS needed to formally set up a political wing. He along with several others agreed with M.S. Golwalkar's view of keeping a close watch on the developments within the Congress, which was in the midst of a churn.

* * *

As mentioned earlier, in November 1949, the Congress Working Committee had adopted a resolution, backed by Deputy Prime Minister Sardar Vallabhbhai Patel, proposing the entry of RSS members into the party. This was recommended not only after the ban on the RSS for its alleged role in the murder of Gandhi, but also in the absence of Prime Minister Nehru who was away on an official tour to the US.

On his return from America, Jawaharlal had promptly reversed the proposal and said that the Congress could only admit members who were part of its volunteer bodies like the Sewa Dal. With the hope of the so-called grand alliance dissipating, Syama Prasad Mookerjee, leader of the Hindu Mahasabha and part of Nehru's interim Cabinet as Minister of Industry and Supplies (who resigned in April 1950), urged the RSS' sarsanghchalak Golwalkar to grant him permission to establish a political party forthwith, which was turned down. Eventually, after Sardar Vallabhbhai Patel's death in December 1950, and with the impending general elections, Mookerjee took the plunge and established in early May 1951 what he called a 'People's Party' in West Bengal.

Despite Golwalkar's scepticism towards mainstream politics, the move by Mookerjee was like a shot in the arm for the cadre, and it was planned that prior to launching the party at a national level, the state units be first established. Subsequently by September 1951, the Bharatiya Jana Sangh's state units were set up in UP, Punjab, PEPSU, Karnataka, Bihar, Rajasthan, Orissa (now Odisha), Madhya Bharat (now Madhya Pradesh), and Delhi. Deendayal Upadhyaya was sent on deputation to the Jana Sangh in UP, where he had begun his career as an RSS pracharak.

In less than a year, he became one of the most trusted lieutenants of Syama Prasad Mookerjee, and by the time of the Jana Sangh's first plenary session in Kanpur in December 1952, he was elevated as the general secretary of the party with the additional responsibility of piloting seven of its fifteen resolutions.

One of the first and most significant resolutions drafted by Deendayal was on the 'cultural revival', which redefined the RSS' philosophy while emphasising on the following: education must be based on national (read Hindu; *emphasis mine*) culture; the revival of Sanskrit and the acceptance of Devanagari script 'for all languages of the country[15]'; rewriting of history on the 'right lines, so that it is the history of the people of India and not of those who committed aggression on her[16]'; and launching a campaign amongst Hindus to 'take up the noble task of Indianisation of general life and of those sections of the Indian national being which were shaken out of national moorings and were made to look outside the country for inspiration.'[17]

In a way, the resolution was a precursor to his booklet, *Akhand Bharat Kyon?* and was viewed by many as a counter to the Congress' emphasis on India's compositeness. In his introduction to the resolution, Upadhyaya proclaimed that in the recent centuries, India's unity was often tested because of the constant reiteration of its diversity which prevented its citizens from being knitted into one nation on the basis of a single or homogenous cultural tradition. Unlike the Hindu Mahasabha which rejected Muslims as part of the Indian mainstream, Upadhyaya referred to them and the Christians as 'different parts of the same body.'

Yet another resolution which bore Deendayal's unmistakable stamp at the Kanpur plenary was one which laid greater emphasis on organisation-building and social issues, as opposed to political activism. As mentioned earlier, unlike Syama Prasad Mookerjee who was insistent that the Jana Sangh plunges into electoral politics, Upadhyaya took a long-term view and pressed for building a robust network of cadre.

The first plenary session of the Jana Sangh was a great success as evidenced by the thunderous applause for Dr Mookerjee's proclamation: 'Give me two Deendayals, and I will completely change the face of this nation.'

The public endorsement by the Jana Sangh chief guaranteed Deendayal Upadhyaya's unhindered rise in the party thereafter. He remained in office as general secretary for fifteen years until December 1967 when he was elevated as Jana Sangh president which was at variance with RSS' philosophy that pracharaks should remain as general secretaries with overall responsibility of the organisation, and not take up the role of a titular head. However, Upadhyaya who had prior experience of setting up the organisation in UP, managed to circumvent every objection that may have come in his way and discharged the twin duties of pracharak and president of the Jana Sangh. In his memoirs, L.K. Advani wrote that although there were several party presidents from 1953 (after Syama Prasad's death) to 1967, everybody knew that 'Deendayalji, its General Secretary in charge of the organisation, was the mind, heart and soul of the party. As a matter of fact, he was more than the organisational head of the party. He was its philosopher, guide and motivator all rolled into one.'[18]

However, if it wasn't for certain extraneous reasons, and most importantly, if history hadn't been unkind to certain men, then Deendayal Upadhyaya may not have become the president of the Jana Sangh. Almost a decade after Deendayal became the axis of the Jana Sangh, the one-time Congress President Purushottam Das Tandon who'd locked horns with Nehru over the 1949 resolution to admit members of the RSS into the Congress party, died in 1962, almost a forgotten man. Deendayal wrote an evocative obituary in the *Organiser,* mentioning that if Tandon had not resigned as Congress president in 1951 (under pressure from Prime Minister Nehru), 'probably the Bharatiya Jana Sangh would not have come into existence.'[19] It was ironical that the internecine squabbles within the Congress over the proposed role of the RSS in the party, and Nehru's striking down of any such suggestion, had indirectly resulted in the birth of the Jana Sangh.

Similarly, but for Deendayal Upadhyaya, the Jana Sangh would have either folded up, or lurched from one crisis to another post

Mookerjee's tragic death in June 1953. As per its constitution, not only did the Jana Sangh restrict the tenure of its president to one year, there was no succession plan for any eventuality in case the founder-president either left the party, or as was proven later, died. Although there were several claimants to the post of president, including N.C. Chatterjee who was one of the founders of the Hindu Mahasabha, nobody came close to S.P. Mookerjee either in stature or erudition. After a few months of his death, the proposal to merge the Jana Sangh with the Hindu Mahasabha was revived yet again, but Deendayal Upadhyaya had rejected it outright. His ideological commitment to the RSS notwithstanding, there were three other reasons which had made the merger impossible—first, there were major differences, albeit nuanced in their definitions of what constituted Hindu nationalism; second, certain influential RSS leaders, especially M.S. Golwalkar, were sceptical about V.D. Savarkar's overt opposition to RSS' continuous efforts in organisation-building; third and most importantly, despite Savarkar's acquittal in Mahatma Gandhi's assassination case, the incident was not only fresh in public memory, but had resulted in a national outrage. It was precisely for these reasons that Upadhyaya had openly declared his opposition to the viewpoint that, 'since the Hindu Mahasbha has a galaxy of leaders and the Jana Sangh none, the two organisations should merge (into one).'[20]

Finally, a couple of months after Syama Prasad Mookerjee's death, Mauli Chandra Sharma, a one-time Congress leader-turned-RSS supporter, was appointed the acting president of the Jana Sangh. The new president was familiar with the internal dynamics of the Jana Sangh which was largely dominated by RSS pracharaks with whom he had once worked closely in Delhi after Partition. Yet, in what was deemed to be unwise, he attempted to seize control of the party—

for instance, his open defiance of Deendayal's move to nominate an executive council which was to function as an independent authority of the party. The power struggle between the two continued for most of 1954, until Sharma was shown the door, and Deendayal inducted the low-profile S.A. Sohoni, who was the sanghchalak of Bihar, as president of the Jana Sangh. With this unusual or rather out-of-turn appointment, Deendayal had ensured the end to the last vestiges of an external influence over the Jana Sangh. In retaliation, several members of the Jana Sangh had decided to quit, but Upadhyaya had paid no heed and remained resolute in ensuring the continuance of RSS' influence over the party.

However, this wasn't the only instance of Upadhyaya forcing his hand on the party. In the decade and a half of managing party affairs, he had handpicked a team of new generation pracharaks. In 1965, at the Jana Sangh's landmark plenary session in Vijayawada—as it was here that Upadhyaya had unveiled his philosophy of Integral Humanism, which has since then been the official doctrine of the BJP—he'd ensured Bachhraj Vyas' elevation as party president. Two of Jana Sangh's senior leaders at the time, Atal Bihari Vajpayee and Balraj Madhok had vehemently opposed the decision and boycotted the session. Yet Deendayal was undeterred, because it was a matter of principle for him which carried more weight than an individual's brilliance, clout, and capacity to sway the public.

Upadhyaya's insistence on retaining Jana Sangh's distinct identity had resurfaced in 1962 when yet another proposal for its merger with the Swatantra Party and Ram Rajya Party (both Right-wing entities) was suggested, and obviously rejected. It may be recalled that in the late 1980s, L.K. Advani had used the phrase 'splendid isolation' while describing BJP's loneliness in Indian politics. In a way, the genesis of this long period of isolation could be attributed to Deendayal who had ensured that every external voice was silenced to protect the distinct ideological base of his party.

It wasn't just the ideas which he had rejected, but Upadhyaya was strongly against forging political alliances for electoral gains. In an article in the *Seminar* magazine, he had written that all such arrangements 'degenerate into a struggle for power by opportunist elements coming together in the interest of expediency.'[21] From the time he had taken charge of the Jana Sangh, Deendayal was guided by the principle of building a 'party with a difference'—another phrase which was resurrected by L.K. Advani in the 1990s. As an aside, it may be worthwhile to mention that when Advani was elected Jana Sangh president in 1973, the *Organiser* had headlined its report on the Kanpur plenary session as: 'Second Deendayal at Helm of BJS.'[22]

Upadhyaya was loathe to the idea of fighting elections and grabbing political power as the means to an end of a political party's existence—social transformation was the kernel of Deendayal's political philosophy, which he viewed as the ultimate objective. He was not only exacting towards party colleagues who were obsessed with the pursuance of power, but curiously, even ordinary voters. In 1955, he wrote in the *Organiser*:

> We do not have to amass popular support but only of those who can follow our ideals...we do not simply want popular support, it must be an idealistic popular support.

His obduracy towards accepting the realities of electoral politics notwithstanding, Deendayal considered even political movements or agitations as deterrents for coercing the State into accepting sundry demands, however unfair. He recommended that dissent of such nature should act as tools for furthering a party's ideology and for securing greater support, than merely as issue-based endorsements. His recommendation of avoiding confrontational politics also extended to Opposition parties who he felt were perennially in conflict with the government of the day. This was strange, considering the Congress was in power at the Centre, and was bitterly opposed to everything that the Jana Sangh stood for. Deendayal attributed the genesis of agitational politics to the Indian freedom struggle which he felt had encouraged 'negative' patriotism, and which needed to be replaced with constructive nation-building in which the government and people could forge a partnership. Amongst all his postulations, what was most significant was his curious belief that a democracy should function in a somewhat 'controlled' manner:

> State suppression may benefit political parties that play the role of political mediator for a short while between the State and the People, but it does not bode good for the nation.[23]

As is obvious, this above-mentioned viewpoint was contradictory to his proposal for a collaboration between the people and State.

But ultimately, it was left to his senior colleagues in the sangh to convince him to view the situation pragmatically in the ongoing tussle between politics and ideology. In the May 1963 by-elections for the four Lok Sabha seats, three in Uttar Pradesh and one in Gujarat, Deendayal finally agreed to contest his maiden election from Jaunpur (UP) after the seat had fallen vacant following the sudden death of a Jana Sangh leader, Thakur Bhramjeet Singh.

Meanwhile, Deendayal found a perfect ally in M.S. Golwalkar

whose antipathy towards conventional politics was well known. He was also of the view that pracharaks should 'organise the organisation,' and maintain a distance from power politics which may result in any form of gain. On the other hand was Balasaheb Deoras, who not only patronised Upadhyaya but was also known to challenge Golwalkar openly, who had stepped in at this crucial juncture to forge an understanding between several non-Congress parties to jointly put up consensus candidates in the elections.

Deendayal Upadhyaya lost the by-election by a substantial margin and for two reasons—first, Deoras had 'not counted on an uncharacteristic pulling together of the factionalized Uttar Pradesh Congress Party[24]'; and second, the Jana Sangh had omitted to notice that all the previous winners from his constituency were local Rajputs, while Deendayal was a Brahmin and had therefore failed to muster votes. The third and possibly the most important reason was that the combined-Opposition candidates from UP were stalwarts in their own right including, Acharya J.B. Kripalani from Amroha, and the Socialist leader, Dr Ram Manohar Lohia, who had contested from Farrukhabad. The fourth seat from Gujarat was also being fought by a leader of considerable repute, the Swatantra Party general secretary, Minoo Masani.

When viewed from the surface, it was a failure for the Jana Sangh, but it also revealed that sixteen years after independence and a year before his death in 1964, Pandit Nehru was perhaps losing his grip over politics. However, Upadhyaya's candidature was the crucial first step in forming an anti-Congress alliance in post-Independent India, which later crystallised into the Janata Party in 1977. But despite the coalition (of which Jana Sangh was a part) which had become a necessity post the Emergency, Deendayal resisted the inevitability of alliances or even if he had acquiesced, as he had done in 1967–68 to the Jana Sangh joining coalition governments in several states, he viewed it as a transitory phenomenon, whereas active practitioners of parliamentary politics like his colleague, Atal Bihari Vajpayee viewed them as essential agents of change.

A year after his failed bid to enter the Lok Sabha, Deendayal Upadhyaya, unbeknownst to himself, realised the advantage of political alliances. In April 1964, ironically just six weeks prior to Nehru's demise on 27 May, he had issued a joint statement with the iconic Socialist leader, Dr Ram Manohar Lohia. This revolutionary, albeit unimaginable coming together of two leaders who represented opposing ideological spectrums, was not only the result of their concurrence on a significant issue, but their joint opposition to the ruling Congress party's stand on nuclear disarmament.

The sworn nationalist that Deendayal Upadhyaya was, he strongly demanded that India seeks US' assistance in developing a nuclear bomb, and obtained Dr Lohia's endorsement. In 1964, the two issued a joint statement in favour of the 'formation of some sort of Indo-Pak Confederation.' Even today, the joint declaration is cited as one of Upadhyaya's major political successes after he had secured Lohia's backing on what was till then two extremely contentious arguments put out by the sangh. First, 'guaranteeing the protection of life and property of Hindus in Pakistan is the responsibility of the government of India,'; second, the assertion that 'the existence of India and Pakistan as two separate entities is an artificial situation.'

While the second point in the declaration was a de facto ratification of the idea of Akhand Bharat, because it questioned the reality of Partition which had happened a decade-and-a-half earlier, the first statement was a geo-political disaster.

A Political Theorist

As an RSS ideologue, Deendayal Upadhyaya continuously stressed on the need to Indianise 'western concepts of the nation, western secularism, western democracy.'[25] For instance, he was sceptical about ushering in adult franchise prior to increasing literacy levels—curiously, a typical elitist argument that links political judgement with formal education, thereby serving as a tool for exclusion. Deendayal viewed Indian democracy as a system which made it imperative for a 'government to be run through mutual discussion,'[26] as enshrined in ancient Indian traditions, but reasoned thereafter that, 'if we carry it to the other extreme, it could prove troublesome.'

Although he had studied European governance systems in detail, his overall hypothesis demonstrated little understanding of the delineation between totalitarian regimes, dictatorships, or even democracies—it stemmed from what was obviously simplistic, that everything western was alien, and therefore unacceptable. His famous argument that 'even dictators like Hitler, Mussolini and Stalin did not go against democratic principles,' was not only self-contradictory, but left a lot to be desired in comprehending political theory.

His open endorsement of the 'controlled democracy' concept also led to his distinctive approach towards public awareness programmes. According to Upadhyaya, building of public opinion 'is a cultural process. In dictatorial communist regimes it is called brainwashing or depriving the dissidents of their rights...in so-called democracies, it leads to chaos...'[27] His unusual views on mass awareness programmes were however in perfect sync with the division of labour that he proposed—that the government must be entrusted with building democracy; campaigns for moulding public opinion should be the preserve of 'selfless' ascetics; and governance was the prerogative of an elected government. Of the lot, the suggestion to entrust renunciates with the responsibility of creating mass awareness programmes was most telling, because that in turn minimised the onus on a particular government in case its policies didn't find favour with the group and vice-versa. The principle of integrating ascetics or sadhus in official programmes was clearly driven by the intent to provide official sanctity to pursuits of faith and evolved from the idea of creating a system based on the 'fusion of both materialism and spiritualism'[28] in contrast to 'Western culture (which) is materialistic.'[29]

Therefore, public opinion which was orchestrated by spiritual or religious leaders was to be honoured by a government after a 'controlled' dialogue. He further hypothesised that such an interaction or relationship was to be governed by three main principles: tolerance and discipline; selflessness; and respect for the rule of law. On the face of it, the ideas seem simply righteous, but on a deeper analysis, flawed and impractical as well. For instance, what Upadhyaya said in reference to the first principle, 'A disciplined person stands between a vocal person and a dumb person...democracy can be successful only (*sic*) when a citizen understands his responsibilities and discharges them to the best of his abilities.'[30] Upadhyaya clearly disapproved of vocalising protest, reflecting his discomfort with democracy and the right to dissent. According to him, for a democratic State to be successful, it wasn't incumbent upon a government to ensure that the rights of its citizens weren't violated in any manner. But he was however silent about the options in case the government did not act according to its brief.

While pontificating about the electoral system, Deendayal argued that for it to succeed, good candidates, good parties, and finally good voters were mandatory. While political parties must be principled, and shun casteism, Upadhyaya held an odd viewpoint about ex-royals as electoral candidates in a democracy, who he said, 'must be active in the country's politics,'[31] but he contradicted it by saying that political parties should avoid nominating them solely for their princely status and wealth.

For voters, Deendayal had a long list of suggestions as follows: do not vote for a party, but for its ideals; don't support an individual, but opt for the party; and opt for an individual, and not for his or her money power, or be 'misled by hype.'[32] In retrospect, these seemingly 'good to do' list seems ironical because much like M.S. Golwalkar, Deendayal didn't consider democracy to be an ideal system of governance in the first place, but was of the view that it was the 'least evil' way of running a government.

Of all his theories, what stood out prominently was his rejection of India's federal system and as a natural corollary, its administrative and governance structure. His recommendation was for a centralised system, and he objected to India being defined as a Union of States, and protested against the enactment of Reorganisation of States on linguistic principles. (He demanded the setting up of a commission to reorganise states, which was eventually established by the Nehru government in 1954.)

While he was in favour of centralisation, Upadhyaya also opposed a 'unitary constitution' and suggested that we should 'decentralise our fiscal and other resources.' It must be mentioned here that the idea of cooperative federalism, which forms a significant part of Prime

Minister Narendra Modi's governance module, is an expansion of the premise.

* * *

Deendayal Upadhyaya shall be best remembered in history for the two seminal texts that he wrote within a span of seven years—*The Two Plans: Promises, Performance and Prospects* (1958), and *Integral Humanism* (1965). However of the two, the latter which is essentially a detailed hypotheses on philosophical issues with a bearing on the larger economic vision, merits greater attention because it has survived for more than half a century as the 'official' philosophy of the Jana Sangh, and later, the BJP.

At one level, the theory of Integral Humanism which was adopted as the 'Principles and Policies of the Jana Sangh' at the plenary session in Vijayawada in February 1965, was considered by the party to be self-sufficient in terms of a well-argued political thought. But according to Deendayal's detractors, one of the biggest shortcomings of the theory was in its assumption that India is a civilisational concept, and not an idea which had evolved over centuries. It was felt that the text reflected Deendayal's very own idea of his party's raison d'être vis-à-vis his position in it. While at a personal level, there was often an overlap and confusion over what he was first and foremost, a swayamsevak or general secretary, there was a complete lack of clarity over whether the party's primary objective was to be part of active politics, or consolidate Hindu society.

As mentioned earlier, Golwalkar had a pathological distaste for politics and considered it an immoral influence on his cadre. Similarly, the RSS was unequivocal in its opinion that a society or nation had greater value than the State, but it was paradoxical for a political party like Jana Sangh to have endorsed such a view. Just as the other affiliates of the RSS—the Bharatiya Mazdoor Sangh (BMS) or Vishwa Hindu Parishad (VHP)—are primarily committed to their respective agendas which are dovetailed into the overall framework of the sangh, the Jana Sangh needed to be more independent than what a pracharak as organising secretary-driven organisation desired it to be. There is enough empirical evidence to prove that since its inception in the mid-Eighties, whenever senior leaders of the BJP have acquiesced to diktats issued from Nagpur, the party has tended to veer off from its primary goals.

As the largest cadre-based party in the world with more than a dozen ideological arms, initially the RSS wasn't known to micro-manage the affairs of its affiliates. However, since the mid-Forties, it began a trend of holding annual meetings with its agencies to ensure adherence to a broad code of conduct. Deendayal attended these meetings regularly, but if one analyses the events of the period, it does appear that there was far greater concurrence between him and Jana Sangh's 'handlers' in the RSS. Upadhyaya also required clarity regarding his twin roles, and was gradually found wanting in his ability to balance between ideology and active politics.

There is no doubt that it was the theory of Integral Humanism which established the theory of Hindu political philosophy in post-Independent India. Upadhyaya began work on it in 1964–65 and after presenting it at the Jana Sangh's Vijayawada plenary session where it was accepted as the party's core philosophy, he elaborated on it in a series of four lectures in Bombay in April 1965.

According to L.K. Advani, Upadhyaya's choice of the title was with the intent of contrasting his party's ideological premise with that of M.N. Roy's philosophical theory of Radical Humanism. For instance, Integral

Humanism rejected the class theory primarily because it was espoused by the Communists. Instead, Upadhyaya's theory recommended that different sections of society should work together, and in this context he referred to a peculiar analogy to elucidate the relationship between the oppressor and the oppressed: 'A flower is what it is because of its petals, and the worth of the petals lies in remaining with the flower and adding to its beauty.'[33] In Upadhyaya's political construct, associations or loyalties were either civilisational, cultural or religious. People were inter-connected not because of class interests, but because of a common religious and cultural heritage. In effect, this meant that a Hindu factory worker would have greater commonalities with his Hindu owner, than his non-Hindu colleagues on a shop floor.

In Anand Gandhi's much acclaimed film, *Ship of Theseus* (2103), the theme explores the notion of whether an object whose parts have been replaced bit by bit can be considered to be the original entity. This was indeed a philosophical poser, and had perhaps left many viewers pondering over a definite answer. In Integral Humanism, Deendayal provides a definite answer to such a conundrum which was fundamental to his concept of what constituted nationhood and the culture of a State. In the text, he narrates a story about a barber who is shaving a customer's beard and boasting about his razor, which he says is sixty years old. The customer stops the barber and asks him how old was the handle of the razor, which was still shining? 'Three months,' says the barber.

'And, the steel?' he asks again.

'Three years old,' he says.

Upadhyaya then argues that although both components of the razor were replaced, 'its identity was intact. Similarly a nation too has a soul,' which he defined as *chiti*. In fact he introduced this concept by first expanding on the concept of dharma or righteousness. According to him, dharma was neither a religion nor sect and also not an entirely personal matter as his detractors had contended. Dharma for him was a 'much wider term with extensive connotation.'[34] Deendayal argued that dharma was 'our chiti, the inner spirit that pervades all of us.'[35] He further introduced the idea of *virat (shakti)* which according to him was the power that energises a nation. While chiti which is 'fundamental and is central to the nation from its very beginning... the soul determines the direction in which the nation is to advance culturally. Whatever is in accordance with chiti, is included in culture.'

When viewed against pluralism and the diverse cultures of India, Deendayal Upadhyaya's thesis seems inadequate, except in endorsing the majoritarian view in the country. His argument is further reinforced by his claim that only a strong virat (shakti) can ensure the success of a democracy, and once it's awakened, then every kind of conflict ceases to exist. Yet, in a country which not only boasts of diversity, but a large workforce, it is a trifle strange why Deendayal had excluded the promise of a collective power.

In conclusion, the core objective of Integral Humanism was to 'create a Bharat which will excel...to achieve through a sense of unity with the entire creation, a state even higher than that of a complete human being; to become Narayan (god) from *nar* (man).' The theory is therefore primarily addressed to a Hindu faithful, and as a result of which it remains an exclusionist philosophy which may not appeal to the adherents of cultural and religious pluralism.

The Economist

In contrast to the philosophical nature of Integral Humanism, *The*

Two Plans: Promises, Performance and Prospects was a general critique of Nehruvian economics, focussing on the First (1951–56) and Second (1956–61) Five Year Plans of the erstwhile Planning Commission, respectively. Interestingly, the assessment while intrinsically economic in nature, was an amalgamation of the four ancient Indian principles or *purusharthas*—artha or wealth, kama or bodily desire, dharma which is righteousness, and finally, moksha, denoting a release from all worldly pleasures or the attainment of salvation. Although the meanings of these four goals have by and large remained constant through centuries, its interpretation and significance in a human being's life have often depended on varying philosophical schools.

Deendayal Upadhyaya placed '*Artha* and *Kama* bracketed between *Dharma* on the left and *Moksha* on the right side of the axis. That raised the thesis that the limits of creating and enjoying *Artha* and *Kama* should be governed by *Dharma* and aimed at *Moksha*.'[36] Therefore, he didn't think that the pursuit of wealth was in anyway unethical, although he did elaborate that both the paucity or excess of it had a negative impact on society. While Deendayal's economic theory was heavily protectionist and had similarities with some of Gandhi's principles, especially his emphasis on encouraging cottage industries to help rural Indian achieve self-sufficiency, his rejection of what he envisaged as the principles governing a 'modern world' were at variance with the Mahatma. Upadhyaya had fundamental disagreements with Nehru's idea of development and in all likelihood wouldn't have seen large dams as the 'temples of modern India'. He argued that it was 'wrong to accept industrialisation as our ultimate objective.' Contrary to his political vision of centralisation of authority in a non-federal set up, the two mainstays of Upadhyaya's economic theory were, decentralisation and the use of technology, which were principally dichotomous in nature.

On the one hand, if he encouraged the use of technology for production, he was against mechanisation and not in favour of using it as a mere tool for speeding up economic progress, which was yet again at variance with Nehru's vision of stepping up growth and infrastructure. His *Two Plans* had a romantic idealism about it, evoking India of the yore in which progress unfolded organically.

As someone who hailed the indigenous sector as a significant element in furthering India's economy, Upadhyaya was not a great votary of the public sector, and criticised the government for constraining the growth of the private sector. His argument being that social justice shall continue to elude India till 'the private sector is encouraged to develop along with the expansion of the public sector and there should be a mechanism to effectively bring this about.'[37] As he was bitterly opposed to Socialism, he recommended the system to encourage individual initiative and enterprise, and wrote that just as 'dictatorship destroys man's creativity in politics, large-scale industrialisation destroys individual enterprise.' Clearly, Upadhyaya did not take into account the factor of individual enterprise in massive industrial projects, and appeared myopically focussed on small-scale enterprises.

As mentioned earlier, as a firm believer in indigenous systems for wealth generation, Deendayal continuously opposed Foreign Direct Investment (FDI) and equally disapproved of Joint Ventures. As one of the earliest votaries of the constitutionally granted, Right to Work, Upadhyaya was of the view that under-employment was bad for society besides of course being detrimental to economic security of an individual; artha as essential for dharma, being his primary belief.

The centrality of village as the engine for economic growth was evident in the first election manifesto of the Jana Sangh in 1951. A short document compared to a long list of promises as is the norm now, it mentioned how villages have been the 'centre of Bharat's life in all times,' and that the 'ideal of *Sarvodaya* cannot be achieved until and unless the village is restored to its original position as the basic economic unit.' The manifesto promised that the Jana Sangh if voted to power, shall usher in *gramtantra* or the hegemony of villages over urban India, which alas didn't come to fruition. Upadhyaya's opposition to Nehruvian economic policies were also evident in his criticism of the Planning Commission, which he said was trying to 'build a pyramid from top.'[38]

Towards the end of his political career, Deendayal Upadhyaya who had made his criticism of public agitations more than evident (yet again) in his seminal Integral Humanism theory, did a volte-face in his maiden presidential speech in 1967. He made a direct reference to 'those who are trying to preserve the *status quo* in the economic and social spheres, are unnerved by popular movement.' Compared to his earlier stance in the early 1950s, Deendayal had now cast his lot with his mentor, Balasaheb Deoras who had a more egalitarian approach to public life in comparison to M.S. Golwalkar. This in effect was the beginning of the 'Leftward turn' that the Jana Sangh was seen to have taken, but the major part of it unfolded after Deendayal's unfortunate death.

The Tragedy

In December 1967, Deendayal Upadhyaya became the president of the Jana Sangh. However, as mentioned earlier, his elevation was fraught with controversy as his colleague and senior member of the party, Balraj Madhok had also thrown his hat in the ring. But the RSS pressed on and besides elevating Deendayal, it also nominated Sunder Singh Bhandari, the lawyer-turned-RSS worker from Rajasthan as vice president of Jana Sangh. Upadhyaya's presidentship coincided with the 1967 general elections in which the Jana Sangh won thirty-five Lok Sabha seats, and 257 seats in the state assemblies. This was up from fourteen and 119 in 1962, and the credit for this was largely attributed to the Deoras–Upadhyaya combine who had eventually chosen the path of political pragmatism as against ideological purity. It would be safe to surmise that much like the personal battle that he had waged throughout the initial years of his career, Deendayal Upadhyaya was once again at the crossroads.

The encouraging results during the elections had forced a debate within the Jana Sangh whether it should join the coalition governments in some states of north India, like Haryana. Finally, Deendayal had sided with the likes of Atal Bihari Vajpayee who was in favour of becoming part of the coalition, but certain voices within the RSS made their protestations loud and clear. As mentioned earlier, Deendayal had past experience of having worked in the United Provinces and had instilled the ideal of bolstering and transforming Hindu society as the sangh's primary objective amongst its members. For most of his fifteen-year-long tenure as a revered member of the Jana Sangh, Deendayal Upadhyaya continued to be viewed as an avowed pracharak, but post 1967 when he had become non-theoretical, his devoted followers who had been nurtured by him on a diet of ideological puritanism, raised objections against his quest for political power.

His presidential address in Calicut (now, Kozhikode) in December 1967 was a clinching evidence of how he was torn between running a party, keeping his core ideological beliefs intact, and facing up to the emerging challenges in Indian politics. Upadhyaya confessed that although with the 1967 general elections, 'the process has started for Congress's gradual withering away,' the 'results left much to be desired.' His reasoning was that it had led to several post-election problems which he classified into three broad categories. First, the 'problems pertaining to the politics of the transition, inter-party relations, instability of coalition ministries and floor-crossing.' Second, how the emerging situation was testing the Indian 'constitutional set-up' as such scenarios were hitherto unknown. Third, how the resultant instability was aiding the 'problems relating to economic, defence, home and foreign affairs,'[39] which he attributed to mishandling by the Congress party. Upadhyaya was of the view that although the first set of concerns were immediate and 'evoke the maximum of public comment and debate,' the other two also required immediate attention.

Despite the absence of political morality which had willy-nilly become incumbent on ensuring political stability, Upadhyaya took no initiative in diluting his party's idealism. It merits mentioning that in 1960 he had ensured the passing of a resolution at the party's annual session that acted as a code of conduct for parliamentarians and legislators. Sadly in recent years, the BJP has also abandoned certain set of rules like, 'walking out of the House and a tendency to create chaos through shouting or sloganeering.'

Deendayal's most innovative and lasting contribution to the Indian political discourse was his proposal to confront the problem of political defection or 'floor-crossing' as he had termed it. The issue had merited focus as a result of the fragmented verdicts in 1967 in Punjab, Bihar, West Bengal, Kerala, Madhya Pradesh, Uttar Pradesh and Rajasthan. The respective state governments were dismissed by the Governors because of the number of defections from a clutch of non-Congress parties. Meanwhile, the Constitution was silent on how Governors should conduct themselves in order to be seen as non-partisan while dismissing a government.

In 1967 during his presidential address, Upadhyaya had drawn attention to the 'arbitrary conduct' of Governors and had demanded that the process of their appointment be made transparent.

He had also added that although India had opted for the Westminster model,

> we should try to mould this to suit our changing politics. A convention can be accepted that no government would resign except on the adoption of a no-confidence vote against it by the legislature. Another convention which may be evolved...is that if a majority of members of a legislature request the Speaker that the House be convened, a meeting of the legislature would be invariably summoned.[40]

Preceding the famous S.R. Bommai judgement by almost three decades, Deendayal's suggestions were brilliantly prescient. Even as recently as May 2018 in Karnataka, the absence of transparent guidelines for Governors over crucial issues following a hung verdict had resulted in questions being raised about the sanctity of such a constitutional position.

Meanwhile in 1967, Deendayal was faced with a challenge of dealing with members who had joined the Jana Sangh from other political parties and were therefore alien to the culture of the RSS. In order to keep them under check, and confined to the acceptable ideological framework, Upadhyaya came up with a two-pronged strategy: first, he inducted large number of pracharaks into the party and second, he decided to 'place the legislative members more closely under the direct support of the organisation.'[41]

He also entrusted the 'party cadre' with the task of taking forward the 'programmes of the party or government to people, translate them into realities for the people. These programmes...become the vehicle to continue to build and take the organisation from strength to strength.'[42] This was in continuation of the process that he had initiated in 1960 when he had spelt out his goal of appointing one pracharak for every district unit of the party.

Although it happened after he was long gone, it was one of Deendayal's initiatives which was at the root of the dual membership controversy in the Janata Party in 1978–79. The dispute which had triggered the collapse of India's first non-Congress government at the Centre, was chiefly due to Upadhyaya mandating that the 'party cadre' be entrusted with the task of taking the 'programmes of the party or government to people, translate them into realities for the people.'

After the bitter experience of the Janata Party experiment, the BJP remained circumspect for many years about its association with the RSS, especially when it was at the helm of the National Democratic Alliance (NDA) from 1998–2004. It was only post-2014 after its spectacular victory led by Narendra Modi that the party leadership stopped being diffident about displaying its association with the RSS.

Ironical though it may sound for a man who lived abstemiously, Deendayal's end was perhaps precipitated by the sudden luxury of comfort which was bestowed upon him by members of his party. All through his life, he had only travelled in a third class train compartment, until he became president in December 1967 when it was decreed that he should now travel only first class.

On 10 February 1968, Deendayal Upadhyaya was in Lucknow when he received news that he was to urgently attend the party's Working Committee meeting in Patna. That same night, his party workers saw him off at the station as he got into the Sealdah–Pathankot Express. However, the train's schedule underwent a last minute change and wasn't any longer bound for Patna. The first class compartment that Deendayal was travelling in was detached from the Sealdah–Pathankot Express, and was instead fastened to the Delhi–Howrah Express at Mughalsarai, the big junction in UP which now bears his name. As scheduled, the train arrived in Patna the next morning, but Deendayal Upadhyaya did not alight from it.

A big commotion had ensued at the Patna station even as party leaders began making frantic enquiries about the missing leader. Meanwhile in Mughalsarai, a body was discovered next to the railway tracks, a short distance away from the platform. A huge crowd had surrounded the unclaimed body when suddenly one voice, belonging incidentally to a Jana Sangh worker, was heard, 'That is Deendayal Upadhyaya ji, the Jana Sangh president.'

He was murdered and the case remains unsolved till date. On 12 February 1968, Deendayal Upadhyaya was cremated in Delhi's Nigambodh Ghat.

In his condolence message, the RSS sarsanghchalak M.S. Golwalkar had likened Deendayal to Yudhishthir's character in the Mahabharata, a man 'who was devoid of any bitterness in word, action and thought.' The comparison was indeed apt because much like the iconic warrior who was torn between righteousness and the horrors of war, Deendayal Upadhyaya was for most part of his life, divided between his commitment to ideology and duty as the head of a political party. However, as one of the most illustrious RSS workers, he had fulfilled what was mandated upon him by his leadership and which was to create a robust space for the organisation in the history of Indian politics. Deendayal Upadhyaya's short octave may have reached an early and macabre end, but with a flourish which remains unmatched in the annals of the RSS.

BALASAHEB DEORAS

In June 1973, at the age of fifty-eight, when he was appointed as sarsanghchalak of the RSS, he had already spent thirty-three years in-waiting. Madhukar Dattatreya Deoras, popularly known as Balasaheb Deoras, was insulin-dependent, which had made him diffident about taking on responsibilities within the sangh.

But as was the norm in the RSS, which espouses strict adherence to authority, when Madhav Sadashiv Golwalkar or Guruji (as he was popularly called) named Balasaheb as his successor, he had accepted it with utmost humility. Despite his initial reluctance, it had turned out to be a wise decision—he presided over the RSS for more than two decades thereafter, and made significant changes to its inherent character and structure. Amongst several other things, his reputation as the quintessential pracharak-activist, the one who is perennially in service of the nation and its people, finally became the reason for his unquestionable supremacy within the RSS.

But that wasn't how it had all begun. Balasaheb Deoras' growth during his initial years in the RSS was limited, and testimony to the internecine squabbles within an organisation which was, as mentioned above, ironically built around the principle of strict adherence to authority*.

The decade-and-a-half beginning the late 1930s was tumultuous for India because in the aftermath of the Second World War, there was no uniformity about its involvement in the effort. Besides, the Muslim League's infamous Lahore Resolution, although conspicuous for its 'glaring absence of details,'[1] had called for a separate country from the Muslim majority parts of undivided India. This was also an equally stormy period for the RSS, marked as it was 'by strong differences between the two most crucial people in the RSS: Golwalkar and Deoras. This is a period that is most guarded in RSS's history.'[2]

Although he was nine years younger than Golwalkar (who was born in 1906), Deoras had reasons for viewing the ascetic-looking Guruji as a usurper. The reason: by the time Golwalkar had entered Hedgewar's charmed circle in the late 1930s, Deoras was already its leading member and was seen by most as a potential successor to his chief (see chapter, Madhav Sadashiv Golwalkar, p. 98).

But it was Golwalkar who had assumed charge of the RSS, about which Balasaheb was openly resentful. In order to subdue his colleague's criticism, Golwalkar often spoke in favour of Deoras and referred to him as Hedgewar's 'alter ego'. But even that didn't cut ice with Deoras who decided to register his protest by staying away from the first meeting called by the newly-anointed chief. His ruse being rather weak—that he was to supervise the official mess in Nagpur to ensure that food was served in time to swayamsevaks. Golwalkar had seen through Deoras' excuse and had responded with a snide remark, 'Real Sarsanghchalak is in the mess. I am the Sarsanghchalak only in

---

* See chapter on Keshav Baliram Hedgewar, p. 1, for the principle of ek chalak anuvartitva or follow one leader.

name, so call him first.'[3] It is however still a mystery if Balasaheb had turned up for the meeting despite the chief's summons. According to a one-time RSS member-turned-critic, 'Absence from the first meeting of the Sarsanghchalak cannot be explained away by innocent anxiety to supervise the kitchen; it is a breach of discipline in an outfit like the RSS.'[4]

The aloofness between the two men continued for a considerable period of time. The veteran RSS leader, M.K. Chauthaiwale, who had a ringside view of the rivalry, gave details of an interesting incident that had occurred between them sometime in 1944–45. Apparently, Golwalkar was once returning to the RSS headquarters—also the dwelling quarters for the top brass—in a tonga with some of his associates, when they had overtaken a group led by Deoras. *'Sacche sarsanghchalak paidal chalte hain,'* (Genuine sarsanghchalaks walk), Balasaheb had said loudly. In return, Golwalkar had responded, *'Aur naqli taange mein'* (And imposters ride in a tonga).[5]

This may sound like light-hearted banter between colleagues, but highlighted the negative undercurrents that existed between two stalwarts of the RSS.

The Beginning

Madhukar Dattatreya Deoras was born in 1915 in Nagpur, and was initiated into the RSS at the young age of eleven. His father, Dattatreya Krishnarao Deoras worked as a junior revenue official and owned a small piece of agricultural land in the district of Balaghat (then part of the Central Provinces, now Madhya Pradesh), adjoining Maharashtra. The large family of eleven (which included nine children) managed within their modest means, and laid a heavy premium on education.

Therefore, the first three children—Diwakar, Bhaskar and Dinkar—followed the traditional career paths and pursued Medicine, Police service, and Law respectively. As a natural corollary, it was expected of Balasaheb to join the civil services, but as mentioned earlier, the young lad had in a way made his intentions clear by joining the RSS. Moreover, he had also initiated his younger brother, Murlidhar aka Bhaurao, to follow him and there came a time when the two were referred to as the 'Deoras brothers' of the RSS, even by serious academicians and scholars. Until his death in 1992, Bhaurao played a significant role in Balasaheb's political career and acted as the 'link man' between the RSS and BJP.[6] It needs to be mentioned here that Balasaheb's entry into the RSS in 1926 as an eleven-year-old was followed by one of the worst episodes of Hindu-Muslim riots in Nagpur in September 1927, when the sangh had trained swayamsevaks in wielding swords, javelins and daggers.[7]

Meanwhile, alongside his political apprenticeship, Balasaheb had continued with his studies and went to the New English High School in Nagpur, and later took a degree in Law.

In 1935, at the young age of Twenty, he was appointed the nagar karyavah or city secretary of the RSS. One of the main reasons for his appointment was his popularity amongst peers—his home would often be abuzz with several swayamsevaks who would spend long hours, and even stay over for dinner.

Balasaheb's father had never forgiven him for opting out of the civil service examination, and his son's large group of political associates bothered him even more. Moreover the family was Brahmin, and the partaking of meals from the kitchen by a motley group of swayamsevaks was a contentious issue, which created a rift between Balasaheb and his mother, Parvathibai.

It must have taken the young man immense courage, but he once confronted his mother and told her firmly that many of his colleagues were not only from the lower castes, but some were even 'untouchables', and added that she shouldn't expect them to either wash the utensils in which they ate, or be served in separate ones. Balasaheb further said that, 'he would never invite his friends home if her treatment of "untouchables" was different. She ultimately gave in, even washing their plates, as the young Deoras would often dine with them.'[8]

In 1937, Balasaheb Deoras obtained his Law degree which coincided with Madhav Golwalkar's rise in the RSS. Two years later in 1939, K.B. Hedgewar sent Balasaheb to Bengal in an effort to widen the organisation's footprint beyond Central India. But within a few months of Balasaheb's arrival, the RSS was struck by a massive tragedy with the passing away of the much-revered K.B. Hedgewar on 21 June 1940. An organisation which had been steered by the grand old sarsanghchalak suddenly felt orphaned, and particularly because he hadn't resolved the issue of succession during his lifetime.

In that seering summer month of June 1940, large number of pracharaks and swayamsevaks had arrived in Nagpur to pay their respects to the patriarch. Balasaheb was also present that day amongst the large gathering of mourners who were also nervous about the future of the RSS which their deceased leader had nurtured with utmost dedication for several years.

On 3 July 1940, the thirteenth day after Hedgewar's passing, the RSS top brass which included the quartet of Dr B.S. Moonje, L.V. Paranjpe, Madhav Golwalkar and Balasaheb Deoras gathered to deliberate about the future*. Dr Moonje's presence in the meeting

* The succession issue within the RSS is detailed in the chapter, Madhav Sadashiv Golwalkar, p. 98.

underscored the fact that the RSS and Hindu Mahasabha had not yet become totally distinct entities, and dual membership in different, particularly rival, organisations was the norm at the time. Secondly, what was also significant was that despite Moonje's disagreements with his one-time protégé, he was present at a crucial meeting and established the fact that amongst Hindu Right-wing groups, political decisions were often influenced by personal relationships.

As mentioned earlier, for many years prior to Hedgewar's death, it was presumed that Balasaheb Deoras would take over the RSS chief's mantle. His early initiation into the organisation was however not the only reason; the other and more significant issue was the reluctance on the part of the other contender, 'Guruji' who was known to be inclined towards eschewing all worldly pursuits. However, when Hedgewar had deputed Balasaheb to proceed to Bengal two months after Golwalkar's appointment as general secretary or sarkaryavah, it seemed like the original plan had been reversed.

Even after eight decades post his death, the mystery of Hedgewar's so-called reneging on his promise to Balasaheb remains unresolved. However, according to some accounts by people within the RSS[9], shortly before Deoras was sent off to Bengal, Hedgewar had summoned him and Golwalkar to his quarters. Thereafter, the ailing sarsanghchalak had told Deoras that although he had wanted to nominate him, he had changed his mind because he had felt that he was still a shade 'immature', and had therefore decided to pass on the baton to Golwalkar. But Hedgewar had also instructed Golwalkar that whenever he wished to pass on the baton, he would have to nominate Deoras as his successor.

As was the norm in the RSS, 'Guruji' had accepted his chief's diktat, albeit reluctantly, laying down two conditions before acquiescing completely—Balasaheb would have to abide by all his decisions, and never refuse a task that was entrusted upon him. The man who was to be sarsanghchalak needed such an reassurance because 'the levers of control had come to his (Deoras') hand during the lifetime of Hedgewar itself,'[10] and it was speculated that Hedgewar had despatched Deoras to Bengal precisely for this reason.

Once Hedgewar had agreed to Golwalkar's conditions, the latter had assumed the mantle of leading the RSS. After this was made public amongst the cadre, a few old associates of Hedgewar had revolted against Golwalkar's nomination, and had even left the RSS in protest.

Meanwhile, the tension between the two men continued unabated. Balasaheb Deoras took occasional barbs at 'Guruji', often displaying his animus publicly, but eventually acknowledged him as the new chief, aided as he was by two men—Appaji Joshi, a key leader from the Vidharbha district in Maharashtra, and the RSS Treasurer, Babasaheb Ghatate. Soon thereafter, Deoras returned to Nagpur from Bengal and decided to 'strengthen his grip over the expanding organisation.'[11]

According to K.N. Govindacharya[12], the former general secretary of the BJP, it had taken several years for Golwalkar to leverage his position in the RSS. His individual efforts notwithstanding, in an attempt to consolidate his position, a posse of pracharaks was sent from Nagpur to establish several units of the RSS in different parts of the country.

The Next Phase

There was no gainsaying the fact that compared to his chief, Balasaheb's popularity index was on the ascendant, and it was primarily because he had succeeded in endearing himself to the rank and file of the organisation. He had joined the RSS in his pre-teens, and understood the workings of it better than 'Guruji', who had had a spiritual tryst with life before finally making up his mind to join the ranks.

Furthermore, Deoras had started his political journey in the Itwari Shakha, an area in Nagpur which not only accounted for almost half the city's population, but was acknowledged as an 'elite' branch of the RSS because it functioned as the training base for prant pracharaks or regional chiefs. Such was its influence that in the early 1940s, three out of four instructors during the annual OTCs in Pune happened to be from the Itwari branch.

In 1937, Balasaheb became the karyavah of the Itwari Shakha, but even before his formal appointment, he had taken the *tarun* or young swayamsevaks under his charge and initiated them into the daily routine of shakha. His efforts in this endeavour are recalled with great reverence, for here was a man who would steer a young bunch of volunteers every evening in a dilapidated house that was routinely used as a public toilet by people living in adjoining houses. The swayamsevaks would gather at the venue in the evening and along with their teacher, begin cleaning the courtyard. Balasaheb's success was also in breaking barriers in an otherwise regimental outfit; he was an equal for his young brigade of volunteers and quite enjoyed being addressed simply as, Bala.[13]

Interestingly, there was a healthy competition amongst the various shakhas in Nagpur, particularly during the annual parade when every branch would vie for the first position. For instance, the Dhantoli-Dharampeth Shakha, which was in focus as it attracted affluent members, and therefore had well-dressed swayamsevaks in crisply-starched shorts and shirts, wearing a clean pair of shoes and socks. On the other hand, the Itwari branch which was recognised as first amongst equals, particularly when it came to adhering to ideology, was ordinary in comparison and had lost the competition a year before Balasaheb had taken over as karyavah. Once he came on board, he set a target for the swayamsevaks, after taking the setback rather seriously, and had said, 'without making any changes in our clothes or footwear (meaning buying fresh pairs), we have to win the contest this time.'[14] This obviously required rigour on the part of young swayamsevaks, but such was Balasaheb's hold over them that they would stay back every evening to practise marching in perfect coordination.

In his pursuit of excellence, Deoras believed in the age-old dictum of (which is now rejected as outdated)—spare the rod and spoil the child. 'While guiding practise sessions, besides giving the standard "left-right" command for marchers, if Balasaheb noticed anyone making a mistake, then he did not shy from using the small *danda* or stick that he brandished in his hand. But no one protested at such punishment.'[15]

In 1937, Balasaheb Deoras' efforts bore fruit and the Itwari Shakha stood first in the annual marching competition.

Much like several political and quasi-political outfits in the decade after independence, the RSS was also dependant on voluntary donations for sustenance. One of the avenues for collecting money was during festivals, camps and other social gatherings, where people would donate voluntarily which the RSS later used for various activities.

The cadre was expected to not only organise such events, but also build the venue from scratch, much like what is done by fabricators during the annual Durga Puja festival in Bengal, and other parts of India, even today. It was yet again Balasaheb who had stepped in to teach the swayamsevaks how to erect tents and build temporary toilets for hosting events. In sum, it was not only seniority, but also extraordinary leadership qualities that had earned the karyavah of Nagpur respect as a dedicated soldier of the RSS.

It was around this time when Madhav Golwalkar had returned to Nagpur from his spiritual sojourn in the Sargachi ashram in Bengal (see chapter, Madhav Sadashiv Golwalkar, p. 98). According to several accounts, oblivious as he was to RSS' culture, it was a curious sight to witness the future sarsanghchalak of the organisation to be guided by the one who was not only nine years younger, but could also have been the chief.

At this juncture in the narrative, it is imperative to understand certain unique internal practises in the RSS. For instance, the rotating hierarchical structure is one of its most distinctive features, unlike other political outfits which normally 'demotes' leading functionaries only for disciplinary reasons. For example, the general secretary in a Left party retires as member of the politburo or central committee, but is seldom relegated to a junior position. Similarly, very rarely is the president of a party subsequently 'appointed' to a lower post—for instance, say a general secretary or vice president of the Congress party. But in the RSS, reassignment of posts is routine. There are examples of a sarkaryavah or general secretary being appointed later as a sah sarkaryavah or joint general secretary. Further, a sah sarkaryavah can even be shunted to a lower position. The only exception being the sarsanghchalak, who as a rule and in principle is never pushed down the organisational ladder.

Yet another unique feature within the ranks of the RSS is that the position held by a leader is seldom reflective of his clout. For instance, although Deoras functioned as the 'critical eyes and ears' of Madhav Golwalkar, he was appointed an office-bearer or sah sarkaryavah only in 1946. (At the time Prabhakar Balwant Dani aka Bhaiyaji Dani was the sarkaryavah. Eventually Deoras was made sarkaryavah but only after Dani's passing in 1965.)

Meanwhile, the conflicting views within the RSS post Hedgewar's death were out in the open, but as mentioned earlier, it had its genesis during his lifetime when there was a growing restlessness within the organisation. One of the main reasons for this was the sangh's contrarian views vis-a-vis the prevailing mood in the nation (see chapter, Keshav Baliram Hedgewar, p. 1). After the passing of the Government of India Act 1935, and the subsequent provincial elections, the RSS found itself split between playing the nationalistic card and focussing on the widening gulf between the Hindus and Muslims in pre-Independent India.

By this time, V.D. Savarkar had also been released from jail and he gave a fresh impetus to the Hindu Mahasabha in mid-1937, even as Hedgewar insisted on staying away from electoral politics. His focus was on reinforcing Hindu society and he believed that any kind of political participation would harm the sangh's long-term objectives.

A Sarsanghchalak with a Difference

While Hindu consolidation was Hedgewar's primary objective, the sanyasin-like Golwalkar was focussed on the spiritual orientation of the RSS. At the time of Hedgewar's death, the RSS was an outfit with limited influence, and this despite a well-oiled and advanced mechanism for the efficient working of its internal processes. For the first ten years of his tenure, Golwalkar maintained status quo and made no changes in its functioning, primarily to tide over the controversy over his appointment. Although it was said that 'the policies and postures of the RSS are contingent upon the personality and predilection of its chief,'[16] Golwalkar was finally able to come into his own only after 1949, i.e., post his release from jail on the charges of complicity in Mahatma Gandhi's assassination.

Although both K.B. Hedgewar and Madhav Golwalkar were essentially adherents of Savarkar's brand of Hindutva, each one approached it differently—Savarkar was clearly in favour of militarisation; Hedgewar wished to channelise the idea through the organisational structure; while Golwalkar was prone to a spiritual interpretation of the idea. Balasaheb Deoras on the other hand, wanted the RSS to plunge headlong into politics. He believed that the 'Hindus did not have an institutional mind. They revelled in destroying this.'[17] In 1965 (seven years prior to his taking over as sarsanghchalak), Balasaheb supported affiliates such as the Bharatiya Mazdoor Sangh (BMS), and the Akhil Bharatiya Vidyarthi Parishad (ABVP) because it was his belief that these organisations had the wherewithal of pursuing grassroots work which could later transform into political activism.[18]

When compared to his predecessor, one of the most important reasons for Balasaheb's contrasting views and pragmatism stemmed from the fact that he was agnostic, and proclaimed it openly. He often referred to himself as a 'Communist' within the RSS, and had a strong dislike for religious rituals. Several insiders have argued that 'it is highly debatable if he (Deoras) believed in God, or if in anyway needed Him. For him, the thread ceremony* was outdated and he disliked attending them.'[19] In fact, it was only after he became the sarsanghchalak that some of his associates had convinced him to

---

* The wearing of the sacred thread is a religious ritual which is followed by the Brahmin community for teenage boys in India. Also called Upanayan, it is also performed for Kshatriyas and Vaishya boys. It is primarily because of this ceremony that the idea of *dvijas*, or twice-born gained currency.

follow basic Hindu prayer rituals like lighting incense sticks, or visiting temples.

It may be recalled that as a young man, he had convinced his mother to give up on outdated caste obligations and admitted swayamsevaks of other castes into his home, and also served them food from the kitchen. Finally, it was this conviction of viewing all Hindus from a common prism which had made Deoras steer the RSS away from the path pursued by Golwalkar.

According to the well-known political scientist and author, Christophe Jaffrelot, Balasaheb Deoras' success in reversing the process had trapped the RSS between what should've been its avowed position or policy on an issue, and what was the 'general will of the Hindu community.' Consequently, from the time he became the sarkaryavah in 1965, Deoras supported 'this strategic change of direction' because he was 'committed to a more egalitarian social order than Golwalkar.'[20]

Interestingly, Deoras also held a modern view of the world and recognised the significance of a post-industrial world, while Golwalkar remained rooted in the world preceding pre-industrialisation. Apart from his pronounced agnosticism, one of the other reasons for Deoras' openness was attributed to his eclectic reading habits; he read voraciously on politics, history, and was especially fond of war memoirs, biographies, novels in Marathi and English, besides of course devouring books by and on V.D. Savarkar. In contrast, Golwalkar only read religious texts. Similarly while Deoras' preference for Hollywood cinema, especially war movies (which he generally watched alone at Regent Theatre, Nagpur) was well known, Golwalkar, in all likelihood, never went to the movies.

However, one cannot attribute Balasaheb's firm hold over the RSS as the only reason for his drifting away from the path chalked out by Golwalkar. He had publicly articulated his discomfort with his chief's position almost three decades prior to becoming the RSS chief in 1945–46 when he had declared, 'organisation, mobilisation and action! Organisation phase does not continue *ad infinitum*.'[21] He had recommended that the organisation must move ahead, or else, the 'RSS will become a sect and loose its relevance to the upliftment and building of society. It will become a ritual.'

This was exactly the issue he had raised during Hedgewar's lifetime. In the mid-1930s, when the national movement was gaining ground after a period of lull post the Civil Disobedience movement, Balasaheb was quoted as saying that when questions were raised about how the daily shakhas would 'fulfil the dream of liberating the *Hindu Rashtra*... we would disagree with doctorji and expressed our doubts.'[22] But at that time, Hedgewar was unrelenting in keeping the RSS out of mainstream politics, and the matter had ended.

In August 1942, when Gandhi gave the call for Quit India, Deoras had approached Golwalkar and presented a very innovative argument as follows:

> In 1931, Hedgewar participated in the Jungle Satyagraha after leaving Paranjpe in charge of the Sangh. You have declared me to be the actual sarsanghchalak and call yourself a mere proxy holder. Since you are already at the helm of affairs, allow me to join the Quit India movement while you remain in charge of RSS.[23]

But Golwalkar would have nothing of it; he had resolved to keep the RSS apolitical, while Deoras had sworn not to transgress his chief's diktat. The incident was yet another example of how the two men had clashed over the future trajectory of the RSS.

After the initial challenges to his leadership, Madhav Sadashiv Golwalkar settled into his role, and continued to evoke respect mainly because of the spiritual halo around his persona. Despite the routine and strong protestations by ideologues that the RSS is principally opposed to personality cult, the first three chiefs of the RSS were revered figures. While Hedgewar's charismatic grip on the organisation was because he had founded it, Golwalkar was the symbol of a peace-loving and detached ascetic, and Deoras in contrast, had not only fought against being elevated to a pedestal, but had insisted on remaining a soldier in the service of the sangh.

The deification of the supreme leader had actually taken root during Hedgewar's tenure, when the sarsanghchalak was given the honorific of *Param Poojaniye* or its acronym in Hindi, *Pa Pu*, to mean His Holiness. After becoming the sarsanghchalak, Balasaheb gave strict instructions that he shouldn't be referred to as *Pa Pu*, or be addressed reverentially at all. He also discontinued with the tradition of keeping sarsanghchalaks' photographs on the mantelpiece, or be hung prominently on the walls of the office. Deoras was of the view that while Hedgewar and Golwalkar's pictures could remain, there should be no space for any more additions.

However, one of the most radical steps in ending the personality cult was his wish that after his death, he be cremated without any fuss, and no memorial ever be erected in his name. As a result, the memorial in Nagpur's Reshimbagh is primarily the resting place of Keshav Baliram Hedgewar, called the Hedgewar Smriti Mandir, with a smaller one in the same compound for Madhav Sadashiv Golwalkar. After Balasaheb Deoras' death on 17 June 1996, his remains were brought from Pune to Nagpur and he was cremated as an ordinary RSS worker and not assigned any special status.

It was obvious that Balasaheb Deoras had broken with convention, and was often perceived as a 'reluctant' sarsanghchalak. It was however quite the contrary, he had lost out once, and had waited for thirty-three long years to assume the mantle. But one thing was certain—he didn't want to follow in his predecessors' footsteps, particularly the one before him. Unlike Golwalkar who believed in the supremacy of the sarsanghchalak, Balasaheb 'believed in the paradigm of centrality of the RSS, not many in the RSS did the same.'[24]

As the supreme leader, Golwalkar may have been cognisant of the fact that following an extraordinary-looking individual, a cult, or dogma was traditionally an inherent part of ancient ritualistic practise. Consequently, he 'offered the RSS cadre that very opportunity, to become his devotees.' He also used his spiritual charisma to advantage by creating the post of prant pracharak who reported directly to him and not to the sanghchalak.

In contrast to the centralisation of power recommended by Hedgewar and later furthered by Golwalkar, wherein the principle of ek chalak anuvartitva (follow one leader) was given great importance, Deoras introduced the twin concepts of *sah chalak anuvartitva* (follow many leaders), and *sarva samaveshak*, or inclusive leadership. Initially there were no takers for Deoras' avant-garde ideas, because 'he didn't offer them (swayamsevaks) spirituality—instead, he criticised traditions and unscientific accumulations in the culture and so on.'[25]

A particular incident mentioned by M.K. Chauthaiwale[26] is reflective of Balasaheb's ingenuity and what conservative Hindus would've considered 'amoral'. As was well known, most swayamsevaks at the time were from lower middle class backgrounds and struggled to pay for their uniforms, or even offer guru dakshina which was mandatory in the RSS. In addition to such expenses, they were also expected to raise funds for the purchase of musical instruments for the RSS band, which accompanied senior leaders during their tours, and also performed during Hindu festivals.

As in the case of erecting tents and building toilets, Deoras came to the swayamsevaks' rescue yet again and encouraged them to 'gate crash' into the *Brahman bhojan* (feast hosted for Brahmins) during the nine-day festival of Janmashtami. Dressed in their best silk dhotis, the swayamsevaks, mainly Brahmins, would arrive at such venues and not only gorge on good food, but also collect the dakshina they received as part of the offering made to Brahmins. The monies thus collected was deposited in the RSS office and was either used to buy musical instruments, or pay for others costs.

Despite his 'modern' outlook to life, Balasaheb's ideological core was intact. Even in the late 1930s when he could have assigned the task to others, he would be present as chief instructor at every OTC. Deoras viewed the conclave as hubs to assimilate swayamsevaks into a single cohesive unit.

In 1947, a few senior leaders had gathered one night at Golwalkar's house to debate on a contentious issue—whether there should be a uniform syllabus for the OTCs, or should it be customised for every region? The question was raised by a senior functionary, Eknath Ranade (the prant pracharak of Central India), who had also suggested that the use of *shool* or trident and *khadag* (the crescent-shaped sword) by the cadre, be made optional for regions.

Even as Golwalkar seemed uneasy taking a stand on the issue, Ranade had second-guessed what the sarsanghchalak was thinking, but stuck to his position. The debate was fast heading towards a stalemate when Balasaheb got up and said, 'We must take a majority view,' but added tactically, 'I will disclose my opinion on the matter and then seek the views of others.'

Balasaheb proceeded to announce what he thought of Ranade's suggestions, and then overturned them saying he was in favour of a combined curriculum. In a single stroke, Deoras had managed to isolate a senior functionary, although the two men had worked closely for many years. But when viewed from the prism of bringing about structural changes in the RSS, Balasaheb considered pluralism as dangerous and divisive. He wished 'complete agreement on belief systems within the organisation.'[27]

Unity & Conflict

It is said that the RSS' finest hour under the leadership of Madhav Golwalkar was in 1946 'when Jinnah's Direct Action gave them the opportunity of a lifetime. Rather than joining hands with Gandhi and nationalist forces to defeat the partition designs, the RSS came into action to finally prove, through proactive as well as retaliatory actions, that Hindus and Muslims could not live together.'[28] Involved as it was in issues relating to the Hindu–Muslim conflict, the Golwalkar-led RSS was oblivious of the fact that independence had become imminent, particularly after the end of the Second World War. The RSS' inability to comprehend that even Partition was a foregone conclusion was evident during an OTC in Punjab when Golwalkar along with Deoras and other senior leaders visited cities like Peshawar, Lahore, Karachi and Multan, which were soon to be part of another country. Golwalkar was later asked to address an OTC in Phagwara on 'this side' of Punjab, and to a question about how the RSS viewed its role in independent India, the chief had retorted, 'Do you think the British will ever leave India?'

Balasaheb Deoras was however cognisant of the tectonic shift in the nation's history. After becoming sarsanghchalak, he was candid enough to point out that Golwalkar was indeed unmindful of facts. This was in response to a question by the *Organiser* magazine as to why the RSS had made no efforts to resist Partition, despite a posse of young men at its disposal? Deoras' reply was unequivocal, and probably the most severe indictment of Golwalkar:

> It must be frankly admitted that senior workers of the Sangh had not given thought to the possible undesirable effects of partition on the future of the country. Nor had the Sangh prepared to stop it. We were taken by surprise. We may even say that we fell short in comprehensive thinking.

On his part, Balasaheb was clear about the inevitability of Partition, and the RSS' role in it. He wanted to alter the raison d'être vis-a-vis the RSS, but it would happen five years later when the Bharatiya Jana Sangh was formed in 1951 to act as the political vanguard of the sangh parivar. But before that, the RSS was faced with serious challenges, the kind it had never experienced previously, and nor would it ever in the future.

Gandhi's Assassination & The Ban

As mentioned earlier, unlike Golwalkar, Deoras did not consider politics to be morally repugnant. His resolve to give shape to a more action-oriented RSS was reinforced after his four-month stint in jail for Mahatma's Gandhi's assassination. By the time Deoras was released, the government had already initiated negotiations to get the RSS to accept certain preconditions for the ban to be rescinded.

But the meetings were making little progress and Deoras let the government representative know that since Golwalkar was in jail, he and Prabhakar Dani as senior leaders of the RSS would take charge of the negotiations. During one of the meetings in the context of curtailing RSS' activities, Balasaheb had almost issued a veiled threat by telling the official that besides satyagraha, the RSS would also resort to more aggressive forms of protest.

When the warning was conveyed to the then Home Minister Sardar Vallabhbhai Patel, he was quick to realise the gravity of the situation and concluded that it would be far safer for the RSS to be conducting the daily shakhas and building Hindu character, than venturing into politics. Although Balasaheb had acted alone without having consulted Golwalkar, Patel was aware that there were chances that the chief may not reject any such plan or project mooted by his deputy, despite his past opposition to such confrontational programmes. The Home Minister was proven right when in May 1949, the government intercepted a letter written by Golwalkar to Deoras in which he had said that because of the tardy progress in the lifting of the ban, the RSS should start another mass movement (see chapter, Madhav Sadashiv Golwalkar, p. 98).

As mentioned earlier in the book, Mauli Chandra Sharma, a former Congress leader who later became president of the Jana Sangh, was enlisted with the task of negotiating with the Deoras–Dani duo. He was later joined by the then chief minister of Central India, D.P. Mishra, and they suggested to Deoras that Golwalkar should write a letter to the government promising that the RSS would keep out of active politics, if he wanted the ban revoked. But Deoras had refused point-blank, knowing full well that a written communication could later be misused by the government.

Eventually, the government was forced to scale down its demands and was content with a letter which was written by Golwalkar to Mauli Chandra Sharma. In time, the ban on the RSS was rescinded, partly with assistance from a few RSS sympathisers within the government, and despite Prime Minister Nehru's objections.

Unfortunately, official records pertaining to the period are hard to find, primarily because of the ban, and also because barring Golwalkar, not many within the RSS were in the habit of writing letters or even recording details of meetings, which forms a major part of any political party's history. For instance, despite his voracious reading habit, Balasaheb Deoras had a peculiar abhorrence for putting pen to paper. In a span of twenty-one years when he was sarsanghchalak, Deoras mustn't have written more than ten letters.[29] For a man who had secured a First Class in college, this was indeed an unusual trait, and also displayed his impatience with an RSS tradition of the chief replying to letters personally. For instance, during Golwalkar's tenure, official communication would be exclusively handled by two senior functionaries—Abbaji Thatte and Krishnarao Mohrir.

On the other hand, Deoras' personal letters, especially during his travels, were penned by Chauthaiwale who often acted as his aide. There is a particular incident in Chauthaiwale's book which provides a significant insight into Deoras' reluctance to deal with official communique, even as his chief, Golwalkar continued to communicate with Sardar Patel discreetly. In early 1950, when Golwalkar was hoping that Patel would part ways with Nehru, he decided to 'send' him a letter (it wasn't sent by regular post, but was hand-delivered by a special representative to the Home Minister). It was also firmed up that Balasaheb should write the letter and also affix his signature on it. Although he had agreed to sign the letter, he had refused to write it. Eventually, Golwalkar had instructed Chauthaiwale to get a letterhead and Deoras agreed to dictate the contents of the missive. Once the task was done, Golwalkar made an official announcement to his close associates forbidding them from revealing the contents of the letter. Balasaheb responded to what was deemed to be top secret as follows: 'Today, I do not remember anything about the contents of the letter.'[30]

Balasaheb's reluctance to write that letter came into focus not only because he was a senior functionary, but also because he was next in line to lead the RSS. Interestingly, not only did he not want to write official letters, but even short messages to his cadre; respond to questionnaires; make speeches during festivals; or even endorse books, etc.

During the Emergency in 1975, Deoras was jailed as were several of his associates who later went on to write books on their experiences. An ingenious method was adopted to tackle the bunch of letters that Balasaheb would receive in prison—a team of swayamsevaks with best handwritings were assigned to him, who would reply to letters and write out other messages on which the chief would affix his signature.

Deoras' disinclination to write and the fact that the Vijaydashami speech by the sarsanghchalak is the most keenly anticipated event of the year*, made him scout for a speech-writer. This was unprecedented

* This speech is significant for several reasons. First, it is an anniversary lecture, as the RSS was established on Dussehra in 1925. Second, over the years, the speech is considered to be the most significant public lecture by a sarsanghchalak.

in the annals of the RSS, because both Hedgewar and Golwalkar would speak extempore. But Balasaheb proceeded to enlist the help of M.G. Vaidya, the then Managing Editor of *Tarun Bharat*, the Marathi newspaper attached to the RSS. Every year, Deoras would summon Vaidya after Ganesh visarjan (the immersion ceremony of Lord Ganesha, after the ten-day long festival of Ganesh Chathurti) and speak at length about his thoughts on various subjects. The arrangement worked rather well for the duo and even for the RSS, except once.

In 1992, the festival of Dussehra fell two months before the horrific demolition of the Babri masjid in Ayodhya. That year, the RSS had invited Arun Shourie, the journalist-turned-author and also, the ex-Disinvestment Minister in Atal Bihari Vajpayee's government, to be the chief guest at the celebrations. Rajendra Singh aka Rajju Bhaiyya, who was the sarkaryavah from 1977–1987, made a concerted effort to ensure that the sarsanghchalak presents strong views on the Ayodhya issue, which was what the Uttar Pradesh unit of the RSS had also wished.

He decided to travel to Nagpur to make sure that Balasaheb dovetails the RSS' aggressive pitch on the Ram Janmabhoomi issue in his speech. Rajju Bhaiyya met with Deoras' private assistant, Shrikant Joshi, and asked for a copy of his Vijaydashami speech, which was as usual written by M.G. Vaidya. Rajju Bhaiyya's fears were confirmed: the section on Ram temple was rather tepid and devoid of the strong pitch that the RSS had recommended. When Vaidya learnt about Rajju Bhaiyya's opinion, he decided to make changes to the speech in deference to a senior functionary. He later turned in the redrafted speech to Balasaheb.

The next morning, Balasaheb summoned Vaidya and told him, 'Do you think it is the tradition in the Sangh for the sarsanghchalak to use such harsh words?' Without taking any names, Vaidya gave his chief the reason for the aggressive pitch, but to no avail. The speech was restored to its original form.

The incident reflected Balasaheb Deoras' insistence on maintaining the dignity of his office, while keeping politics out of the sarsanghchalak's purview. In the context of the Ram Janmabhoomi issue, Deoras was of the view that the RSS had already expressed its position in a series of resolutions since the late 1980s—for instance in 1991, when it was suggested that the Hindus must 'brace themselves up for any amount of sacrifice and hardship and take forward this agitation with all the earnestness and dedication. Victory is assured.' After such an affirmation, aided by the election results in 1991 when the BJP had secured a majority in Uttar Pradesh, Deoras had felt that the RSS had already endorsed the demand for building the Ram temple in Ayodhya.

The demolition of the Babri masjid on 6 December 1992 marked a watershed moment in the evolution of the RSS. In more ways than one, this was the crowning glory of Deoras' tenure, but more of which later.

The Activist in Trouble

After the ban on the RSS was lifted, Balasaheb Deoras felt that it was time it evolves into a full-fledged political organisation. Throughout the mid-1940s, he had displayed great resolve when faced with Golwalkar's insistence on not only remaining distant from politics, but also refusing to accept the impending reality of the subcontinent's partition. As mentioned earlier, he had made his views clear in his interview to the *Organiser* after taking over as sarsanghchalak.

But Balasaheb stuck to his ground and made an attempt to convince his chief about the RSS' relevance in mainstream politics. For instance, in the early Fifties, coinciding with the setting up of the Bharatiya Jana Sangh, Deoras had requested that he be sent on deputation to the party, but Golwalkar had turned down his request. The second time around in the aftermath of Syama Prasad Mookerjee's death in 1953, Balasaheb had yet again submitted that he be transferred to the Jana Sangh, but it was rejected yet again.

It was inexplicable why Golwalkar had refused to depute Deoras to the new party, knowing full well that his vast experience would have only aided it to evolve better. However, the sarsanghchalak had later reasoned that it was because he had pledged to Hedgewar that Balasaheb would eventually be nominated his successor, and therefore his deputation to another organisation, however ideologically similar, would have been a breach.

Balasaheb Deoras however found a way to be involved with the Jana Sangh and assisted the party in raising funds for the first general elections in 1951–52. He was known for procuring monies and once earlier during the ban on the RSS, when all its resources were seized, Deoras had managed to raise loans from moneylenders after signing personal *hundis* (financial agreements).[31] The need for loans had also arisen because Golwalkar had prohibited voluntary donations from patrons.

That Guruji had a spiritual bent of mind was a given, and therefore his strict adherence to propriety even while running an outfit, was evidenced several times. Once during K.B. Hedgewar's tenure as sarsanghchalak, a noted industrialist and philanthropist called Jugal Kishore Birla, who was also an RSS supporter, had requested that he be allowed to buy land in Nagpur. The sarsanghchalak had given him permission, but had died before the deal could be finalised. When Golwalkar had taken over as the chief, Birla had sent his secretary to discuss the matter with him. But the newly-appointed sarsanghchalak made it clear to him that he was against receiving donations, either in person or even when directly given to the institution. He said that it was incumbent upon all patrons to place the gifts before the bhagwa dhwaj on Vijaydashami day in full public glare. Birla's emissary had heard him out and promised to get back, which he never did.

Unfortunately for Balasaheb, the Jana Sangh performed abysmally in the first general elections, even as the RSS was floundering in its endeavour to emerge as a major force. The money-lenders were worried about making little or no recoveries, and began chasing Deoras for repayment of loans. Deoras reported the matter to his colleagues, including Appaji, the Teasurer who had shirked all responsibility claiming that no one had asked him to take loans in the first place.

Eventually, Deoras had taken up the matter with Golwalkar, but the sarsanghchalak took the plea that since Deoras had acted of his own accord, he would have to personally bear the burden of repaying loans. According to several accounts in the RSS, a bitter clash had ensued between the two men—Deoras had accused Golwalkar of duplicitousness. He argued that on the one hand, the sarsanghchalak eulogised him by constantly comparing him to Hedgewar, but was now leaving him to his own mercies.

It needs to be mentioned here that although Deoras was not charged with corruption or in this case, embezzlement, his colleagues in the RSS had refused to take issue with Golwalkar to bail him out. The incident had left a bad taste in Deoras' mouth and he was left with no option but to withdraw from the RSS. He left Nagpur and set up a small business in his village, and also began overseeing his farmlands. Balasaheb therefore stayed away from the RSS for seven long years between 1953 and 1960.

Meanwhile, efforts were on within the RSS to bring him back into the fold. In early 1956, Bhaiyaji Dani and Eknath Ranade came up with a unique plan to raise donations—Golwalkar was turning fifty-one that year and the duo approached him with a proposal that they would seek donations for the celebratory functions. They further submitted that a portion of the funds be presented to the sarsanghchalak and the remainder be used to pay off the twenty-one lakh rupees that Deoras had loaned from moneylenders.

But as was expected, Golwalkar rejected the proposal, adding that as a sanyasi, he didn't believe in *vibhooti puja* or personal deification. He was firm in his conviction that neither would he accept any donations in his name, nor allow it to be utilised for clearing debts. Even his biographer, C.P. Bhishikar had noted that he 'was so averse to personal name, fame and publicity that it was an onerous task to get his consent for such an idea.' But Dani and Ranade anticipating such a response had come ready with an answer and told him, 'Granted you are a sanyasi and do not believe in such idolatry, but then if you are a true sanyasi then your *aham* or pride should not be there. But your pride is at an all time high and you are not allowing the sangh to use your persona for its cause and clear off loans. You have become an obstacle for the further growth of RSS.'

The sarsanghchalak did not take well to what was obviously an open revolt and retorted, 'If you are so unhappy with my ways, why do you not find another sarsanghchalak?'[32]

'If the need be we will look for one. We are unable to find anyone at the moment that's why we are bearing with you,' Ranade had said jocularly. The reason Ranade could take such liberties was because Golwalkar would often joke around with his senior colleagues and this kind of camaraderie wasn't viewed as insolence. But perhaps things had come to a head this time around—the episode led to bad blood between Golwalkar and Ranade and the latter was never pardoned for the transgression. In early 1960, Ranade was despatched to Kanya Kumari to set up the Vivekananda Rock Memorial and returned to Nagpur only after Deoras was appointed sarsanghchalak.

Eventually, it fell upon Dani to convince Golwalkar to agree to the felicitation plan. As planned, a committee was established and donations were raised for the event. The Akhil Bharatiya Pratinidhi Sabha or ABPS also passed a resolution and expressed 'deep sense of gratitude to all the people for their association with and unreserved contribution to the Samarpana Nidhi offered to Shri Guruji.'

Despite the successful conclusion of the felicitation ceremony and the raising of funds, the loans were still outstanding in Deoras' name. In due course, Balasaheb had to pay off the creditors from his personal money and eventually returned to the fold.

Curiously, whenever Balasaheb visited Nagpur during this phase, he would stay at the RSS headquarters and even attend the Vijaydashami celebrations dressed in full uniform, but would have no verbal communication with Golwalkar. Instead, Deoras would send his chief written questions through a close friend and an important functionary in the RSS, Babasaheb Talatule. Golwalkar received the questions, but made no effort to break the ice; he would send his replies 'orally' through Talatule, but not before checking if his replies were reproduced verbatim.

Eventually, Golwalkar had his way and Deoras returned to the sangh after being persuaded by his close associates, Dani and Ranade. Initially, he was appointed the joint prant pracharak of the Nagpur division, and was later promoted as the all-India sah sarkaryavah. After Dani's death in 1965, Deoras was appointed general secretary of the RSS.

Although Balasaheb's return was a vindication of sorts, all wasn't well within the RSS. His departure from the fold for reasons which were seen to be legitimate, had caused a tremendous upheaval amongst the cadre who were confused and were at a loss to 'understand if Deoras had left the RSS altogether, or was still part of the organisation.'[33] That he was a figure who evoked respect from his colleagues was evident—when he was approached by some of them to discuss the matter, he had firmly brushed them off, 'Do not be after me and bother me. It is a matter between me and Guruji.' On being pressurised further, he had once said, 'Whatever it may be, but I will not allow the sangh to split into a Guru Golwalkar sangh and a Deoras sangh; this is not what Dr Hedgewar has taught me.'[34]

The fact was that neither had Deoras split the parent body, nor formed a parallel front, but he had certainly carved out a niche for himself. Prior to his return to the fold, Deoras had started working as the publisher for the pro-RSS Marathi newspaper, *Tarun Bharat*. This was a well-thought-out strategy because there was no better tool than a Marathi newspaper to propagate RSS' ideology. Although he wasn't involved in the day-to-day running of the paper, he kept a close watch on the content and would often tick off reporters or even the editor if he found certain anomalies in the newspaper.[35] I once recall M.G. Vaidya telling me how Deoras preferred subtlety over the use of negative or even offensive words, especially while writing about a political adversary, and insisted on maintaining old-fashioned conventions.

In all likelihood, Balasaheb's stint with *Tarun Bharat* had made him aware of the ways of the Indian press. I remember it was he who had started the practise of distributing cyclostyled copies of his Vijaydashami speech to journalists, prior to his annual address in Nagpur.

While Deoras immersed himself in activities which furthered his mission in the RSS, the conflict between him and his chief continued, albeit indirectly. It was an open secret in the RSS that Golwalkar and Savarkar had serious differences, and Balasaheb used every opportunity to display his fondness for the latter, whom he considered several notches above the rest. In 1960, the government had enacted the Reorganisation of States Act, leading to Bombay state being divided into Maharashtra and Gujarat. As a result, not only was the Itwari Shakha in Nagpur impacted, but many swayamsevaks who were attached to western Maharashtra and Mahakaushal (in Madhya Pradesh), were forced to shift to new colonies. In 1961, a reunion was planned for the volunteers at the Koradi Devi temple complex in Nagpur. That evening, Balasaheb Deoras had mesmerised the cadre by reciting *Majhe Mrutyupatra* or My Final Testament, which is still considered to a classic Marathi poem by V.D. Savarkar. The poem, written in the form of a letter from Savarkar to his sister-in-law, has twenty-five stanzas, of which Deoras had recited a particular one with great emotion:

Oh Motherland! I have dedicated my intellect to you,
To you I have dedicated my oratory,
To you I have dedicated my new poem,
You have become the sole subject of my prose

Although there is no record of Golwalkar's reaction to Deoras' open veneration of Savarkar, it was well established that while Golwalkar had routinely questioned Savarkar's writings, the Mahasabha leader had also kept his distance from him. Deoras' act of invoking Savarkar through his poem at a time when the personality cult of Guruji within the RSS reigned supreme was indication that he wanted to keep his individuality intact, despite having returned to the fold.

Yet another instance of Deoras' ratification of Savarkar's viewpoint was mentioned by Shreerang Godbole, a medical practitioner who was also well known for his writings on the sangh parivar. 'In an interview given to the Marathi daily *Sobat*, Deoras was asked whether the Sangh accepted Savarkar's definition of a Hindu. After waiting for some time, Deoras answered in the affirmative.'

Direct Intervention in Politics

In April 1962, Balasaheb Deoras was appointed the joint general secretary, one day before what was considered to be auspicious by the RSS—the inauguration of the Hedgewar Memorial in Reshimbagh, Nagpur. As mentioned earlier, such events held little significance for Deoras, and moreover, he was at the time singularly focussed on making the RSS politically and ideologically relevant. In 1957 (even when he had withdrawn from the RSS), Deoras had succeeded in creating pressure on Golwalkar to support the Jana Sangh in the second general elections. Apparently, late one evening, Deoras had addressed a closed door meeting in the RSS headquarters in Nagpur to drive home the point that rallying behind the Jana Sangh had become mandatory for the RSS.

This meeting was almost like a precursor to the 1962 Jana Sangh plenary session in Bhopal, which Deoras had wanted to address, but Golwalkar had denied him permission. Later, a compromise was struck between the two—Deoras was allowed to deliver a RSS baudhik at a shakha in an adjacent venue which was attended by Jana Sangh leaders. Thus began the tradition of the RSS holding simultaneous sessions during Jana Sangh's plenary sessions. As a consequence, any degree of separation between the RSS and Jana Sangh was consigned to the backburner by Deoras, and Golwalkar could do nothing but acquiesce.

Meanwhile in April1962, Deoras played an active role in assisting the Jana Sangh during its campaign for the third general elections, which were held in end-February that year. Chauthaiwale wrote that it was Balasaheb who had finalised the list of candidates as a result of which, members of the Jana Sangh who normally kept a distance from RSS leaders, would often be seen in Nagpur.[36]

It was Deoras who was also instrumental in putting up Deendayal Upadhyaya as the Jana Sangh candidate in 1963 for the by-election in Jaunpur, Uttar Pradesh. Although Upadhyaya had never before contested elections, Deoras had nominated him with an eye on sending him to the Lok Sabha. (Deendayal's nomination was over yet another stalwart of the RSS, who was recognised for his exemplary oratorical skills and later became India's prime minister, Atal Bihari Vajpayee.)

The decision to nominate Deendayal Upadhyaya was deemed controversial by traditionalists within the RSS mainly for two reasons. First, his nomination over a talented and dedicated soldier of the sangh like Atal Bihari Vajpayee, and second, the induction of a man who was supposed to remain focussed on organisational and ideological matters. Deoras obviously wanted to blur the lines between what was considered to be political and apolitical principles in the RSS, but Golwalkar, as was well known, had always been opposed to the premise for more than a decade or so. He was of the view that pracharaks are only to 'organise the organisation.'[37] It was for the same reason that the sarsanghchalak was also against Deendayal Upadhyaya taking over as president of the Jana Sangh till 1967; he felt that pracharaks should limit their role to running the party as general secretaries. Be that as it may, Upadhyaya eventually lost the elections and wrote in his diary that the reason for his defeat was because he was projected as 'an outsider by the Congress party.'[38]

In the aftermath of the third general elections, Deoras' clout in the political circles increased manifold, and a decade later in 1977 when the Janata Party formed the government at the Centre, several ministers were routinely sighted in RSS offices in Nagpur and Delhi.

Balasaheb Deoras revelled in the power that he exerted on political leaders. According to the writer Sanjeev Kelkar, the well-known journalist Dilip Deodhar had once told him in 2007–08 that Deoras would often confide in his close associates that, 'Wherever I go, I will be the number one, and that would include being a General Secretary or a Prime Minister.'[39] In my conversations with Dilip Deodhar, it was evident that people within the sangh were aware of Deoras' feeling that Golwalkar should have acquiesced to his request of deputation to Jana Sangh, particularly because several RSS loyalists were of the opinion that it would have empowered the RSS in more ways than one.

Thereafter, Balasaheb Deoras shifted his attention to certain significant initiatives which were started at the behest of Golwalkar, but had so far not yielded results. This included RSS' interest in the labour movement and trade unions in the country. In an effort to recover lost ground in the aftermath of the ban, Golwalkar had chosen one of his close associates, Dattopant Thengadi to work with the Congress-affiliated Indian National Trade Union Congress (INTUC), in order to estalish a labour body affiliated to the RSS. In July 1955, the Bharatiya Mazdoor Sangh (BMS) came into existence, but it was only in 1964 when Thengadi was elected to the Rajya Sabha, that it was finally decided that the moribund network be revived. Deoras was at the forefront of this initiative and as a consequence, the first all-India BMS conference was held in Delhi in 1967. Nearly two decades later, in 1984, it emerged as the second largest trade union and in 1996, it overtook every other trade union in the country.

Yet another crucial initiative undertaken by Balasaheb was the setting up of the Bharatiya Shikshan Mandal (BSM), which later became one of the most potent ideological platforms for furthering the sangh parivar's cause. This affiliate was set up in Bombay on the day of Ram Navami in August 1969, and Deoras continued to be its leading light even after he had taken over as sarsanghchalak.

As the Sarsanghchalak

Within a month of Madhav Sadashiv Golwalkar's death on 5 June 1973, Balasaheb Deoras made an important speech in Nagpur sharing his optimism for the RSS, 'not so much on its "sanatan philosophy" as was the wont of his predecessor, but on the "army of workers which would be the envy of gods".'[40] With that statement, not only had Deoras dropped a hint about the impending changes in the RSS, but had also lent his final stamp on the significance of human endeavour over the power of ideas and ideology.

Unlike his predecessors, Golwalkar and Hedgewar, Balasaheb had succeeded in bringing the RSS firmly under his control. As mentioned previously, this was possible because he had invested several years in the organisation and had effected some of the most significant changes in its structure.

Meanwhile, for the first time after independence, India was yet again on the threshold of a massive crisis despite the two unprecedented victories—the first, in a major war against Pakistan in 1971 resulting in the creation of Bangladesh, and second, Prime Minister Indira Gandhi's fabulous electoral victory in March the same year. But there was a simmering anger amongst people who felt that corruption and hubris had made her and her government apathetic to their needs.

Sensing a great political opportunity, Balasaheb Deoras sent out instructions to Jana Sangh leaders that they should 'utilise the mass discontent for discrediting the adversary Indira Gandhi and to win the sympathy of the masses.'[41] Within weeks, at its plenary session in Kanpur in February 1973, the Jana Sangh under the leadership of its new president, L.K. Advani resolved to 'organise mass unrest and to lead the struggle on the economic and social fronts for all aggrieved sections of society.'[42]

Never before in its history had the RSS witnessed such a situation. More than the space that it intended to cede, this was the first time when it was working this closely with an affiliate: the Jana Sangh. The opportunity had literally fallen into its lap considering the ruling government at the Centre was reeling under major crises, including price rise with inflation exceeding twenty-three per cent; successive failure of the monsoons resulting in food shortages; and a massive industrial unrest leading to strikes and lockouts. Balasaheb moved with great alacrity to strike at the very roots of Mrs Gandhi's government and decided to take it beyond the realm of activism. His entire approach was 'tinged with populism, a tendency that grew out of his wish to speed up RSS' penetration of the whole body of society by combining the Sangathanist method with the propaganda of a kind that could rally whole sections of public opinion *en bloc*.'[43]

In the twenty-one years of his career as RSS sarsanghchalak, Balasaheb Deoras shall be best remembered for three major achievements. The first was the agitation launched against the misdemeanours of Mrs Gandhi's government which led her amongst other reasons, to impose the Emergency in June 1975. The second was in bringing to power the first non-Congress government at the Centre and thereby catapulting the sangh parivar to the mainstream. Third and finally two decades later, his grandiose plan of making the Ram Janmabhoomi agitation the kernel of India's Right-wing politics in the twenty-first century.

Although there was no doubt that the newly-appointed sarsanghchalak had affected major changes, the cadre in far-flung areas had not only been unable to come to terms with the death of Golwalkar, but had failed to fully comprehend whether the transition 'was to mean a complete change in the style, functioning and thinking of Golwalkar's RSS.'[44]

Balasaheb was aware of the latent resentment amongst several of his peers and in order to restore faith, he brought back a few veterans who had been forced to exist in the periphery of the sangh, including Eknath Ranade, Vasantrao Oke, Madhukar Deval, and V.V. Pendsey. Of the lot, Deval's return to the fold was extremely significant as he withdrew from regular sangh activities and proceeded to work amongst Dalits, a move which was not only ratified by Balasaheb, but he also donated a princely sum of one lakh rupees (that he had been awarded as prize money) to the project.

A few months later in December 1974, in a bitter indictment of the Golwalkar era, Balasaheb spoke about a 'crisis of character and credibility' in the organisation. He went on to add that 'the responsibility of what needs to be done will come over to us and we will have to accept that.' He continued in the same vein, adding that, 'We,' had avoided taking responsibility previously, but now 'this will not do.' Within six months of taking charge, Deoras had infused his cadre with a renewed sense of purpose, brought in loyalists, and eased out those who were reluctant to accept his leadership.

This was manifest when the students' affiliate of the RSS, the ABVP had plunged into the Gujarat Navnirman agitation which soon galvanised into a nationwide protest movement against the Congress, with Jayaprakash Narayan or JP at its helm. In the same period, the ABPS passed a very important resolution, portions of which read as follows:

> The RSS believes that the present atmosphere of all-round corruption and selfishness can be cleansed only by the generation of such a pure stream of patriotism. Having directed all its energies towards that end, the Sangh hereby extends its hearty co-operation to every such effort from any direction.

This was an important resolution because the RSS was finally clear that there was merit in engaging in active politics. It was now ready to shed the yoke of being a mere socio-cultural outfit that it was made out to be. There were three other extremely remarkable events witnessed in 1974–75 which had unfolded against the backdrop of an unprecedented display of camaraderie between JP and Balasaheb.

In March 1975, Jayaprakash Narayan consented to attend the Jana Sangh's plenary session in Delhi; he had already invited the party to participate in the Opposition's protest march to parliament, much to the consternation of other anti-Congress leaders. At the meeting in Delhi, JP gave the party, what decades later its leaders would term, a 'clean chit'. Jayaprakash had said to the RSS, 'If you are fascist, then I too am a fascist.'

Thereafter it was the turn of the RSS chief to praise JP when he compared him to Mahatma Gandhi, Acharya Vinoba Bhave, and Golwalkar. 'He (JP) is like sanyasins of old who remained aloof and yet did not hesitate to lead the people when the rulers went astray.' By elevating JP to the pedestal of the Mahatma, Deoras had with one stroke overturned the Congress' allegation that the leader from Bihar was destabilising India at the behest of foreign powers. But by placing Golwalkar in the exalted gallery of the greats, Deoras had deftly attempted to rid the RSS of its links with Nathuram Godse. This shift in eulogising Gandhi, albeit indirectly, was a significant step for the RSS. But before detailing how Deoras went about building what *The Economist* once described as the 'only non Left-wing revolutionary force in the world,' we shall turn our attention to the third most important event of 1974—Deoras' speech at an annual event in Pune.

A Watershed Lecture

The annual Vasant Vyakhanmala (or the Spring Lecture Series) was started by the multi-faceted, Justice M.G. Ranade in 1875 along with Bal Gangadhar Tilak. Amongst other things, the series which was held in the second half of April in Pune, was aimed at reviving intellectual discourse in society, and provided a platform for speakers to exchange ideas on various topics.

In 1974, Balasaheb Deoras was invited to deliver the lecture and his topic for the series' centenary year was, 'Social Equality and Hindu Consolidation'. It was no wonder that his lecture had evoked a lot of curiosity amongst the intelligentsia, but most importantly, about how he would address the issue of forging Hindu consolidation at a time when major caste distinctions existed in the community, etc.

In his address of 8 May 1974, Deoras told his audience at the outset that he had selected the topic because:

> Hindu consolidation is a must for the welfare of the nation. Hence all aspects of it are important. Even among them, the aspect of social equality being a delicate and currently relevant one, appealed to me.[45]

He then proceeded to position himself more as a grassroots leader, and said:

> I do not claim to be one among the thinkers and scholars of the society. But I have moved much amongst our people. That has given me many experiences and ideas and also a peep into the feelings of the people.

Thereafter Balasaheb threw a question to the audience: 'Who is a Hindu?' Although several hands had gone up and many definitions were put forward, Deoras argued that none of them were perfect, since each one, however carefully worded, 'suffers from the defect of being either "too short/brief" (*avyapti*) or "too expansive" (*ativyapti*).' In his explanation, Deoras submitted that he first wished to detail which communities were excluded from Hindu society. In order to expand on the premise, he referred to the Hindu Code Bills which were passed in 1956 and argued that because they were applicable to all, except Muslims, Christians and Jews, every citizen whose personal matters were governed by them, were Hindus, including, 'Sanatanis, Lingayats, Arya Samajists, Jains, Sikhs and Buddhists and even others who did not come under any of these categories.' Deoras was upfront about his objective:

> We want to organize or consolidate all the Hindus. Organization does not merely mean a crowd, a front or a meeting. Organization implies bringing and keeping the people together and making them realize the purpose for their remaining together.

Deoras however accepted that this wasn't an easy task, and how it had become necessary to 'furnish some basis for it. And some of those basic factors of unity will have to be necessarily emotional in content.' He then added that there was no better way to enlist support from people than evoke 'our motherland, we are its children and we have been living here for the past thousands of years.'

After gauging the mood of his audience, Balasaheb became aware that many may perhaps squirm at his attempts to deify the nation, and provided a justification as follows:

> Even Stalin had to remind his compatriots that they all belonged to a single, great nation, when Russia faced a terrible ordeal during the Second World War. He had to invoke the spirit of 'nationalism' and 'fatherland.' The necessity of such an emotional inspiration is beyond controversy.

It may be recalled that right at the outset, Deoras had excluded Muslims, Christians and Jews from his 'project consolidation'. Yet, despite the Hindu Code Bills which had created a *de facto* Hindu society, he highlighted how the community was still divided on several lines. The sarsanghchalak argued that there were enough instances in the history of India to show how,

> just a handful of Muslims and even fewer Englishmen could rule over us and could forcibly convert many of our brethren

> to their religions. They also created controversies like 'Brahmin and non-Brahmin', '*Savarna* and *Asprishya*'.
>
> We have to admit that social inequality amongst us has been a reason for our downfall. Fissiparous tendencies like caste and sub-caste rivalries and untouchability have all been the manifestation of this social inequality.

Balasaheb acknowledged that although members of the sangh parivar were 'immensely proud of our Dharma and our Sanskriti,' it was sheer lip service in the face of the larger problem of caste divisions in society. The RSS chief acknowledged that not everything was sacrosanct anyway, and, 'while cherishing this pride (in heritage) it would not do to think that all that is old is gold...Just because something is old, it need not necessarily be good or eternal or the gospel truth.' He was emphatic about the need to end caste divisions and recommended introducing reforms within Hindu society.

As mentioned earlier, Deoras was a sworn agnostic from a young age, and was severely critical of the tendency to blindly follow Hindu scriptures. He elaborated on the point during the lecture, adding,

> it has been said in the Puranas that the lunar and solar eclipses are a result of "*Raahu* and *Ketu* swallowing the Moon and the Sun". But should we, in order to affirm our devotion to our old religious texts, incorporate this story in the school text books to explain to the children why the eclipses take place?

But what stood out in his lecture prominently was his focus on the caste system and its effects on social stratification, which many felt had a larger purpose. Although Balasaheb had cleverly sidestepped the reason for his focus on the scourge of casteism, there was little doubt that much of what he spoke in Pune was to eclipse the controversy which had erupted after Golwalkar's interview to the Marathi newspaper *Nava Kal* in which he had expounded on the chaturvarna or the four-tiered caste system. In an article in the *Mainstream*, Subhash Ghatade wrote that the then RSS chief, 'had extolled the virtues of Chaturvarnya (the division of the Hindus in four Varnas) and had also glorified Manusmriti, the ancient edicts of the Hindus.'[46]

In what was an interesting reference, Balasaheb Deoras had mentioned Milovan Djilas (the Vice President of Yugoslavia under Josip Broz Tito) and his book titled, *New Class* and said that although 'communism aimed at the removal of all types of inequalities... a new class has come up in all communist countries,' demonstrating how Communism also encourages an inequitable system. Varna vyavastha or the caste system, argued Deoras was similar because it was,

> no exception to this human weakness and as a result it became distorted and it collapsed. But none can say that the originators of the system had any such perverse intentions in their mind when they introduced it.

Drawing on the colloquial *roti-beti-vyavahaar* dictum, meaning eating and marrying outside one's caste, Deoras said that in the past this may have invited severe social penalties, but with time, particularly with the Jhunka-Bhakar Sangh in Maharashtra, this barrier was lowered.

In sharp contrast to Deoras' view of removing caste discrimination in Hindu society, his predecessor, M.S. Golwalkar had remained unconcerned about it throughout his tenure as sarsanghchalak. In an interaction with journalists in Bangalore (now, Bengaluru) in February

1973, he had spoken about reservations for the Scheduled Castes and Tribes and said, 'We are opposed to continued special privileges on the basis of caste only, as it would create vested interests in them in remaining as a separate entity. That would harm their integration with the rest of the society.' In yet another interview in 1969 when Golwalkar was asked if 'samskaars' (values) could be imparted to nomadic tribes, his reply was startling:

> If we could domesticate even the wild animals roaming the jungles, can we not persuade our own people to take to better and more stabilized ways of life? Certainly we can, provided we display the human touch.[47]

The two contrasting approaches in alleviating social discrimination was indicative of the serious ideological split in the sangh parivar. But Balasaheb was undeterred and adhered to his core beliefs which was manifest at various levels within the organisation. For instance, in the 1974 OTC, a special session was devoted to the Vyakhanmala lecture series; at the ABPS meeting, the issue of reservation was discussed at length and references were made to the use of inappropriate language by Dalit leaders. Deoras had intervened in the debate, and while accepting its relevance, he had added that if members of the upper castes had been ostracised for centuries and subjected to all kinds of humiliation and discrimination, they may have also used objectionable language.

That Deoras had to continue waging a political battle against caste-based inequalities a decade and a half after the Pune lecture demonstrated the inherent prejudice within the RSS towards the lower castes. In 1974, the reaction 'in the dominant and majority psyche of the Sangh was at variance with the way Deoras thought.'[48] The new sarsanghchalak had to wait for more than a decade before there was some semblance of a change in the dominant sections of the RSS when a few Dalits of Meenakshipuram in Tamil Nadu had converted to Islam and had thereby rejected the caste biases in Hindu society.

Expanding the Horizons

In February 1967, when the Jana Sangh had notched its best electoral performance in history by winning thirty-five of the 520 parliamentary seats in Lok Sabha, and more than 250 seats in state assemblies, it was attributed to Deoras' far-sightedness in appointing Deendayal Upadhyaya as party president. Going against conventional wisdom, the Jana Sangh had promptly joined the coalition governments in Uttar Pradesh, Rajasthan and Madhya Pradesh. Balasaheb Deoras and Deendayal Upadhyaya saw these governments as temporary arrangements, although many in the party, including Atal Bihari Vajpayee, were euphoric that they had finally secured a place in electoral politics. Although Deoras viewed Vajpayee as an 'indulgent child,'[49] he guided him into taking certain radical steps, for example, extending support to Indira Gandhi's move of nationalising banks, and the abolition of privy purses.

This resulted in a 'revolt on the Right'[50] with the former president of Jana Sangh, Balraj Madhok filing a petition in the Supreme Court against what he thought was a reversal of the party's official principles. A few months before he became the RSS chief in 1973, Deoras saw logic in Vajpayee's and his close associate, L.K. Advani's point of view and supported their decision to expel Balraj Madhok from the Jana Sangh. For more than a year after his expulsion, Madhok who was one of the founder members of the Jana Sangh, continued his tirade against Deoras alleging that he was instrumental for his eviction from the party. Initially, Deoras would respond to every accusation made by Madhok, but when his broadside did not subside, he quit acknowledging his letters.

While the core ideology and programmes of the Jana Sangh was at variance with those of its coalition partners, this wasn't the only reason for the demise of India's first major experiment with a confederation of parties. Deoras had been closely observing the political developments in the run-up to the coalition government and had deputed the then general secretary of Jana Sangh, Nanaji Deshmukh to reach out to Jayaprakash Narayan.

In March 1974, K.N. Govindacharya and Sushil Modi (now Deputy Chief Minister of Bihar) approached Jayaprakash Narayan. 'JP finally agreed to take charge of the entire movement, but on two conditions—the movement will be entirely non-violent and his leadership will be absolute,' reminisced Govindacharya in an article to mark the fortieth anniversary of the Emergency.[51]

Balasaheb agreed to JP's preconditions, but not before placing his on the table tacitly and that being the validation for the RSS. Despite his own stated objective of remaining clear of power politics, JP was aware that without the massive RSS network, the sampoorna kranti or total revolution movement that he had launched against Indira Gandhi would remain a non-starter.

While JP appointed key members of the RSS in crucial committees, Balasaheb began meeting influencers who had in the past been critical of the RSS. His first stop was the Paunar Ashram in Wardha district to meet Acharya Vinoba Bhave, who at the end of the meeting declared himself to be 'an unofficial member of the Sangh.'

Meanwhile, Prime Minister Indira Gandhi who was hemmed-in from all sides decided to mount an aggressive campaign to rein in her adversaries, including JP, the RSS and other motley groups which had joined hands to destabilise her government. Amongst several other charges, they were accused of acting at the behest of Western imperialists, primarily America, which led to violent agitations across the country. While the RSS vehemently rejected the charges, the ABPS adopted a resolution saying that 'the people will not be carried away by such false and malicious propaganda.'[52]

On 1 December 1974, Balasaheb Deoras in his speech in Delhi's Ramlila Maidan criticised Indira Gandhi's government for its reiteration of 'hard days ahead, critical days ahead' citing the global financial crisis, repeated failure of the monsoons, and heavy spends during the 1971 war as factors for the political crisis in the country. He ridiculed the Congress government and commented that 'nations make progress in spite of the adversity of circumstances. It is no use giving explanations.'[53] Even as Indira Gandhi's failures were at the centre of the political narrative, Deoras was deftly moving the RSS away from its ideological core and creating the most audacious political strategy ever witnessed in the history of the sangh.

On 12 June 1975, the Allahabad High Court charged Indira Gandhi with electoral malpractices and set aside her 1971 election. By now, most of her political adversaries, including Deoras knew that in the aftermath of the judgement, preceded by the consolidation of Opposition forces, Mrs Gandhi would take drastic steps to secure her position.

Balasaheb called a meeting of the RSS' top brass in Firozabad, UP, which was attended by Nanaji Deshmukh and Madhavrao Mule to discuss pre-emptive measures in case the government swooped down to arrest any of them. Meanwhile, there was hectic activity in JP's camp as well, for he along with his associates were readying themselves for a large gathering in the capital on 25 June 1975. Prior to the public meeting, JP constituted a Lok Sangharsh Samiti (LSS; or the People's Struggle Committee) with Morarji Desai as president and Nanaji Deshmukh as general secretary. Although Ravindra Verma, a leader of the Madhya Pradesh Congress (O) was appointed to the post, the RSS regained control over the LSS when Verma was arrested and Dattopant Thengadi took over after his resignation from the Bharatiya Mazdoor Sangh. Finally, Deoras' strategy of backing JP had paid him rich dividends.

On 25 June 1975, although a galaxy of leaders took turns in delivering thundering speeches against Mrs Gandhi, it fell upon Nanaji Deshmukh to announce the next phase of the agitation which included a satyagraha at the prime minister's residence, exhorting her to resign.

However, on the midnight of 26 June, Indira Gandhi imposed the Emergency and the Opposition's plans came to naught. Hundreds of senior Opposition leaders, including Lal Krishna Advani and others were thrown into jail. Balasaheb was arrested in the most dramatic fashion a few days later at Nagpur railway station while he was on board the GT Express. On 4 July 1975, the RSS was proscribed for the second time in history. But unlike the first time when it was banned in the aftermath of Mahatma Gandhi's assassination in 1948, in 1975, 'the RSS was not isolated like in 1948, and had formed a close working relationship with other opposition parties.'[54]

In the last week of July 1975, senior office-bearers of the RSS who had either gone underground or had evaded arrest, met in Bombay to discuss the future course of action. With Balasaheb in jail,

Madhavrao Mule was designated as the RSS chief, while a temporary zonal hierarchical structure was set up as follows—Yadav Rao Joshi (south; he was later credited with setting up the RSS in Karnataka); Moreshwar Moropant Pingle (west); Bhaurao Deoras (east); and Rajju Bhaiyya (north). Besides these zonal heads, Rambhau Godbole, the organising secretary for Bihar and West Bengal was given the additional responsibility of coordinating with Opposition parties; Moropant Pingle was made responsible for liaising with the LSS; while Eknath Ranade was given the crucial task of handling negotiations with the government.[55] What seemed like a school roster was in fact a significant step in RSS' history as it heralded a complete break from the past. In 1975–76, the RSS of the Fifties was not only a forgotten chapter, but under Deoras was very much discarded as well.

The July meeting also devised a four-pronged plan to tackle the Emergency: to keep the volunteers' morale high; setting up an underground network to print and distribute literature; planning for a nationwide satyagraha; and establishing an overseas network. There was a fifth one, which was not only treated as top priority but kept a closely guarded secret and handed over to Eknath Ranade: to liaise with Indira Gandhi. It may be recalled that even in 1948–49, it was Ranade, who along with Dani, had negotiated with the government about rescinding the ban on the RSS.

However this time around, the RSS was faced with a woman prime minister who was known to put her adversaries in place. The imposition of Emergency notwithstanding, Indira Gandhi was known to be ruthless when faced with any kind of opposition. On 5 August 1975, she imposed the draconian Maintenance of Internal Security Act (MISA) and in a nationwide swoop arrested more than twenty-three thousand swayamsevaks.

Balasaheb Deoras who was himself languishing in jail, was stunned by her action and was forced to placate the prime minister in order to get the RSS back on track. He wrote two letters to the prime minister—the first in August, and the second in November. In his first missive, Deoras praised her Independence Day speech, while in his second letter, he congratulated her after the Supreme Court upheld her 1971 election from Raebareli.

However, while researching for this book, I discovered that the impact of these letters from the sarsanghchalak to Prime Minister Indira Gandhi is seldom discussed in the RSS. There was a third letter which Balasaheb had written in July 1976 enquiring about Mrs Gandhi's efforts to improve relations with Islamabad and Peking (now, Beijing).

In this entire letter-writing exercise, Eknath Ranade had acted as a bridge between the two—while his chief reposed his trust in him, Indira Gandhi was appreciative of his work at the Vivekananda Kendra in Kanya Kumari. In early 1970s, she had even suggested to Ranade that instead of propagating the sangh's idea of Vivekananda as the symbol of Hindu India, he should collaborate with the Centre to promote the seer-philosopher as an Indian icon across the world.

Even as the pretence of civility was maintained by both Balasaheb and Indira Gandhi, the RSS went ahead with their plan of launching a nationwide satyagraha on 14 November, a date they chose carefully as it happened to be Pandit Nehru's birth anniversary, in which more than forty thousand swayamsevaks courted arrested from different parts of the country. What was interesting about the protest was that although the RSS was at the forefront of the campaign and the majority of arrests were of its cadre, the LSS which had also participated in the agitation, didn't ask for the removal of the ban on the RSS. This was so typical of Deoras who wanted to convey the impression that the RSS was motivated by pure national interest, than by reasons of opportunism.[56]

Balasaheb had also succeeded in bringing to fruition a rather dubious game plan—the infiltration of RSS men into the Youth Congress, which was helmed by Sanjay Gandhi. Prime Minister Indira Gandhi had later admitted that 'there had been large-scale infiltration of RSS men into the Youth Congress ranks.'[57] Additionally and rather startlingly, 'RSS leaders were of the opinion that Sanjay, with his confirmed enmity towards communists and opposition to measures like nationalisation, was nearer to their own ideology and politics.'[58] There were also reports that in order to forge an alliance with the Congress party, the RSS had proposed making fundamental changes to its structure which included appointing a president in place of a sarsanghchalak, and even the 'admission to non-Hindus was decided upon and conveyed to Sanjay Gandhi.'[59]

It was probably a result of this so-called infiltration that the government had hoped that it would succeed in neutralising the RSS after the Emergency in January 1977 and hold fresh elections. In what was a blatant act of volte-face, all the political prisoners were released, except those belonging to the RSS. In the weeks before the poll process had picked up steam, Indira Gandhi directed that meetings be held with underground RSS leaders. It was clear that she had succeeded in creating panic amongst swayamsevaks by extending their detention, and when a government representative met with them she had fanned it further by saying that in the event of a Congress victory, the RSS and its cadre could see worse days.

In return for the unconditional release of its members and rescinding the ban, the RSS was advised to stay away from the poll process, and also exert pressure on the Jana Sangh to stay out of the Janata alliance. But it was rejected by the RSS negotiators who contended that the Congress had lost a golden chance by not responding to Deoras' missives to Indira Gandhi in 1975.[60]

Eventually, Balasaheb Deoras was released from jail on 21 March 1977 and the ban on the RSS was also lifted the same day. After spending two days in Bombay, Deoras took a train to Nagpur and was given a hero's welcome at a huge gathering in the city. As sarsanghchalak, Deoras had effected major changes in the RSS, and could have rested on his laurels. But that was not to be.

* * *

Despite her conduct during the Emergency, Indira Gandhi had somehow succeeded in endearing herself to the RSS. The reason: her unique talent of resorting to jingoism. According to several political commentators, although Balasaheb Deoras' letters to the prime minister were cited as evidence of his lack of political courage and conviction, it's most likely that this was part of a tactical ploy, much like what the RSS had planned vis-a-vis the Congress in 1948–50.

Initially, Deoras may have worked on the premise that a besieged Indira Gandhi may respond favourably to his offer of a friendship and therefore wrote her letters, particularly the one praising her for her Independence Day speech. What was however most perplexing was not so much his extending an olive branch to her, but that he was well aware of the LSS' plan of launching a nationwide stir against the Emergency. In the end, it was not so much servility, but his duplicitousness in the entire incident which had come to the forefront.

Truth be told, no one had any illusions about Deoras' friendly overtures towards Indira Gandhi—it wasn't for any other reason, save the fact that she carried the reputation of being a strong leader, which was given more credence after the 1971 Indo-Pak war when Atal Bihari Vajpayee had apparently described her as the very incarnate of goddess Durga. However, Advani had later disputed this claim and argued that although Vajpayee had supported her for the war effort in a Lok Sabha speech, the Durga comparison was made by a member of the Jana Sangh Working Committee at the Ghaziabad national session in 1971. Be that as it may, it only goes to prove that sections of the sangh parivar held Indira Gandhi in high esteem. The pop-nationalism rhetoric which Indira had mastered over the years, was lapped up by the sangh—for instance, she had no qualms about lavishing praise on the Rajput king Maharana Pratap during one of her visits to Haldighati in Rajasthan, much like what a typical RSS member was wont to do. Despite similarities such as this, there was no question of a truck between the lady and the RSS, simply because both were at one level indulging in power politics which had little or nothing to do with ideology.

Although Deoras was still in jail during the 1977 election campaign, he kept abreast of every political development and was insistent that the Jana Sangh be part of the coalition. In April 1977, when a group of MPs who had won the elections held a reception for Deoras, he had said in his speech that the, 'ban and imprisonment has been regarded by the Sangh as a blessing in disguise as this sojourn (in jail) has helped in dispelling many misgivings about the RSS which has provided beneficial to national unity of the new party.' It was clear that Deoras wanted others to recognise that the RSS was not unacceptable any longer and was in fact a preferred partner in the coalition. It had taken Deoras an entire decade to end the sangh parivar's ostracisation which had begun with Gandhi's assassination, and he had resolved not to thwart it for anything in the world.

However, Deoras was forced to begin his new sojourn with a compromise. The Janata Party had firmed up on its prime ministerial candidate prior to the elections, and while Morarji Desai and Charan Singh were the front-runners for the post, Deoras had personally rooted for Jagjivan Ram because he had felt that his departure from the Congress, along with Hemvati Nandan Bahuguna, had given a fillip to the anti-Indira campaign. This claim was however disputed by Madhu Limaye who wrote in 1979 that the RSS 'simultaneously dangled the carrot of the prime minister's chair before several Janata Party leaders. On the one hand, they went on assuring Morarji Desai to the end that he was their choice for prime minister. Every now and then they would promise Chaudhary Charan Singh that they would support his claim to be prime minister. Concurrently, they kept giving similar assurances to Chandra Shekhar, Jagjivan Ram and George Fernandes.'

There is no record to prove if Deoras was playing a devious game. But according to M.K. Chauthaiwale, Deoras had had a tough time convincing his core team that it was expedient to put the politics of Hindu consolidation on the back-burner and allow the Jana Sangh to become part of the political mainstream. Besides what was obviously an ideological compromise, the Jana Sangh had to settle for a lesser role in the Cabinet, and Deoras had attributed that to the sacrifice made by the sangh in providing stability to the Janata government.[61] According to some members of the RSS, Morarji Desai had offered a Cabinet berth to Nanaji Deshmukh, but it was politely turned down because Deoras did not wish the organising secretary of the Jana

Sangh to accept a ministerial berth. For a man who had once pushed Deendayal Upadhyaya into mainstream politics, the decision to keep Deshmukh out of the government was most puzzling.

Meanwhile, the Janata Party experiment was turning out to be a disaster. The 'Socialist' group within the coalition had begun to rear its head and demanded to know why the RSS must not throw open its membership to non-Hindus; abandon Hindu consolidation as one of its objectives; jettison the bhagwa dhwaj; and introduce intra-organisation polls to elect office-bearers, including the sarsanghchalak. The sangh viewed it as typical Muslim appeasement politics practised by some of the groups within the coalition who were seeking to consolidate the Muslim vote bank which had shifted from the Congress after the forced sterilisation drive led by Sanjay Gandhi during the Emergency. Balasaheb was obviously in a bind because he had encouraged his cadre for months to rise above their ideological moorings to assimilate with the new government at the Centre. But there was little he could have done to salvage the situation.

Main Challenges

Balasaheb was faced with three main challenges during the Janata years. First, to formulate the RSS' response to demands for altering its core principle of Hindu consolidation. According to several accounts, this was manifest prominently in two ways—the RSS' refusal in allowing non-Hindus (read Muslims) to become members, and second, the Jana Sangh's hot pursuit for introducing legislations banning cow slaughter; prohibition of religious conversions; and championing other Hindu revivalist agendas like the revision of school textbooks on Social Sciences.

The second challenge that Deoras faced was actually a conundrum—over the relationship dynamics with members of the Jana Sangh after it was dissolved in 1977—whether to maintain a status quo or detach completely. Critics of the RSS within the Janata government gave this dilemma a name—'dual membership' and demanded that members of the erstwhile Jana Sangh sever all links with the RSS.

The final obstacle for Deoras was about orchestrating the RSS' future trajectory in Indian politics. In the past, whenever his advise was sought on the subject, he would say in Hindi, *'Dason dishaon mein jao'* (Go in every direction; the word, dason denotes the numerical ten in Hindi, but also the multiple hands of certain Hindu gods). The crucial question for any ordinary pracharak at the time was which direction should the beleaguered RSS be now taking, considering it was hemmed-in from all sides.

After the Socialists in the government, several others followed and demanded that the RSS must allow Muslims (also Christians and Parsis) to become members. Apart from what they felt went against the grain of a secular democratic republic, they were also apprehensive that the Muslims may go back to the Congress' fold. The RSS had deliberated over this issue during the Emergency, and Madahvrao Mule had even announced that such a proposal was under consideration. After his release from jail, although Deoras had made a passing mention of it, he was quoted as saying that he hadn't given it much thought.[62] During the anti-Emergency struggle, a few RSS and Jamaat-e-Islami leaders were forced to share space in prisons, and the criticism of the Congress' forced sterilisation campaign by the former had interestingly secured the support of even the Imam Bukhari of Delhi's Jama Masjid. Once the Muslims' membership issue was made public, the Imam obviously expected Deoras to deliver on the promise.

Similarly, in so far as JP was concerned, it wasn't as if he was unaware that the RSS had succeeded in getting political legitimacy by partnering with him. In return, he expected them to make his task of managing a fractious coalition easier. As a result, he also wrote a letter in September 1977 demanding that the RSS must throw open its doors to Muslims. Eventually, before the year was over, Deoras made a startling announcement that the RSS was now open to non-Hindus. But this so-called declaration was obviously a smokescreen because the 'RSS did not change its traditional Hindu revivalist goals.'[63] Moreover in a speech that he later made, Deoras worded his intent rather smartly by saying that the 'doors (of RSS) were open' for them 'if Muslims believed that India (read Bharatvarsha—*emphasis mine*) was their country, that their past was in this land and they were ready to comply with the minimum demands of the rituals of the shakha.'[64]

Even today, the RSS maintains that:

> Christians and Muslims who live in Bharat have not come from an alien land, rather they are all children of this nation. All our forefathers and ancestors are from this country. If for any reason, a person changes his religion then that does not mean that they should change their values and vision towards life. So Christians, Muslims or people following any other religion who live in Bharat and who subscribe to the world view of Bharat are all 'Hindus'. They are welcome to be in the RSS.[65]

Meanwhile, the clamour for the RSS to abandon its objective of Hindu consolidation was getting louder by the day. The government then decided to assign the Janata Party president, Chandrashekhar to open talks with Deoras on the issue. The 'Young Turk' who later became prime minister of India, was travelling to Chennai en route Nagpur and met Deoras in the VIP lounge of the airport where the two held a brief one-on-one session. It was made known to the press that certain key decisions were arrived at during the meeting, but neither leader was willing to reveal the details.

But in the next eighteen months or so, Deoras was seen to be making several concessions, of which some were as follows:

> while insisting that there would be no dilution in RSS' ideology, he agreed to imposing no conditions on swayamsevaks who wished to be associated with other organisations.
>
> former members of the Jana Sangh should conform to the code of conduct of the Janata Party, and that the RSS shall not interfere in the matter.
>
> there was no necessity for swayamsevaks in politics to retain close contact with the RSS.
>
> they must avoid advocating the idea of Hindutva in the government.
>
> dilution of the RSS ideology and its programmes—OTCs, winter camps, speeches etc.

On witnessing that Deoras had yielded appreciably, the critics upped their ante, suggesting that ex-Jana Sangh lawmakers must secure a declaration from the RSS that they would not be bound by any directions or expectations from the sangh. In order to ensure the continued presence of RSS in the ruling party, albeit obliquely, Deoras accepted even this demand stating that all legislators at the Central and state levels would henceforth be free from all obligations of the RSS. Yet, he refused to direct any swayamsevak to stay away from either the shakhas or any other activity associated with the RSS, if done voluntarily. He also declared with confidence that despite the declaration, none of the elected representatives would 'ever give up their loyalty to the RSS.'[66]

Two decades after the collapse of the Janata Party government, while on a state visit to the US, Prime Minister Atal Bihari Vajpayee had famously said, 'Once a swayamsevak, always a swayamsevak.' There couldn't have been a more apt description of what Balasaheb Deoras had said, and really meant.

However, Balasaheb's long list of concessions to the Janata Party government was severely resented by many of his peers. It was noticed how during his public speeches, Deoras would take extra precaution to steer clear of three key words, which still form the kernel of the RSS—Hindu, Hindutva and Hindu Rashtra.

Finally, it took a senior leader and sanghchalak of Maharashtra, Kakasaheb Limaye to caution Deoras. In a letter to him, Kakasaheb wrote that the chief should stick to his brief of running the sangh on the guidelines laid down by K.B. Hedgewar. 'Do not alter that sangh,' Limaye chastised Balasaheb and added for good measure, 'if you still wish to make alterations, then kindly go and develop an alternate sangh.' Following Limaye's stern letter, other voices of protests also joined in and it was recommended that the matter be cleared before things got out of hand. It finally fell upon Rajju Bhaiyya to clarify that there was no change in the RSS' ideology, but for the nation's good, it was decided to take a temporary break from advocating its core principles.[67]

Deoras' tactical retreat paid rich dividends—the government began to involve the RSS in crucial sectors like External Affairs, Education and media. A large international conference backed by the foreign ministry was held in New Delhi under the aegis of the Friends of India Society International, headed by north India sanghchalak, Hans Raj Gupta. The ministry of External Affairs even acceded to 'polite suggestions for taking the sangh men on foreign trips.'[68] Those criticising the RSS were blocked out; the history curriculum and related research bodies were specifically targeted. An anonymous memorandum began making the rounds alleging that the Communists had 'colonised' autonomous educational bodies like the Indian Council of Historical Research (ICHR), Indian Council of Social Science Research (ICSSR), the National Council Of Educational Research And Training (NCERT), and the University Grants Commission or UGC. Several history text books for school children were put under the scanner, and although efforts to proscribe them had failed, there were only a few copies available in the market. An organisation parallel to the Indian History Congress, backed by the Deendayal Research Institute was promoted by the government as a rival to ICHR.

The RSS was mighty impressed with the government's efforts. The ABPS had even passed a resolution appreciating the fact that the Ministry of Education had invited RSS' representatives for a meeting to discuss an adult education programme. Bhaurao Deoras and Rajju Bhaiyya pledged to 'extend their active and whole hearted co-operation' for it which included the 'use of the fabulous funds meant for adult education to promote the "national cause".'

From late 1978 onwards, Balasaheb Deoras had reconciled to the end of the Janata Party rule. Apart from internecine skirmishes made worse by personality clashes, the issue of 'dual membership' had severely impacted the party. The RSS baiters within Janata Party were hell bent on alienating the RSS, little realising that it would also sound the death knell for the government. Balasaheb decided to move on from this setback and decided to revive the Vishwa Hindu Parishad (VHP) which was established by M.S. Golwalkar amidst great enthusiasm in 1964, but had since languished. After the First World Hindu Conference in 1966, Deoras organised its second chapter after more than a decade in January 1979 in Allahabad.

The conference turned out to be a roaring success insofar as it had included representatives from sections which were listed as 'Hindus' by the RSS—the inaugural session was addressed by the Dalai Lama, and was attended by almost all the important Hindu seers of India. The three-day conclave adopted what it called the 'Minimum Code of Religious Conduct' listing six tenets.[69] Foremost among them was the pledge to accord the sun the status of an 'eternal god', and a commitment to do 'vandana' (prayers) to it every day; the 'Om' syllable was accepted as the 'universal symbol of divinity'; and the holy Gita was declared as the 'non-sectarian scripture of Hindu society'. Unless proven otherwise, the genesis of the curious term, 'political Hindu' could easily be attributed to this very conference. As Deoras had said without mincing his words:

> Hindus must now awaken themselves to such an extent that even from the election point of view the politicians will have to respect the Hindu sentiments and change their policies accordingly...If others put up their demands, they were accepted, but, even genuine demands by Hindus are ignored. This is because Muslims and other minorities usually vote *en bloc* while Hindus are divided. Once Hindus get united, the government would start caring for them also.

However, the decision to reactivate the VHP was not taken overnight, and it becomes imperative here to understand what had made Deoras shift his focus. As mentioned above, the VHP was set up by M.S. Golwalkar along with S.S. Apte, and the global yoga guru, Chinmayananda to primarily carry out the RSS' tribal outreach programme. However in 1977, it had handed over the baton to the Bharatiya Vanvasi Kalyan Ashram (BVKA), which was also established by Golwalkar in 1952 in Chhattisgarh (then part of the Central Provinces). Thereafter, although the BVKA had spread out to a few other states, its performance was laggard, and it was for this reason that Deoras had stepped in revive it in order to ensure that the affiliates stayed focussed on one area of work. Gradually, the BVKA became well known for propagating the belief that Christian missionaries in India were focussed on converting Hindu-tribals and other lower castes to Christianity.

As mentioned in the beginning of this chapter, Balasaheb Deoras' long stint in the RSS notwithstanding, his image of a dedicated soldier in the service of the nation and its people was the reason which had made him synonymous with the sangh. It may be recalled that in its commitment to sewa or service, when thousands of displaced people had arrived from across the border during Partition, it was the RSS which had set up relief camps for refugees in Delhi and other parts of India. Several accounts of the period have chronicled the extraordinary work done by the RSS, but the camps also doubled up as sites for indoctrination which had led to the increase in the number of shakhas in the late Forties. Balasaheb wanted the sangh's service-oriented activities to continue unabated, but with greater involvement in politics.

He set the ball rolling in April 1978 when he told a large gathering of swayamsevaks to 'start service activities among the neglected sections of the society,' and this had led to the setting up of the Sewa Bharati on Vijaydashami day in 1979.[70] What Balasaheb had meant by service amongst weaker sections was that the activities be initially targeted towards the Scheduled Castes. As was its wont, the RSS likened the Delhi initiative to being,

> no different from the River Ganga which after originating from the Gaumukh assumes a gigantic form before joining the Yamuna and the Saraswati in Prayag. Who had thought that a tiny project started way back in 1979 with 4-5 kids would become the flagship of entire Sewa Bharati work and stand as the talking monument of social reforms and development?[71]

Over time, Sewa Bharati expanded its activities to other areas such as running hostels and residential schools, *matrichhaya* or orphanages, helping street children, setting up tailoring centres, computer literacy programmes, adult education, mass marriages, supporting children from terror-affected regions and finally, to the setting up of *bhajan mandalis* (groups which sang religious songs) in order to bring all the initiatives under the common umbrella of religion.

Even before the RSS had overtly begun to focus on the sphere of education during the Janata period, Balasaheb had initiated steps in this direction several decades ago. The background was Golwalkar's decision to establish a school in Gorakhpur way back in 1952. Prior to his assuming the mantle of sarsanghchalak, Deoras had given a fillip to his chief's initiative by expanding the single-school project into a statewide network of schools. Called the Saraswati Shishu Mandir, or the temple of learning, named after the goddess of learning,

Saraswati, these schools worked as perfect alternatives for parents who desired quality education for their children, but did not have the financial means to afford expensive schools. The Saraswati Shishu Mandir schools were steeped in Hindu ethos which mandated that the students chant the Saraswati Vandana, Shanti path and the Gayatri Mantra. By 1977, there were almost 700 Shishu Mandirs in India, at which point, Deoras decided to bring them all under a common programme called, Vidya Bharti.

Gradually, Vidya Bharti became an important vehicle to carry the RSS' ideology to Hindu families. Currently, Vidya Bharti runs more than twelve thousand schools in India, an equal number of sewa kendras, and employs almost one and a half lakh teachers who teach nearly thirty-five lakh students. It is the largest educational institution in the non-governmental sector and unambiguously carries the stamp of Balasaheb Deoras' efforts.

The setting up of the Shishu Shiksha Samiti in Assam in 1979 could be held out as the perfect example of what Deoras had intended to do—the assimilation of socially-driven activities with politics. The Samiti later ran several schools called the Sankardev (one of Assam's most revered saints) Shishu Kunja and by early 2016, its number had increased to 490.[72] The clutch of schools had come up at a crucial period in the state's history when the All Assam Students' Union (AASU) had started a movement against non-Assamese settlers, a sizeable number of whom were both Hindus and Muslims from Bangladesh. Gradually, with the tacit support of the RSS, what had originally begun purely as an ethnicity issue had transformed into a communal conflict. While addressing the issue of illegal migrants from Bangladesh, Balasaheb had argued that 'infiltrators and refugees can't be put on par,' and elaborated that the case of Hindus coming from

Bangladesh was different, because they were 'refugees' who had fled their homes after being persecuted by an Islamic dispensation. While addressing the Assamese Hindus in the state, Deoras had exhorted them to accommodate Hindus from Bangladesh and forewarned that the traffic of Bangladeshi Muslims could lead to the gradual alteration of their demographic profile.[73] This argument made in 1979 found resonance twenty-seven years later during the assembly elections in the state in 2016 when the agitation for ethnicity had developed overt anti-Muslim overtones.[74]

Within two years of its formation, the RSS had begun to exert undue influence over the Janata Party, acting as a kind of 'supra-party' with extra-constitutional powers. With their backs against the wall, both Balasaheb Deoras and Atal Bihari Vajpayee had made several concerted bids to salvage the Jana Sangh and its status within the Janata government. However, such were the pressures from both within the Janata Party and the RSS that in March 1979, Deoras was finally forced to direct former Jana Sangh members to attend a meeting of the RSS' Delhi unit.

Vajpayee had turned up for the meeting, but had chosen not to sit in the front row indicating that all wasn't well between him and Deoras. In a further embarrassment to the RSS chief a few months later, Vajpayee had stated in a speech that the former Jana Sangh members had 'left the politics of the Jana Sangh forever. We should forget these things now and participate in the only nationalist stream of the Janata Party based upon the four principles of nationalism, democracy, religious equality and social equality.'

On 2 August 1979, by which time the Janata Party had split and Charan Singh had become prime minister at the head of a breakaway Janata faction, Vajpayee wrote a signed article in *The Indian Express* and amongst other things, made three assertions. First, that the RSS-sponsored publications must stop taking sides in political power games; second, the RSS should sever all links with youth organisations which worked with political parties. Finally, that the RSS should clarify that Hindu Rashtra actually meant, 'Bharatiya Rashtra'. Within weeks, Deoras also retaliated and in no small measure during his annual Vijaydashami speech in Nagpur. He accepted that organisations must change, but that it 'should not take place by cutting itself from the arteries of life-sap.'

Exactly eight months later on 6 April 1980, Atal Bihari Vajpayee along with his most trusted lieutenant, Lal Krishna Advani, founded the Bharatiya Janata Party or BJP. At the BJP's first conference on 5–6 April 1980, Vajpayee in his maiden presidential speech refuted rumours of the Jana Sangh being revived under a new name. 'We will make use of our experience in the Janata Party. We are proud to have been associated with it.' Even the party's credo—Gandhian Socialism, which was coined by Vajpayee, was far removed from what the RSS stood for. It was clear that the BJP had willy-nilly abandoned the principle of Integral Humanism propounded by the RSS stalwart, Deendayal Upadhyaya. Although Balasaheb had showed considerable restraint in the matter, it hadn't gone down well with his cadre who urged him to rein in the BJP. While Deoras was still chairman of *Tarun Bharat*, its editor wrote signed pieces accusing the BJP of abandoning Upadhyaya's principles. Finally, the sarsanghchalak made his opinion known to his colleagues as follows:

> BJP leaders like Vajpayee and Advani are experienced with sufficient years in politics behind them and have the requisite understanding to decide for themselves. Politics is a tricky game and it is not wise to offer explanation at every step. Instead of

> being concerned about BJP's deviation, focus on strengthening the sangh and try to reach a situation where you can influence more than one party. Eventually the BJP will have to face consequences of its own leaders. It is best to follow a wait and watch approach for the moment.[75]

It was apparent that although Deoras had maintained that Vajpayee and Advani were well within their rights to start a new party, but deep within, he was sceptical about their move to disassociate themselves from the RSS. Eventually however, he was left with no option but to agree that ex-Jana Sangh members must be allowed to chart their own political destinies. After going past the problem, Deoras decided to, 'turn his energies back towards sangathanism by calling on the activist network to explain—and to establish—the organisation in as many places as possible.'[76]

Within the next three months, members of the RSS hit the road, traversing through more than ten thousand villages to give their version of the sequence of events. It had been a tumultuous three years for Deoras when he had attempted to take the RSS closer to power than what his predecessors could have ever imagined. After the passing of three years however, the RSS was back to where it had begun—an insular entity, but with a difference. It had come to be acknowledged as a force which was capable of influencing electoral politics, mainly because of a proactive sarchangchalak who was even then preparing for the next round.

Beyond the Janata Debris

It was in the Eighties when religion had first begun to make its mark as a mandatory tool for mobilising Indian electoral politics. Although political parties had resorted to selecting candidates on the basis of religious and caste identities even during the first general elections in 1951–52, but the assimilation of religion to appropriate political space was first witnessed after Indira Gandhi had returned to power in 1980.

Punjab, once acknowledged as the most prosperous state in north India, was in the grip of militancy with separatist Sikhs demanding to secede from the Indian Union to form their own homeland called, Khalistan. It is rather well documented how Indira Gandhi had mismanaged Punjab, mainly by playing into the hands of Jarnail Singh Bhindranwale who was at the head of a separatist movement in order to push back the Akalis in the state. She repeated this during the 1983 elections in Jammu & Kashmir which was already struggling with a contentious history since independence.

In contrast, the RSS held a different viewpoint on Punjab and Deoras articulated it by saying that the Sikhs were part of Hindu society as they had waged wars against Muslim rulers in the past. In any case, as Article 25 of the Indian Constitution classifies Sikhs, Jains and Buddhists as Hindus, it was therefore rather puzzling for the RSS chief to have made the reference to context. In all probability, Deoras may have intended to educate the Hindus and Sikhs of Punjab that regardless of anything, Muslim deception is universal and has been a recurring theme since the medieval period.

By the time Indira Gandhi stormed back into office in January 1980, it was almost three years since Balasaheb had taken charge of the VHP which had 300 units spread over 437 of the 534 Indian districts at the time (this number went up to more than 700 in 2018). More significantly, the VHP was being managed by 150 full-time pracharaks and had witnessed a marked improvement from the time Balasaheb's younger brother, Bhaurao was given charge. In his time, much like the RSS, the VHP also fell outside the purview of politics and was therefore limited to activities such as, 'running hostels, orphanages, medical centres, and publishing journals that raised fears of Hindus being swamped by "non-Hindu foreigners".'

It is noteworthy that the VHP is the only affiliate of the RSS in which the sarsanghchalak is a trustee of a board (called the Nyasi Mandal) and therefore has a say in its decision-making. After Golwalkar's death, Balasaheb had joined the board, but towards the latter part of his tenure when his health had begun deteriorating, he had inducted Moropant Pingle into the Mandal.

By late 1980, the VHP had evolved into a well-oiled machinery, but it still lacked a central emotive issue that could mobilise Hindus at a mass level. Deoras was of the view that the RSS narrative should become part of the day-to-day social discourse amongst Hindus in order for them to have a stake in the sangh's attempt to establish Hindu hegemony across the nation. In early 1981, the RSS and its subsidiaries were handed over an issue on a platter for them to occupy centre stage and work towards harnessing their goal of Hindu consolidation.

On 9 February, an obscure village called Meenakshipuram in Tirunelveli district, Tamil Nadu had shot into prominence for a reason most unpleasant when nearly 800 Hindus belonging to the untouchable Pallas caste had converted to Islam because of continued harassment from the upper castes in their village.

Deoras saw the Meenakshipuram incident as the perfect opportunity for fortifying the Hindu community, and considering he was familiar with the ways of the VHP, he decided that it should plunge into the mass conversion episode without any further delay.

He had at the outset acknowledged the fact that the mass conversions in Meenakshipuram were the result of upper caste discrimination which he had mentioned at length in his Vasant Vyakhanmala lecture in Pune. He had felt strongly that such incidents obstructed the RSS' objective of Hindu consolidation, and historically, the Dalits had therefore stayed away from the sangh's purview. Balasaheb instructed the VHP to work among the lower castes, and it consequently launched a fund-raising campaign in January 1983 and collected fifty million rupees in donations. Additionally in the winter of 1983, the VHP made its maiden attempt at mass mobilisation by organising a nationwide Ekatmata Yagna Yatra during which the holy water of the Ganga was carried in giant urns to different parts of the country. The yatra was conducted on cow-driven carts which were decorated with giant maps of India and the image of Bharat Mata to drive home the significance of three *matas* or mother goddesses for every Hindu—Ganga, Bharat, and Gau Mata. K.S. Sudarshan, who later went on to become the sarsaghchalak of the RSS in 2000, commented about the yatra as follows:

> When people were told that Ganga Mata is coming, thousands of people came there. It was a thing to be seen to be believed... Even in Kerala which is Leftist ideology...even if they could get just a few drops on their body, they thought, 'we shall definitely go to heaven'...All these things evoke a nationalist sentiment.

Such was the popular appeal of the yatra that even Prime Minister Indira Gandhi had considered attending a public meeting when the procession had reached Delhi on 17 November 1983, but had backed out at the last minute. By the time the programme had concluded one month later on 16 December, Deoras must have felt vindicated in the way the VHP had shaped up under his supervision.

It wasn't only the RSS and its affiliates that had expressed shock at Hindus embracing Islam in Meenakshipuram, but even leaders such as Dr Karan Singh (described as the 'on-and-off' Congressman and a confidant of Indira Gandhi), who was extremely agitated over the incident. In September 1981, the erstwhile king of Jammu, and an erudite scholar of Sanskrit, established the Virat Hindu Samaj (VHS) and became its founding president, while the then VHP president, Ashok Singhal was nominated as its general secretary. Within a month of its formation, the VHS organised several public meetings in north India, the most significant of these being in Delhi in October. While Karan Singh was the star of the moment, Singhal was among the *nepathya nayaks* or backstage heroes.[77] When asked for his reason for setting up the VHS and his association with the VHP, Dr Singh had said:

> The real, proximate cause (for establishing VHS) was the conversions in Meenakshipuram...The Hindu opinion was divided, even before independence, into two streams, one is the RSS Parivar, the other may be called Congress Parivar.... the Virat Hindu Samaj was a sort of an attempt to bridge. I, having been in the Congress all my life, felt that there were people who may be turned off, who may not go to the RSS Parivar, but would come here.[78]

Alas, the RSS was unwilling to work with an organisation whose antecedents were doubtful, and Dr Karan Singh had to subsequently wind up the VHS.

On Track

The Ram Janmabhoomi agitation for constructing a Ram temple in Ayodhya is acknowledged as one of the largest religio-political mass movements in Independent India. As is well known, it was after L.K. Advani's rath yatra from Somnath to Ayodhya in 1991 that the BJP was catapulted from the margins of Indian politics to the centre stage. Since the agitation was spearheaded by the VHP, Balasaheb Deoras had insisted that its controls remain firmly in the hands of the top brass of the RSS and its nominees.

There is no doubt that the Indian Right-wing has a natural proclivity towards godmen and renunciates, evidenced as it was in one of the icons of the RSS, M.S. Golwalkar. The reason for this has less to do with enlightenment or knowledge, and more with including men of god who can influence the electorate. While many such men were part of the VHP, it was felt that parallel bodies be set up to ensure that religious leaders joined the political campaign without being part of decision-making bodies. In March 1981, the VHP set up the Kendriya Margdarshak Mandal and a few months later a larger organisation had come up called the Dharam Sansad which was described as the 'supreme deliberative body to decide on issues pertaining to the interests of the Hindus.' Yet, and on this point Deoras had insisted even when the issue was debated by the core handlers, that 'the VHP made it clear from the beginning, that while it would allow itself to be "guided" by the Mandal and the Sansad, the decisions of the VHP would be taken by its office bearers alone.' (Even today, barring the 'notional' advisors and patrons, all the office-bearers of the VHP are RSS functionaries who are handpicked by the top brass. Both the Mandal and the Sansad remain active currently and function as the VHP's representative arms among religious leaders, reaffirming the fact that the structures created during Deoras' tenure have indeed stood the test of time.)

Ironically, although the construction of the Ram temple was the leitmotif of the RSS, VHP, and later the BJP, it was first brought into focus by a former Congress leader. In the early 1980s, Gulzarilal Nanda who had stewarded India twice after the demise of Nehru and Shastri, joined the VHP. In May 1983, he wrote a letter to Indira Gandhi demanding the restoration of temples in Ayodhya, Mathura and Varanasi. When there was no response from her office, the *Organiser* 'took up the theme,'[79] but fearing the charge of fomenting communal violence, it had treaded cautiously and said, 'according to hearsay', such a structure had existed in the past etc. What this proved was that the agitation around the Ram temple wasn't even part of the RSS' narrative either during Hedgewar's tenure, or when Golwalkar was the sarsanghchalak.

Later, when the building of the temple became the lynchpin of the Indian Right-wing, Balasaheb Deoras had recommended that an attempt be made to secure the support of the Congress party, much like his predecessor Golwalkar had done by seeking help from Sardar Patel and his group for rebuilding the Somnath temple. Both Deoras, and before him, Golwalkar knew well that despite the Congress' secular credentials, a particular section in the party had always acknowledged that the idea of Hindu vulnerability was real, and could only be reversed by restoring temples which had been destroyed by 'outsiders'. Therefore, Deoras' concern that the Congress party may hijack the temple movement was somewhat genuine.

In the late 1980s as a young reporter on the Ayodhya beat, I would spend time at the VHP's Lucknow office. During one such visit in July 1989, I recall asking Onkar Bhave who was the organising secretary of Central Zone, how the Ram temple agitation had come to occupy such an important place in the sangh's programmes. He told me that in early January 1984, an important meeting of the RSS was held in Lucknow after which a few senior leaders had come visiting the temple town. Unfortunately, I hadn't stopped him midway to ask who these leaders were and he continued with his narrative adding that when the leaders had witnessed the state of Ram Lalla (the idol of Lord Ram as a child), they had cried copious tears. It was post that visit, said Bhave, that the issue of constructing a brand new temple on the same site was discussed internally and became part of the RSS' agenda. It goes without saying that a decision of such import could not have been made without consulting Deoras.

Thereafter, things had moved at a lightning speed—a two-day meeting of the Dharam Sansad was held in Delhi's Vigyan Bhavan in April 1984 in which a large number of saints demanded the 'restoration' of temples in Ayodhya, Mathura and Kashi. Yet another organisation called the Ram Janmabhoomi Mukti Yagna Samiti was formed with the sole purpose of 'liberating' Lord Ram's 'birthplace', with Mahant Avaidyanath (a former member of the Hindu Mahasabha from Gorakhpur and chief of the powerful Gorakhnath Mutt) as its president. Deoras had succeeded in achieving his primary objective—the Hindu bandwagon was set rolling, even as he had succeeded in drawing religious leaders and several others belonging to other political parties like the Congress. It was only a matter of time before the temple in Ayodhya became the tool for Hindu consolidation.

For Deoras and the RSS, 1984 was a bitter-sweet year. On the one hand, if the Ekatmata Yagna Yatra had demonstrated how such processions could successfully convert devotees into political supporters, the next one ended almost in a disaster although for no fault of the organisers.

In September 1984, the VHP launched yet another yatra called the Ram-Janaki Rath Yatra, named after Lord Ram and Sita (Janaki being another name for her). It was flagged off from Sitamarhi in Bihar and arrived on the outskirts of Delhi on 30 October after traversing through Ayodhya and Lucknow, in UP. Earlier in the year, a youth wing of the VHP was established called the Bajrang Dal, named after Lord Hanuman, which was at the forefront of attracting support for the Ram-Janaki Rath Yatra. According to H.V Seshadri the yatra had resulted in an 'unprecedented Hindu upsurge'. However, the procession had to be rolled back as Indira Gandhi was assassinated a day later, and the country was besieged by murderous assaults on Sikhs in Delhi, and elsewhere.

The festival of Vijaydashami was celebrated a week into the Ram-Janaki Rath Yatra. What had begun as a routine speech on the occasion, later turned out be a 'bombshell' because never before in his entire career had Deoras made such shocking assertions. Amongst other things, which included his observations about the threat of terrorism, the Centre-state relations, and highlighting the contributions made by leaders such as Nehru, Patel and Rajendra Prasad, it was his comments on Indira Gandhi which became the focus of the speech.

He accused Indira Gandhi of many things—labelling her as 'self-centred'; a prime minister who owed no 'allegiance to principles and ideology. The only objective was to be in power forever'; presiding over a party which was 'disorganised with internal conflicts'; and on the 'brink of destruction.' Yet, the RSS chief saw the Congress party as irreplaceable: 'We do not see any other party which can capably take the place of Congress,'[80] he had said. For the Opposition parties, and also the BJP, there was worse to come because he accused them of infighting: 'They cannot come together and work. Nor can they project a strong alternative to the Congress. And such a possibility does not seem apparent in the near future.'

Deoras' speech had had a rippling effect because it was interpreted as his tacit support for the Congress, and an attempt to coerce Indira Gandhi into forming a political association with the RSS. There was recent history to this entire premise as a large chunk of the RSS believed, albeit erroneously, that it was Deoras who had helped Mrs Gandhi win the 1980 elections.

Immediately thereafter, the RSS chief toured the country and further sharpened his rhetoric and eventually cast the die by openly asking Hindus to vote for those who upheld their interests.

The Vijaydashami address of Balasaheb was controversial because of three main points—first, there was genuinely no real alternative to the Congress at that point of time. Second, and also linked to the first point, the Opposition parties were not only at loggerheads, but were also unlikely to resolve their differences in the immediate future to evolve a mechanism of cooperating with each other. Third and finally, was his advice to Hindus to vote as a block and keep their religious interest uppermost immediately after his address to the Congress, which political experts felt was an invitation to the ruling party to form an alliance with the RSS.

Even before the dust could settle on Deoras' speech, the polls were announced and the campaigning by political parties came into sharp focus. The Rajiv Gandhi-led Congress party launched its massive juggernaut, but it was obvious that their narrative had undergone a major change after Indira Gandhi's assassination—it was upfront and divisive in nature. Even as many saw it as a negative portent for the future of Indian politics, it found resonance with the RSS. For instance, Nanaji Deshmukh, who for all practical purposes had withdrawn from active politics, declared that Rajiv Gandhi needed the support of patriotic forces. Deoras' stoic silence throughout the campaign, and the complete rout of the BJP in the polls (the party managed to win only two seats, and even Vajpayee had faced defeat) gave rise to the speculation that several members of the RSS had voted for Congress candidates and had contributed to the party's landslide victory.

The End of Expectations

On several occasions in its history spanning six decades, the RSS had made several attempts to form an alliance with the Congress, or even with a section of it. Sample this: since its inception in 1925, the RSS was with the Congress until 1937; a decade later in 1949–50, M.S. Golwalkar had approached Sardar Patel and his loyalists within the Congress party for rescinding the ban on RSS. In the 1970s, Balasaheb Deoras had openly praised Mrs Gandhi's contribution in liberating Bangladesh; the RSS had initiated back channel negotiations with the government during the Emergency, and finally, Deoras' speech of 1984 which had sent out a signal that the Congress and RSS could explore to partner by focussing on the Hindu vote.

After Rajiv Gandhi assumed the mantle of prime minister in the aftermath of his mother's killing, Deoras presented him with a list of demands—scrap Article 370 of the Constitution; evict infiltrators in Assam; deport foreign missions and missionaries engaged in religious conversions; establish a Human Rights Commission in place of the proposed Minority Rights Commission (which was under consideration after the Gopal Singh Committee's recommendation in June 1983). Eventually, none of these demands were met. To add to Deoras' disenchantment, Rajiv Gandhi had succumbed to pressure from the Muslim orthodoxy and obtained parliamentary approval for the Muslim Women (Protection of Rights on Divorce) Bill to quash the Supreme Court's verdict in the Shah Bano case*. On the one hand, if the Congress was riding roughshod over the RSS, and which was expected given the history, even the BJP seemed to pay less and less attention to the men in Nagpur.

Such was the atmosphere of hopelessness in the RSS circles that several swayamsevaks had approached Balasaheb suggesting they form another party. But the sarsangchalak had instead given them an assurance that he shall solve the impasse by holding a dialogue with BJP leaders warning them to not deviate from the core principles of the sangh.

Meanwhile, as a consequence of the apex court's verdict in April 1985, Rajiv Gandhi was caught in a dilemma—whether he should side with progressive Muslims (ironically backed by the RSS for obvious reasons), or go with the conservatives who controlled the Muslim vote bank. The RSS was watching the developments keenly, and when it was reasonably certain that the Centre would catapult to Muslim obscurantism, it decided to revive the campaign for the Ram temple in Ayodhya. But not before it accused Rajiv Gandhi of

---

* The Supreme Court had delivered the Shah Bano judgement on 23 April 1985 and triggered protests from the Muslim clergy and conservatives in the community. The government had legislated the new law to address this, but the move had antagonised Hindu groups.

succumbing to the 'planned anti-national manoeuvre,' of the 'fanatic Muslim leadership'.[81]

In May 1986—three months after the disputed shrine was unlocked at the instruction of Rajiv Gandhi—L.K. Advani was appointed BJP president and he revived his party's ties with the RSS. The samanvaya samitis, which were established by Deoras after the Emergency, were brought back into the reckoning, and RSS pracharaks were loaned to work for the BJP, including K.N. Govindacharya and Narendra Modi. In 1987, Advani and Vajpayee met Deoras to draw out a strategy for the Ram temple. Deoras advised them to play it smartly—first, hijack the Congress' plan which had initiated the opening up of the disputed site, and second, instruct party workers to adopt guerrilla tactics while accomplishing the task. Ironically, his advise was completely ignored when the kar sevaks had clambered on to the dome of the disputed mosque and were seen demolishing it, and finally razing it to the ground on 6 December 1992.

Throughout the late 1980s, the VHP was majorly focussed on the Ayodhya agitation, while Balasaheb had moved on to other pressing issues, like the grand celebrations to mark Hedgewar's birth centenary in 1988. Deoras 'undertook a whirlwind tour of the country in failing health,'[82] and ensured that every detail for the event was 'imaginatively and meticulously planned.' The level at which it had panned out, made the intent clear—it wasn't just a grandiose plan to celebrate the founder's birth anniversary, but to establish him as the fountainhead of a movement that had come into its own. The iconic status of Hedgewar even found mention in Narendra Modi's book, *Jyotipunj*, in a chapter in which he was compared with Swami Vivekananda: 'Right since childhood, both Vivekananda and Doctor Saheb continuously struggled for their respective goals...'[83]

In India, 50,000 committees were formed for the anniversary celebrations, while 80,000 public meetings were held between November 1988 and April 1989, targeting 1.5 crore families drawn from 2.16 lakh villages. The RSS also took the programme abroad—a gathering at Milton Keynes in the UK was held for two days in August 1989, and was attended by almost 80,000 people.

The other, but long-term objective of the campaign was to firm up the unification of Hindus, and it happened without eulogising either the RSS or any of its icons. It was a slogan which has since then become synonymous with the Hindu Right, but at the time all it had intended to do was to lend a sense of pride to every member of the community: *Garv se kaho hum Hindu hain* (Say it with pride that I am a Hindu).

Apart from the fact that Deoras had wanted Hedgewar to get his due in the pantheon of the greats, it was also a period in Indian politics when the RSS was on the upsurge, primarily because of the Ram temple agitation. As mentioned earlier, the VHP had its game plan chalked out, and was drawing people to its fold; the Bharatiya Mazdoor Sangh had become the second largest trade union in the country and was poised to overtake rivals; and the Bharatiya Vanvasi Kalyan Ashram had developed into an impressive outfit across India. But alas, there was no coordination amongst the affiliates, and they often worked at cross purposes, locked as they were in personal rivalries.

An internal document written by Bapurao Varadpande, an important RSS functionary of the time, claimed that Deoras had decided to remedy the situation after veering around to the viewpoint that the sangh parivar's collective consciousness had been diluted and the organisation was facing the threat of fragmentation, afflicted as it was by 'institutional egoism'.[84] According to Varadpande, the sarsanghchalak had suggested that the only way to rectify the anomalies was by offering the allurement of political power, but before that all the affiliates would have to work in tandem with each other. The only way that was achievable in 1988 was to bring them to jointly celebrate Hedgewar's birth centenary.

In order to bring Deoras' suggestion of cohesiveness to fruition, it had become incumbent upon the BJP to make a clean break from its past when it had joined the Janata Party government. In 1987, it delivered on its promise and refused to join Devi Lal's party, the Lok Dal in Haryana. Later, at the BJP's National Executive meeting in Ahmedabad in October 1988, party president L.K. Advani sounded a warning to his colleagues when he said that the 'mere aggregation of disparate groups without a coherent set of policies' to bind them shall fail to inspire people. He stressed on the importance of Opposition unity, than mere 'Opposition credibility'.[85] At long last, Balasaheb Deoras was somewhat reassured and the headline in the RSS' mouthpiece, *Organiser*, put it rather succinctly: 'RSS Chief Backs BJP'.[86]

The Final Years

In the early 1990s, when L.K Advani was Leader of the Opposition, he had once remarked to a group of journalists, including me, that the post-Bofors period in Indian politics was on a perpetual fast-forward mode. In the context of the BJP, this was proven true because from a party which had just two members in the Lok Sabha between 1984–1989, it went on to win 85 seats in 1989, and 120 in 1991. However to solely attribute this rise to the Bofors kickback scandal was a bit of a stretch—its ascent between 1989–1991 was also because of the Ram temple issue. As mentioned earlier, it was to the credit of Balasaheb that he had accelerated the Ram temple movement by not only mobilising the VHP, but also by prudently advising his flock to snatch it away from the Congress' mouth.

Meanwhile in 1989, there were indications that Rajiv Gandhi's political graph was on a decline. As a result, all the anti-Congress parties had come together to form a united front called the Janata Dal in the month of October that year. Apart from their common cause of defeating the Congress, they were also united by the fact that they were inimical to the sangh's ideology, and there were doubts if they would even consider accommodating the BJP in the alliance.

In order to resolve the problem which had seemed impossible at the time, a meeting was arranged by the media baron and owner of the Indian Express Group, Ramnath Goenka at his Nariman Point office in Bombay. Amongst others, in attendance was V.P. Singh, and three senior members of the RSS, Bhaurao Deoras, Rajju Bhaiyya and Nanaji Deshmukh. But the most distinguished guest at the gathering was a sworn RSS supporter and a multi-faceted man—a chartered accountant-turned-editor-turned-crusader, S. Gurumurthy, who had played a crucial role in investigating the Bofors scam, a story which was broken by *The Indian Express*. The presence of the RSS' top brass in the meeting was a clear departure from the past, because not only was the RSS deemed to be an apolitical outfit, its direct participation in political negotiations was hitherto unknown. It was therefore clear that the three leaders would have obtained the prior permission of their sarsanghchalak, Balasaheb to be part of this backroom parley. Unlike the past, when all the RSS did was to advise the BJP during the Janata Party years, it was now part of a crucial meeting to strategise for the impending elections that year.

It was partly as a consequence of this meeting that the BJP came to be recognised as part of the anti-Congress front, especially in the Hindi heartland and western India. The strategy however reaped rich dividends for the BJP and it announced its dramatic arrival with a tally of 85 seats in the Lok Sabha—up from the mere two in the previous year. In comparison to his predecessor, Deoras' strategy of being an activist-sarsanghchalak had proven to be a success. Although the BJP had chosen not to become part of the unwieldy coalition, its influence was overtly noticeable because of its support to the minority government 'from the outside'.

Even as the RSS had chosen not to comment on the BJP's election results officially, it did make its stand clear on certain pressing issues at its Akhil Bharatiya Pratinidhi Sabha meeting when it had passed a resolution on the events pertaining to Ayodhya after the fall of the V.P. Singh government and the state government's action against the VHP on 30 October 1990, in which a few activists were killed in police firing. In one of the minutes of the meeting, it was stated that the 'offering of karseva for the renovation (sic) of the Sri Ram temple is the dharmic and national right of the Hindu society.'

By the time this meeting was held, the BJP had parted ways with every significant political party, barring the Shiv Sena, that it had allied with in 1989, and decided to contest the mid-term elections on its own steam and performed credibly than ever before. More significantly, the BJP secured a majority in Uttar Pradesh, and formed its maiden government in the state. As against 1989 when it had fought on 225 seats, it contested on 477 seats in 1991, raising its tally from 85 to 120. Even its vote share rose from 18.11 per cent to 31.45 per cent, while the number of seats in the 425-strong state assembly rose from 57 to 221.

A few months later, Deoras was once again at the helm of the RSS' Karyakarini Mandal meeting which passed a resolution stating that the success of the BJP in the polls was an 'unambiguous verdict' on Ayodhya, and was a firm message to the Centre and the state of Uttar Pradesh to remove every hurdle in the way of constructing a temple. The resolution also sent out a message to the 'Muslim brothers opposed to the temple renovation to appreciate the national mood and desist from the path of confrontation.'[87]

Once it was acknowledged that the RSS had delivered on its promise of bringing the BJP to mainstream politics, there was no way that its leaders could be kept out of future negotiations on Ayodhya. On 30 October 1992, the Dharam Sansad made an important announcement—the kar seva for the construction of the Ram temple was to be undertaken on 6 December 1992, a date which had been ratified by the VHP. Within three days of the announcement, the RSS was invited for talks by the government. Rajju Bhaiyya and Moropant Pingle arrived, along with yet another colleague, Bhairon Singh Shekhawat who was then the chief minister of Rajasthan, and who later became the Vice President of India. Even Prime Minister Narasimha Rao had held negotiations with Rajju Bhaiyya on at least two occasions in November and early December 1992.

In his memoirs, *My Country My Life*, L.K. Advani recounted what had transpired at that meeting between Rao and Rajju Bhaiyya. The RSS leader had told the prime minister:

> Lakhs of people will be assembling at Ayodhya. We have made elaborate arrangements to see that they conduct *kar sewa* within the parameters of the court order. But what if the court order (allowing the programme) does not come and something

> untoward happens? I hope this does not happen. It is, therefore I am impressing upon the government the need to secure a verdict before December 6.

In response, Narasimha Rao is supposed to have said, 'I am confident that with you in control, nothing untoward will happen.'[88]

The Demolition: Planned to Perfection

For almost a quarter of a century, there has been speculation whether the demolition of the Babri masjid was a planned operation, or a spontaneous outburst. It had taken the Justice Liberhan Commission seventeen years and forty-eight extensions before presenting a report to the Manmohan Singh government in June 2009, in which it ruled out the demolition as being a spontaneous act by a frenzied mob. The Commission stated that because all the men at the site that day were seen sporting 'distinctive coloured headbands identifying them as RSS Bajrang Dal cadres, it cannot be inferred or concluded that it was without the knowledge of K.S. Sudarshan.' The Commission named several other RSS leaders, including H.V. Sheshadri, and K.N. Govindacharya as culpable, and concluded that even the trio of Vajpayee, Advani and Dr Murli Manohar Joshi would have to bear the responsibility for the demolition of the mosque. The report described the sangh parivar as 'a highly successful and corporatized model of a political party and the Ayodhya campaign demonstrates, has developed a highly efficient organisational structure.'[89] Although the Liberhan Commission report had several factual inaccuracies and was submitted thirteen years after Balasaheb Deoras' demise, it nevertheless acknowledged his role in transforming the sangh parivar from a politically pretentious club into one of the most well-oiled and politically-savvy outfits in the country.

My conclusions of what had transpired on that crucial morning of 6 December 1992 in Ayodhya, as also the decisions taken in the preceding weeks, are based on a series of taped conversations with several important people within the sangh, who shall remain unnamed here. These conversations have altered many of my earlier views on the Babri masjid demolition—including some conclusions in my book, *Demolition: India at the Crossroads*—and they can be further altered in the eventuality of fresh evidence in the case.

The government archives would undoubtedly have records of the negotiations that were conducted with representatives of the RSS, VHP and BJP, but they are currently not in public domain. But quite like the Gandhi assassination, aspects of which are still in the realm of speculation, the demolition of the Babri masjid is still obscured by several conflicting theories. It may be recalled that K.R. Narayanan, who was the Vice President at the time of the demolition, had said that the demolition of the sixteenth-century mosque was the greatest political tragedy in India after Gandhi's assassination.

There is no gainsaying the fact that the Babri masjid demolition was a planned operation, and was known to a select group of people in the RSS, VHP and BJP, including of course the sarsanghchalak, Balasaheb Deoras. A senior leader of the RSS who as I said earlier, shall remain unnamed, told me that the entire demolition issue needed to be understood from Deoras' point of view. In November 1989, when the volunteers had proceeded to Ayodhya for the first time, as also on two other occasions, in October–November 1990 and July 1992, there was little progress made. If this had repeated on 6 December, a day which was carefully chosen by the VHP, and ratified by the

RSS, it would have meant a terrible loss of face for the leadership in Nagpur. Something had to be done, and nothing would have been acceptable save the razing of the mosque to the ground.

Not only was the execution of the plan kept top secret, but it was handed over to men who had earned the trust of the RSS. On 6 December, Moropant Pingle, the 'chief operational commander' was comfortably ensconced in one of the numerous bhawans or ashrams close to the Babri masjid. Although he hadn't stepped out even once to oversee the goings-on, he was surrounded by a band of loyalists who were keeping a close track on the events. Once the first group of fifty-odd volunteers began chipping at the mosque, thousands who had surrounded the precincts began attacking it. Thereafter, it was just a matter of time before the mosque was pulled down, and turned into mounds of debris.

The first group of activists who lead the attack were personally picked out by Pingle, and it was a given that Deoras was in the know of this brigade; he was stationed at Nagpur when the decision was taken. Thereafter, the men literally came out from the dark and disappeared into it once the task was completed. These nameless people chose anonymity over recognition because of the seriousness of their commitment and conviction to the cause of Hindu consolidation, and were driven by a deep-seated sense of revenge for what was perceived as injustice meted out to Hindus in the medieval era.

What was most astounding was that Pingle had created an organisational chart for the operation for different parts of India. These handpicked activists in turn identified local-level volunteers, who then coordinated with functionaries belonging to the RSS, VHP, and the BJP. Senior party leaders in various states were also drawn in, including Advani and Dr Joshi. The Liberhan Commission said in its report that it 'cannot be assumed even for a moment that Advani, Vajpayee or Joshi did not know about the designs of the Sangh Parivar.'[90]

In the aftermath of the demolition, Balasaheb had also expressed his disappointment, but had added that at least, the 'Muslims will know how it feels when a place of worship and faith gets demolished at the hands of others.'[91]

The Legacy

In an organisation which was based on the principle of ek chalak anuvartitva, Balasaheb Deoras had created a paradigm of change when he had made his displeasure known after being superseded by Madhav Sadashiv Golwalkar. In due course, by accepting the sarsanghchalak as his supreme leader, Deoras had proved that he was first and foremost, a dedicated worker in the cadre-based outfit. Later, by affecting major alterations to the RSS' functioning, most importantly, by giving it a political purpose, Deoras had managed the impossible.

At the end of his career, he had yet again resorted to a major deviation from tradition on an issue that had been at the centre of several debates since the RSS' inception: succession. In March 1994, suffering as he was from acute diabetes, he decided to nominate his successor and did what was unprecedented in RSS' history by stepping down for Rajju Bhaiyya to assume charge. This tradition was later carried forward by Rajju Bhaiyya and his successor, K.S. Sudarshan. There was another very important directive which he had issued—that no memorial be constructed for him and he should be cremated like an ordinary man without much fanfare. Barring the odd photo of Deoras in RSS offices, the organisation therefore remains focused on two icons—K.B. Hedgewar, the founder, and Madhav Sadashiv Golwalkar or 'Guruji'.

As is universally proven, ushering in change is always fraught with dangers. In the context of the RSS, the biggest challenge was in transiting from a cadre-based outfit to a mass-based party. For instance, even today, the RSS adheres to the policy of restricting entries, unlike its other affiliates which are overtly political and hence accept members easily. However, even the limited expansion that Deoras had initiated, meant maintaining the integrity and commitment of swayamsevaks in the Hedgewar-Golwalkar era. Over the decades this has resulted in a situation where many of them have become leaders simply because they followed a routine—attending the daily shakha, going to camps and OTCs, lobbying with those outside the fold to attract them etc. Therefore, the standard routine of the RSS became detrimental to Hedgewar's objective of strengthening its inner core.

Till the end, Balasaheb insisted on maintaining the ordinariness that he felt was the greatest attribute of an RSS pracharak. As mentioned earlier, in what was viewed as a shocking divergence from the core of the RSS, his agnosticism was a topic of discussion, as he had not only rejected the kernel of Brahminism by refusing to attend the sundry sacred thread ceremony celebrations, but he had also categorically stated that his death be treated as ordinary and no memorial be erected in his name.

It was only later when his associates had pressed upon him that he had started to follow the basics in Hindu prayers by lighting incense sticks etc. But over the years, the RSS culture overtook his personal choices and he began to inch closer to symbols of organised religion and even ended his letters with, 'I pray to the Almighty for a long illness-free healthy life for you.'[92] He also began attending religious congregations like kirtans and yagnas etc. This became a regular feature particularly at the dawn of the Eighties after he realised the electoral potential of religion in politics. Balasaheb was in regular attendance at the ashrams and mathas of several gurus, and also began accepting invitations for quasi-religious functions at swayamsevaks' homes. There also came a time during his tenure when vedic prayers began to be recited in RSS offices, including the headquarters in Nagpur. In conclusion, despite his attempts and several of his own volition and however revolutionary, Balasaheb Deoras was as Atal Bihari Vajpayee had said, albeit in a different context: once a sarsanghchalak, always a sarsanghchalak.

VIJAYA RAJE SCINDIA

On 25 January 2001, death proved that it was indeed a great leveller. A senior leader of the Congress party, a former Union minister for Civil Aviation, and an ex-maharaja-turned politician, had stood in front of a funeral pyre with his tonsured head bowed in reverence, with tears in his eyes. It was his mother who lay in front of him, a woman he was estranged from for almost quarter of a century.

The dead woman lying on the pyre, draped in a rust-and-gold sari was Vijaya Raje Scindia, the erstwhile Queen Mother or Rajmata of Gwalior. The man who was about to light the funeral pyre was her son, the late Madhavrao Scindia.

A few days after her death, her personal secretary and close confidant, Sardar Sambhajirao Angre, had likened her to Ahilyabai Holkar, the medieval queen of Indore. Legend has it that Ahilyabai had ordered her only son to be trampled by elephants because he had tried to poison the recipients of her munificence. Amongst other things, Angre drew the comparison to suggest that Vijaya Raje hadn't parted ways with her son because of the property dispute which was in focus after her death, but on issues of morality.

If by some divine intervention had she had her way, she wouldn't have wanted Madhavrao to perform her last rites. In her will that was drawn in 1985, she had stated that her son had, 'rendered himself unfit even to the right to cremate his mother's dead body and do the last rites (*kriyas*), which is the religious duty of every son.'[1] But alas, no one raised an objection when Madhavrao had lit her pyre. Even the menagerie of gods which sat on her bedside, and accompanied her everywhere, were a mute witness to the spectacle that day. After all, she had succumbed to tradition and one she had endorsed all her life as the queen regent of Gwalior.

Despite the Instrument of Accession promulgated by Sardar Patel in 1947, and the abolition of privy purses by Prime Minister Indira Gandhi in 1971, Vijaya Raje Scindia was the quintessential royal. Although she took to politics in a democratic India, she always imagined herself to be the 'benefactor'. Ironically, she was addressed as Rajmata even in her own party which was in principle opposed to dynastic rule, empowering instead its cadre who were instructed not to attach any importance to honorifics.

* * *

A descendent of Nepalese royalty, Vijaya Raje's family was banished from Nepal and later settled down in Sagar, Madhya Pradesh where she was born in 1919. She was married at twenty-two to one of the most powerful and richest Maratha rulers of the time, Maharaja Jivajirao Scindia of Gwalior. The newly-wed divided their time between Gwalior and Bombay, where the Maharaja was a regular in the horse-racing circuit, and owned some of the best breeds in his personal stable.

With India's independence, much like other Indian royals, Jivajirao began feeling the heat of joining the Republic of India at the cost of giving up on the luxuries of monarchy. As the Indian National Congress was at the helm of affairs, Jivajirao turned deeply antagonistic towards the party and viewed it as an exploitative force which was coercing him and other royals to acquiesce to its demands. As a result, the Maharaja was naturally drawn towards the other emerging political force in Gwalior, the Hindu Mahasabha, but he was careful not to formalise it in any fashion out of fear of a political reprisal from the Congress.

A decade after independence, when the Central provinces (CP) or Madhya Bharat was reorganised as Madhya Pradesh in 1956, the Congress party which was aware of the erstwhile Maharaja's proclivity towards the Hindu Mahasabha, convinced him to contest for the second general elections in 1957. It needs to be mentioned here that despite the Congress' unquestionable dominance across India, the party was unsure about winning elections in Gwalior because it was home to Dr Dattatraya Parchure who had set up the Hindu Mahasabha in the state, and was later acquitted in the Mahatma Gandhi assassination case. The second and more important reason for getting the Maharaja on its side was the sheer size of Gwalior state, which was spread over eight parliamentary and sixty assembly seats and would have substantially added to the Congress party's victory margin.

Meanwhile, Jivajirao was least inclined to fight elections, to the manor born as he was. The Congress party however kept up its pressure on the erstwhile king, but to no avail as he was 'immersed in the racing season.'[2] As was expected, his wife came to his rescue and informed the Congress party that the Scindias wanted to keep away from electoral politics.

Vijaya Raje had even travelled to Delhi to meet with Prime Minister Nehru to convince him of her husband's reluctance to fight elections. However, Jawaharlal Nehru was in no mood to listen to her reasoning and promptly sent her off to see Indira Gandhi, who in turn took her to meet the then Minister for Railways, Lal Bahadur Shastri, and the Union Minister for Home Affairs, Pandit Govind Ballabh Pant.

As the conversation proceeded, Vijaya Raje Scindia tried convincing the group yet again that neither had she come to fight her husband's case, nor was she seeking a ticket for herself in his place. But the men in Nehru's Cabinet dismissed her pleas and told her firmly, 'Either your husband or you.'

Finally, a phone call and several parleys between Shastri and Pant made the Maharaja see reason and he agreed to fight the elections, but with the rider that the Congress' candidate would be his wife, Vijaya Raje Scindia.

The Maharani was thus thrown into the deep end of politics and was fielded from Guna (part of the erstwhile state of Gwalior) in 1957. That the royals still commanded respect and a near-cult following was proven when she trounced her opponent, V.G. Deshpande of the Hindu Mahasabha by 60,000 votes, winning 67 per cent of the vote share. Although her political career had begun with a fabulous victory, she somehow felt 'responsible for throttling a party (Hindu Mahasabha) with which I and my husband had much in common.'[3] Thereafter, her political career extended for more than four decades of which a major part was spent to 'undo the consequences of my impulsive mission to Delhi.'[4] It was therefore more than evident from the very beginning that Vijaya Raje Scindia was never inclined towards the Congress.

Her first few years in parliament were lacklustre as she was constrained by her husband's deteriorating health. Four years after her victory in the 1957 elections, Jivajirao Scindia died due to diabetes-related complications at the age of forty-five in July 1961. Vijaya Raje retreated into a shell with little or no interest in politics. Despite a prolonged period of mourning and adhering to the ritual of not appearing in public, as was the custom for widows in certain Hindu families, the Congress leadership convinced her to contest the general elections in 1962, and she won yet again with an impressive margin of 1,48,820 votes.

Within a few months, the dowager queen was disgruntled with the Congress yet again. The disagreement began with the then Finance Minister, Morarji Desai introducing the Gold Control Act in 1963 which put an embargo on the possession of gold with individuals and families* up to four kilograms, and permitted the manufacture and sale of only fourteen-carat gold jewellery (as against the prevailing twenty-two carats). The Rajmata thought the measure to be a 'venomous sister of prohibition,'[5] and finally, the 11.7 kilograms of gold that she was forced to surrender, became the reason for her decision to abandon the Congress party in 1967. There were of course other mitigating factors, for instance her conflict with the then chief minister of the state, D.P. Mishra, but the principal trigger was what she felt was a draconian step.

Therefore, during the 1967 general elections, Vijaya Raje was still ambivalent about her political future, and decided to sail in two boats—for the Lok Sabha, she chose to fight from Guna on behalf of the Right-wing Swatantra Party, while choosing the Jana Sangh for

* Hindu United Families, the legal name for joint families, were permitted to hold up to four kgs of gold, while individuals could possess up to two kgs.

the assembly elections from Karera in Shivpuri district. In the decade post her initiation into politics, Vijaya Raje had gone from being a reluctant royal to a seasoned politician managing two parties. In her autobiography, she had stated candidly how she 'looked upon all parties with suspicion,' and was therefore unable to decide 'between Jana Sangh and the Swatantra, the two parties with those programmes I was broadly in agreement.'

It later turned out that her decision to engage with two parties was part of a strategy devised by her trusted loyalist, Sardar Angre who'd apparently advised her that owing to her royal status, she should demand for seat adjustments from both parties. The Jana Sangh readily agreed to Angre's proposal because the Scindias' support meant a sure-shot victory for its candidates. In exchange, Vijaya Raje secured their support for her candidates, including the owner of the Indian Express Group, Ramnath Goenka (who addressed her as Rajmata, despite being older), who was sent to the Lok Sabha from Vidisha.

It needs to be mentioned here that despite her discontentment with the Congress party, Vijaya Raje had initially made an offer to the party's leaders in the state that 'she would select candidates from her riyasat,'[6] and that they 'should obtain Congress tickets for them.' Apparently when she was informed that the Congress followed a set procedure for selecting candidates, she is supposed to have demanded that her nominees be 'adopted by the Congress.'[7] However, her offer to the Congress was eventually turned down and she fielded her own candidates from territories that were part of the former 'state' of Gwalior, and also from other regions in Madhya Pradesh.

Whether it was the result of political pragmatism or rank opportunism, Vijaya Raje vacated her parliamentary seat despite an impressive tally of 1,87,000 votes, while retaining her seat in the state assembly. The running duel with D.P. Mishra was proving to be a thorn in her flesh and in a matter of a few months, she played a pivotal role in propping up a rebel Congress leader, Govind Narayan Singh against Mishra, which resulted in the Congress' split in the state. Under the leadership of Vijaya Raje, all the rebel legislators were shepherded to Delhi and kept confined in a hotel. They were later paraded in front of the then President, Dr Zakir Hussain, who after ascertaining their numbers decreed that the Congress party had ceased to be in majority and had therefore lost the moral and legal right to rule Madhya Pradesh.

In the aftermath of the Congress' ouster, the rebel leaders swiftly cobbled up a coalition of anti-Congress parties and named it the Samyukta Vidhayak Dal with Govind Narayan Singh as president, and Rajmata Vijaya Raje Scindia as the leader of the House. Although the experiment had failed to sustain beyond March 1969, it had helped Vijaya Raje to finally firm up her mind to remain in mainstream politics.

* * *

It was ten years since her husband had passed away, and Vijaya Raje had already spent a decade in the thick of politics with Sardar Angre as her able advisor. In the 1971 snap-polls, the mother and son were given tickets by the Jana Sangh—Madhavrao was to fight from where his mother had started her political career, Guna, while she was fielded from Bhind.

If the Gold Control Act had triggered her decision to forsake the Congress, Indira Gandhi's move to abolish the privy purses had made Vijaya Raje go towards the Jana Sangh. There was of course an ideological affinity, as was manifest right at the beginning of her political life, but it was also because of Jana Sangh's stated, albeit strategic ambiguity on the issue. While one group of Jana Sanghis had appealed to the ex-royals to voluntarily forsake their purses, another section had canvassed to secure their support to counter Indira Gandhi and her party.

But as mentioned earlier, it was mainly her ideological commitment to Right-wing politics which was of greater significance, and which after her husband's death was further sharpened by her secretary, Sardar Angre. After her formal initiation into the Vishwa Hindu Parishad in May 1968, she began to take an active interest in its activities and presided over a conference of its units from MP, Gujarat, and Rajasthan. In one of her speeches, Vijaya Raje slammed the Congress for its 'sham secularism' and declared that the need of the hour was to accept the 'true meaning of Hindutva.' While in the 1971 mid-term polls, the Jana Sangh had used her influence to campaign in seats other than where her family's writ ran large, in a matter of four years, she was being considered for the post of party president. The two most powerful leaders in the party at the time, Atal Bihari Vajpayee and L.K. Advani visited her in Gwalior and had even succeeded in getting her to accept the offer. However, she had made it clear to them that her final acquiescence depended on the advise of her spiritual guru who lived in the small town of Datia, some distance away in Gwalior. The next day, she informed them that she was refused permission, and L.K. Advani was made president of the Jana Sangh.

There was no doubt that in a span of a decade and a half in politics, Vijaya Raje had succeeded in carving out a niche for herself in the pantheon of eminent anti-Congress leaders. Yet, her erstwhile royal status came to the forefront in all her future choices and decisions in public life. During the Emergency, unlike other Opposition leaders and activists, Vijaya Raje had kept away from protests with the sole intent of avoiding arrest. In order to avoid detection, she had even discarded wearing the customary widow's white sari and began wearing not only other colours, but also clothes other than the sari.

Much like many of her peers, she was often forced to change her location and during one such sojourn, she'd arrived at the doorstep of senior journalist, Tavleen Singh, who was at that time working with *The Statesman* and whose father, a former Brigadier in the Indian Army, was a close friend of Jaswant Singh. Ironically, on the same day, unware that Vijaya Raje was hiding in her house, Tavleen Singh was waiting in Old Delhi's Chandni Chowk area after a tip-off that the dowager queen would make an appearance.

After playing hide-and-seek with the police who were in hot pursuit of every Opposition leader, Vijaya Raje Scindia had escaped to the country of her origin, Nepal, before her 'inner voice' suddenly made her return to India and face Indira Gandhi. Her original plan was not to escape like her son, Madhavrao had, but surrender to authorities in her native country. Be that as it may, in what was a political master stroke, she returned to India and went to Gwalior to surrender to the police and was hailed as a true and fearless worker of the Jana Sangh. Meanwhile, Madhavrao Scindia had not only crossed over to Nepal, but had also stepped out of the Jana Sangh and his mother's life permanently.

Vijaya Raje Scindia had a tough time in jail—the ex-Queen Mother was obviously not used to the mental, physical, and emotional stress of a prison life, after having spent years in the fabulous Jai Mahal palace in Gwalior.

Meanwhile her daughters, Vasundhara Raje Scindia (ex-chief

minister of Rajasthan), and Yashodhara (also a member of the BJP and an ex-minister in Madhya Pradesh) were working frenetically to secure their mother's release. Unlike other prisoners, the Rajmata had an expansive network of influencers who had volunteered to agitate for her release. Finally, after submitting an application to grant her temporary reprieve on health grounds, Vijaya Raje Scindia was released from Delhi's Tihar Jail.

* * *

Two years after her release, Vijaya Raje Scindia was somewhat vindicated when her bete noire, Indira Gandhi was defeated in the 1977 elections. It was the dawn of a new era in the history of Indian politics with a coalition of anti-Congress forces at the Centre, with Morarji Desai as prime minister. But during this phase, Vijaya Raje was also preoccupied with her son's open defiance, as he had not only abandoned the Jana Sangh and severed all ties with her, but was now looking to join the Congress party. In 1977, Madhavrao Scindia contested as an independent candidate (backed by the Congress) from Guna and retained the seat despite his estrangement from his mother. Three years later in 1980, Madhavrao formally joined the Congress party after winning from Guna yet again and in a way, made his distance from Vijaya Raje permanent. The mother and son would often cross paths in parliament, as the Rajmata was nominated to the Rajya Sabha by the Janata Party in 1978, but they would refuse to acknowledge each other. The estrangement was complete after Madhavrao Scindia filed a legal suit and seized control of some portions of the Jai Mahal palace in 1983.

Vijaya Raje Scindia spent the post-Emergency years in a hiatus, carefully gauging the political developments in the country. Her nomination to the Rajya Sabha gave her the necessary respite from the rough and tumble of active politics, but she was a woman-in-waiting for the right opportunity to knock on her door.

In 1980, the spotlight was turned on her yet again, although much against her wishes, when she was fielded from Raebareli against Indira Gandhi. As was expected, she lost the election with a huge margin—garnering a mere 13 per cent vote share—and faced a temporary setback in her career which was accentuated by the collapse of the Janata Party and a virtual decimation of the faction that once comprised the Jana Sangh. But a few months thereafter when the Bharatiya Janata Party (BJP) was founded in April 1980, Vijaya Raje Scindia was appointed the vice president of the new outfit; a position which was bereft of any decision-making, while all the powers were vested in Vajpayee and Advani, as president and general secretary of the party, respectively.

At the party's first plenary session in Mumbai, Rajmata's discomfort with Gandhian Socialism* as the primary tenet of the party came to the fore. It was well known that she was more aligned to the concept of Hindutva, and exhibited a distinct unease with the idea of Socialism as the core principle of the newly-established party.

When the BJP had inducted leaders from outside its fold, including Sikander Bhakt, Ram Jethmalani, Shanti Bhushan, and K.S. Hegde, Vijaya Raje had made her displeasure known to party

---

* As a new philosophy, Gandhian Socialism was coined to delineate the BJP from Jana Sangh, and was rejected by the traditionalists. The BJP at its inception wanted to position itself as the inheritor of Jayaprakash Narayan's legacy, but had eventually reverted to its core ideology and has now declared Deendayal Upadhyaya's Integral Humanism as its core philosophy.

elders. In December 1980, coinciding with the party's maiden plenary, she circulated a note expressing her disappointment with the BJP for having abandoned Deendayal Upadhyaya's idea of Integral Humanism. Her primary objection being that the BJP was following in the footsteps of the Congress and appeared to be a mere 'photocopy' of the party. She argued that Atal Bihari Vajpayee was erroneously aligning the BJP with Gandhian symbols and Marxist concepts which was based on the theories of class conflict, while Upadhyaya's philosophy was sworn to greater social harmony and viewed Indian society as an extended family based on ancient Indian precepts. Gandhian philosophy and Socialism, she further elaborated, were conflicting principles because while Gandhi's focus was on decentralistion (euphemistically referred to as Ram Rajya or an ideal State; associating it with the god as the king of Ayodhya) and self-sufficiency, Socialism made the involvement of State mandatory for the socio-economic upliftment of its people.

Vijaya Raje's impassioned speech was impactful and received strong support from certain sections of the BJP who suggested that the party must revisit its core philosophy and adopt the concept of Ram Rajya as its central article of faith. However, after hectic backroom parleys, and as mentioned by L.K. Advani in his book, after 'an elaborate inner-party discussion re-emphasised the "Indian content" of (our) economic Philosophy" she withdrew the note.'[8]

Post the objections raised by Vijaya Raje Scindia, although Atal Bihari Vajpayee's presidential address did attempt to allay the fears amongst members of the BJP, he remained steadfast in creating a distinct identity for the newly-established party. Vajpayee claimed that the concept of Gandhian Socialism was far removed from Marxism and made three important points in its support: first, that the BJP did not believe that materialism shaped all ideas; second, that the party did not accept violence as a tool to further its political strategy; and finally, that the BJP was against the concentration of political and economic power in the hands of a particular group.

Even as thousands at the Mumbai plenary had applauded Vajpayee's speech, it had failed to convince Vijaya Raje who felt that the BJP had strayed from the path of Hindutva. It was at this juncture that she began to inch closer towards the VHP, which had launched the agitation for the Ram temple in Ayodhya. As mentioned earlier, her association with the organisation dated back to May 1968 when she was initiated into the organisation and invited to preside over the conference of VHP units from MP, Gujarat and Rajasthan. With its resurgence in the Eighties after adopting the Ram temple as its core agenda, the Rajmata found the VHP the perfect avenue for realising her political ambitions.

However, in her three-and-a-half decades-long association with the VHP, not once had she held any official position of significance, except as Trustee, which entailed raising funds for the organisation. But the presence of an ex-royal and a matronly figure certainly added heft to the VHP, and the various programmes that were launched as part of the Ram temple movement.

Vijaya Raje also played a crucial role in identifying and grooming new talent for the VHP, and one of them was none other than the child prodigy-turned-fiery sanyasin who later went on to become the chief minister of Madhya Pradesh, Uma Bharti. It was Vijaya Raje who had first spotted the exceptional talent in Uma who as a child could recite several verses from the Bhagavad Gita which she had learnt by rote. Vijaya Raje took a young Uma under her wings and later helped her get a ticket from the temple town of Khajuraho during the 1984 general elections. Uma Bharti lost her maiden election but won the next time in 1989, and as a woman-renunciate dressed in saffron robes, she made the agenda of her party a visual reality, which till then was merely ideological and therefore eclipsed from the people.

Meanwhile, Vijaya Raje Scindia who was an office-bearer of the BJP, was openly seen participating in several programmes of the VHP. In September 1990, she was present in Somnath, Gujarat, to flag off L.K. Advani's rath yatra, which had changed the political landscape of India by catapulting the BJP to the centre stage, while 6 December 1992 presented her with the opportunity to go down in Right-wing politics as a major player in bringing its core ideology to fruition.

After having made a pledge on behalf of the VHP that the disputed Babri masjid would be secured on all counts, and only a symbolic kar seva would be conducted at the site, she was present in the 'viewing gallery' cheering the mob who were inching towards the structure 'as if she was a football fan watching her team win the World Cup.'[9] Later, when she was asked how she had felt when the three domes of the mosque were pulled down, all she had said was that, 'this is what God wanted. It was His will.'[10]

Ironically, with the demolition of the Babri masjid, Vijaya Raje Scindia also became politically irrelevant. While she was still revered as the Rajmata of Gwalior, her son, Madhavrao was much sought after in the Congress party, particularly after Rajiv Gandhi's gruesome assassination in May 1991.

Vijaya Raje continued in the Lok Sabha till ill-health prevented her from being re-nominated for the thirteenth general elections in 1999. Although she was an eight-time member of the Lok Sabha, and was even nominated to the Rajya Sabha for a single term, Vijaya Raje Scindia never made it as Union minister in the BJP. One of the main reasons for her limited rise in the party and its affiliate, the VHP, was because of her reluctance to alter her political vision. Despite her political engagement, she never ceased to be the Rajmata of Gwalior, a leader whose top-down approach to politics was rooted in the 1950s and Sixties, and most importantly, out of step in the post-Mandal phase of Indian politics. As a strong votary of Hindutva, eventually her strength became her primary weakness as the BJP under Atal Bihari Vajpayee was seeking to expand its base beyond the Ram temple.

When the Jana Sangh was a fledgling outfit and nervous of merging with the Janata Party in 1977, Vijaya Raje had supported it and lent it enough gravitas to be part of the national narrative; her presence on the day of the Babri masjid demolition will always be recalled by many as culpability in an incident which had shaken the foundations of a secular India. But if there is one thing for which she may not be recalled often, but which was indeed an achievement, it was that Rajmata Vijaya Raje Scindia was the only woman in the sangh parivar, which is inherently patriarchal, and it seems impossible for any other woman leader in the future to match up to her charisma.

ATAL BIHARI VAJPAYEE

Before he had faded away from public life in 2007, the late Atal Bihari Vajpayee was perceived as different things by different people—*mukhauta*, a mask, one of BJP's general secretaries, K.N. Govindacharya had said way back in 1997. He is the 'right man in a wrong party,' said many of his peers, especially those in the Opposition. Then there were others who were convinced that he was the 'wrong man in the right party', but chose not to announce it in deference to a leader who was mourned by the nation on 16 August 2018. What was remarkable was that most of the analyses was seldom trite; even his worst detractors meant what they had said on the passing of Atal Bihari Vajpayee.

In June 2018, when the ninety-four-year-old Vajpayee was admitted to AIIMS in Delhi, several senior leaders had come enquiring after his health, including Congress president, Rahul Gandhi. The vicious political barbs notwithstanding, his visit, as also of others, had little to do with politics. Simply put, Atal Bihari Vajpayee deserved the attention because he was one of the few left from a bygone era of Indian politics when personal vendettas were deemed irrelevant in the face of an individual's contribution to national politics.

The best way to recall Atal Bihari Vajpayee would be to say that here was a man who was a moderate amongst Hindutva hardliners; also a leader who was but of course a Right-winger amongst liberals. However, it would be unfair not to mention that even though he had friends in the Opposition benches, there was an element of mistrust which followed him, because despite his staunch pragmatism vis-à-vis his party's ideology, he remained the quintessential RSS apparatchik all his working life.

In a way, Atal Bihari Vajpayee was no one's man, but his own. Yet, the sangh owned him, not only because he belonged to it, but he had lent an intellectual heft to the organisation which until then existed on the fringes of Indian politics. An instance of how only Vajpayee could take liberties with the unyielding RSS was manifest when he was Foreign minister in 1977. On his first day in office, he had noticed that a portrait of Jawaharlal Nehru which for many years had occupied prime space on the wall, had been removed by his office staff in anticipation of his so-called antipathy for a man at the other end of the ideological spectrum.

'This is where Panditji's portrait used to be,' he had promptly told his secretary. 'I remember it from my earlier visits to the room. Where has it gone? I want it back.'[1]

As a young man, Atal Bihari Vajpayee's decision to plunge into India's struggle for independence was influenced by two main reasons—the first was RSS' indifference towards Mahatma Gandhi's call for the Quit India movement in 1942. Atal Bihari had joined the RSS as a fifteen-year-old in 1939 and was perhaps puzzled why the organisation had kept its distance from a movement which was unifying India like never before; the second was his family's decision to shift him from Gwalior where he had finished school and had joined Victoria College (now, Laxmi Bai College), as he was displaying signs of joining the agitation at a very young age.

However, when the Quit India procession had arrived in his village, Bateshwar (district Agra), a young Atal Bihari was enthused to join the throng, but had slipped out immediately thereafter indicating no further commitment in the agitation. But a police officer who was stationed at the site had noticed the young man and put him in jail for twenty-three days. Atal Bihari was released after he had signed a statement before a Class II Magistrate in which he had stated that neither did he share the objectives of the protest, nor had he participated in the 'culpable act'. The police officer released him forthwith after failing to produce 'sufficient evidence or reasonable ground of suspicion to justify the forwarding of the accused to a magistrate.'

In retrospect, there is enough evidence to conclude that although his release from custody was not due to any surety against future participation in such protests, Vajpayee 'did not participate in the Quit India movement as a "freedom fighter" in his home village of Bateshwar. In his own characterisation...he was "a part of the crowd" with no role to play in the militant events...'[2]

After more than three decades of an illustrious career in the RSS, the issue had resurfaced to haunt Vajpayee in 1974 when he was president of the Bharatiya Jana Sangh. A news report in the Left-wing newspaper, *Blitz*, had accused him of providing evidence against a freedom fighter by signing a confessional statement in the presence of a magistrate. The report was challenged by Vajpayee's colleague, the revered Nanaji Deshmukh, who had filed a defamation suit against the paper. It had taken another nine years before it was finally established that Atal Bihari Vajpayee hadn't betrayed the nationalists, but also that he had not participated in India's struggle for independence.

* * *

Atal Bihari Vajpayee's political career can be neatly divided into distinct phases. The first was in 1946 when at the age of twenty-two, he was appointed the editor of a Hindi monthly called, *Rashtradharma*. This was the time when Bhaurao Deoras (Balasaheb's younger brother), and Deendayal Upadhyaya were setting up the RSS in the United Provinces and were soliciting support to disseminate the organisation's ideology amongst people. The young Atal Bihari had relocated to Lucknow to pursue his Ph.D after securing a First Class in Political Science from DAV College, Kanpur. But at the call of his seniors in the RSS, Vajpayee decided to abandon his doctoral thesis midway and plunged deep into writing and editing for the newspaper which propagated the sangh's ideology. It was perhaps then that he had earned the sobriquet of a politician-poet, which was attributed to him even after his death, with several books on poetry that he had subsequently written in his life. This stint was later followed by his editorship of the *Panchjanya*, which exists till date as the RSS' official mouthpiece.

The second chapter of his political life unfolded in 1957 when he was elected to the Lok Sabha from Balarampur (UP), which was preceded by his losing the 1952 by-election in Lucknow. This period which lasted a decade, included his five-year stint in the Rajya Sabha from 1962 onwards, after he was defeated by B.K. Dhaon of the

Congress party by 30,000 odd votes in the election to the third Lok Sabha.

Meanwhile in 1957, the Bharatiya Jana Sangh (which was set up in 1951 as the political arm of the RSS) had only five members in the Lok Sabha and as a consequence of which, the time allotted for it during parliamentary debates was limited. L.K. Advani, who was working as a pracharak in Rajasthan at the time, was asked by the then general secretary of the Jana Sangh, Deendayal Upadhyaya to shift to Delhi and assist the parliamentary party with research. Thus began a lifelong association between Advani and Vajpayee which for most part was based on mutual respect for each other. The thirty-year-old Advani was an apprentice to Vajpayee, and his task was to purely assist him and not tread beyond the assigned brief. Advani was in a way following tradition—in 1951, Vajpayee was assigned as the political aide to Syama Prasad Mookerjee.

Years later, L.K. Advani wrote in his memoirs[3] how Prime Minister Jawaharlal Nehru had noticed Vajpayee in parliament not only for his eloquence in Hindi, but also for his erudition on a range of subjects. Once after Atal Bihari had finished speaking, Nehru had sought the Chair's permission to speak in Hindi and while acknowledging the points made by Vajpayee, he had proceeded to clarify certain issues involving India's foreign policy.

The prime minister had 'remarked to his colleagues that he saw in Vajpayee signs of a man who might well step into the Prime Minister's shoes one day.'[4] In 1958, Nehru had included Vajpayee in an official delegation to the UN General Assembly and personally instructed M.K. Rasgotra, who was then an officer in India's Permanent Mission to the UN, to not only chaperone Vajpayee, but also ensure that he was introduced to world leaders.

However Nehru's fondness for the young man dissipated soon thereafter when Vajpayee began questioning the government on the controversial issue of the Tibetan uprising, or rather its repression by the Chinese. Although Nehru was forced to speak on the matter by Opposition leaders on 17 March 1959, the same day when the Dalai Lama was forced to flee Lhasa, Atal Bihari Vajpayee tabled an Adjournment Motion six days later. The Speaker of the Rajya Sabha while disallowing the Foreign Minister, had allowed Prime Minister Nehru to make yet another statement on the issue. Meanwhile, the situation in Tibet had worsened, even as the Indian parliament routinely erupted in impassioned debates led by Vajpayee. The poet-turned-politician while presenting yet another Adjournment Motion spoke lucidly, demanding a 'review of India China relations where Tibet could be revived into its past Indian friendly form.'[5] He also insisted that India must assist the Dalai Lama in his fight for Tibet's liberation and termed the Chinese persecution as an example of 'yellow imperialism'. In the same Motion, Vajpayee also declared that 'the agreement of Panchsheel between India and China was meaningless as China had violated all its promises towards Tibet. He asked the government to review its China policy and withdraw all diplomatic relations with China.'

Vajpayee's intervention drew criticism not only from the government, but also from a stalwart of the Indian Left, S.A. Dange, who denounced his theory and contended that the uprising against the Chinese government was a class struggle led by vested groups in a feudal setting, and exhorted Nehru not to acquiesce to any demands. In his reply on the debate, Prime Minister Nehru had rebutted Vajpayee's points arguing that his proposal of openly backing the Tibetans would lead to an armed conflict with China.

However, the Jana Sangh and Vajpayee were relentless in their campaign against the Chinese and in a few months moved another resolution in parliament demanding that the Tibet issue be referred to the United Nations. In initiating what had become an unending debate, Vajpayee showcased his prodigious oratorical skills yet again. He had also proven his deftness at evolving strategies, including moving amendments to resolutions and using multiple instruments for interventions in parliament.

At this juncture, Lal Krishna Advani as Vajpayee's able associate had intervened and quoted the practise amongst members of the British House of Commons of using their right to seek a White Paper, and demanded the same from the government of India. After acknowledging the past precedent, Prime Minister Nehru agreed to the request and on 7 September 1959, the first ever White Paper in the history of Indian politics was presented in parliament.

The mutual respect and admiration between Nehru and Vajpayee manifested itself on several occasions, and most importantly and rather poignantly after the former's death on 27 May 1964. Atal Bihari made one of the most stirring speeches in parliament, while eschewing the normal practise of resorting to trite statements at the death of a statesman. In his tribute he said that in Nehru's death:

> Bharat Mata is stricken with grief today—she has lost her favourite prince. Humanity is sad today—it has lost its devotee. Peace is restless today—its protector is no more. The down-trodden have lost their refuge. The common man has lost the light in his eyes. The curtain has come down. The leading actor on the stage of the world displayed his final role and taken the bow....

Despite his strong criticism of Nehru's foreign policy, particularly in the context of China, Vajpayee recalled:

> I once saw him very angry during the days of the Chinese aggression when our Western friends were trying to prevail upon us to arrive at some compromise with Pakistan on Kashmir. When he was told that we would have to fight on two fronts if there was no compromise on the Kashmir problem, he flared up and said we would fight on both fronts if necessary. He was against negotiating under any pressure.

In reference to the 1962 war, Vajpayee said in his condolence speech that,

> the freedom of which he (Nehru) was the general and protector is today in danger. We have to protect it with all our might. The national unity and integrity of which he was the apostle is also in danger today. We have to preserve it at any cost. The Indian democracy he established, and of which he made a success, is also faced with a doubtful future. With our unity, discipline and self-confidence we have to make this democracy a success. The leader is gone, the followers remain. The sun has set, now we have to find our way by the light of the stars.

Vajpayee's respect for a political adversary was not only limited to Prime Minister Nehru, he had the unique ability to assess his colleagues strictly on political points, without resorting to personal attacks. His criticism had sarcasm, satire, harmless banter, but it was never disparaging. That was one reason why his colleagues—Communists, Socialists, and even leaders of the Congress party—were often seen sharing a light moment with him in the Central Hall of parliament before trooping back into the House to continue with the slanging matches.

As mentioned earlier, Atal Bihari was different while being the same man. Therefore, despite the camaraderie, he was unwavering about his political convictions. He seldom lost an opportunity in criticising the Nehruvian viewpoint on both politics and policy; as a dyed-in-the wool politician, he knew that the fledgling Jana Sangh would fail as an alternative unless Nehru's political theories were debunked.

That was the only reason why he and the party he headed attacked India's first prime minister relentlessly, both as a man, and his ideas. For instance, the Jana Sangh's campaign projecting Nehru as the 'Brown sahib' who had agreed to the subcontinent's partition, which the Right-wing saw as Bharat Mata, was according to them only to secure the political *gaddi* or chair. To say that Vajpayee was also part of such scathing attacks on a man he admired would be scurrilous, primarily because he kept his criticisms within the boundaries of civility, and this was what gave rise to him being perceived as a 'right man in a wrong party' and vice-versa.

By now, it was acknowledged across political parties that Atal Bihari Vajpayee had a way with words and an unusual ability to sway people with his riveting speeches. By the early 1960s when political parties did not have designated spokespersons, he was tasked with explaining his party's position on various issues, and a practise which had stood him in good stead after he became president of the Jana Sangh in 1968.

One of the first challenges he faced was from his colleague, also an ex-president of the Jana Sangh, Balraj Madhok, which was a continuation from what had unfolded during Upadhyaya's era. It may be recalled that it was Madhok who had raised a strong objection against Deendayal Upadhyaya's nomination as president of the Jana Sangh (see chapter, Deendayal Upadhyaya, p. 211).

Later, Balraj Madhok had trained his guns on Atal Bihari Vajpayee and accused him of lending the Jana Sangh a 'Leftist' push on issues such as the government employees' strike in 1968, and the nationalisation of banks a year later, in July 1969.

The strike is recalled as a major milestone in Indian working class' history because never before had forty lakh government employees descended on the streets to protest against the government of the day. Workers from different sectors, including, railways and defence demanded need-based minimum wage; neutralisation of price rise; merger of DA with Basic Pay; withdrawal of the proposal to retire employees at fifty or at the completion of twenty-five years of service; and the abolition of contract and casual labour system. Unfortunately, albeit expectedly, every attempt was made to quell the strike and the striking leaders were victimised for many months thereafter. A year later, the Indira Gandhi-led Congress government nationalised fourteen commercial banks by first introducing an ordinance and later seeking approval in parliament.

It was against this backdrop that Balraj Madhok along with Minoo Masani of the Right-wing Swatantra Party had filed a petition challenging the presidential ordinance. The two leaders had even secured a stay from the Supreme Court, but Indira Gandhi had it deftly replaced with a Bill and had also managed to secure the assent of the then acting President of India.

In the ensuing debate between the two stalwarts, while Madhok was clearly in favour of the Jana Sangh merging with the Swatantra Party, Vajpayee wanted to retain its distinct identity with a marked populist thrust.

Eventually, when L.K. Advani took over as president of the Jana Sangh in early 1973, he along with Vajpayee collaborated to expel Madhok and remained firm on the path of economic and political populism. By the time the Vajpayee–Advani duo had succeeded in silencing the internal dissensions within the party, there was a change of guard in the RSS. The Jana Sangh's participation in the emerging anti-Congress coalition had become a reality, and after the 1977 Lok Sabha polls, Atal Bihari Vajpayee became the Foreign minister.

Atal Bihari Vajpayee's foreign policy largely operated within the Nehruvian framework. According to an insider account[6], as Prime Minister Morarji Desai 'had carefully calibrated the normalisation of India's relations with China,' Vajpayee was extended an invitation to visit China in October 1978. The Foreign minister had however cancelled the visit citing what was thought to be an innocuous reason—a 'stomach ache', while it was an open secret that the 'real reason' behind his reluctance was that 'the Soviet Union and the Soviet lobby within the Janata Party had opposed tooth and nail the process of normalisation of Sino-Indian relations. Vajpayee was afraid of annoying them.' Eventually, Vajpayee did travel to Beijing in February 1979, but he 'had to come scurrying back home because China had—as Deng Xiaoping had vowed to do—militarily intervened in Vietnam while Vajpayee was in China. The whole world knew that China was going to take this action and so did Vajpayee before he departed, but the howl in Parliament of the now-defunct 'Friends of the Soviet Union' about 'Chinese aggression' made him cut short his visit.'

Vajpayee's excellent speech in Hindi at the United Nations General Assembly (UNGA) in 1977 is now legendary. As India's Foreign minister, he took the lead in sending the jurist-economist and a free-market champion, Nani Palkhivala as the Indian Ambassador to the

US in 1977. A year later in 1978, Jimmy Carter became the first American President to visit Delhi since Richard Nixon in 1969.

Atal Bihari later shifted his focus to India's immediate neighbours and was of the firm view that unless India mends its ties with them, its geopolitical status would remain globally tenuous. In 1977, he travelled to Bangladesh and met with President Zia-ur-Rahman and signed the Farakka Accord to settle the contentious issue of Ganga river waters. A year later in February 1978, even as Pakistan was struggling to come to terms with the chief martial administrator, Zia-ul-Haq, Vajpayee went to Islamabad and was invited by the unyielding General to his Colonial-style bungalow for talks. As evidenced in later years, Vajpayee had made repeated efforts to normalise India's ties with Islamabad, first with his historic Lahore visit and later by extending an impromptu invitation to General Pervez Musharraf for the Agra summit. Vajpayee was eulogised by the BJP for long, including by the current government headed by Narendra Modi. But as was observed, turning him 'into a national icon does not necessarily mean the BJP and RSS appreciates his diplomatic legacy, especially towards the neighbours.'[7]

With the collapse of the Janata government in mid-1979, Atal Bihari Vajpayee's stint as India's Foreign minister came to an end. What had started off as an ambitious, and a hitherto unknown phenomenon of forming a coalition of disparate political forces with a singular mission to stand against the monolithic Congress party, had also ended rather abysmally due to the internecine skirmishes between stakeholders. Atal Bihari Vajpayee was faced with severe ignominy as he along with his colleagues were seen as suspect for their ideological commitment to the RSS while running a government with the Socialists and others who questioned them on the dual membership issue. It was indeed ironical when Vajpayee and his colleagues were pilloried by a section of Socialists who were the former associates of Ram Manohar Lohia. The reason: in the past, Vajpayee and some of his Jana Sangh colleagues were at loggerheads with Balraj Madhok who had accused him of being in cahoots with the Leftists. Finally, Atal Bihari Vajpayee and a few others from the Jana Sangh chose to go alone and formed the Bharatiya Janata Party in April 1980.

In his maiden speech at the BJP's first plenary session in Delhi, he had openly distanced the party from Jana Sangh's ideological legacy. He proposed that the newly-established party adopt Gandhian Socialism, which was unacceptable to the RSS and amongst other reasons because it was, as the name suggested, associated with the Mahatma and the Socialists.

But Vajpayee had stuck to his guns in lending the BJP a pan-Indian appeal rather than restricting it to just being an offshoot of the Jana Sangh. Sikander Bhakt, a one-time Congress (O) leader, was made vice president of the party even though sections of the sangh parivar had launched a scurrilous campaign against him in the late 1950s for having married a Hindu woman.

However by the early Eighties, Vajpayee's grand plans for the BJP were eclipsed by the shadow of militancy in Punjab leading to the assassination of Indira Gandhi in October 1984. In the elections held in the aftermath of her murder, Atal Bihari Vajpayee was defeated in his home turf by the erstwhile Maharaja of Gwalior, Madhavrao Scindia by a huge margin of two lakh votes. The worse was yet to come—in May 1986, L.K Advani replaced Atal Bihari Vajpayee as president. But while the change of guard was justified as a 'lesson for other parties', what was apparent was the party's return to its core principles—Vajpayee's 'wishy-washy' credo of Gandhian Socialism was swiftly abandoned, and Deendayal Upadhyaya's Integral Humanism was back as the guiding philosophy of the Jana Sangh.

The RSS resumed the practise of deputing pracharaks; the stage was readied for the party's revival as a pro-Hindutva party; it was back to the basics, the only difference being that Atal Bihari Vajpayee was absent from the scheme of things.

* * *

Sometime in 1987, as a young freelance journalist, I was asked by the editor of a magazine to interview Atal Bihari Vajpayee. I was briefed on all the questions, including the one about him being sidelined in the BJP and his future course of action.

Even as I was approaching the end of the interview, I had asked Vajpayee with great trepidation about his so-called isolation. He had immediately lapsed into one of his legendary pauses and while pointing towards my tape recorder, he had said, 'Switch that off.' Once he was sure that I had stopped recording, he had smiled at me and asked if I was fond of Hindi film music. When I had nodded in the affirmative, Vajpayee asked me another question. 'Have you heard that song, *Jayen toh jayen kahan?*' (Literally, where should one go, even if one wants to? This song is from the 1954 Dev Anand starrer, *Taxi Driver*). He had then burst into laughter and ended the interview. I was struck by his brilliant response—the manner in which he had almost said what was most controversial about his position in the BJP and second, his ability to laugh at himself, which is still a rare trait in politicians.

Even as the BJP was surging forward with its plans to build a grand Ram temple in Ayodhya, Atal Bihari Vajpayee treaded with utmost caution on the issue. L.K. Advani had already launched his famous Somnath to Ayodhya rath yatra in 1990 and had traversed thousands of miles to mobilise support for the temple, and clearly without the overt support of his one-time senior and comrade-in-arms.

One would have thought that with the BJP's focus on the temple under the leadership of L.K. Advani, Atal Bihari may have as well walked into the sunset, but that was not to be. In 1991, although he was a member of the Rajya Sabha with one whole year to go, Atal Bihari Vajpayee returned to Lucknow to contest the Lok Sabha polls after having 'publicly declared that I won't stand for election to the Lok Sabha.'[8] He also contested simultaneously from Vidisha, but had eventually retained his Lucknow seat.

The BJP had opted to field both L.K. Advani and Vajpayee from two seats (the former from Gandhinagar in Gujarat and New Delhi) to 'give momentum and acceleration to our election,' and chose Lucknow for Vajpayee because it was certain that his presence in UP would help the party in securing a majority in the simultaneous assembly polls. The ploy worked, for the BJP won fifty-one out of eight-five seats in UP, and 221 seats in a 425-member assembly. Although Vajpayee returned to the Lok Sabha after seven long years, it was clear that it was Advani who was the man of the moment and in charge of the party.

In 1992, when the Congress government gave Atal Bihari Vajpayee the Padma Vibhushan, followed by the Best Parliamentarian Award in 1994, it seemed as if his political career was virtually over. At the Padma awards ceremony, Atal Bihari read from his poem titled, *Oonchai* (meaning, Height), which almost reflected his state of mind:

Jo jitna ooncha,
Utna ekaki hota hai,
Har bhaar ko swayam dhota hai,
Chehre par muskan chipka,
Mann hee mann rota hai.

(He who reaches the acme,
Is the most lonely,
Burdened by his own weight,
Forced to keep a smile,
But his heart within weeps.)

The lines sounded like a lament, but it was certainly not a swansong from a stalwart of Vajpayee's stature. A year after receiving the awards, and what many had presumed was his period of retirement, Atal Bihari Vajpayee was back in the reckoning. In November 1995, the sangh parivar's top brass recommended his name for prime minister in order for the BJP to transit from being the 'government in waiting' to becoming the ruling dispensation at the Centre. It was felt that the 'inclusive' Vajpayee was a better option than L.K. Advani, the unabashed hardliner who had catapulted the BJP to centre stage with his rath yatra. But most importantly, Vajpayee's candidature was considered mandatory to secure the support of regional parties which were more inclined to throw their weight behind him.

In *My Country My Life*, L.K. Advani mentions that it was he who had announced Vajpayee's candidature without consulting either his party colleagues or the RSS, which seems implausible as it was they who had wanted Vajpayee to be fielded as the incumbent prime minister in the first place. Be that as it may, the BJP emerged as the single largest party in 1996 and Atal Bihari Vajpayee was sworn in as India's tenth prime minister. At long last, the sangh parivar's long cherished dream of installing one of its own as India's prime minister had come to fruition, but it lasted a mere thirteen days—Atal Bihari Vajpayee was forced to resign after failing to muster a majority in parliament.

But from then to the 1998 elections, Vajpayee had come a long way and after the BJP emerged as the single largest party yet again, its task of cobbling together a coalition had become far easier because it had firmed up fourteen alliances with parties (compared to 1996 when the party had fielded 471 candidates, and later went for a more realistic estimate by fielding only 388).

In December 1997, the party unleashed an advertisement blitzkrieg with 'The Man India Awaits' as its tagline. In the ensuing election, although the magic figure of 272 had eluded the BJP one more time, Vajpayee's charm was firmly intact and he was sworn in as prime minister in March 1998. As the head of the National Democratic Alliance (NDA), he had insisted on a written programme for the coalition almost like a statement of intent called the National Agenda for Governance (NAG). After the failure of the Janata Party experiment, and his thirteen-day tenure in 1996, Vajpayee had become alert to contrarian views within the coalition. He was also aware that a certain hard line Hindutva faction within the sangh parivar would step up the demand for the construction of the Ram temple, and hence as a pre-emptive measure, the NAG had not only excluded the Ayodhya issue, but also two other potentially polarising electoral promises—the Uniform Civil Code, and the abrogation of Article 370 of the Constitution. In the 1999 NDA manifesto, there was no reference made to the three contentious issues. In 2004, there was a covert reference to the Ram temple issue while the other two issues were omitted; but in 2009, by the time Vajpayee had retreated from political life due to his illness, the BJP's manifesto had stated its position most unequivocally.

Much has been said and written about Vajpayee's premiership which lasted for six years from 1999–2004. If there was one issue on which he invited the wrath of the sangh, it was in accelerating economic liberalisation which Nagpur viewed as an extension of the steps initiated by P.V. Narasimha Rao and Dr Manmohan Singh, and later pursued by the United Progressive Alliance or UPA (I) government.

By weeding out the 'Hindu nationalistic' programmes from the list of objectives in the NAG, Vajpayee had achieved his first major win as India's prime minister. It was however also true that Vajpayee had to literally genuflect to the RSS when it came to the choice of appointing his council of ministers. It was no secret that Jaswant Singh was his closest aide, and Vajpayee was keen that he becomes the Finance minister. The RSS wanted Yashwant Sinha to be entrusted with the portfolio because he had joined the BJP after his stint with the Swadeshi Jagran Manch and was thus more in tune with the sangh's economic vision. The RSS was also of the view that the choice of Jaswant Singh would also send out a wrong signal for the party as he had lost the Lok Sabha elections.

The message was conveyed to Prime Minister Vajpayee at midnight by the RSS sarsanghchalak, K.S. Sudarshan. Although Vajpayee was not pleased with this unwarranted intervention, neither Jaswant Singh nor the late Pramod Mahajan were sworn in as ministers for they had lost from Chittorgarh and Mumbai respectively.

The choice of Yashwant Sinha came as a shot in the arm for the champions of 'economic nationalism' within the NDA, like the Swadeshi Jagran Manch and the RSS-affiliated trade union, Bharatiya

Mazdoor Sangh which had campaigned against multinationals; the privatisation of public enterprises; mechanisation and automation in sectors which they felt had led to job cuts; and the increased influence of international monetary agencies in policy formulation.

In May 1998, Atal Bihari Vajpayee's decision to conduct nuclear tests, code-named Operation Shakti which was more popularly known as Pokhran-II, was considered to be one of his finest moments because it had put to an end what was perceived to be his so-called 'political weakness'. However, it had also marked the beginning of the idea of 'ultra-nationalism', which had terrible consequences a decade later. Much like Atal Bihari Vajpayee's first stint in the ministry of External Affairs, his initiatives as prime minister had a few hits, but many glaring misses as well. It was under him that India's foreign policy was given a fresh impetus in the post-cold war world. With Bill Clinton's India visit in early 2000, Vajpayee was feted for renewing ties with the United States. Although his 1979 visit to China was a disaster, as prime minister he had succeeded in transforming the contentious border dispute with China by naming special representatives as interlocutors on both sides.

However, Vajpayee's two biggest initiatives with Pakistan had resulted in terrible embarrassments—the historic Lahore bus journey in February 1999 which was launched with much hype of connecting people across borders had ended in a 'betrayal' with the Kargil war in May 1999. Similarly, two years later, the Agra Summit which was seen as a unique initiative with Pakistan's General Pervez Musharraf, had not only ended in a terrible public spectacle, but the attack on the Indian parliament within a few months had pushed the sub-continent to the brink of a nuclear war.

Atal Bihari Vajpayee continued to have a troubled relationship with the Vishwa Hindu Parishad (VHP) and other hard line elements within his fraternity. Amongst several other things, the VHP was most unwilling to accept his argument that the Ayodhya dispute should be left to the court's discretion. Despite his long years in the RSS, he remained distanced from K.S. Sudarshan, who had succeeded Rajju Bhaiyya in 2000; but most importantly, Vajpayee had failed to contain Narendra Modi after the 2002 Gujarat riots. As the patriarch of the BJP, he had nevertheless lectured Modi on adhering to the principles of democracy, but it finally had had little or no impact.

It is now well documented that the defeat of the BJP in the 2004 elections was mainly due to its unrealistic and over-ambitious India Shining campaign, which in retrospect, is viewed as a disaster considering the poor and the marginalised had voted against it and shifted to the Congress party. However, there was yet another crucial reason which has always had a direct bearing on BJP's electoral gains—the disinterest of the RSS cadre in securing a victory for the party. The man in the middle of it all was none other than Atal Bihari Vajpayee. In 1980, after the collapse of the Janata Party, Atal Bihari Vajpayee had written a poem titled, *Sapna Toot Gaya* (The Dream is Shattered). Although it was seen as his response to the failure of the Janata experiment, the following lines could very well have been the swansong of the poet-prime minister:

Strange are the ways of the damsel called Destiny.
Always ready to spell ruin.
The caravan has marched two steps
And, the companion has fallen by the wayside.
The dream is shattered.

LAL KRISHNA ADVANI

It is trite, but nowhere is it more manifest than in politics. A man who had driven thousands of miles on a rath to make his party relevant for the people of India, and succeeded in catapulting it to the centre stage, was uncharitably referred to as the 'forever-in-waiting-PM'. In the years leading to the emergence of Narendra Modi as the Bharatiya Janata Party's invincible leader, every attempt by the man to put off the inevitable generational change had fallen by the wayside.

This failure to see the writing on the wall was one of the several paradoxes which characterised Lal Kishinchand Advani (this is his original name, but the middle name was later legally altered to, Krishna). Had his first and only boss been alive today, he would have rued over how his apprentice had turned out eventually. K.R. Malkani, the late journalist-turned-senior leader of the BJP, who was editor of the *Organiser,* had spoken to me years ago when I was working on a profile of L.K. Advani (who was then Union Home Minister) for the now defunct *Sunday* magazine.

'When I saw Lal for the first time, I was struck by his obvious astuteness and clarity of thought.'[1] And this was in 1942, in Hyderabad, Sindh (now in Pakistan) when Advani was a young man and like Malkani had put it, he 'didn't even have facial hair.'

It was his earnestness which had helped him move up the ladder, first in the RSS, later in the Jana Sangh, and eventually in the BJP. His family background however was very 'un-swayamsevak like'. Son of a businessman, Lal Krishna studied in St. Patrick High School, Karachi, hardly the place for stentorian Hindutva arguments that he had so deftly adapted to in his youth. Moreover, Sindh had a syncretic tradition, followed by both Muslims and Hindus alike who revered the eighteenth-century Sufi poet, Sain Sachal Sarmast. In a party which was built around ancient Hindu precepts, Lal Krishna's early years in Pakistan was often quoted to highlight the schism between his childhood values, and what he eventually practised. Even in the years when he reigned supreme in the BJP, there would be snide remarks on his brand of Hindutva which some said, 'begins with his kurta and ends with his dhoti.'

In fact, at the time of his initiation into the Jana Sangh in Rajasthan, where he had settled after Partition under somewhat 'questionable' circumstances (see, chapter, Madhav Sadashiv Golwalkar, p. 98), he was perceived as extremely polished for the rough and tumble of politics, and was therefore considered more suitable for organisational tasks, than the chaos associated with mass politics. In fact, for a major part of his political career, L.K. Advani was not the quintessential mass leader, a trait which was best understood by Deendayal Upadhyaya who had successfully established the RSS in Uttar Pradesh.

In 1957, Upadhyaya ordered that Lal Krishna be moved to Delhi and perform the role of a parliamentary secretary (which wasn't an official appointment) for the four-member Jana Sangh team in the

Lok Sabha. It was during this phase when the legendary Atal–Advani friendship had taken root. As mentioned elsewhere in the book, Lal Krishna was an industrious worker of the party and although Vajpayee was only three years older, he held him in great esteem.

Within a span of less than two decades and coinciding with a period when he was elected as president of the Jana Sangh, L.K. Advani was labelled the next Deendayal and mainly for his ability to stay out of mainstream politics and focus on building the core ideology through clever intellectuality. In the early years, along with acting as the de facto parliamentary secretary, Advani also doubled up as a correspondent for the *Organiser,* which helped Vajpayee bolster his arguments in parliament.

It was only four decades later after the BJP was formed in 1980 that the first signs of a disagreement began to manifest between the two men and particularly after Lal Krishna Advani made the construction of the Ram temple in Ayodhya the core of his party's politics.

* * *

In 1970, L.K. Advani was nominated to the Rajya Sabha and after nineteen long years, he made an 'uneasy' transition into the Lok Sabha in November 1989. The reason: he was more at ease addressing small gatherings at party meetings than facing thousands at public rallies. But behind the genteel image of the man lay the archetypal organisational worker of the RSS and a trait which stood him in good stead as president of the Jana Sangh. In 1973, it was under his leadership that the revolt within the Jana Sangh was crushed most successfully. The one-time Praja Parishad leader, also a former party president, Balraj Madhok was evicted from the Jana Sangh without as much as a chance to plead his case with RSS sarsanghchalak, Balasaheb Deoras. Thirteen years later in 1986, after the BJP was routed in the 1984 elections, L.K. Advani was not only given the charge to resurrect the party, but also to firm up its core ideology.

In the next five years, he deftly created the leitmotif around which the BJP built its politics. Even as the issue of building the Ram temple in Ayodhya was under discussion prior to independence, it was in 1990 when L.K. Advani had given his party a compelling reason to fight the Congress party on an equal footing. Although he was equated with Deendayal Upadhyaya owing to nostalgia and a deep emotional connect on the part of the cadre, Advani had fulfilled what his mentor had recommended as early as the early Forties: to strengthen the ideological core of the RSS. Despite his so-called 'unswayamsevak-like' aptitude and his failure to connect with the masses, L.K. Advani succeeded in securing the BJP firmly into the Sangh fold and put an end to any discussion on adopting Gandhian Socialism, which was strongly supported by his closest ally, Atal Bihari at one time.

If one were to analyse Advani's role in giving the BJP a strong political purpose in its fight against the monolithic Congress party, then it was the loftiness that he had lent to an agitation which was till then appropriated by lumpen foot-soldiers and bigoted leaders of the Right-wing who typically resorted to 'hate speeches' and disparaging slogans such as, *Mein Babur ka damaad hoon* (I am the son-in-law of Babur, denoting sexual domination over single Muslim women). It may be recalled that the Ayodhya agitation was spearheaded by the Vishwa Hindu Parishad under the guidance of the RSS leadership (see chapter, Balasaheb Deoras, p. 247) in the mid-Sixties. It had reared its head yet again in 1984, but was soon eclipsed in the aftermath of

Indira Gandhi's assassination. Four years later in 1989, it had acquired a pan-Indian character due to several innovative campaigns, the most virulent being the Ram shila pujan accompanied by a yatra in which specially consecrated bricks with 'Jai Shri Ram' inscribed on them were taken out in processions through the hinterland and trunk routes to Ayodhya, resulting in more than 700 communal riots in Gujarat, Rajasthan, Madhya Pradesh, Uttar Pradesh and Bihar which was the worst affected, with more than 1,700 people dead.

Despite one of the worst episodes of sectarian violence in post-Independent India, and also the BJP's dramatic rise in 1989 when its tally had increased from an abysmal two in 1984 to 85, the building of the Ram temple in Ayodhya was yet to become a significant electoral issue for the party. In retrospect, the centrality that the Ram temple came to assume in India's political discourse during the following year was only due to Advani's Somnath to Ayodhya rath yatra which he had kick started between September and October 1990.

The itinerary for the rath yatra was drawn up with the intention of ensuring L.K. Advani's grand entry into the temple town to coincide with the VHP's pre-planned programme to launch the construction at the disputed site. Meanwhile, the VHP also supported this grand initiative by taking out Ram Jyoti yatras during which devotees carried torches from the other two disputed temple towns—Varanasi and Mathura. It was the season of Hindu festivals where traditionally large crowds walk in processions, and the VHP's march succeeded in creating the right pitch for the religio-political fervour across many cities in north India. In a matter of two years, Lord Ram, the hero of the Ramayana, was transformed into a political icon and mainly because of the efforts of Lal Krishna Advani.

There is no doubt that the rath yatra and its accompanying

background around one of the most revered gods of the Hindu pantheon had attracted hordes to come out on the streets and pay obeisance, but it was L.K. Advani's presence which gave it a kind of legitimacy that was hitherto unknown. I recall the spectacle so vividly when Advani wearing a large *tika* (a vermillion mark on the forehead) would stand atop the LCV-turned-rath which was painted with popular motifs from the Ramayana, almost like a character from the mythological world who had descended from the heavens to rescue the 'lost' temple and its devotees.

In the initial years of the VHP's campaign, its leaders had argued that the claim of a Ram temple at the disputed site would be eventually 'proven'. However, the findings by the Archaeological Survey of India (ASI) as part of its Archaeology of Ramayana Sites project, suggested that there was no evidence of any human settlement in contemporary Ayodhya before eleventh century BC. What this meant was that if events described in the epic did occur as believed by several Hindus, they perhaps may have, but not necessarily in the location that the VHP insisted they did. At a time when the sangh parivar was in a conundrum over faith and fact, it was Advani who had come to their rescue by proclaiming that Ram was a matter of faith.[2] His master stroke of a statement, which was in a way an assertion of belief over rationality, gave the RSS and its affiliates instant nirvana from the burden of confronting historical facts.

Much like phrases which have become part of the urban political narrative today—'Libtard' to mean someone who is an unyielding liberal and therefore, biased, or 'bhakt' to mean a blind devotee of the current ruling dispensation, it was Advani who was instrumental in coining a phrase which not only became a significant part of the Indian political lexicon, but helped the BJP to gain further acceptance amongst its supporters—pseudo-secularism. His argument being that the sangh parivar and its subsidiaries believed in genuine secularism which was built on the principle of 'equality for all, but appeasement of none'; while the rest of the parties appeased religious minorities, especially Muslims, thereby being anti-Hindu and were therefore deemed to be pseudo-secular.

At one point during the Ram temple agitation, and especially after the demolition of the Babri masjid in 1992, Advani had layered his original argument even further and said that their campaign wasn't just limited to building the Ram temple in Ayodhya, but was part of a larger plan to propagate the idea of cultural nationalism. This wasn't an original idea by any standards. What Lal Krishna Advani had managed to do was astutely repackage a core Hindutva ideal for modern India. He had turned the idea of cultural nationalism on its head, while juxtaposing his idea of a nation with territorial nationalism, and redefined ancient religious codes for Hindus to take pride in their religious identity.

While the majority of VHP leaders spoke in a rhetorical fashion, L.K. Advani loved a good argument and constantly emphasised on buttressing the political thought behind Hindutva. He was perhaps the first RSS leader who could hold his own with the intelligentsia and was therefore used by the sangh parivar to address a section amongst Hindus which was distinctly uncomfortable with the Congress' approach towards the minorities, but also found the sangh parivar either too coarse or incomprehensible because of their insistence in speaking in highly Sanskritised Hindi. Advani succeeded in creating a vocabulary that appeared coherent and logical. Even those who disagreed with him found it difficult to dislike him, for such was his charm which hid an extremely tough interior.

The year 1990 clearly belonged to L.K. Advani. The BJP was waiting in the wings to act as per a pre-meditated plan. On 23 October, when Chief Minister Lalu Prasad Yadav arrested Advani in Samastipur, Bihar (under sub-section [2] of Section 3, National Security Act, 1980) to 'prevent him from acting in a manner prejudicial to the maintenance of public order,' Vajpayee was tasked with informing the then President, R. Venkataraman that his party was withdrawing support to V.P. Singh's coalition government.

Meanwhile in end 1990, the British Broadcasting Corporation or BBC had sought nominations for its annual Man of the Year award. Decades before the existence of social media platforms, the BBC had discovered that several supporters of L.K. Advani had made multiple nominations to ensure his selection. His name was consequently struck off the list, but there was no denying the fact that Advani was clearly the man of the moment for his cadre.

Two years later, when he was in 'partial' confinement in a government guest house in Jhansi, Advani had written two signed articles in *The Indian Express* stating that 6 December had been the 'saddest day' of his life. After his release from detention when he was asked if it was correct to presume that he had actually apologised to the nation for the demolition of the sixteenth-century mosque, he had replied in the negative. However in his memoirs, Advani wrote that his regret had stemmed from the inability of the sangh parivar in controlling the mob, and how it had resulted in a personal loss of face for him.[3] The reason being that he had all along claimed that some form of symbolic or even shambolic construction activity would be undertaken at the site without incurring any damage to the structure. Advani also wrote that he was not only criticised within the sangh parivar for having expressed his sorrow, but also by secular groups who had heaped scorn on him for his refusal to express regret. He had further explained that the incident had hurt him the most because it had eroded his personal and professional credibility within the organisation. It needs to be questioned and owing to the personality that Lal Krishna Advani is—was Advani being truthful when he had clarified about his controversial statement in the newspaper articles? Was he actually showing remorse, and if so, then why?

It is my belief that memoirs of well-known political leaders, especially when they are still active in public life, are more often written with the sole intention of leveraging their last years. In retrospect, Advani's statement terming 6 December as the saddest day of his life has to be viewed contextually and by juxtaposing it with the past and future events in his career. For instance, he had proclaimed that the Ayodhya agitation was not so much about constructing the temple, but for a larger political agenda. Therefore, one wonders if the Babri demolition had actually taken the sangh parivar closer to its objective? Thirty-five months after the demolition, why did he cede space to Atal Bihari Vajpayee by resurrecting the party's old slogan – '*Agli baari*, Atal Bihari' (The next time around, it shall be Atal Bihari), clearly indicating that the BJP would contest the next elections under Vajpayee's leadership? However, this was in effect L.K. Advani's acceptance of the fact that despite the success of the Ram temple agitation in Ayodhya, it was prudent to promote a comparatively liberal and more acceptable face such as Atal Bihari Vajpayee.

In the years preceding the Ayodhya agitation, the Right-wing had relentlessly presented the disputed mosque as a symbol of Hindu subjugation, and avowed to build a grand temple almost as an act of penance towards the community. Ironically, with the demolition of the disputed mosque, the object for invoking hostility towards the minority community had suddenly disappeared and impacted the sangh parivar and L.K Advani's collective cause. While introspecting in the guest house, Advani must have perhaps realised that henceforth it would be nigh impossible to enthuse the Hindus towards a cause that they were sworn to for decades. For some time, the movement for building the Ram temple was de-escalated, but no one in the sangh parivar had the gumption to declare that the Ayodhya agitation had accomplished its mission once a makeshift temple was constructed, and henceforth it would rest on the Indian courts to decide if a permanent structure could be built at the site or not. But more importantly, the cause of Hindutva had to now find a more relevant peg to consolidate the community and there was concern over how this could be achieved.

It was therefore sheer political necessity which had made L.K. Advani vacate the top spot for Atal Bihari Vajpayee in the run up to the elections. According to several insiders of the time, he had hoped to influence his old comrade with assistance from the sangh affiliates, which had worked but for a short while before Vajpayee became his own master. In later years, L.K. Advani had conceded that he was most definitely the second-in-command to the late Vajpayee. After Vajpayee had lost the elections in 2004 and openly attributed it to the 2002 Gujarat riots and the decision in allowing Modi to remain in office, Advani's assumption was further buttressed. Consequently, with an eye on India's secular consciousness, he had discovered the secular credentials of Mohammed Ali Jinnah during a tour to Pakistan in June 2005. But the ploy had backfired: for secularists, Advani remained the quintessential driver of the rath, a man who had mobilised Hindus to pledge their allegiance for the Ram temple in Ayodhya. On the other hand, he was alienated by the RSS and the entire rank and file of the sangh parivar.

From early 2005 onwards, whether it was by design or naïvete, but L.K. Advani refused to read the signals from Nagpur—it was time for him to call it a day, and which had eventually resulted in humiliation that a leader of his stature did not deserve.

One afternoon in June 2013 at the party conclave in Goa when Advani was all by himself after Modi was named the BJP's prime ministerial candidate, there was no one around to share his pain. From an entire generation of leaders who had been virtually mentored by him, this was a tragic payback. But politics is cruel and seldom leaves room for niceties, even if it means disrespecting a party elder, and in a party which insists on adhering to ancient Indian values. Today, when one sees him being ignored by his associates in the BJP, one has to be reminded that this was the man who had in a way contributed to the demolition of the Babri masjid.

ASHOK SINGHAL

Any political organisation which sustains for decades needs effective leadership and vice-versa. One of the best examples of this well known argument was Mahatma Gandhi's decision to synergise the Non-cooperation and Khilafat movements under the platform of the Indian National Congress in 1919–20. In one single stroke, he had succeeded in bringing the nation's focus on to the Congress party as being in the vanguard of fighting the British. The impact of Gandhi's action was indicative of the fact that there existed no other powerful tool for political agitations than an effective mass movement.

In a completely different context, while juxtaposing it almost four decades thereafter, was the Vishwa Hindu Parishad (VHP) which was set up in 1964 at the initiative of the then RSS sarsanghchalak, M.S. Golwalkar, but it was only in the late Seventies when it had begun to make an impact on Indian politics. For close to two decades, the VHP had meandered around in a rudderless fashion, until a man called Ashok Singhal had appeared and changed its destiny.

In the early 1980s, India was on the threshold of a political churn—the Janata Party experiment was over, and with it the opportunity to create an alternative to challenge the Congress' hegemony; the Jana Sangh, RSS' political affiliate, had ceased to exist; and most importantly, RSS chief Balasaheb Deoras had an extremely difficult task on hand. He had resolved to reinvent the sangh parivar knowing full well that not only had the Jana Sangh's bid to merge with the Janata Party failed, but the RSS still carried the stigma of being a communal organisation, perceived to be culpable in Gandhi's murder.

Deoras had therefore decided to proceed prudently and using his long and illustrious record of working with pracharaks, he carefully handpicked a few who had the special talent of mobilising Hindus. Ashok Singhal, who joined the RSS as a sixteen-year-old in 1942, was one amongst the chosen ones who became a full-time pracharak shortly after he had completed his degree in Metallurgical Engineering from the Banaras Hindu University or BHU.

However, the RSS wasn't the only political force in the 1980s to use religion to its political advantage. Even the Indira Gandhi-led Congress party had willy-nilly accepted that in order to sustain in the political atmosphere, it was imperative to dovetail religion with mainstream politics. As a result, one of her key loyalists, the erstwhile ruler of Jammu & Kashmir, also an erudite Sanskrit scholar, Dr Karan Singh had swung into action and in September 1981 launched a 'socio-religious' outfit called the Virat Hindu Samaj or VHS. Ashok Singhal who was then the RSS' Delhi prant pracharak, was appointed its general secretary; Lala Hans Raj Gupta, yet another seasoned RSS member and publisher, became its vice president; and one of India's top industrialist, Vishnu Hari Dalmia (who later became president of the VHP) was appointed its treasurer. The irony of this strange amalgamation was that although Karan Singh belonged to the other end of politics, the RSS' influence over the VHS was seen to be complete, especially with Singhal occupying a key position in the hierarchy. The Samaj began by holding Virat Hindu Sammelans, literally large Hindu conclaves, in several parts of north and east India which were also addressed by senior Congress leaders, including Dr Shankar Dayal Sharma who later went on to become the President of India in 1987. It required no great political acumen to infer that the arrangement was for the mutual benefit of both parties—Karan Singh wanted to use the sangh's network to widen the scope of his newly-established organisation, while the RSS hoped for legitimacy with the presence of Congress stalwarts on a shared platform.

By 1982, Ashok Singhal was relieved of his charge in the RSS and deputed full-time to the VHP as joint general secretary. For two years thereafter, he played an active role in both the VHP and VHS (see chapter, Balasaheb Deoras, p. 247). However, according to several political accounts of the time, by late 1983, he was keen to play a more decisive role in politics than merely convening large Hindu congregations.

During his early years in the VHP, he had made a strong case for forging Hindu solidarity by running two campaigns: first, the need for reforms in Hindu society apropos the horrific Meenakshipuram conversion episode*; and cow protection.

In March 1983, when the demand for the building of the

---

* In February 1981, Meenakshipuram, a small village in Tamil Nadu's Tirunelveli district, was witness to a large number of Hindu Dalits converting to Islam. The incident had forced Hindu organisations like the RSS to campaign for the social inclusion of Dalits, which in more ways than one had also sharpened the latent communal divide within society.

Ram temple in Ayodhya was made openly at a public meeting in Muzaffarnagar (Uttar Pradesh), and which was attended by several Congress leaders including, Gulzarilal Nanda who had served as the acting prime minister twice (after the demise of Nehru in 1964, and Lal Bahadur Shastri in 1966), Ashok Singhal had found the right cause for his rebellion and decided to give it a formal structure by co-opting religious leaders into the movement. He set up a committee to celebrate the festival of Ram Navami in the same year, and in 1984, established the Ram Janmabhoomi Mukti Yagna Samiti (in an attempt to 'liberate' the site of Lord Ram's birth) at a two-day long Dharam Sansad (religious conference) in Delhi.

What had begun as an offshoot of the mighty RSS, the VHP gradually came to occupy centre stage in the nation's narrative by making Lord Ram central to its movement.

* * *

If one were to apply the archetypal profile of an RSS pracharak to Ashok Singhal, then he might as well have failed the test. A gold medallist in Metallurgical Engineering from the renowned Banaras Hindu University, he belonged to an affluent business family in Allahabad. It was perhaps his conviction of dedicating his life to the unification of the Hindus that one of his brothers, Bharatendu Prakash Singhal, an ex-Indian Police Service officer, also followed in his footsteps and led several VHP campaigns including one against decriminalising gay sex.

If his degree in Engineering made him an odd candidate for the rigour associated with a cadre-based party such as the RSS, then it was his political avatar of a monk-warrior which made him stand out amongst his peers. In comparison to an average pracharak or swayamsevak, Ashok Singhal displayed an enhanced sense of religiosity, but he was neither a Hindu seer nor a religious leader; he was a mix between a political activist and a self-appointed messenger of god. When Singhal appealed to various religious leaders to become part of the VHP, he succeeded in convincing them by donning the avatar of a man who didn't carry the amoral baggage of politics; when he met political leaders, he insisted that he was in no way swayed by the impracticality of religious leaders.

When the RSS launched a nationwide anti-cow slaughter campaign in the 1960s, the young Ashok Singhal mobilised support from vast number of saints who were until then never counted as part of any mainstream political agitation. As men of god, they were often part of religious congregations held by political organisations, but the anti-cow slaughter campaign, and the Ram Janmabhoomi agitation had all of a sudden given them the feeling of being an integral part of the country's political discourse.

Ashok Singhal drew them out in droves by reposing his trust in them for raising the pitch for the temple in Ayodhya. In September 1984, the VHP flagged the Ram-Janaki Rath Yatra (which began its journey from Sitamarhi in Bihar and arrived in Delhi on 30 October) to muster support for the Ram temple. However a day later, Prime Minister Indira Gandhi's assassination by her Sikh bodyguards had thrown the yatra off-kilter. According to insiders, not for a moment was Ashok Singhal disheartened with the setback, because he believed that the Ram temple issue had gained a unique momentum of its own, which was now tough to curtail.

He was proven right two years later—in 1985, Prime Minister Rajiv Gandhi overturned a Supreme Court ruling which had recommended that the sixty-two-year-old divorced Muslim woman, Shah Bano be given maintenance by her husband. While this was clearly a move to appease the conservatives amongst the Muslim community, Rajiv Gandhi later 'facilitated' the opening of the locks at the disputed Babri mosque for worship, in order to consolidate his position amongst the Hindus. Until then, Rajiv Gandhi was viewed as a reluctant politician who relied on the advice of his clique who had little or no experience in realpolitik, but with these two controversial steps, it was clear that the Congress party had erroneously played into the hands of communal elements in the country.

Ashok Singhal accelerated the agitation by commandeering the VHP to 'rescue' Lord Ram from 'captivity'—he negotiated with the government to ensure that mass mobilisation programmes like shilanyas or the foundation-laying ceremony be allowed on the eve of the 1989 Lok Sabha elections; he solicited support from prominent Jain, Buddhist and Sikh religious leaders and their respective communities for the movement.

From 1986 onwards, when he was appointed general secretary of the VHP, until his death in 2015, Ashok Singhal was undoubtedly the face of the Ayodhya agitation. Although it was L.K. Advani who had kick started the famous Somnath to Ayodhya rath yatra in 1990, and propelled the BJP from near-oblivion to prominence, it was Ashok Singhal who had worked tirelessly to ready the ground which eventually resulted in the Ram temple agitation evolving into a political launch pad for the BJP and its principal Hindutva ideology.

In terms of conceptualising programmes, Ashok Singhal had some of the most ingenious ideas. I remember one day in early 1989 when the news ticker at work had made me particularly anxious—the VHP had made an announcement that it shall proceed with the shilanyas for the Ram temple on 9 November that year. Even as the ticker moved, I read that this was part of Ashok Singhal's statement during the kumbh mela in Allahabad, in which he had exhorted people to head towards Ayodhya for the foundation-laying ceremony. However as a precursor to the shilanyas was yet another event called the shila pujan in which customised and consecrated bricks with 'Jai Shri Ram' inscribed on them were to be taken out in processions throughout India—almost like 'awakening' the consciousness of every citizen to participate in the building of a grand temple for Lord Ram.

That same afternoon, I had trooped into Syed Shahabuddin's (an ex-IFS officer-turned-politician, who had spearheaded the movement to protect the Babri masjid) home and sought his opinion about the shilanyas and shila pujan. I remember how shaken he was and had said to me after a long pause: 'With these programmes, the VHP has ensured that it shall never have to look backwards on the road to Ayodhya.'

As part of the Ashok Singhal-led twin programmes of shilanyas and shila pujan, the brick consecration ceremonies were held in more than half a million locations—mostly local temples—and then carried in processions for people to pay their obeisance. As a next step, the VHP devised plans to raise funds for the additional manufacture of customised bricks and decided to approach industrialists who were perceived to be supportive of the endeavour. But Ashok Singhal was not in favour of restricting the fund collection to a select group and had said that 'every Hindu should feel that he or she has built it and not one businessman.'[1]

As a result, at a public rally in Delhi's Boat Club, coupons valued at Rs. 1.25, five and ten rupees were sold to large numbers. This was not only a well thought out plan to raise extra funds for the religio-political movement, but also provided a sense of participation for those who were unable to travel to Ayodhya, and were enabled to perform their 'duties' from other locations.

Once he had concluded his public rallies, Ashok Singhal began inching towards the event with great precision. On the morning of 9 November 1989, he'd sent his aide to request the VHP joint general secretary in-charge of the tribal-dominated districts in Bihar, Kameshwar Chaupal who happened to be a Dalit, to accompany him to the site. When the prayers for laying the foundation stone for the Ram temple had begun amidst the chanting of mantras, Chaupal was asked to place the first brick and thereby initiate the building of a grand temple for Lord Ram.

With that one master stroke, Ashok Singhal had ensured that the Ram temple agitation transcends the scourge of caste discrimination which since time immemorial has been a limiting factor for the sangh parivar's efforts at Hindu consolidation. At long last, it was felt in the RSS and VHP that their ultimate goal of uniting Hindus across caste barriers had been successfully conveyed to the people by not only laying the foundation stone for the Ram temple, but at the hands of a Dalit worker.

The impact of the shilanyas movement was such that Rajiv Gandhi who was battling corruption charges in the Bofors gun deal, decided to most unwisely kickstart his 1989 electoral campaign from Ayodhya. As expected, the VHP had succeeded in making the Ram temple the focal point of their campaign, and targeted the Congress, even as the multi-million Bofors howitzer deal was weighing it down.

For all his aggression during the movement, Ashok Singhal was a polite and soft-spoken man. His hostile demeanour was strictly reserved for achieving his political goals and which was undoubtedly the building of the Ram temple in Ayodhya. Behind the veneer of a master puppeteer, Singhal is ironically remembered for his 'soft-spoken manner and his strong conviction about the organisation's goals. Boisterous, loud, hostile, aggressive, short-tempered—he was none of these. On the contrary, he gently and calmly answered the most incisive or unsympathetic of questions. Never once did he raise his voice.'[2]

Yet, this was a convenient veneer. It was indeed true, and I recall how he displayed a great sense of equanimity each time I met him, but the portent of his statements revealed the ideology he represented. For instance in January 1990, a month after the V.P. Singh government assumed office, he had asked the Muslim community to find an 'alternative site' for the Babri masjid.[3]

As a VHP leader who had achieved a near-cult status post the shilanyas ceremony in 1989, Ashok Singhal was prone to ignore parliamentary procedures, and had once even violated the Model Code of Conduct. In 1995, he had declared in Badaun, Uttar Pradesh that there shall come a time when not a single non-Hindu convert shall be found in India, once they were reconverted by the VHP. He had also added that if the Christians were well within their rights to give up everything for religion and culture, so could the Hindus. Amongst other things, these and several other statements thereafter made two things clear—first, he wasn't so much the self-effacing character that he was made out to be, and second, he had failed to exorcise the ghost of the 1981 Meenakshipuram conversions despite his success with the shilanyas ceremony in Ayodhya.

This trait was evident in an interview that he had granted to one of India's front-ranking television news channels, Aaj Tak, a few days after BJP's fabulous victory in 2014. While heaping praise on Narendra Modi, Singhal had compared the prime minister to the Maratha king, Chhatrapati Shivaji. He reiterated about BJP's ability to secure a victory with support from sections which were allied to its principles, which is how elections are won, but there was an insinuation that the party was self-sufficient and didn't require to solicit help from any other section.[4]

* * *

As mentioned earlier, there was no doubt that Ashok Singhal had indeed given the VHP a mission to build the Ram temple in Ayodhya, but it had paled in comparison to L.K Advani who had given the issue a pan-Indian dimension. For Advani, the temple was an agency for electoral gains; for Ashok Singhal it was about delivering on a promise made to scores of Hindus and as such, bereft of any politics.

This clear divergence in approaches between the party and VHP often led to clashes, the sharpest in 2002 when the VHP had initiated yet another programme for the symbolic construction of the temple in Ayodhya.

It had been a decade since the disputed Babri masjid had been razed to the ground by those who were motivated by the spirit of reinstating Lord Ram to His rightful place; the Liberhan Commission was also in the midst of bringing the guilty to book; the syncretic culture of India had taken a blow by the demolition, and there was all-round condemnation of such an act; and most importantly, the late Atal Bihari Vajpayee was disturbed by the VHP's move and had taken up the matter with the RSS leadership.

But the temple agenda was nevertheless taken forward, and on

27 February 2002, a jatha (religious group) owing allegiance to the VHP was returning to Ahmedabad after participating in the symbolic temple-building ritual in Ayodhya. At 8 a.m., even as the train pulled out from a non-descript station called Godhra, a mob of approximately 2,000 people had surrounded the coach carrying VHP activists and set it on fire, killing fifty-nine people.

Thereafter, what came to be known as the 'Gujarat riots', in which Narendra Modi was eventually exonerated by the courts, the Ram temple rhetoric had somehow lost steam. As prime minister, Modi was extremely focussed on development, the building of Ram temple was not top priority. By the end of 2018 however, the focus on Ram temple was back with the obvious intent of consolidating Hindus in the run up to the 2019 elections.

Like several others in the sangh parivar, Ashok Singhal was prescient enough to realise that the potential of the Ayodhya issue to mobilise crowds would dwindle after the demolition of the disputed mosque.

Consequently, from mid-1990s, Ashok Singhal began broadening the VHP's area of engagement. It was in 1995 when he had declared that the VHP would 'reconvert those who had by fraud or force were being made non-Hindus.'[5] He called the initiative, Paravartan (in 2014, Paravartan metamorphosed into the ghar wapsi programme), which was a step beyond the shuddhi programme run by the Arya Samaj since the late nineteenth century, and not aimed at just reconverting (*sic*) Muslims and Christians, but was especially directed at tribals. Although Ashok Singhal had pushed for Paravartan to be a time-bound mission, he had however remained fixated on the Ram temple and this more than any other reason had prevented him from reinventing the VHP.

This was also the reason why since the middle of the millennium, the number of pracharaks from the RSS who were sent on deputation to the VHP had declined progressively. Further, the VHP's 'demotion' within the sangh parivar was also linked to the rise of Modi's old bête noire, Pravin Togadia. Consequently, the focus had shifted to other organisations like the Hindu Jagran Manch and on agendas such as, 'love jihad'.

However, by the end of 2018, the Ram temple agitation in Ayodhya made a comeback—the sarsanghchalak, Mohan Bhagwat openly expressed his exasperation about the Supreme Court declaring that the issue was not a priority. In the run up to 2019 elections, the BJP has enough issues to sway the electorate to vote for the party, but its dependence on the revival of building the Ram temple was testimony to the fact that had it not been for Ashok Singhal's single-mindedness, the BJP in all probability, would have been a different party than what it is today.

BAL THACKERAY

Chances are that each time someone mispronounced his name, it wouldn't have been to his liking. The reason: the first half of the surname, 'Thack' should be pronounced as 'back', and not as 'Thaak', which is the more Indian way. For a man whose politics was rooted in the 'son of the soil' principle, his preference for the Anglicised version was one of the several incongruities associated with Bal Keshav Thackeray.

However, the spelling and pronunciation of his surname wasn't his doing. It was 'bequeathed' to him by this father[1], Keshav Sitaram Thackeray, who had discarded his Indian-sounding family name, Thakre, and borrowed the last name from the author of *Vanity Fair*, William Makepeace Thackeray.

There were other anomalies in Bal Thackeray's persona which require mentioning, considering he had a four-and-a-half decades-long career in public life. His preferred drink was a glass of warm beer; he smoked only Cuban cigars; idolised Adolf Hitler[2]; and played host to Michael Jackson—all of which would still be construed as most inappropriate, particularly for an Indian politician. Very much the anti-hero, and of course, 'unpolitician like', Bal Thackeray was conspicuous amongst his peers because despite his long and deep engagement with mainstream politics, not only did he ever assume any official position, he was upfront and honest to the point of being brusque.

For a man who grew up with books around him (his father, who was better known by his nom de plume, Prabodhankar Thackeray, was a well-known editor and political activist), Bal Thackeray was street-smart, and had no pretentions about being sophisticated. His eldest daughter-in-law (wife of Bindumadhav Thackeray) had once mentioned how her sons had picked up profanities from their grandfather. In an attempt to impress a large group of hangers-on at Matoshree, the Thackerays' residence in Mumbai, the children would repeat those words, but instead of checking them, the men would burst into loud laughter.[3]

Strangely, Bal Thackeray was a school drop-out and this despite the fact that he was not only financially well off, but had a writer for a father. It was quite likely that the young Bal had already made up his mind to make a profession out of his talent for drawing, and therefore took up a job as a cartoonist with the *Free Press Journal* (or *FPJ*, as it was popularly known) when he had just turned twenty, before he ventured out on his own first as an owner-editor, and later as a political leader. At work, Thackeray made friends with a fellow-cartoonist, who later went on to become one of the icons in the field—R.K. Laxman. Apart from their love for political satire, the two shared a strong dislike for Communists, whom the *FPJ* back then promoted.

His initiation into politics was no surprise for he belonged to a political family. His father, Keshav Thackeray was an active participant in the linguistic agitation launched by the Marathi-speaking people of Bombay presidency who thought of themselves as the original inhabitants of the state and demanded that it be rightfully restored to them. As a member of Maharashtra Navnirman Samiti, Keshav Thackeray had fought alongside his peers and as a result of which on 1 May 1960, the Bombay presidency was cleaved into two halves—Maharashtra and Gujarat.

Bal Thackeray (who was born in 1926) had turned thirty-four at the time of the formation of Bombay state. He had witnessed his father's close involvement with the Samiti's movement, and started a Marathi magazine called *Marmik* (meaning, poignant) in 1960 in collaboration with his younger brother, Shrikant Thackeray.

After dropping out from school and a short stint with the *Free Press Journal*, Bal Thackeray discovered a cause which subsequently formed the core of his politics—the furthering of Maratha nationalism by restoring the pride of the 'Marathi *manoos*' (or a Marathi-speaking person from Maharashtra).

Week after week, the magazine would rail against one group or the other—first the south Indians, then the Communists, and eventually, the Muslims. The revulsion for the minority community was something Bal Thackeray shared with the RSS, but his campaign against 'Madrasis' (a disparaging term used to denote anyone belonging to the four states of south India) was virulent, for he saw them as a monolithic block who had undeservingly taken away jobs from the Marathi manoos in Bombay.

As was expected, the magazine was a huge success, mainly because it was viewed as an extension of the Navnirman Samiti movement, and most significantly, as a potent tool for reinstating Maharashtrian dignity. Six years later in June 1966, *Marmik* metamorphosed into a full-fledged political party which was named after the Maratha warrior king, Chhatrapati Shivaji Bhonsle. Finally on 30 October 1966, the Shiv Sena held its first public rally on Dussehra day, much like the RSS which had also made its debut on the same day forty-one years ago.

The estimated half a million people who had gathered in Shivaji Park that morning was proof that Bal Thackeray had successfully preyed upon the insecurities of the Marathi-speaking people. Thereafter, it was just a matter of time and soon the Sena's mascot, the snarling tiger 'began to stalk Bombay,'[4] and *Marmik* became the Sena's mouthpiece. In its issue dated 12 June 1966 titled, 'Prolegomena to the Birth of Shiv Sena', the magazine reported that,

> ...in the city of Mumbai, in Maharashtra, people of other provinces (para-prantiya), 'non-locals' or 'outsiders' have managed to establish themselves everywhere, in the name of 'cosmopolitanism'. As a result, the Marathi (speaking) people are being deprived of job opportunities and housing. Both the State Government and the Marathi people themselves have so far been rather generously accommodative and foolhardy not to have taken note of the situation. The Marathi people earned their claim to the city of Mumbai as the capital of their states only after a long-drawn struggle and the martyrdom of many. Was this all for living a life of the unprivileged and of the deprived in the city?

Like most demagogues, Thackeray used falsehoods to prey upon the insecurities of Maharashtrians.[5] While Keshav Thackeray had mobilised the Marathi-speaking people as a political community, his son used them as an 'anti-immigrant' force. In 1965, when the anti-Hindi agitation had raged on in Madras (as the city was then known;

now, Chennai), and cinema theatres had stopped screening Hindi films in protest, Shiv Sena activists had picked up the gauntlet for the Hindi film industry and coerced Bombay theatre-owners to boycott Tamil films. Thackeray's new-found love for Hindi was early evidence of a trait that was so typically part of his persona—he always found reasons to hate ever so easily, but his admiration or support for an issue or a person was solely determined by opportunity. Over time, Thackeray's objects of hate altered with great alacrity—after the Madrasis had outlived their purpose, the next on the list were north Indians—first the 'bhaiyyas' (an objectionable term to describe men from Uttar Pradesh) and then the Biharis. He also spewed venom against the Communists because apart from the obvious ideological clash, he saw them as a serious impediment to his growth in Bombay where the trade union movement was strong and people were organised mainly on class lines and not on caste, community or creed. In 1967, an opportunity had fallen into his lap to target both south Indians and Communists in one go—V.K. Krishna Menon, the one-time Defence minister in Jawaharlal Nehru's Cabinet, was denied a Congress party nomination from Bombay and opted to contest elections as an independent candidate backed by the Communists. Bal Thackeray deployed his band of sainiks to secure a victory for the Congress (a party he was strongly opposed to) candidate and ensured that his city rejected the 'Madrasi' Menon.

After the 1967 Lok Sabha polls, Bal Thackeray shifted the focus of his narrative and deftly replaced the anti-south Indian campaign with an anti-Muslim tirade. Through a sustained and offensive campaign, he had succeeded in labelling Bhiwandi, a suburb in Bombay which was the site of a major communal conflagration in 1970, as 'mini-Pakistan' by collaborating with groups affiliated to the sangh parivar.

However, not once did he lose sight of his original game plan and launched a simultaneous campaign against the Centre on the issue of securing Marathi-speaking districts of Karnataka state.

By the early 1970s, the Shiv Sena had emerged as a significant political force in and around Maharashtra. As a result of which, not only political parties, but even business groups began using its influence as a counter to crush trade union agitations in the state. It was clear that the Sena was viewed as a coercive force in the state, but Bal Thackeray cleverly nipped the perception in the bud, and instead used the party's patron status to gain a pan-Indian acceptance. He was slowly emerging as a cult figure in the pantheon of local Maharashtrian leaders, and several years before Amitabh Bachchan came to be synonymous with the 'Angry Young Man' of Hindi cinema, representing the angst of lakhs of youth in the country through films like *Deewar* (1971), Bal Thackeray beat him to it.[6]

But many felt that behind the image of the snarling tiger lay a curled-up cat which mewed harmlessly. As quoted by the bestselling author, Suketu Mehta in *Maximum City: Bombay Lost And Found*, the *tiger* roared only from its safe confines—for instance, a posse of 179 policemen had guarded Bal Thackeray's home in the aftermath of the 1993 riots. Yet, every word he uttered from behind the walls of his fortress-like home was treated like the gospel truth by his followers.

Gradually, it became clear that Bal Thackeray was different from the quintessential Indian politician—he was someone who had a firm grip over his people, albeit in absentia, primarily because of the mysterious and fearsome aura which was far removed from reality. The more one got to know him, the better one understood his insecurities—he covered up for his weaknesses by staying away from public glare, and constantly shifted goal posts so that barring his band of loyal sainiks, his constituency of supporters lived in perennial fear of the man.

* * *

By the mid-1980s, Bal Thackeray had friends in both the BJP as well as the Congress party. As mentioned earlier, he was bitterly opposed to India's oldest party, but his friendship with the late and ex-Maharashtra chief minister A.R. Antulay was an open secret, as was his admiration for Prime Minister Indira Gandhi. After her assassination in October 1984, Bal had exhorted the Sikh community in Bombay to pressurise local religious leaders to issue strong diktats against militants.

Thackeray's bonhomie with the sangh parivar requires no particular elaboration. In terms of personal ties, few could boast of better access amongst its top leadership, but in the context of sheer political mileage, much of it came to naught because of his focus on his state and its people—the Marathi manoos.

In the decade of the Eighties however, Bal Thackeray had decided to expand his base and joined the BJP in what was to become its political leitmotif—the building of the Ram temple at the disputed site in Ayodhya. He participated in the Ram shila pujan ceremonies and plunged headlong into the agitation hoping to widen his influence outside his state. His efforts bore fruit in September 1989 when he was asked by the BJP to address its National Executive meeting in Bombay as a 'special guest'. Exactly a year later, in what was to become a watershed moment in BJP's history, when L.K. Advani had embarked on his Somnath to Ayodhya rath yatra, Thackeray played host to him in Bombay. Even as the BJP president, a man who had sworn to alter his party's image, addressed nine meetings in the city, he had Bal Thackeray by his side to indicate that the Sena–BJP alliance was final and poised to be a long standing one.

The sewing up of the alliance was undoubtedly Bal Thackeray's biggest political achievement: never before had any regional leader succeeded in making his provincial, and most importantly, a parochial party, acceptable to a political outfit which professed a 'national vision'. In every which way thereafter, he was ahead of those who had appropriated the Hindutva space in the first place. For instance, not only did the Shiv Sena join the ABVP and Bajrang Dal's campaigns against celebrating Valentine's Day, which they felt went against the grain of 'Indian values', but it outdid the two outfits by driving terror amongst the local youth by attacking greeting card shops and sundry restaurants, while swooping down on the city's parks in search of 'lovers'. Thackeray's soldiers, much like their other counterparts in different parts of the country, argued that their war was against Western culture which was being forcibly injected into the impressionable minds of the youth in post-liberalisation India. Their mission of restoring Indian culture notwithstanding, they were blatantly seen to be playing politics when they had omitted a chain of restaurants run by one of Bal Thackeray's close relatives. But no one dared question either the leader or the workers of the Shiv Sena, for it would have invited unprecedented wrath.

In October 1991, when the champions of Hindutva were in the midst of the Ram Janmabhoomi controversy, Thackeray had ordered his sainiks to dig up the Wankhede Stadium in Mumbai in protest against the impending Indo–Pak cricket series. The Shiv Sainiks had not only vandalised the stadium but also lit parts of it with engine oil to register their leader's pathological hatred towards the neighbouring country. Shishir Shinde[7] who had led the gang of pitch-diggers was subsequently elected to the Brihanmumbai Municipal Corporation (BMS), and later became a member of the Maharashtra Legislative Council.

However, the sainiks' campaign against Valentine's Day celebrations wasn't just a show of ideological camaraderie, but had a more potent precedent and that being their role in orchestrating the post-Babri masjid demolition riots in 1993. Bal Thackeray had allowed his vicious imagination to run riot by arguing that if the Muslims could offer Friday prayers or namaaz on the streets, then nothing should stop the Hindus from offering aartis in public places. If one were to go by different interpretations of Hinduism, it has no set tradition of offering prayers in a congregation, but the sainiks in deference to their leader had organised them with the objective of giving the issue a communal tinge, and to mobilise large number of Hindus at one place. In the backdrop of Thackeray's claim that the Sena was responsible for the demolition of the Babri masjid, these maha aartis became flash points in a city which was already simmering with communal tension.

Soon, the venues for the aartis or maha aartis became theatres for launching attacks on Muslims.[8] Thackeray's deft coordination with the marauding brigades had the makings of a thriller. The Justice B.N. Srikrishna Commission which had probed the 1993 riots commented as follows:

> From 8th January 1993 at least there is no doubt that the Shiv Sena and Shiv Sainiks took the lead in organising attacks on Muslims and their properties under the guidance of several leaders of the Shiv Sena from the level of Shakha Pramukh

> to the Shiv Sena Pramukh Bal Thackeray who, like a veteran General, commanded his loyal Shiv Sainiks to retaliate by organising attacks against Muslims. The communal violence and rioting triggered off by the Shiv Sena was hijacked by local criminal elements who saw in it an opportunity to make quick gains. By the time the Shiv Sena realised that enough had been done by way of 'retaliation', the violence and rioting was beyond the control of its leaders...

Despite the Sena's culpability in the gruesome string of tragedies, there were only three convictions in the 1992–93 Bombay riots case. In contrast, in the 1993 Mumbai bomb blasts case, 'as many as 100 people have been convicted for the 1993 Bombay serial blasts which took 257 lives. However, in the 1992-93 Mumbai riots, an act of mass violence that killed 900 people, just three convictions have been achieved.'[9]

This blatant anomaly underscored the preferential treatment given by the investigating agencies to Bal Thackeray and his sainiks.

In 1995, the Sena–BJP alliance came to power in Maharashtra. Bal Thackeray proclaimed unapologetically that he was India's first 'remote control' chief minister[10], meaning the one who ran the government by proxy, headed as it was by a member of his party, Manohar Joshi.

However, it was another matter that the four-year-long BJP–Shiv Sena alliance also marked the beginning of Bal Thackeray's decline. Like several other past experiments (for instance, the Janata coalition in the aftermath of the Emergency in 1977), the Shiv Sena neither had the rigour nor the discipline for running a government. Secondly, and more importantly, Bal Thackeray was suddenly faced with several internecine power struggles within his own family and the famous

Matoshree at the time was witness to several disputes. Finally, a man whose word was taken as final in Bombay failed to manage the affairs within his own family. In December 2005, his nephew Raj Thackeray resigned from the Shiv Sena and was quoted as saying, 'What I suffered should not be inflicted even on my enemies. I was caught between the party on the one side and my family, on the other.'[11] He later formed the Maharashtra Navnirman Sena and in a way carried forward his uncle's legacy. Raj's disgruntlement against his paternal uncle stemmed from the fact that his cousin, Uddhav (Bal Thackeray's youngest son) was appointed as working president of the Shiv Sena in January 2003.

On 17 November 2012, Bal Keshav Thackeray died in Mumbai at the age of eighty-six. Even in his death and particularly after a bitter family feud over succession, he continued to be the invincible and undisputed leader for lakhs of followers—a sea of over 5,000 Shiv sainiks openly crying outside Matoshree was evidence of his unprecedented influence. Furthermore, although Bal Thackeray was neither a member of either Houses of parliament nor held any official position in his life, yet he was remembered in obituary references in both the Houses. His cremation in Shivaji Park, the first public funeral in Mumbai after Bal Gangadhar Tilak's death in 1920, was attended amongst others by the then chief minister of Gujarat and a man who had assumed the mantle of the new age Hindu Hriday Samrat, Narendra Modi. Thackeray had once declared that Modi and he complemented each other: Gujarat's lion and Maharashtra's tiger. He also claimed to have stood by Modi when he was under attack by his own party men after the 2002 Godhra riots.

Yet, three years after Thackeray's death, Modi gave the go-ahead to party president Amit Shah to end BJP's alliance with the Shiv Sena and contest the assembly election on its own mettle. However, the two most important leaders in the BJP would not have in all probability taken such a step, had Bal Thackeray been alive and 'roaring' from Matoshree. Be that as it may, despite the BJP's tenuous relationship with the Shiv Sena after Thackeray's death, the party may still find it difficult to exorcise the ghost of a man who was undoubtedly the original 'Samrat', pugnacious and grandiloquent till his last day.

NATHURAM GODSE

Within months of Narendra Modi assuming office as Prime Minister for the first time in May 2014, when his idea of 'New India' was almost three years away from conceptualisation, early indications of the icons of this metamorphosed nation-to-be emerged from the district of Sitapur in Uttar Pradesh. Local leaders of the Hindu Mahasabha had not only the unabashed gall to declare that they would construct a temple for Nathuram Godse in a village within the district, but also asserted that work on it would begin on 30 January 2015, the sixty-seventh death anniversary of Mohandas Karamchand Gandhi (who had been bestowed the moniker of 'Mahatma' for the first time by Rabindranath Tagore a few decades prior to his assassination). It was not even necessary to acquire land for this purpose because the selected plot belonged to a Mahasabha leader.[1] The Hindu Mahasabha, whose members celebrated the day of Gandhi's assassination as Shaurya Diwas (Valour Day) and not as a day of mourning, added that the urn containing Nathuram Godse's mortal remains—in custody of his niece, Himani Savarkar,[2] in Pune—would be taken in a public procession across the country. In deference to

Godse's last wishes, his ashes had remained in the safekeeping of his family. He had not wanted the remnants to be immersed in any sacred rivers until India had been declared a Hindu rashtra (nation). Modi becoming Prime Minister was the watershed moment people like the Mahasabha activists had been waiting for to scatter Godse's symbolic bits and pieces across rivers in the country. It was also considered a moment appropriately ripe for displaying fervent admiration for Godse (and its polar opposite, contempt, for Gandhi) on the streets of a reconfigured India. Modi never publicly endorsed any such act. Yet, him becoming the country's premier was sufficient to encourage hundreds of thousands of Indians into following the path of the motley lot in Sitapur.

Within days of this announcement, the Meerut unit of the Mahasabha in Uttar Pradesh shared its plans of installing a bust of Godse in its office. These declarations were made barely a couple of weeks after BJP lawmaker from Uttar Pradesh, Sakshi Maharaj, termed Godse a 'nationalist just like Gandhi'.[3] A furore erupted and the government neither allowed the programme in Sitapur, nor did it permit the installation of the bust in Meerut. It also pre-emptively thwarted the nationwide yatra with Godse's remains. Yet, active politicians owing allegiance to the Hindu Right-wing continued making statements eulogising Gandhi's assassin. In March 2016, then Union Home Minister Rajnath Singh distanced his government from the Godse acolytes on one hand but, at the same time, asked rhetorically without condemning the act: 'How can anyone worship Nathuram Godse?' Veneration for Godse was frequently voiced by a few BJP lawmakers even after such initial controversies. For instance, when she did not stop from making statements glorifying Godse, BJP member of Lok Sabha and terror accused, Sadhvi Pragya Thakur, was dropped from a parliamentary standing committee in 2019.[4]

But despite Thakur being penalised to set an example, admiration for Godse and others who had allegedly been part of the conspiracy to assassinate Gandhi continued to be in vogue. In February 2022, I drove to the city of Gwalior in Madhya Pradesh and went to the office of the Hindu Mahasabha in a building located in the midst of a cacophonic marketplace. The building was regarded with some reverence by people in the locality. Barely a couple of years ago, the custodians of the office had converted, with raucous confidence, an area within the building into a temple of sorts. Their brazenness stemmed from how they, after all, saw themselves in Modi's India as the ones who would arrange the various pieces of the show. Idols and portraits of Godse, Vinayak Damodar Savarkar, Narayan Dattatreya Apte and Dattatreya Sadashiv Parchure were put up on shelves and walls of the room; prayers were offered daily by 'devotees' before the state government removed them. When I visited the office, the busts and portraits of Savarkar and Parchure still remained on display while the busts of the assassin and his aide had been 'taken into custody' by the state government. Proudly standing next to one of his role models while flexing his biceps, Aditya Sharma, a Hindu Mahasabha activist in his late twenties, threw a rhetorical question at me: 'How can anyone be Bharat Mata's father?' He did not want an answer because his question was effectively an opinion: Gandhi should not be called 'Father of the Nation'. A much older Haridas Agarwal, with whom I had set up this rendezvous, supplemented that assassinating Gandhi had been Godse's 'national duty'. With a slow drawl that underscored his conviction, he insisted that Godse's assassination of Gandhi was similar to the mythological account of

Arjun killing Bhishma Pitamah in the Mahabharata. The third of the group that had escorted me up the narrow flight of stairs remained silent, but unmistakably commanded the respect of the other two. He was my first contact and had connected me with Agarwal and requested anonymity in return. The reason? He had been moved from the Mahasabha to the BJP by local 'sangh karyakartas' (RSS functionaries) and had become a local area office bearer. 'It is tough for me to now sing paeans to Godse ... you know this very well ... after becoming part of BJP, it is difficult to speak on these matters ...' and he tapered off with that. I promised to be part of his secret in return for an unrestrained interaction with those who had no qualms or faced no political backlash in declaring that Godse, to them, was a revered demigod.

Not A New Quandary

This unnamed BJP leader from Gwalior exemplifies the predicament of his party and its leaders: in their hearts, they back the act of Gandhi's assassins and hero-worship Godse, his associates and the Hindutva guru V.D. Savarkar, but in public, they have to shun them. It is only in recent decades that Savarkar's figure has been brought out from the closet and his memory lavished with praise. The predicament is not new and has dogged Hindu Right-wing forces since Gandhi's assassination when thousands of RSS and Mahasabha members, including senior leaders, M.S. Golwalkar and V.D. Savarkar, were arrested on charges of conspiring to assassinate Gandhi. Despite its ideological ascendance triggered by the spectacular win in 2014 and furthered by the bigger victory in 2019, why is Gandhi's assassination still something that plagues the BJP? Why does the party not formally accept the assassins of Gandhi as their iconic heroes even though they continue to advance the careers of the likes of Sakshi Maharaj and Sadhvi Pragya Thakur? Why has the BJP-RSS duo consciously signalled that Godse ceased to be part of their organisation when he killed Gandhi while failing to camouflage the sneaking sympathy for him in rank and file? Does Godse's status of an 'awkward' icon of the saffron fold have anything to do with his defence statement in court? It is well-known that many of Godse's assertions at that time continue being endorsed by the leadership even though they are unable to publicly state this.

Part of the reason is the fear that public sympathy continues to lie with Gandhi and not his assassins. This worry stems from the events of 1 February 1948, when a grieving and enraged mob attacked Savarkar's home in Bombay alongside the offices of the Mahasabha and RSS in several parts of India. For the cadres and its leaders, this outpouring of rage had been a forewarning that any attempts to support Nathuram Godse would not only jeopardise their political ambitions, but also put their lives in acute danger. As a result, Gandhi's assassination put Right-wing organisations in a spot and hastened the decline of Savarkar's political aspirations. Although he lived for another eighteen years after the calamitous event, his impact on independent India's politics was inconsequential.

Paradoxically, every time anyone speaks of Mahatma Gandhi, Nathuram Godse also segues into the conversation. If the nation recalls the Mahatma for his greatness, Godse is also remembered and revered by his supporters in equal measure. In a way, Nathuram Godse began to 'live' in public memory following his death, after having lived in virtual obscurity for thirty-eight years before the evening of 30 January 1948. Despite the Indian government's initial clampdown on his 'last testament' in court, why is it that no public debate over Gandhi's assassination in the recent past has ever concluded without a defence for Godse's actions? Why was Gopal Godse, Nathuram's younger brother, publicly feted and his family hailed for 'national service'[5] on his release in November 1964 after being confined for fifteen years to a prison for his involvement in the conspiracy? Why is it that on the internet, the comments section under every news report on Nathuram Godse has several views supporting his action? How can one explain the fact that despite the obvious abhorrence for the assassination, a section has succeeded in creating a romantic aura around this man who would have had, but for his heinous action, no place in history? Does this have anything to do with the fact that like several other infamous assassins and his own associates, Godse made no efforts to escape and embraced his 'guilt', making him a martyr-like figure?

Their destinies were inexorably linked; one may have killed the other but both continue to 'live' amongst their admirers. In a way, both died for their principles without fearing the consequences. Gandhi lived a voluminous life, so great that decades before he was felled, he was already revered as the Mahatma. Godse's life, in comparison, was one that had consisted of negligible accomplishments. Even the newspapers—*Dainik Agrani* or *Hindu Rashtra*—that he edited and published, the latter after shutting the former, in partnership with Narayan Apte, his friend-turned-fellow-assassin, were essentially a means to end their financial woes. The duo launched the newspaper in 1944 and since its inception, it acted as little but an 'in-house journal' of the Hindu Mahasabha with V.D. Savarkar's photo prominently displayed on its masthead. Consequently, if anything, Godse was only viewed as Savarkar's pamphleteer, although it seemed as if he was in search of an issue which would catapult him to the centre stage of national politics. On 15 August 1947, Nathuram Godse left the front page of his newspaper blank with just a black border, denoting mourning. The same day, he led a group of five hundred people to hoist the symbol of Hindu Rashtra, the *bhagwa dhwaj*—the triangular, saffron petard—which fluttered in air, but with a slight variation. Inscribed on it prominently was the swastika, the ancient religious symbol that had been revered before Hitler appropriated it as an insignia of fascism. Godse's address was short but served to release pent-up emotions that he had wallowed in over the weeks after Lord Mountbatten announced, on 3 June, the plan to partition India. With a shriek, he reminded people that Gandhi had once said that India would be partitioned over his dead body. Yet, Gandhi was still alive. Not only had the motherland been 'vivisected' but the 'chastity of Hindu women' was being 'violated in open streets while Congress eunuchs watch'. Almost as if he had rehearsed his lines, Godse stood taut and with a tremble in his voice asked: 'How long, oh, how long can one bear this?' His performance at the gathering was described by writers Dominique Lapierre and Larry Collins as one where he appeared to experience a 'sexual climax' and thereafter 'seemed to deflate from a ranting orator to a meek journalist'.[6] But this was not before he promised the assembled crowd that he would become a 'vengeful spirit, purifying India of the foes of a militant Hindu resurrection'.[7]

Early Days

Nathuram Godse's early childhood was dysfunctional from when he became aware of the need to cope with the duality of his identity

Almost universally, across different languages and cultures, the nose is associated with pride or arrogance. As a child, Godse grew up with a piercing in his nose that should not have been there in a male child of the culture he was raised in. But very early, before he had any awareness of it being performed upon him, his nose was pierced to create an opening for a ring to dangle as an adornment. As a young child, he was a boy trapped in the family's decision to bring him up as a girl without ever taking his consent. This was deeply embarrassing to him and he attempted, as an adult, to ensure that this truth did not exit the confines of the family home, though these attempts were ultimately futile following his infamy in his later years.

Godse had two names—one before his nose was pierced and the other given thereafter. His first publicised name, Ramchandra, was forgotten till his biographers recalled the story. The first part of his second and better-known name was taken from 'Nath'—the word for a nose ring in Hindi and Marathi—while the second part 'Ram' was drawn from his actual name. The two parts were conjoined with the vowel 'u' and that is how he became Nathuram. Godse was raised as a girl till he was seven by his parents, Vinayak and Lakshmi. They hid his gender identity because three sons born prior to him died in infancy. Superstition made them believe that male children of their family were ill-fated but that, perhaps, the divine 'curse' could be surmounted if the child's gender was camouflaged and he was brought up as a girl. Whether the Almighty was pleased or hoodwinked is a matter of subjective assessment, but the boy grew up to be a healthy child—and he went on to have younger male siblings. When his father, who worked as a postal clerk, was transferred to Lonavala, Maharashtra, he freed the seven-year-old boy from the burden of false identity. Yet, the trauma of living his initial years as a girl scarred the boy permanently and the experience was greatly responsible for his troubled sexuality. He never entered into relationships with women, remained unmarried and eventually turned celibate. For decades, the rumour mill was agog with salacious tales of Godse's homosexual relationship with Savarkar. In the first edition of *Freedom at Midnight*, authors Lapierre and Collins attributed the disclosure of this relationship to Godse's younger brother, Gopal. Several years later, veteran journalist, one-time editor and former minister in Modi's government M.J. Akbar described Godse as a '... homosexual, fanatic, ascetic (addicted only to coffee), follower of Veer Savarkar ...'[8]

Shortly after *Freedom at Midnight* was published in India, Gopal Godse denied speaking to the authors either about Nathuram's homosexuality or his sexual relationship with Savarkar. Eventually, Lapierre and Collins provided an undertaking to Gopal Godse's lawyer that the reference would be removed from future editions of the book. The noted sociologist Ashis Nandy also focused on this controversy in his book, *Edge of Psychology*, but expressed reservations about its veracity. Koenraad Elst, a Belgian writer not so unsympathetic to Hindutva issues, also argued[9] that the burden of proof lay with those making claims regarding Godse's homosexual orientation and their assertion that he had 'only one sexual experience, with his political mentor Veer Savarkar, as initiator'. (Elst translated this quote from the French edition of *Freedom at Midnight*).

The *nath* was not the only falsity heaped on the child by Godse's parents. He was drilled into believing in his 'power' to confer with the supernatural. Because of this, he was often made to be the human centrepiece in a ritual wherein he would become the 'medium' for the family goddess to supposedly manifest her divine presence through him. The boy was made to sit for hours in front of the idol and stare fixedly on a black circle drawn with soot on a copper plate. Till a few decades ago, such rituals were commonplace in India—they still are among followers of obscurantist practices—with the accompanying ritualistic clanging of bells, chanting of mantras and profusion of incense sticks, enabling the 'medium' to convince his audiences of his 'special' powers. When he slipped into the trance-like condition, his family members asked specific questions and his responses were attributed to the goddess. He chanted indecipherable mantras which may have been little beyond gibberish but this ensured that he was treated as a special person. Traditionally, the following of such bizarre rituals in many Brahmin families warranted benefits since they were regarded as superior to other families, within their own as well as other castes, for having power to act as intermediaries between humans and gods.

Despite his status as a divine intermediary, Nathuram's childhood was constantly disrupted his father's job was transferable. The family had to move to a new city every few years and forge new friendships amongst peers. Nathuram dreaded his father's transfer orders for it entailed making new friends every time, a daunting task because of his introverted nature, and also because he had to explain his 'divinity' and previous life as a girl child.

He eventually hurdled past primary school and was sent to Poona to his aunt's house to study for his matriculation level examination. Nathuram severed all links his with oracularity (although he was asked to act as an intermediary on a few occasions when at home during vacations) and attempted to make sense of textbooks. However, if there was one subject that gave him more trouble than what he felt from within, it was the English language—the young boy struggled with it for days on end. In deference to his father, Nathuram made a few sincere attempts at clearing the examination, but to no avail. He returned to his family which had by now shifted to another town, Karjat, close to Bombay. Years later, Godse's defence statement in English, read out during the Gandhi assassination case in the special court on 8 November 1948, was appreciated for its lucidity of thought as well as linguistic coherence. It was certainly odd that a person whose 'marks in English were so poor that he could not get a matriculation certificate,'[10] could have written such a high-quality text. Yet, this incongruence was ignored for decades and the Godse speech has instead been listed alongside the finest speeches made in independent India.

The Initiation

After failing to clear his matriculation examination, Nathuram started working as a carpenter to supplement his family's income. But even as he was just about finding his feet in the new city, his father was transferred to Ratnagiri, another town in the Konkan region. Unlike previously when he had found moving homes an agonising experience, Nathuram adjusted to the new surroundings easily. Ratnagiri was famous as a town which housed the last Burmese ruler, Thibaw Min, who had been exiled by the British. But what enthused the young Nathuram was not the charm of sighting an exiled king, but a man who was serving a prison term in the same city—Vinayak Damodar Savarkar. He had been allotted a government bungalow and his family was allowed to live with him. He was also allowed to travel within the district. And while he was permitted to write, he was barred from participating in or writing about any kind of political activity or subject.

Within three days of his arrival in Ratnagiri, the nineteen-year-old Nathuram became part of a small group of men who visited Savarkar's house to hear him discuss a variety of subjects. The first time he heard the elderly man speak, Nathuram was spellbound and returned to hear Savarkar's views on issues effecting Hindus every day: the evils of the caste system which prevented the community from coming to the aid of others, how Muslims and Christians were converting Hindus, how the Hindus were humiliated in their own land for more than a millennium and so on.

One of the primary reasons for the teenaged Nathuram being easily drawn to Savarkar was because of his own upbringing in a strict, ritualistic Brahminical family. His father, Vinayak Godse, was an austere man who stuck to every convention governing Brahmins specified through generations in families. For instance, only his wife was allowed to cook and serve him and after a ritualistic bath, he would change into clothes 'unsullied' by a donkey, a pig or a menstruating woman. As a young boy, Nathuram was initiated into Brahminhood (following the 'twice-born' ceremony) by wearing the sacred thread which was mandatory for every male child in the community. Despite his rejection of caste during his adulthood, this ceremony, one which heralded a rite of passage for Brahmins, remained an integral part of his personality, much like the stories eulogising the valour of the Peshwas. In the Maratha kingdom, after Shivaji's reign, the Brahmin ministers (known as Peshwas) were the de facto repositories of all political power, with the chattrapati (the king) reduced to a titular head. As the Maratha empire was locked in wars with the Mughals for a major part of its existence, Nathuram developed a strong antipathy towards Muslims, much like several upper-caste Hindus in western India.

Within a few weeks, the high school dropout became an ardent admirer of Savarkar and developed an interest in politics. Soon enough, he even began espousing Savarkar's principles on Hindus and Hinduism and, most importantly, his ideas of a nation, nationhood as well as his emphasis on establishing a Hindu sangathan (organisation) for strengthening Hindu society.

Savarkar needed a personal secretary to help him with his everyday work and found a willing candidate in Nathuram Godse. Apart from his proximity to a man he so revered, the apprenticeship helped Godse in picking up reading and writing the English language in which he had been a miserable failure while studying for his matriculation certificate. Constant interaction with Savarkar also helped Godse to hone his skills in public speaking—something Savarkar was known for across India. To a young Godse, Savarkar appeared to be the oracle that he had served as a 'miracle' child when called upon to act as an intermediary between ordinary mortals and the supreme power. The teacher and his pupil could not meet for long periods of time because of restrictions on Savarkar's movements and interactions, but Godse was clearly imbibing every word when they did, which later manifested particularly in the context of his hatred towards Mahatma Gandhi. Eventually, it was his 'blind devotion' to Savarkar and the 'potent teachings of the master and his shattering disillusionment at the way everything in Savarkar's scenario had gone wrong'[11] that took Godse on the path which culminated in Gandhi's assassination.

New Beginnings

It is tough to prepare a comprehensive timeline of Godse's life but it can be surmised that his interactions with Savarkar lasted almost two years between 1930 when he arrived in Ratnagiri till 1932 when he went away to Itarsi, a large railway junction, with his elder sister Mathura and her railway employee husband who had arranged a job for Nathuram. But the two years that he was under Savarkar's spell resulted in Godse being influenced by Savarkar for his entire life. As mentioned, there were periods when Godse could not remain in close touch with Savarkar. The first occasion was between 1932 and 1934 and for a brief period thereafter. This was when Godse tried to not just ensure his own upkeep with his earnings, but also send money regularly to his father. Vinayak Godse had retired by then and was perennially low on funds. He had little earnings, received no pension or perks like official accommodation and had several dependants to take care of—the younger siblings of Nathuram besides his own wife. The father often chastised the son for failing to step into his shoes.

Despite his intractable ways and inability to hold on to work, Godse continued living in Itarsi till 1934, doing odd jobs after a failed attempt at business. Eventually, the family summoned Godse, this time in 1934 to Sangli where his father shifted after retirement because the cost of living was relatively low. But he had fallen ill and there was no way out but to ask Nathuram to come home and take care of all. At Sangli, it initially appeared that the indoctrination he had received from Savarkar had ebbed out and he made no effort to establish contact with anyone remotely advocating the Hindutva ideology.[12] To contribute to the family's earnings, he learnt tailoring; an interesting choice because the vocation was essentially the domain of women and Muslim men. He appeared to have outlived his flirtations with political ideas in the past but it soon became clear that nothing was ever 'past' for Godse. Savarkar may not have been present in Sangli but Nathuram soon found a new father figure (or an ideological guru) in Kashinath Bhaskar Limaye, the sanghchalak or regional head of the RSS in Maharashtra. Like many others of his generation of swayamsevaks, Limaye too had embarked into the world of politics by first becoming part of the Congress and then shifting to the RSS. It was just a matter of time before Godse became a permanent fixture, first at places where Limaye was present, and later wherever he was directed to go as part of his responsibilities as an RSS swayamsevak. It was a relationship that would last a lifetime. Limaye remained his mentor right until the end. The association between the two did not cease even after Godse 'rediscovered' Savarkar in 1937 after the latter was free to participate in any activity of his choice.

Limaye found Godse suitable for shouldering the responsibility of attracting potential young men into the RSS because the latter was not interested in either the freedom struggle or in women. This reasoning of Limaye, although odd and demonstrative of the former's view of young, urban Indian men in the 1930s, was mentioned by Godse in his statement in Marathi which he made and affirmed during police interrogation after Gandhi's assassination in February-March 1948. The statement, which is a vital link in understanding the complete political affiliations of Godse, especially his continued association with the RSS, has rarely been referred to by scholars and writers who have researched and written about Godse.[13]

Godse had responsibilities towards his family but was attracted towards political canvassing and working to establish Hindu hegemony in various walks of life. While there was need to find a balance between his private household duties and chosen public interest activities, quite often, Godse neglected the former and completely devoted himself to the latter. This was happening again in Sangli and so he proposed to shift to Poona where, as said in his statement to investigators, he would be free 'from the area of my public activity, so that I could concentrate only on earning money'.

By the time Godse arrived in Poona, the city had emerged as an important centre of Hindu revivalism. He had also become successful in his tailoring business, owing greatly to a partnership with an RSS activist, a contact that enabled the enterprise to emerge as the shop where swayamsevaks came to get their uniform stitched. Journalist and writer Dhirendra Jha is of the view that while a definite date cannot be affixed to Godse's relocation to Poona, 'a likely date would be 1937'.[14] This was the year when Savarkar was finally released from all forms of captivity and permitted to participate in all public activities. But Godse did not immediately flock to his old guru, choosing instead to stay focused on whatever work was allocated to him by local RSS functionaries and on making his business more profitable so he could contribute to his father's kitty.

The Coordinator

Nathuram's engagement with the RSS had increased and he hoped that the organisation and the Savarkar-led Hindu Mahasabha would collaborate on issues, programmes and agitations. Hoping to bring about a tactical unity, he wrote to Savarkar sometime after he began touring different parts of the country: '... your goal is the achievement of the Hindu Rashtra. There are 50,000 disciplined RSS cadres who carry the same aspiration in their hearts. These swayamsevaks are spread from Punjab to Karnataka. What they lack is your leadership and guidance and are waiting for it.'[15] In possibly a different missive, he wrote: 'It is a fact generally accepted that if there is to be a Hindu Sangathan not only in Maharashtra but in the whole of India, it would be systematically brought about by one, and the only powerful institution, that is the RSS.'[16]

In another letter to Savarkar, Godse mentioned that he had 'started the work of enlisting new members,' without specifying the organisation he was getting them to join. There is risk of drawing definitive conclusions about Nathuram's exact affiliation but it is possible that Godse was referring to recruiting newcomers to the RSS, a job he had already done on record at Sangli and probably continued in Poona. In any case, it would appear that he viewed the RSS and the Mahasabha not as distinct organisations, but as a monolith.

The twenty-eight-year-old Nathuram Godse of 1938 comes across as an impatient young man who appreciated the RSS for its robust organisational framework and perhaps wanted the Mahasabha to follow a similar trajectory along with its leader, Savarkar. In order to keep Godse engaged with the Mahasabha, Savarkar, in the winter of 1938, gave him a vital responsibility which not only kept him preoccupied but also tested his mettle. It was, however, a responsibility effectively solicited by Godse himself, so to say, as he had suggested that the Mahasabha join an agitation, a thought which may not have crossed Savarkar's mind as he continued his visits to various parts of the country while developing the Mahasabha's organisational structure.

Since the mid-1930s, the Arya Samaj (a Hindu reformist and revivalist movement) had begun agitating for greater rights for Hindus in the state of Hyderabad, which was under the reign of the Nizams. This actually began in the early 1920s over the Nizam's refusal to allow the adoption of a resolution in Telugu at the Social Reforms Conference in November 1921. It went through several modification and matters had come to head when, in his August 1938 letter to his guru, Nathuram wrote: '... unless we take upon ourselves the task of undertaking such ordeals on behalf of Hindu Mahasabha, its strength would not increase.'[17] Whatever his position was at that time in either the Mahasabha or the RSS, he certainly was aware of the potential of a campaign against the ruler in Hyderabad. There were several parallel agitations, including one under the aegis of the Congress, but Godse was of the view that it was strategically most prudent to hitch the Mahasabha wagon to the one initiated by the Arya Samaj, which was the strongest in the two provinces where Hindus were in the minority: Punjab and Hyderabad. Although the Mahasabha and the Arya Samaj were polar opposites within the Hindu order—the former being Sanatan Dharmis while the Arya Samaj was against idol worship and opposed to the caste system—they were united against the common 'enemy' and, of course, religious conversion, which both alleged was rampant in the Nizam's territory.

This signifies two things. Firstly, a substantial level of political and tactical awareness in Godse and secondly, the fluidity (or porosity) of the relationship between the RSS and the Mahasabha. Godse knew that Hedgewar was deeply committed to strengthening the sangathan and would not organisationally commit to political activism. Savarkar, in contrast, eager to make a splash in public after twenty-six years of being politically stifled, would possibly take the bait, which he did. And although Godse had no past experience in waging an agitation, Savarkar shouldered him with the responsibility of leading one of the early jathas of the Mahasabha to the Nizam's territory.

In October 1938, the Hindu Mahasabha joined the protests, which included long marches. Savarkar had entrusted Godse with the task of leading the first batch of Mahasabha volunteers into Hyderabad. Because of a clear violation of the rules imposed by the state of Hyderabad, Nathuram was arrested and spent one year in jail. According to some accounts, he cherished his time in prison and felt a greater sense of purpose, for he believed it meant that he was no longer viewed as an underling, but acknowledged as a leader of standing. Godse's resolve against Gandhi also sharpened for the former was of the opinion that latter had tried to influence the Arya Samaj into withdrawing from the satyagraha because Gandhi wanted to have the Nizam on his side. A hatred for Gandhi continued to build.

Meanwhile, Savarkar's backing for the Hyderabad agitation coincided with his appeal to support the British efforts during the Second World War. He firmly believed that the war should be utilised by the Hindu youth to train for battle against forces inimical to Hindu society and he exhorted them to enrol in the British army. Nathuram's younger brother, Gopal, responded to the call of his sibling's guru and served in the Persia and Iraq Force (PAI Force) through the war years.

Preparing for Onslaught

Upon release from the Nizam's jail as part of a gesture of goodwill, Godse returned to Poona in August 1939 to a hero's welcome. He was recognised by the RSS leadership and cadre for motivating jailed satyagrahis to be part of the shakha that he organised in prison. Nathuram may have been the chief of a Hindu Mahasabha jatha but had proved himself as an RSS loyalist with this act. Such a dual political identity or affiliation was common place at that time (many were even members of the Congress and Hindu Mahasabha simultaneously) and Godse remained part of both organisations till his last breath. Political stardom for Godse, however, had pushed his family to near penury in his absence. He spent the next few months reviving the sagging tailoring business in Poona, no longer participated in daily activities of the RSS and attended only crucial meetings.

Soon after release from prison, while Godse was attending to a few pending chores in the Poona office of the Mahasabha, he met a man who was a year younger and an active member of the Hindu Mahasabha in Ahmednagar, a nondescript town in Maharashtra. Of all the relationships, barring his ties with Savarkar, Godse's association with this young man—Narayan Apte—was the most significant in his life. From the time they got acquainted, the two were inseparable except for when Apte was away frolicking with women in seedy hotels. This eventually was the reason for his arrest in the aftermath of Gandhi's assassination. But that is a different story.

Although both the men were Brahmins, Narayan Apte was Nathuram Godse's anti-thesis. While the latter was known to be reclusive, introverted, shy in the presence of women, an avowed celibate, non-smoker and teetotaller, Apte was sharp, quick-witted, fond of cigarettes, drink and, most importantly, women. While Nathuram Godse took abstinence to another level, declaring his fondness for coffee as his only vice, Narayan Apte often bragged about his prowess in attracting women. Godse was certainly more ethical that his partner—it was assumed that he would not even consider 'reusing a postage stamp that remained unfranked'.[18] Despite such sharp contrasts between the two, they struck a perfect partnership solely based on their political commitment to the idea of a Hindu sangathan.

No portrait of Apte's life can be complete without mentioning his amorous interludes. He went to such extreme lengths to be with his women that oftentimes, he would leave his political missions midway and disappear for a considerable length of time. As was the custom at the time, Narayan was married off early, but it was a relationship of convenience, and after his son was diagnosed with a psychological condition, he became estranged from his wife. Narayan taught in the co-educational American Mission High School and also ran a rifle club in the town as a pastime. However, this innocent pursuit was mistaken as a symbol of power by the locals who spoke of him in hushed tones of deference. As it is now, to possess a gun then, even a simple airgun, denoted an authority which was seen as an extension of the colonial power. Since the British viewed these clubs with apprehension, the idea caught on amongst the nationalist youth and such clubs were established in several towns of Maharashtra, including Poona. In the interim, Apte joined the Hindu Mahasabha in 1938, attracted to it for the same reasons as Godse: Savarkar's charisma, the idea of Hindutva and a deep-seated dislike for Muslims. By the time he met Godse, Narayan had already become acquainted with Vishnu Karkare, a Brahmin who had been orphaned at an early age and ran a tea shop for sustenance. From a humble tea seller, he eventually shifted to playing a crucial role in hatching the plan to assassinate Gandhi, for which he spent fifteen years in jail. But ironically, when the two met for the first time sometime in 1942, Karkare viewed Apte with suspicion because he worked in a school run by Christians!

Despite his extracurricular activities, Apte soon began feeling stifled in Ahmednagar—a streak of impatience that he shared with Godse—and found the activities in the town extremely limiting. Therefore, when he was presented with an opportunity to escape his mundane existence and join the civilian wing of the Royal Air Force as a recruiting officer based out of Poona, he grabbed it. By that time, during his periodic visits to Poona, he and Nathuram had begun partnering (with the blessings of Savarkar and the RSS) in an effort to establish a subversive outfit: the Hindu Rashtra Dal (HRD). Once formed, Apte was to play a more involved role in it. This was not possible while living 120 kilometres away and a shift became warranted. And before moving out of Ahmednagar, Apte bid goodbye to the school where his 'real interest had been introducing his female students to the erotic message of Kama Sutra rather than the principles of algebra'.[19]

Activism Beckons

The Hindu Rashtra Dal's first camp was held in Poona in the summer of 1942 and was attended by more than 150 swayamsevaks of the RSS, as well as sympathisers of the two organisations. RSS leadership, despite an insistence of sticking to the organisational programmes, did not disallow its members from also being part of the HRD. The body that Godse and Apte fronted was a virtual replica of the RSS not just by way of structural arrangement but also in terms of its personnel—Kashinath Limaye, who had been sanghchalak of the RSS since 1934 (a post he retained till 1965), was also asked by Godse and Apte to be HRD's prantpramukh. There is little doubt that the formation of the HRD was a forerunner to the subsequent post-independence practice of establishing affiliated organisations that were symbiotically connected with the RSS but had no legal association to it on paper. It was also the absence of a constitution and any formal membership which enabled the RSS to claim, in the immediate aftermath of Gandhi's assassination (and even after), that Godse had 'ceased' to be a member of the RSS.

The truth is that the assassin was as much a member of the RSS as well as the Mahasabha from the early 1930s right up until 1948 when he shot Gandhi. As it is, Godse had, since his association with the Mahasabha's Hyderabad programme, also been a part of an umbrella organisation, Pratikar Sahayak Mandal, headed by G.V. Ketkar, journalist and grandson of Lokmanya Tilak; it was a body formed to coordinate the agitation.[20] Ketkar played the role of an intermediary between the government and RSS (when the latter was asked to frame its constitution in order to be allowed to operate as a legal outfit again) by getting the ban imposed on it in the aftermath of Gandhi's assassination revoked. Never one to camouflage his ideological sympathies, he came under a cloud following Gandhi's assassination—but more on this later.

In May 1943, when Congress leaders were in jail in the wake of British repression following Gandhi's Quit India movement, Savarkar directed his disciples to arrange a training camp for volunteers from Bombay and other districts in Maharashtra. The J.L. Kapur Commission, which investigated Mahatma Gandhi's assassination in the 1960s, concluded that:

> 'Savarkar was the Chief architect and force behind the Dal, almost its Fuhrer. He laid down the policy and exhorted its volunteers to show and give implicit allegiance to him as the sole director.'[21]

As the committed followers of Savarkar, Nathuram and Narayan not only swore allegiance to their master's ideologies, but acquiesced to every command of his, including the appointment of provincial and district level heads of the outfit. Savarkar encouraged members of the Hindu Rashtra Dal to establish mass contact and 'inculcate in the villagers a spirit of aggression; to protect themselves from Muslim atrocities.' He also asked his volunteers to 'assist the villagers to secure arms licences'. He frequently exhorted Godse and others that they should not 'stop until you retaliate in the same spirit and manner. If Hindu women were raped and Hindu temples damaged, equal number of mosques should be destroyed. He advised the volunteers to oppose the Constitution if it was detrimental to the interests of Hindus and the "Hindudom".'[22]

Despite leading a brigade of protestors to Hyderabad and being in a position of authority in the Hindu Rashtra Dal, Nathuram Godse's ambition was to play a significant role on the national stage and be immortalised in history. He was also looking for possible ways of increasing his earnings to meet his personal and family's needs. While he was weighing various options, his counterpart, Narayan Apte, was also on the lookout for a professional engagement, as his father's death and the deteriorating mental health of his son had forced him to turn down the Royal Air Force offer of a permanent commission. Eventually, Godse zeroed in on the idea of starting a newspaper to advocate the politics of the Hindu Mahasabha. He would be editor and he asked Apte to look after the business as the publisher. But obviously, as both had no money to start the venture, they 'met a number of prominent Hindu Sanghatanist leaders and after securing sympathy and financial help from them, met Veer Savarkar as the President of the Mahasabha'[23] and briefed him about their plan. Finding great merit in the idea, Savarkar did not just bless the venture but also donated a not so insignificant amount of Rs 15,000 to the kitty. He, however, laid down one condition: Godse would have to establish a limited company and Sarvarkar's donation and that of others must be converted into shares of the company. Godse did as instructed at the earliest and the capital was translated into shares of Rs 500 each. The shareholders and directors of the paper were almost part of the crème de la crème in society and besides Savarkar, included men from leading business families like, Seth Gulabchand Hirachand (among the ten largest business houses at the time of India's independence) and Bhalji Pendharkar, the well-known film magnate who set up the Prabhat Film Company.

On 28 March 1944, on the auspicious day of the Hindu New Year, the *Dainik Agrani* ('Forerunner' in Marathi) was launched with great fanfare. The newspaper carried Savarkar's picture on its masthead, along with a slogan in Sanskrit which when translated meant 'Public Good, Not Mere Popularity'. Unfortunately, the paper was beset with problems from the outset, forever grappling with shortages of newsprint and resources, besides coping with police surveillance. But nothing deterred Nathuram, for he was committed to turning the newspaper into an instrument of political activism, and to provide a legitimate cover for his campaigns and protest movements. They utilised this to the hilt and within months of the paper's launch, Godse and Apte had made up their minds and drawn up a plan which changed the course of Indian history.

Big Jump

A horrified uproar was let out a few months after Jawaharlal Nehru's death in May 1964. Grieving Indians were struggling to imagine a future without him. At that vulnerable point in India's history, Mahatma Gandhi, his meticulously planned assassination and Nathuram Godse were back in the headlines. It was a culmination of a sequence of events since the late 1950s when citizens began coming to terms with the impending release of three men who had been sentenced to life imprisonment for assassinating the Mahatma—Gopal Godse, Vishnu Karkare and Madanlal Pahwa. Several petitions and pleas were submitted by their supporters to the government that they be treated like other prisoners and set free at the conclusion of their jail term in December 1962. Foremost among the campaigners was G.V. Ketkar, mentioned previously as the man who acted as a bridge between RSS, the Mahasabha and the government. He wrote several articles in *Tarun Bharat*, a newspaper he edited, arguing that the 'usual remission of sentence which is awarded to other prisoners, should not be denied to Godse and Karkare.'[24] The government was however disinclined to do so, and when the due date passed, Godse and Karkare petitioned the Supreme Court for their release. The apex court heard the matter and eventually ruled in their favour, and on 13 October 1964, the younger brother of Gandhi's assassin stepped into freedom after sixteen years in captivity. On 12 November 1964, one of the many admirers of the Godses and others accused in the Mahatma's assassination organised a Satyavinayak Puja, an invocation for Lord Ganesha. The invitation card for the event was distributed 'out of joy', and referred to Nathuram as a 'patriot'. The invitees were requested to 'remain present with your friends circle' for 'offering congratulations' to Gopal Godse, Vishnu Karkare and Madanlal Pahwa.[25]

G.V. Ketkar also attended the function, although he arrived late. Puja over, while addressing the gathering, he made a startling revelation. He told a stunned audience that 'it was his misfortune that he could not dissuade Nathuram Godse from the idea of murdering of Gandhiji'[26] and went on to disclose that he had even given advance information about Godse's intentions to the then chief minister of Bombay State, B.G. Kher. Ketkar further claimed that he had sent the letter by registered post and through an important Congress functionary called Balukaka Kanitkar. Ketkar repeated the statement at another meeting three days later on 15 November 1964 at Poona to mark the death anniversary of the assassin of Mahatma Gandhi. These shocking disclosures by a man of reputation such as Ketkar resulted in a raucous political uproar and the government was forced to appoint a judicial commission headed by a leading advocate and member of parliament, Gopal Swarup Pathak, eventually the fourth Vice President of India. But much before that, Indira Gandhi inducted Justice Pathak into her cabinet as the Union Law Minister in 1966-67. As a result of this, the inquiry commission became headless. The government then chose Justice J.L. Kapur to preside over the commission and it began its task in November 1966. The final report was submitted to the government in September 1969.

Although Ketkar had stirred the hornet's nest, a fresh controversy exploded over the issue fifty days prior to Justice Kapur taking over the commission. On Gandhi's 97th birth anniversary, the *Poona Herald* ran what in journalistic parlance is called a banner headline—'A Story That was Never Told: The Day Godse Made His Attempt to Assassinate Mahatma Gandhi'. The report, written by Abel David, editor of the paper, made a shocking revelation—as early as July 1944, Godse had tried to run a knife through Gandhi's stomach, but had been overpowered by vigilant men who had disarmed him. It would have greatly harmed the objectivity of the Kapur Commission if it had glossed over the newspaper report because it would have been interpreted as an omission to absolve the Indian state, albeit under British control, of its lapse. Critics would have immediately argued that the Kapur Commission was whitewashing the investigations by not looking into the reasons behind inadequate intelligence input regarding Godse's previous attempt on Gandhi's life.

For a nation which was coming to grips with Ketkar's allegation that the Congress government in Bombay did precious little to save the Mahatma's life, the Poona newspaper's report was doubly embarrassing. However, if one were to compare the two allegations, Ketkar's disclosure was of critical importance because it suggested that Gandhi could have been saved, had the government and its agencies acted swiftly. Moreover, it pointed towards a larger conspiracy than what was proved at the trial stage in 1949. On the other hand, the report in the *Poona Herald* had greater significance for scholars and writers to pinpoint Godse's calibrated hatred in targeting the Mahatma. Ketkar was detained towards the end of November 1964 because he was accused of keeping silent about the assassination plot instead of sharing information with the government. He remained in custody well into 1965. Although he had been part of the Salt March, was arrested after having participated in the Dandi March and had initially been a part of the Congress (even the president of the Maharashtra Provincial Congress Committee) before becoming a Hindu Mahasabha regular, Ketkar is one of the thousands of forgotten people who contributed during the national movement. His name now surfaces as a lost footnote in history on the periphery of the Hindu sectarian discourse. Despite Ketkar being a nearly-forgotten public figure and journalist, his account establishes that Nathuram Godse's act of assassinating Gandhi was neither the result of a spontaneous outburst of emotions nor politically unmotivated. The Kapur Commission succinctly concluded as follows:

i) G.V. Ketkar of Poona did have prior information about danger to the life of Mahatma Gandhi in October or November 1947.

ii) He did have information of Godse's conspiracy to commit the assassination which he learnt of from his talk with D.R. Badge on or around 23 January 1948.

iii) Up to the time he met Badge, he did not know that Apte and Badge were involved in the conspiracy to assassinate Mahatma Gandhi but he must have known about Nathuram Godse's complicity as Nathuram had told him in October or November of his intention to do so.

iv) G.V. Ketkar did not communicate any information regarding the plot to the Government of Bombay or to the Government of India or any other authorities.

v) In particular, Ketkar did not get any information conveyed to the late B.G. Kher through the late Balukaka Kanitkar. This claim made by him is not established. Balukaka Kanitkar conveyed the information regarding the danger to the life of Mahatma Gandhi and other top leaders of the Congress out of his own volition.

Panchgani Offensive

Nathuram took a major step, albeit by proxy, towards his destiny from Panchgani, the quaint hill station in Maharashtra. The town was famous as Gandhi's annual retreat and the Mahatma was particularly keen to retire to the hills during the monsoon months of 1944 as he was recovering from a bout of malaria.

Meanwhile, Godse was plagued by disturbing thoughts—he was tired of being the pamphleteer-editor of the *Dainik Agrani* and wanted to bring his plans to fruition by staging public protests against Gandhi. He concluded that the move would not only give fillip to the political ideology of the Hindu Mahasabha but also amplify his public image as a serious player in politics. By now, the Mahatma had made it a practise to hold sabhas or daily evening meetings in public where he shared his views on a variety of subjects. Godse decided that the meeting venue would be the perfect spot for staging a demonstration against Gandhi and his policies.

One evening, prior to the daily meeting, the Mahatma was told that a bus-load of people who had arrived from Poona were protesting against him. Further enquiries revealed that the commotion was the handiwork of a group of Poona Brahmins led by a man called N.D. Apte and that they were protesting against Gandhi's endorsement of the CR Formula (see chapter on SP Mookerjee). The protestors waved flags and attempted to surge forward but were stopped by volunteers loyal to Gandhi.[27] According to Deputy Superintendent Deulkar, a police officer present at the venue and deputed to the Panchgani region, Apte was accompanied by twenty young Hindus and attended the prayer meeting in the hall of a school. After the prayer, Apte 'accosted' Gandhi 'in a challenging mood and asked if he had consented to the Rajaji Formula'. Gandhi replied in the affirmative and extended an invitation to Apte for a discussion at his residence. But the angry protestor rejected him and began shouting anti-Gandhi and anti-Pakistan slogans instead. Apte obviously did not have the calibre to rationally debate the issue with Gandhi and after giving vent to his anger, left with his supporters in the same bus that had brought them to the venue.

Little did Gandhi know that prior to the group leaving for his evening prayer meeting, Nathuram Godse had bragged to his associates that they would soon hear something dramatic from Panchgani about the Mahatma. Those days, not every piece of news made it to the papers, especially something that may have occurred in distant Panchgani. Consequently, only one mainstream newspaper, *The Times of India*, reported the incident on 23 July 1944. But there was a detailed report in the *Dainik Agrani* that displayed the editor and publisher's partisan views while reporting an incident which had been orchestrated by the duo in the first place. The paper printed Narayan Apte's photograph against Gandhi's and ran an incendiary headline: 'I denounce you a hundred times because you have conceded Pakistan'. More importantly, the accompanying report accused Gandhi of 'stabbing the nation' and issued a warning that if he did not change his behaviour, then 'more difficult situations and ill fame are awaiting you. We will treat them as traitors who will try to vivisect our motherland'.[28]

There couldn't have been a more direct threat to Gandhi. Yet, both intelligence agencies and the police did not think it necessary to keep Godse and his ilk on their radar. As mentioned earlier, this incident corroborated the report published in *Poona Herald*—Godse had conspired to kill Gandhi as early as 1944 and had perhaps retracted, waiting for a better opportunity to strike at the old man.

Godse and Apte were among many within the Hindutva supporters who believed that Gandhi was on the verge of conceding the Muslim League's demand for Pakistan, even though the Indian subcontinent was still three years away from being partitioned. In his deposition during the murder trial, Godse had claimed that Gandhi had conceded to the League's demand for Pakistan in a series of meetings with Muhammad Ali Jinnah as early as 1944. These meetings, Godse stated, were arranged by none other than India's last governor-general, C. Rajagopalachari.

Further, Godse's deployment of Narayan Apte to the prayer meeting that evening of 1944 had been nothing more than part of his recce to test the readiness of police and other authorities in the event of an attack on Gandhi. Following the incident, there was a fear in the minds of *Dainik Agrani* management that the British administration would clamp down on the newspaper, but there was no such action and the fledgling paper continued to survive.

However, there is little doubt that colonial intelligence agencies (and later those under independent India's first government) were fully aware that Gandhi had been attacked according to a pre-meditated plan by members sympathetic to the Hindu Mahasabha and that Godse was the mastermind of the incident. Without any doubt, Savarkar was also aware of the plan as well as the controversial write-up in the *Dainik Agrani*. After all, following the launch of the newspaper, Godse would often visit Savarkar's home in Bombay for press releases and articles which the Mahasabha leader wrote for the broadsheet. Although Savarkar, in his statements to the police, had reiterated that he had had little contact with Godse after investing the initial capital in the newspaper, several events firmly established that Godse had kept his one-time guru well-informed about every development related to the *Dainik Agrani* at least up until 1946. Even if one were to agree that Godse distanced himself from Savarkar following 1946, it is difficult to accept that the latter ceased to keep tabs on his favourite disciple's plans.

Amorous Apte

Meanwhile, Narayan Apte was emotionally drained out after his shenanigans in Panchgani and was desperately looking for an outlet to loosen up. This was the time that he took his relationship with Manorama Salvi, his erstwhile student, one step forward.

Apte's not so secretive dalliance with his former student began in 1943 when the Ahmednagar school he worked in organised a farewell party for him because he decided to take up the wartime job of a recruiting officer with the Royal Air Force. It was a 'touching farewell'[29] during which he assured his pupils that he wasn't exactly going to the other end of the globe and even provided them with an address where he could be reached.

This was the beginning of his relationship with Manorama Salvi, who was a Christian and fifteen. She began writing to Apte and the two exchanged several letters for almost a year before Narayan travelled to Bombay to see her as after she'd taken admission in a college there and was staying in a students' hostel. After a few dates, Apte escalated the relationship and began setting up regular rendezvous with Manorama in seedy hotels and other questionable areas in Bombay. For these overnight trysts, the couple always checked in as man and wife—Mr and Mrs Apte—and Narayan began neglecting his work. Godse obviously frowned at Apte's conduct, but did not severe ties with his friend and comrade.

Paper Problems and Beyond

For the first two years, bringing out *Dainik Agrani* proved to be extremely tough for Godse and his veritable Sancho Panza, who displayed none of the humour and ironic wit that the fictional character is known for. Godse was completely dedicated to the newspaper and tended to it like a mother cares for an infant. He kept Savarkar informed about the paper's monthly progress even as he kept his ears to the ground. India was reeling under the scourge of communalism and Godse, as editor of *Dainik Agrani*, decided that his paper's focus on spreading paranoia about the 'other' because, amongst other things, it would also ensure a rise in its circulation.

He was proven right. As the strategy paid dividends, *Dainik Agrani's* circulation rose exponentially, as did its revenues from advertisement. Godse ushered in 1946 on a cheerful note: the newspaper had enabled an elevation in Godse's social status; he was seen as an eminent Hindutva leader by people who gathered at places where Hindu nationalists met regularly. The paper now had a printing press of its own and a teleprinter line and he, along with Narayan Apte, began scouting for a plot to set up office and move the press there.

But politically, things were not looking so bright for Godse and his organisation. The dismal results of the 1946 elections for the central and provincial assemblies demonstrated that despite the veneer of confidence amongst several members of the Mahasabha, the organisation had little mass support. India's independence, along with the Partition, was soon to be a reality, although there was no clarity over which parts of the subcontinent would constitute the two countries that were to be cleaved from one single entity. The Congress formed a government in Bombay yet again and cracked down on organisations and newspapers which promoted communalism. The *Dainik Agrani* was one such entity since it routinely defied the Press Act which forbade communal propaganda against any religious community. Godse, however, believed that his paper's primary duty was to keep its' readers informed about what it alleged, atrocities that the Muslims were committing upon the Hindus all over the sub-continent, to censure the government for its inability to protect the Hindus, and above all, to exhort the Hindus to stand up for themselves.[30]

In June 1946, Savarkar received a letter from Godse informing him that the British government had stopped its advertisement to *Dainik Agrani* and was now planning to support a rival newspaper called, *Lokashakti*, which was published from Nagpur. The *Dainik Agrani* was also served a notice to pay Rs 6,000 as damages for spreading communal hatred. Although the newspaper had few resources to tide over this crisis, Godse succeeded in raising the amount thanks to influential friends and other professional associates.

The alacrity with which Godse raised the necessary funds rankled the Congress leaders in the Bombay government and they retaliated by seizing the security money and ordering the closure of the newspaper. Godse and Apte had anticipated this because within a day, the *Dainik Agrani* was back on the stands, but with a new name—the *Hindu Rashtra*. This cat-and-mouse game with the Congress government continued and yet another notice was served, this time for Rs 5,000 rupees, but 'much to the government's surprise, the editor and manager were able to put up the money in time'.[31]

It became unmistakably clear that the *Hindu Rashtra* was flush with money provided by the burgeoning mercantile class which endorsed the Mahasabha's policies in the wake of rising communal riots in the country. The list of admirers grew, including those from outside as well as within the newspaper—people who were drawn to Godse for his malevolent, vitriolic views. Besides spending money on themselves 'more freely' the diabolical duo also 'branched out into the clandestine buying of arms and explosives'[32] to pursue their objective.

That the Hindu Rashtra had proven to be a successful venture was for everyone to witness for it did not cease publication even for a day up until 31 January 1948, when the last edition carried the news of Gandhi's assassination. It was evident that once the newspaper venture had succeeded in crossing the threshold early in 1946, it was just a small hop to infamy or glory, depending on one's primary position, in 1947 before the proverbial leap to 1948.

The Assassination

It was the evening of 30 January 1948. The sun in Delhi was to set; the clocks struck 5.17 p.m. The verdant lawns of Birla House, well-manicured and curated by its affluent owners, had become the backdrop of an awful scene. A nightmare had unfolded against the fading sunlight: the Mahatma, Bapu, Father of the Nation, a man millions of Indians considered infallible, lay piteously on the ground in a pool of warm blood. A man in a blue-grey shirt hovered over him, holding his head high, gripping a pistol tightly in his hand. The minor activist of yore who had turned into an editor and protestor had finally secured an eternal identity for himself. He was the first one to shatter the silence which followed the firing of three bullets: 'Police ... police!'

Nathuram later told his brother, Gopal: 'I wanted everyone to see that this was something premeditated, something deliberate – that I had not acted in a fit of passion. I wanted no one to say that I tried to run away or to get rid of the pistol, but wanted to be caught, complete with the pistol.'[33] Yet, not a single person came forward for almost a minute, which seemed like eternity. The crowd around the murderer was coming to grips with the moment. The pistol in Godse's hand, which had killed a man just a few minutes ago, was a terrifying sight. Eventually, a man in an Air Force uniform gripped Godse's wrist firmly and extricated the weapon. Godse had wished it this way.

Several people on the lawn of Birla House suddenly gathered courage and found their voices. Abuse and fisticuffs followed as a posse of policemen took Nathuram Godse into custody. Even as he was being led through a sea of people, he seemed happy, pausing every now and then to look at people who were throwing several questions at him.

Why did Godse not run away and melt into the crowd in the aftermath? After all, Narayan Apte and Vishnu Karkare had slunk away quietly. Evidently, Godse had arrived at the Birla House that evening with a dual purpose: he wanted Gandhi dead and secondly, he desired to be recognised as India's most famous assassin. But was it just craving for recognition, or was there something more to Godse's actions?

The precision with which Godse went about the task of assassinating Gandhi and collecting arms and ammunitions for his mission has been well-documented in several accounts.[34] The failed assassination attempt, ten days before Gandhi's death, on 20 January 1948 when Madanlal Pahwa lit a crude bomb and the countrywide search for a suitable murder weapon has also been elaborately chronicled. Although it is widely believed that Nathuram Godse was provoked by Gandhi's last fast-unto-death seeking peace in the city, an end to retributive killings in the capital and a demand that India must release the instalment due to Pakistan under the agreement between the two countries, he had certainly planned much ahead of 1948 with some of his close associates. The indoctrination he received in Savarkar's sectarian factory and his own searing ambition to leave an indelible mark on history sealed Gandhi's fate and with that, a nation witnessed the violent death of the Mahatma, an anti-thesis of Godse's lifelong values.

There was no doubt that Godse had cold-bloodedly drawn up a meticulous plan and was ruthless in using his associates as mere pawns in the mission. Yet, because he had stuck to the claim that his was an individual enterprise, it is clear that he wished to be seen as the sole initiator of the most diabolical plot in Indian history. That Apte, Karkare and others were detained and prosecuted was proof that Godse had failed in ensuring that his accomplices' alibis do not come unstuck within days of the assassination. As a matter of fact, he had been naive enough to believe that after the killing, the group would be able to return to their respective homes and return to normal lives.

During the investigations and the trial, a couple of photographs were released to the press that belied Godse's claim that he had acted as the proverbial lone-wolf in the conspiracy. The camaraderie in one of the pictures (which looked like a family portrait) was proof that each member of the group was in the know of the other's role in the Mahasabha's hierarchy. Almost invariably, except when they were photographed in the courtroom, V.D. Savarkar was seated in the middle with Godse to his right. Only Digamber Badge was seated at a distance and seemed disconnected from the group; he later turned approver and this probably explains his discomfort in the picture.

Apart from Badge's obvious uneasiness and his subsequent 'treachery', all the other men seemed at complete ease with each other, likely owing to their decade-long associations. It may be recalled that the collaboration was not only restricted to routine political activity, but extended to a common mission including the formation of militant brigades, attacks and protests against Gandhi and, most importantly, the publication of *Dainik Agrani* or the *Hindu Rashtra*.

The trajectory of Godse's plan, starting July 1944, through the failed murder attempt on 20 January 1948 and to the eventual assassination ten days later, is a textbook case of how zealots are sworn to their mission despite initial failures. The first incident in 1944 at Panchgani was aimed at checking the feistiness of his group and to assess the administration's response. Had the government cracked down on *Dainik Agrani* and forced the closure of the paper the moment it violated the clauses under the Press Act, 1910, Gandhi's assassination could have been prevented. There were many such occasions for the government to act with alacrity, the last being just nine days before the assassination when a jailed Madanlal Pahwa had ominously uttered on 21 January three words to his interrogators: '*Woh phir aayega*' (He will return). The three portentous words were callously unheeded and no investigations were launched which could have saved Gandhi's life. It remains among the unpardonable blemishes in securing one of the most abhorred political icons.

Incidentally, Nathuram had first met Madanlal barely a month prior to Gandhi's assassination. Godse was shrewd to gauge that this refugee from West Punjab, who had been severely traumatised by the Partition and constantly yearned for his ancestral land, will come handy. Madanlal Pahwa had a deep-seated hatred for Gandhi which became manifest in a slogan that he would often shout, almost like a lament, both chilling and poignant at the same time: 'Gandhi *ko marne do, hum ko makan do*' (Let Gandhi die, give back our homes). Another was, '*Marta hai to marne do! Khoon ka badla khoon se!*' (If he so wishes, let him die! We just want blood for blood!).

Despite all his bluster, Nathuram Godse was pusillanimous—he would often act from behind the scenes, not risking any confrontation. This trait was first witnessed in July 1944 when he propped up Narayan Apte as the head of the protestors while he chose the relative comforts of the editor's chamber. The second time he did this was during the aborted attempt on 20 January 1948. According to this plan, Madanlal Pahwa, Vishnu Karkare, Digambar Badge and Shankar Kistaiya were to be the main attackers—thereby risking the maximum—while Nathuram, Gopal and Narayan Apte were to hurl grenades, but only if the plan fell through. Despite all the careful planning before and during the attack, the plan was for naught and Madanlal Pahwa was taken into custody because, at the last minute, he baulked at hurling the grenade. During the interrogation, he led the investigating officers to Marina Hotel (now Radisson Blu) in New Delhi's Connaught Place—the hotel where Godse had also stayed and later vacated when the plan had gone awry.

After the failed assassination bid, Godse and Apte fled Delhi and caught a train to Kanpur, instead of their original destination, Bombay—the duo realised that the usual route would be crawling with police teams and was best avoided. That night aboard the train, Nathuram Godse began introspecting and concluded that if he wanted his mission fulfilled, he would have to act on his own, unlike previously when he had deputed others to finish the task. Narayan and Nathuram were travelling in a first-class cubicle which guaranteed privacy, but when the former tried to draw his friend into a conversation around future plans, Godse seemed reluctant to talk. Narayan was stunned by Nathuram's silence and later narrated that night's events to Vishnu Karkare, explaining how he had evinced no response from Godse for his proposal of acquiring more men, resources and money. He was swift to gauge that his partner was reluctant in endorsing his plan. Something was brewing in his mind, Apte knew.

The next morning, he found Godse awake. Once Apte was fully alert, Godse told him about his intention to kill Gandhi. 'I don't need any help, not another man. No recruiting people, no depending on anyone else.'[35] He added that he only needed the right gun for carrying out the assassination. Apte later confessed to Karkare that it was in that precise moment when he knew that Gandhi was as good as dead.

If there was a defining period in Nathuram Godse's life, it was the hiatus of a mere ten days, between 20 and 30 January 1948. Even though Mahatma Gandhi's great-grandson Tushar Gandhi argued in his book, *Let's Kill Gandhi*, as well as in subsequent articles and interviews, that it was Narayan Apte who was the ring leader till 20 January 1948, the argument precludes the factor of the natural leadership position which an ideologue takes in a mission of this nature. It may be recalled that Nathuram Godse, from his earliest days in the Hindu Mahasabha, viewed himself as superior when compared to the rest. Even Savarkar had accepted Godse as one of his brightest apprentices and had made it clear on three occasions—first, when he appointed Nathuram as his personal secretary; second, when he placed Godse as the head of the first batch of protestors against Nizam's Hyderabad and finally, when he extended both moral and financial support for the *Dainik Agrani*.

Curtains on Gandhi, Spotlight on Godse

Godse returned just as Madanlal Pahwa had predicted. Shooting

Gandhi was just been one part of the task. The next bit to explain the reasons that had prompted him to undertake such an act. The assassination was merely a way of gaining political mileage and drawing attention to an abominable ideology. With his 'brave' posturing and ready surrender to police, Nathuram Godse appropriated a haloed space in the folklore of Hindu sectarian groups.

After his arrest, Godse wanted the State to try him, so that he could counter—not by denying charges, but by using the occasion as an opportunity to publicise a political theory first expounded by Savarkar about nation, nationhood and cultural nationalism as against the territorial definition of nationalism. After all, it isn't as if Nathuram Godse shot Gandhi only because he was driven by megalomania and wanted to be remembered in history as a brave assassin. It wasn't also only because he aspired to be remembered as a 'freedom fighter' who had liberated India's political soul from the clutches of the 'Muslim appeasers'. It was Vishnu Karkare who provided a vital clue as to why Godse had taken it upon himself to kill Gandhi. 'He was an orator and writer and would be in a position to impress upon the Government and the Court as to why he killed Gandhi,'[36] said Karkare to his interrogators. His open endorsement of Godse's oratorical skill was backed by another man—Justice G.D. Khosla, Chief Justice of Punjab High Court, who, after hearing Godse's appeal against his sentence, wrote:

> The audience was visibly and audibly moved. There was a deep silence when he ceased speaking. Many women were in tears and men were coughing and searching for their handkerchiefs. The silence was accentuated and made deeper by the sound of an occasional subdued sniff or a muffled cough. It seemed to

> me that I was taking part in some kind of melodrama or in a scene out of a Hollywood feature film. Once or twice, I had interrupted Godse and pointed out the irrelevance of what he was saying, but my colleagues seemed inclined to hear him and the audience most certainly thought that Godse's performance was the only worth-while part of the lengthy proceedings.[37]

Godse gave a good fight and matched the State with his well-rehearsed defence, point by point. He was aware that the intelligence agencies, a significant part and parcel of the Indian State, were on the defensive, considering they had bungled several times in fobbing off the threat to the Mahatma's life. As there was no way in which the 'system' could absolve itself or compensate for its failure, it was forced to mount the trial as a huge spectacle. Consequent to this decision, the government chose the historic Red Fort as the venue of the trial because it was symbolic of the State's might. India was on its way to becoming a nation state and committed to a republican path, but in the face of having been exposed for its vulnerability, the government was forced to draw power from India's impressive medieval past. The assassination and trial were independent India's first major crisis, brought upon by its own frailties. By designating the iconic Red Fort as the venue of the trial, the government sought to underscore the continuity of authority from the imperial powers into the hands of an Indian dispensation. It may be recalled that the British had also held Bahadur Shah Zafar's trial at the same venue almost a century ago, a place from where he had once ruled Hindustan. Furthermore, the trial at the Red Fort was also to convey the message that the guilty were charged with regicide—in this case, Gandhi, the people's king.

Although the proceedings were held within the Fort, the hall where it was actually held was a modern British structure, thereby indicative of the imperial power. The Indian State was prosecuting Gandhi's killer but the setting was reminiscent of India's colonial past. In fact, the Indian State even fought the case in the name of the British monarch: *Rex vs Nathuram Vinayak Godse and others*.

But, as it turned out later, the Indian State had got its symbolism wrong. The reason was that the British government had conducted the INA trails at the same venue barely a few years ago, in 1945-46. In prosecuting men and women who were viewed by the nation as committed patriots who had sacrificed their lives for the freedom of the nation, the Red Fort had come to acquire the image of a location where 'unjust trials' were conducted. The government had made 'every attempt to ensure that the proceedings were aimed towards the external audience of the trial and not those within the courtroom'[38] yet, as we shall analyse later, the final thunder was stolen by none other than the main accused, Nathuram Vinayak Godse, because he claimed that his action was on behalf of a community that had been wronged in history, especially during the medieval period, and its 'correction' was prevented by Gandhi.

Gandhi's assassination put the RSS and Hindu Mahasabha on the back foot. Savarkar was also tried in the conspiracy case and although he pleaded not guilty, the needle of suspicion that pointed to him is yet to be completely shifted away from his direction. The BJP has failed in this endeavour despite being cumulatively in power for more than a decade and half at the time of this writing. The public embrace by the Sangh Parivar points to a silent acquiescence of the reasons why Gandhi was assassinated in the first place. If this had not been the case, the BJP would not have kept within its ranks (in important positions to boot) those leaders who glorified Godse by acts or statements. Even as the RSS had conveniently declared itself as a 'cultural body' with its top leaders washing their hands off the accused, Nathuram had brazenly pleaded guilty, declared that he had killed Gandhi and was justified in doing so. The only objection that he registered was the government's claim of a conspiracy and argued vociferously that the killing was solely his handiwork. Although this was a planned tactic to ensure that the leadership of the Mahasabha (and possibly some within the RSS) were absolved of all charges, the unequivocal espousal of his political views made him a hero among a section of the people and this explains the continuing adulation for him.

The Court as Proscenium

The courtroom was the next site after the Birla House where Gandhi was killed for the second time, albeit in absentia. Instead of his physical body, Nathuram Godse proceeded to demolish the Gandhian worldview, the idea of a nation advocated by forces antagonistic to the political theory propounded by Savarkar, Hedgewar, Golwalkar and several others in the Mahasabha and RSS. While Godse converted the court into a bully pulpit to spread his idea of a nation that he had imbibed from his guru, Savarkar distanced himself from the accused in an attempt to get acquitted. In his defence statement, Godse made it clear to the court that he had not made 'any attempt to run away; in fact, I never entertained any idea of running away. I did not try to shoot myself. It was never my intention to do so, for it was my ardent desire to give vent to my thoughts in an open Court'.[39]

While the court had become an arena for Godse to immortalise himself, Savarkar's intent was to maintain his position as an intellectual and political thinker. On the first day of the trial, when press photographers were permitted to shoot the accused, Savarkar had protested, arguing that he had not given consent for being photographed alongside others. He was a trained lawyer and because he was 'aware of the iconology of the court and the trial syntax',[40] he pleaded that, owing to his ill health, he may be permitted to sit in a separate chair placed outside the dock. By ensuring that his plea was accepted by the presiding judge, Savarkar succeeded in creating a physical barrier between him and the others accused.

However, while this ploy may have strengthened his case for acquittal, he was to lose his political credibility forever. Savarkar lived for more than a decade after the trial, but was never able to regain the eminence that he once commanded in the Indian political arena. In the public's eye, Savarkar was as guilty. And even amongst his admirers, he remained a defeated man who had no role to play in the removal of a scourge called Gandhi—a gutless man who could not stand up for his beliefs. The subtle difference between the lives of Godse and Savarkar following Gandhi's murder is in the fact that while the former has been elevated as a doer, so to say, the latter is revered as an ideologue or thinker. Savarkar's bravado, his Veer title, is because of his actions prior to arrest, conviction and sentencing in 1910-11 whereas Godse's gallantry comes from his stalking of Gandhi till his end.

In contrast to Savarkar, Godse had the easier task because all he wanted was to 'explain his guilt'. During the trial, all the accused decided to read out their defence statements, which enabled their legal teams to weigh each word, examine nuances and lay exclusive emphasis on significant aspects. Nathuram Godse's statement was predictably the most voluminous of the lot—out of the ninety pages of his defence testimony, almost two-thirds were a critique of Gandhian ideology and the Mahatma's relevance (or rather, the absence of it) in politics.[41] Godse's statement also devoted considerable time in explaining how he had little or no synergy with the other accused and had acted on his own in planning and executing the assassination. Not surprisingly, only a fraction of his statement pertained to act of the murder itself. In his statement, he justified his action by claiming that 'accumulating provocation of 32 years culminating in his last pro-Muslim fast at last goaded me to the conclusion that the existence of Gandhiji should be brought to an end immediately'. Gandhi's fast for peace was depicted as a concession to Muslims.

After his conviction in the trial court on 10 February 1949, Godse opted to challenge it in the Punjab High Court, but didn't dispute the death sentence which was awarded to him. 'His appeal was confined to the finding that there was a conspiracy. He assumed complete and sole responsibility for the death of Mahatma Gandhi,' wrote Justice Khosla. However, what seemed strange to many at the time was that if Godse had refrained from challenging the trial court's verdict, then why was he appealing in the High Court?

As it turns out, Nathuram Godse viewed the ballroom at the Viceregal Lodge in Shimla, once used as the summer retreat for viceroys and later as a holiday home for the president of India, as yet another proscenium for a jaw-dropping performance. His ploy worked and this was discernible from the elaborate bandobast for the trial, including the decision by the presiding judges to revive an anachronistic practice. In the aftermath of the Partition, judges of the Punjab High Court had adopted a relaxed and easy code of dressing so as not to evoke the horrors of the past. But during

Godse's appeal, the three assigned judges decided to 'resume the old practice of wearing wigs, and that on our entry into the court-room we should, as in the olden days, be preceded by our liveried ushers carrying silver-mounted staffs'.[42]

When the hearing on the appeal of the accused began on 2 May 1949, Godse expressed his financial inability to hire a lawyer, as a result of which he was the only accused to be personally present in court. Admission to the courtroom was restricted owing to security concerns, but also to ensure that the ballroom, unlike the trial court a few months earlier, was not treated like a loud marketplace, with several people speaking and commenting at will.

On 2 May 1949, as the hearing on the appeal got underway, every practising lawyer in the High Court who did not have a case listed in another court that day was present and grabbed the best seats. The audience included Shimla's gentry—wives and even children of eminent judges and government officials. There was no doubt that everyone wanted to carry a slice of history along; to be part of a case which had rattled the soul of India. Justice Khosla wrote that Godse had manipulated his way into Shimla because of a 'morbid desire to watch the process of his disintegration at first hand'. This argument, however, sounds flawed, as Godse did not see his fate as decaying, decomposing or being annihilated. This was his moment of nirvana, of freeing himself from the routine cycle of life and death and elevating himself to a stature of a martyr. He knew that the people were present in court only to witness his performance and he delivered with aplomb, portraying himself, in Justice Khosla's words, as 'a fearless patriot and a passionate protagonist of Hindu ideology. He had remained completely unrepentant of his atrocious crime, and whether out of a deep conviction in his beliefs or merely in order to make a last public apology, he had sought this opportunity of displaying his talents before he dissolved into oblivion'.[43]

Even in distant Shimla, the government failed in its endeavour to demonise Godse. The excitement in the Viceregal Lodge matched the jamboree which had unfolded earlier in the trial courtroom of the Red Fort. Kanika Sharma recalled Harper Lee's depiction of the first day of Tom Robinson's trial as a 'gala occasion', comparing it with the proceedings of the Red Fort trial. In what was simply ridiculous, men serving water in the courtroom presented a strange sight as they balanced the earthen surahis on their heads while pouring out water for the thirsty from metal glasses which were refilled with intricate manoeuvres without putting the pots on the ground. People constantly complained about faulty loudspeakers and not being able to hear a word of what the judge and the lawyers said. But even in the chaos, although no one could comprehend the proceedings of the day, a 'House Full' sign was displayed outside the courtroom the moment Godse began testifying.

Godse's statements (first in the trial court and later in his arguments between 5–12 May 1949) in the High Court formed the centrepiece of the opera that he split into two acts. The intent, as mentioned before, was to portray himself as the sole assassin of the event. As such, on 8 November 1948, several months into the trial, when the judge had asked Godse if he had anything to say, he affirmed that he wished to read a statement. The prosecution protested, but was overruled by the court. Godse had known all along that the prime accused in the case would not be denied the opportunity to present a case and, as part of the strategy, had cleverly opted for a written statement for two main reasons. First, it left room for improvement in any number of drafts and second, once a written statement was submitted, it would become a permanent part of history. He chose to make two statements, one in the trial court, and other in the form of arguments in the High Court. About the second, Justice Khosla wrote in his book how he, 'pursued the same line (what prompted him to take Mahatma Gandhi's life) in the long, written statement which he had filed in the trial court'. Both speeches were equally evocative and invariably found a place in compendiums on the most powerful political speeches of India. Justice Khosla's viewpoint that if 'the audience of that day been constituted into a jury and entrusted with the task of deciding Godse's appeal, they would have brought in a verdict of "not guilty" by an overwhelming majority,' was echoed by Verrier Elwin, a close friend of Gandhi and a noted anthropologist. According to him, Godse's speech 'was the finest by a condemned man since Socrates' trial speech'.[44] Elwin would have certainly disagreed with Godse's viewpoint and his political clan's interpretation of history, politics and much more, but that did not prevent him from accepting Godse's charismatic presence on the witness stand and the seductive capacity of his words.

Earlier on 8 November 1948, Nathuram Godse began reading his speech in the trial court at about 10.15 a.m. and faltered just once after almost an hour when he fell after feeling a shade giddy. After recovering from the setback, his performance thereafter was a tour de force. For five hours, people in the courtroom were spellbound, much like they would be later in Shimla. While reviewing the book on a selection of important speeches in modern India, the *Business Standard* argued that despite the 'controversy and the stigma' surrounding Godse, this speech is one that 'every Indian must read. Not to sympathise with Godse, but to gain a better insight into Gandhi as a leader'.[45] That may not just be the reviewer's judgement, but also that of the majority of those who reach out for those ninety-odd pages.

Although Godse began his speech by refuting the conspiracy charges, his speech was essentially a diatribe against Gandhi. Godse strung together a series of polemical arguments and clarified at the outset that he had 'never made a secret about the fact that I supported the ideology or the school which was opposed to that of Gandhiji'. By way of introduction, he told the audience how he had 'worked for several years in RSS and subsequently joined the Hindu Mahasabha and volunteered myself to fight as a soldier under its pan Hindu flag'. In what was clearly his attempt to distance himself from his mentor and project himself as the sole actor in eliminating Gandhi, he said that since the mid-1940s he had been disillusioned with Savarkar because of his political pacifism and acceptance of the inevitability of Partition. 'Veer Savarkar setting aside the will of the majority of Hindu Sanghatanists hoisted this new flag with the wheel, as a National Flag, on his house along with the Bhagwa (on 15 August 1947).' However, what Godse chose to omit deliberately were his regular meetings, even the last one before departing for Delhi, with the Mahasabha leader and the support Savarker had extended to each of his initiatives to further the Hindutva argument. Moreover, if the relationship was no longer anchored on Godse's reverence for Savarkar, why did he seek, and get, the latter's support for the newspaper?

As was expected, Godse focused on tearing Gandhi down. He accused the Mahatma of advocating views which 'always showed or evinced a bias for Muslims, prejudicial and detrimental to the Hindu community and its interests'. He thundered how 'during more than thirty years of the undisputed leadership of the Mahatma, there were more desecration of temples, more forcible and fraudulent conversions, more outrages on women and finally the loss of one third of the country'. Godse's judgement on Gandhi was damning, that he was 'a mere pygmy before Shivaji, Rana Pratap and Guru Govind'.

Thereafter, Godse asked the court for permission to present a political critique of Gandhi, which the prosecution objected to but the judge overruled. He then meticulously divided the Mahatma's political career into three distinct phases: from 1915 to 1939-40; thereafter till 3 June 1947 and finally, from then onwards till his death. Godse had a definite viewpoint on each of these three phases, although he clarified that they were interwoven by a unifying theme which he said was the 'infatuation of Gandhiji for the Muslims and his incorrigible craving for Muslim leadership without any regard for right or wrong for truth or justice and in utter contempt of the sentiments of the Hindus as a whole was the high watermark of the Mahatmic (sic) benevolence'. The quote abundantly establishes the kernel of Godse-Gandhi divide—while the Mahatma firmly believed in the idea of an India that was as much Muslim as it was Hindu, Godse believed in a Hindu Rashtra, a nation which was legitimately and culturally Hindu.

There were two issues that Godse raised unwaveringly that have resonated loudly in all statements and actions of the RSS, its branches and subsidiaries (including the BJP) over the past seven decades. The first was about the national anthem—an unresolved debate since the 1940s—a toss-up between *Vande Mataram* and *Jana Gana Mana*. Godse's contention was that the 'Muslims disliked the celebrated song of "Vande Mataram" and the Mahatma forthwith stopped its singing or recital wherever he could' and that he had instead 'asked to adopt Rabindranath Tagore's "Jana Gana Mana", as a substitute for "Vande Mataram"'. Could anything be more demoralising or pitiful than this brazen-faced action against a song of worldwide fame simply because one ignorant fanatic disliked it?[46]

The second issue revolved around the tricolour. Godse claimed that 'if any Hindu attached any importance to Shivaji's Hindu flag, Bhagwa Jhanda, the flag which freed India from the Muslim-domination, it was considered communal'. Godse was extremely critical of the Congress flag, which formed the basis for the national flag. He called it 'Gandhiji's tricoloured flag' and denounced it for reasons which not only sounded illogical, but also bizarre, stating the flag 'never protected any Hindu woman from outrage or a Hindu temple from desecration'.

In the final analysis, Godse achieved what he had set out to do during the trial and appeal. He had presented a forceful critique of Gandhi and pressurised the government to enter a mode of panic. The government responded to Godse's written statement by gagging the press. However, as the text of the speech had unofficially been in circulation for long, the Congress government's censorship further aided in the deification of Godse.

On 15 November 1949, even as Nathuram and Narayan were led to the gallows in Ambala jail, he left behind a will in the form of a letter for his younger brother, Dattatraya. His ashes, willed Nathuram, should be preserved till they could be 'sunk in the Holy Sindhu River (Indus River) when she will again flow freely under the aegis of the flag of Hindustan'. He also authorised Dattatreya to publish his final testimony once the proscription order was lifted. He then proceeded to donate Rs 101 for the construction of the Somnath temple. This temple in the erstwhile Junagadh Princely State had been destroyed by invading armies but, after its accession to India, was in the process of rebuilt when the trial and the appeal against it was heard. This initiative provided the template to the Sangh Parivar to justify its demand to demolish or 'shift' the Babri Masjid from Ayodhya to allow a grand temple dedicated to Rama to come up. Over the years, Nathuram Godse's dying wish has assumed an epic proportion, with several layers added to it by his admirers.

On 15 November 1949, as the hangman prepared his tools, Godse burst into the RSS morning prayer (or hymn) in Sanskrit, adopted in 1939: *Namaste sada vatsale matribhume* (Oh Motherland, ever-affectionate to your children—salutation to thee). With that, it seemed as if the life he had chosen had come a full circle. Earlier, his statement in the trial court had ended with in the shouts of, '*Akhanda Bharat amar rahe*' (Long live undivided India) and '*Vande Mataram*'. Godse had embarked on his project to assassinate Gandhi after being inspired by Savarkar. Having successfully accomplished his mission, Godse chose to walk into the night of his life with the RSS prayer, an ode to the nation as a goddess or motherland. In the process, he connected the dots that appear on paper as rupture points between the RSS and the person who inspired its formation, Savarkar. Godse remained as much a swayamsevak as an acolyte of the Mahasabha leader, the codifier of Hindutva.

Godse had lived up to his pledge of working to strengthen the Hindu sanghathan and succeeded in bridging the gap between the RSS and Hindu Mahasabha at the time of his death. Almost seventy years later, his memory is being evoked yet again to bring all the affiliates of the Right-wing BJP under the common cause of supporting a Hindu nationhood. The iconic status of Godse sits uncomfortably in the consciousness of several Hindu sectarian groups. Only the creation of an alternate iconography will alter this.

ENDNOTES

KESHAV BALIRAM HEDGEWAR

1. *Dr. Hedgewar, the Epoch Maker: A Biography*, B.V. Deshpande & S.R. Ramaswamy, Sahitya Sindhu, Bengaluru, 1981, p.3. Accessed online from the official site—www.rss.org/Encyc/2015/8/8/334_12_29_25_Dr.Hedgewar_The_Epoch_Maker.pdf
2. op.cit., p.10. Accessed online from the official site www.rss.org/Encyc/2015/8/8/334_12_29_25_Dr.Hedgewar_The_Epoch_Maker.pdf
3. op. cit., p. 9.
4. op. cit., p. 12.
5. *Builders of Modern India, Dr. Keshav Baliram Hedgewar*, Rakesh Sinha, Publications Division, Government of India, 2016. Accessed online: https://books.google.co.in/books?id=LSHiDQAAQBAJ&pg=PT30&dq=hedgewar+cocaine&hl=en&sa=X&ved=0ahUKEwjC0ZWx0obgAhVIk3AKHcsxB9UQuwUIMDAA#v=onepage&q=hedgewar%20cocaine&f=false or (for short) https://goo.gl/ZwzFJC
6. *Militant Hinduism in Indian Politics: A Study of the RSS*, J.A. Curran, International Secretariat, Institute of Pacific Relations, New York, p. 13. Cited by D.R. Goyal in *Rashtriya Swayamsevak Sangh*, Radha Krishna, 1979; revised edition, 2000. He claimed that Curran was

once a 'senior official of the CIA' and his study was sponsored by the Institute of Pacific Relations. It remained a mimeographed document till its publication in 1979 by the All India Quami Ekta Sammelan which was led by Raj Narain.

7. *Rashtriya Swayamsevak Sangh*, D.R. Goyal, Radha Krishna, 1979; revised edition, 2000, p. 54.
8. *Dr. Hedgewar, the Epoch Maker: A Biography*, B.V. Deshpande & S.R. Ramaswamy, Sahitya Sindhu, Bengaluru, 1981, p. 18.
9. op. cit., p. 20.
10. *The Myth of the Lokamanya: Tilak and Mass Politics in Maharashtra*, Richard I. Cashman, University of California Press, 1975, pp.198-99.
11. *Dr. Hedgewar, the Epoch Maker: A Biography*, B.V. Deshpande & S.R. Ramaswamy, Sahitya Sindhu, Bengaluru, 1981, p. 24.
12. op. cit., p. 26.
13. *Rashtriya Swayamsevak Sangh*, D.R. Goyal, Radha Krishna, 1979; revised edition, 2000, p. 57.
14. ibid.
15. Hedgewar's original written statement was reproduced in *Dr. Hedgewar, the Epoch Maker: A Biography*, B.V. Deshpande & S.R. Ramaswamy, Sahitya Sindhu, Bengaluru, 1981, p. 29.
16. *Sangh Nirmata*, C. P. Bhishikar, Suruchi Prakashna, p. 30, cited by D. R. Goyal, *Rashtriya Swayamsevak Sangh*, Radha Krishna, 1979; revised edition, 2000, p. 57.
17. *Dr. Hedgewar, the Epoch Maker: A Biography*, B.V. Deshpande & S.R. Ramaswamy, Sahitya Sindhu, Bengaluru, 1981, p. 66.
18. op. cit., p. 29.
19. *Emergence of Hindu Nationalism in India*, John Zavos, Oxford University Press (OUP), 2000, p. 148.
20. *Dr. Hedgewar, the Epoch Maker: A Biography*, B.V. Deshpande & S.R. Ramaswamy, Sahitya Sindhu, Bengaluru, 1981, p. 29.
21. op. cit., p. 30.

22. *Encyclopedia of Eminent Thinker: The Political Thought of K.B. Hedgewar*, Jai Narain Sharma, Concept, 2008, pp. 33-34 &117.

23. *Rashtriya Swayamsevak Sangh*, D.R. Goyal, Radha Krishna, 1979; revised edition, 2000, p. 58.

24. *Emergence of Hindu Nationalism in India*, John Zavos, Oxford University Press, 2000, p. 152.

25. ibid.

26. *Dr. Hedgewar, the Epoch Maker: A Biography*, B.V. Deshpande & S.R. Ramaswamy, Sahitya Sindhu, Bengaluru, 1981, p. 33.

27. op. cit., p. 34.

28. *Dr Hedgewar Charitra*, N.H. Palkar, Bharatiya Vichar Sadhana, p. 129, cited by Walter K. Andersen & Sridhar Damle in *The Brotherhood in Saffron*, Vistaar, 1987.

29. op. cit., p. 154.

30. *The Brotherhood in Saffron*, Walter K. Andersen & Sridhar Damle, Vistaar, 1987, p. 34.

31. *Dr Hedgewar Charitra*, N.H. Palkar, Bharatiya Vichar Sadhana p. 168.

32. ibid.

33. *Dr. Hedgewar, the Epoch Maker: A Biography*, B.V. Deshpande & S.R. Ramaswamy, Sahitya Sindhu, Bengaluru, 1981, p. 45.

34. *The Brotherhood in Saffron*, Walter K. Andersen & Sridhar Damle, Vistaar, 1987, p. 37.

35. *Rashtriya Swayamsevak Sangh*, D.R. Goyal, Radha Krishna, 1979; revised edition, 2000, p. 78.

36. *Khaki Shorts and Saffron Flags: A Critique of the Hindu Right*, Tapan Basu, Pradip Datta, Sumit Sarkar, Tanika Sarkar, Sambuddha Sen, Orient Longman (now, Orient Blackswan), 1993, p. 18.

37. *Dr. Hedgewar, the Epoch Maker: A Biography*, B.V. Deshpande & S.R. Ramaswamy, Sahitya Sindhu, Bengaluru, 1981, p. 41.

38. *Fundamentalisms and the State: Remaking Polities, Economies, and Militance*, eds. Martin E. Marty & R. Scott Appleby, University of Chicago Press, 1993, pp. 241-42.

39. *Rashtriya Swayamsevak Sangh*, D. R. Goyal, Radha Krishna, 1979; revised edition, 2000, p. 80.
40. *Dr. Hedgewar, the Epoch Maker: A Biography*, B.V. Deshpande & S.R. Ramaswamy, Sahitya Sindhu, Bengaluru, 1981, p. 52.
41. op.cit., p. 50.
42. op.cit., p. 51.
43. Op.cit., p. 52.
44. *Khaki Shorts and Saffron Flags: A Critique of the Hindu Right*, Tapan Basu, Pradip Datta, Sumit Sarkar, Tanika Sarkar, Sambuddha Sen, Orient Longman, 1993, p. 22.
45. op. cit., pp. 22-23.
46. 'Hindutva's Foreign Tie-up in the 1930s: Archival Evidence', Marzia Casolari, *Economic and Political Weekly*, 22 January 2000.
47. ibid.
48. ibid.
49. *Khaki Shorts and Saffron Flags: A Critique of the Hindu Right*, Tapan Basu, Pradip Datta, Sumit Sarkar, Tanika Sarkar, Sambuddha Sen, Orient Longman, 1993, p. 24.

VINAYAK DAMODAR SAVARKAR

1. https://www.economist.com/news/christmas-specials/21636599-controversial-mentor-hindu-right-man-who-thought-gandhi-sissy. See also, Jyotirmaya Sharma, *Imagining Incommensurables: The Hindu Rashtra and the Indian Nation; Grounding Morality: Freedom, Knowledge and the Plurality of Cultures*, eds., Jyotirmaya Sharma & A. Raghuramaraju, Routledge, 2010, p. 298.
2. *Collected Works*, Mahatma Gandhi, Vol. 10, p. 201.
3. Ibid.
4. *Complete Works*, Gandhi, Vol. 9, https://www.gandhiashramsevagram.org/gandhi-literature/mahatma-gandhi-collected-works-volume-9.pdf

5. https://www.gandhiashramsevagram.org/gandhi-literature/mahatma-gandhi-collected-works-volume-37.pdf.
6. Report of Commission of Inquiry into Conspiracy to Murder Mahatma Gandhi, Part II, p. 303.
7. *Divine Enterprise: Gurus and the Hindu Nationalist Movement*, Lise McKean, University of Chicago Press, p. 72.
8. *Emergence of Hindu Nationalism in India*, John Zavos, Oxford University Press, 2000, p. 177.
9. *Veer Savarkar*, Dhananjay Keer, Popular Prakashan (first published in May 1950 as *Savarkar and His Times*); this taken from the third edition, 2012, p. 2.
10. op. cit., p. 4.
11. Ibid.
12. https://ethnomusicologyreview.ucla.edu/journal/volume/17/piece/603
13. '150 years of heroism, via Kala Pani', *The Indian Express*, 10 May 2007; http://archive.indianexpress.com/news/150-yrs-of-heroism-via-kala-pani/ 30503/0
14. *Hindutva and Violence, V.D. Savarkar and the Politics of History*, pp. 51-54.
15. *Collected Works of Mahatma Gandhi*, Vol. 4, pp. 366-367.
16. Rajmohan Gandhi in *The Hindu*, 8 July 2003; http://www.thehindu.com/2003/07/08/stories/2003070801391000.htm
17. Ibid.
18. 'V.D. Savarkar and the Indian War of Independence: Contrasting Perspectives of an Emergent Composite State', John Pincince, Department of History, Loyola University, Chicago, http://www.csas. ed.ac.uk/mutiny/confpapers/Pincince-Paper.pdf.
19. *Divine Enterprise: Gurus and the Hindu Nationalist Movement*, Lise McKean, University of Chicago Press, p. 77.
20. Ibid.
21. Ibid.

22. *Indian War of Independence: 1857*, V.D. Savarkar, Abhishek Publications, 2012, p. 52; this extract can also be found in www.savarkar.org

23. Op. cit., pp. 216-17.

24. Ibid.

25. *Veer Savarkar*, Dhananjay Keer, Popular Prakashan (first published in May 1950 as *Savarkar and His Times*); this taken from the third edition, 2012, p. 171.

26. Op. cit., p. 139.

27. Op. cit., p. 143.

28. *Hindutva: Exploring the Idea of Hindu Nationalism*, Jyotirmaya Sharma, Penguin Books India, 2003 & 2011, p. 94.

29. *Hindutva! Who is a Hindu?* V. D. Savarkar, Veer Savarkar Publications, 1989, sixth edition, pp. 91-92. 'It is clear that though their (Muslims and Christians) original Hindu blood is thus almost unaffected by an alien adulteration, yet they cannot be called Hindus in the sense in which that term is actually understood, because, we Hindus are bound together not only by the tie of the love we bear to a common fatherland and by the common blood that courses through our veins and keeps our hearts throbbing and our affections warm, but also by the tie of the common homage we pay to our great civilization—our Hindu culture, which could not be better rendered than by the word Sanskriti, suggestive as it is of that language, Sanskrit, which has been the chosen means of expression and preservation of that culture, of all that was best and worth-preserving in the history of our race. We are one because we are a nation a race and own a common Sanskriti (civilization).'

30. Op. cit., p.70. 'India alone had to face Arabs, Persians, Pathans, Baluchis, Tartars, Turks, Moguls—a veritable human Sahara whirling and columning up bodily in a furious world storm! Religion is a mighty motive force. So is rapine. But where religion is goaded on by rapine and rapine serves as a handmaid to religion, the propelling force that is generated by these together is only equaled by the profundity of human misery and devastation they leave behind them in their

march. Heaven and hell making a common cause–such were the forces, overwhelmingly furious, that took India by surprise the day Mohammad crossed the Indus and invaded her. Day after day, decade after decade, century after century, the ghastly conflict continued and India single-handed kept up the fight morally and militarily.'

31. *Veer Savarkar*, Dhananjay Keer, Popular Prakashan (first published in May 1950 as *Savarkar and His Times*); this taken from the third edition, 2012, p. 143.

32. *Hindutva! Who is a Hindu?* V. D. Savarkar, Veer Savarkar Publications, 1989, sixth edition, p. 115.

33. http://www.frontline.in/static/html/fl2207/stories/20050408001903700.htm

34. https://www.youtube.com/watch?v=lIl1AhOWDI8&t=3s.

35. *Frontline*, 8 April 2013, http://www.frontline.in/books/savarkars-unparalleledrecord/article4328693.ece.

36. https://timesofindia.indiatimes.com/india/savarkar-was-strategic-affairs-expert-gave-robust-defence-and-diplomatic-doctrine-rajnath/articleshow/86983820.cms.

37. *Veer Savarkar*, Dhananjay Keer, Popular Prakashan (first published in May 1950 as *Savarkar and His Times*); this taken from the third edition, 2012, pp. 158-59.

38. Op. cit., 163.

39. *Hindu Pad-Padashahi* (or A Review of the Hindu Empire of Maharashtra), V.D. Savarkar, B.G.Paul & Co, Madras, 1925, p. xiii.

40. 'Savarkar, Hinduness and the Aryan Homeland', Koenraad Elst; http://koenraadelst.bharatvani.org/articles/fascism/replytopv.html. According to Elst, Savarkar claimed that, 'When the foremost band of the intrepid Aryans made it their home and lighted their first sacrificial fire on the banks of the Sindhu, the Indus, yet certain it is that long before the ancient Egyptians, and Babylonians had built their magnificent civilization, the holy waters of the Indus were daily witnessing the lucid and curling columns of the scented sacrificial smokes and the valleys resounding with the chants of Vedic hymns–

the spiritual fervor that animated their souls.' However, Savarkar's views regarding Aryan settlers is considered flawed as the 'Hindutva school, as we know it today, argues that the Aryans were the natives of the country.'

41. Accessed from the judgement, https://indiankanoon.org/doc/726232/
42. *Veer Savarkar: Father of Hindu Nationalism*, Jaywant Joglekar, English edition accessed from https://books.google.co.in/books?id=1J3uk3x_k6sC&pr int sec=f rontcover&dq=Jaywant+Joglekar&hl=en&sa=X&ved=0ahUKEwiSlbnDxIngAhVHbysKHTS4BfcQ6AEIKDAA#v=onepage&q=Jaywant%20Joglekar&f=false, p. 113
43. *Hindutva: Exploring the Idea of Hindu Nationalism*, Jyotirmaya Sharma, Penguin Books India, 2003 & 2011, p. 141.
44. *Veer Savarkar*, Dhananjay Keer, Popular Prakashan (first published in May 1950 as *Savarkar and His Times*); this taken from the third edition, 2012, p. 220.
45. Marzia Casolari, *In the Shadow of the Swastika: The Relationships Between Indian Radical Nationalism, Italian Fascism and Nazism*, Routledge Studies in Modern History, 2020, p. 86.
46. Op. cit., p. 222.
47. Op. cit., p. 227.
48. http://www.thehindu.com/2004/09/21/stories/2004092109381100.htm
49. *Hindu Rashtra-Darshan*, V.D. Savarkar; sourced online from the Maharashtra Prantik Hindu Sabha, Pune, p. 9.
50. From Savarkar papers cited by Marzia Casolari, same as above, p. 88
51. From Savarkar papers cited by Marzia Casolari, same as above, p. 88
52. Ibid.
53. Casolari, p. 93.
54. Ibid. V.D. Savarkar in his presidential speech, in Madurai 1940, '... then the war broke out and the British Government, to serve their own interests, were compelled to raise new military forces in India on a large scale. Naturally, the Hindu Mahasabha with a true insight into

practical politics decided to participate in all war efforts of the British Government in so far as they concerned directly with the question of the Indian defence and raising new military forces in India. I emphatically maintain that the results of that policy even within a year of its trial are positively encouraging ...' see p. 86. Also see, p. 87, 'While in the old army the proportion of the Moslems had risen in some parts even to 75% we find amongst these new recruits, there are nearly sixty thousand Hindus and thirty thousand Moslems. The strength of the air force also is terribly increased and is being daily increased. It is very encouraging a fact that the Hindus are evincing a special interest and ability in the aircraft and are getting themselves enlisted in large numbers in the air forces.'

55. *Veer Savarkar*, Dhananjay Keer, Popular Prakashan (first published in May 1950 as *Savarkar and His Times*); this taken from the third edition, 2012, p. 246.
56. *Hindu Rashtra-Darshan*, V.D. Savarkar, his presidential speech, Nagpur, 1938, p. 15.
57. *Divine Enterprise: Gurus and the Hindu Nationalist Movement*, Lise McKean, University of Chicago Press, p. 89.
58. *Veer Savarkar*, Dhananjay Keer, Popular Prakashan (first published in May 1950 as *Savarkar and His Times*); this taken from the third edition, 2012, p. 341.
59. Ibid.
60. *Veer Savarkar*, Dhananjay Keer, Popular Prakashan (first published in May 1950 as *Savarkar and His Times*); this taken from the third edition, 2012, p. 416.
61. Op. cit., p. 420.
62. Op. cit., p. 448.
63. Op. cit., p. 500.
64. Op. cit., p. 530.
65. *Divine Enterprise: Gurus and the Hindu Nationalist Movement*, Lise McKean, University of Chicago Press, pp. 86-87.
66. *Veer Savarkar*, Dhananjay Keer, Popular Prakashan (first published in

May 1950 as *Savarkar and His Times*); this taken from the third edition, 2012, p. 230.

MADHAV SADASHIV GOLWALKAR

1. *The Making of Exile: Sindhi Hindus and The Partition Of India*, Nandita Bhavnani, Tranquebar Press, 2014, pp. 47-50.
2. ibid.
3. ibid., this incident is also referred to in *My Country My Life*, L.K. Advani, Rupa & Co, Delhi, 2008, p. 51, and also in *The Telegraph*, 'Pak Digs Into Advani Case', 1 February 2002, https://www.telegraphindia.com/india/pak-digs-into-advani-case/cid/902729
4. L. K. Advani refers to this rally of 5 August as a 'morale booster' in *My Country My Life*, Rupa & Co, Delhi, 2008, p. 51.
5. L.K. Advani's speech on the release of the Marathi edition of *My Country My Life*, 19 July 2009, in which he had said that he had joined the RSS at fourteen and quoted M.S. Golwalkar; http://www.bjp.org/en/media-resources/speeches/shri-l-k-advaniji-s-speech-on-the-release-of-the-marathi-edition-of-my-country-my-life
6. *Shri Guruji: Pioneer of A New Era*, C. P. Bhishikar, translated into the English by Sudhakar Raje, Sahitya Sindhu Prakashana, Bengaluru; accessed online from www.golwalkarguruji.org, pp. 56-57.
7. Cited by A.G. Noorani, *The RSS and the BJP: A Division of Labour*, Leftword, 2000, p. 55.
8. *The Making of Exile: Sindhi Hindus and The Partition Of India*, Nandita Bhavnani, Tranquebar Press, 2014, p. 50.
9. Multiple sources, but this is accessed from https://www.mkgandhi.org/journalist/rssmember.htm
10. Full text of *Mahatma: Life of Mohandas Karamchand Gandhi*, vol. 8, D.G. Tendulkar, p. 154, accessed from https://archive.org/stream/mahatmalifeofmoh08tend/mahatmalifeofmoh08tend_djvu.txt
11. C.P. Bhishikar wrote in *Shri Guruji: Pioneer of A New Era*, translated into the English by Sudhakar Raje, Sahitya Sindhu Prakashana, Bengaluru,

accessed online from www.golwalkarguruji.org, that Gandhi was misrepresented, p. 56.

12. https://www.dawn.com/news/17522 & https://www.telegraphindia.com/1020202/front_pa.htm
13. C. P. Bhishikar in *Shri Guruji: Pioneer of A New Era,* translated into the English by Sudhakar Raje, Sahitya Sindhu Prakashana, Bengaluru, India, accessed online from www.golwalkarguruji.org, p. 20.
14. ibid.
15. ibid.
16. ibid.
17. ibid.
18. *The Brotherhood in Saffron*, Walter K. Andersen & Sridhar Damle, Vistaar, 1987, p. 41.
19. C. P. Bhishikar in *Shri Guruji: Pioneer of A New Era,* translated into the English by Sudhakar Raje, Sahitya Sindhu Prakashana, Bengaluru, India, accessed online from www.golwalkarguruji.org, p. 21.
20. ibid.
21. ibid.
22. ibid.
23. *Terrifying Vision: M.S. Golwalkar, The RSS, and India*, Jyotirmaya Sharma, Penguin Books India, 2007, p. xiv.
24. C. P. Bhishikar in *Shri Guruji: Pioneer of A New Era,* translated into the English by Sudhakar Raje, Sahitya Sindhu Prakashana, Bengaluru, India, accessed online from www.golwalkarguruji.org, p. 16.
25. op.cit., p. 22.
26. op. cit., p. 24.
27. op. cit., p. 25.
28. *The Brotherhood in Saffron*, Walter K. Andersen & Sridhar Damle, Vistaar, 1987, p. 42.
29. C. P. Bhishikar in *Shri Guruji: Pioneer of A New Era,* translated into the English by Sudhakar Raje, Sahitya Sindhu Prakashana, Bengaluru, India, accessed online from www.golwalkarguruji.org, p. 131.

30. op. cit., p. 27.
31. ibid.
32. *The Brotherhood in Saffron*, Walter K. Andersen & Sridhar Damle, Vistaar, 1987, p. 42.
33. *Dr Hedgewar Charitra*, N.H. Palkar, Bharatiya Vichar Sadhna, pp. 360-61, cited by Walter K. Andersen & Sridhar Damle, *The Brotherhood in Saffron*, Vistaar, 1987, p. 42, and note 90, p. 64.
34. The RSS pamphlet, Justice on Trial, p. 96.
35. C. P. Bhishikar in *Shri Guruji: Pioneer of A New Era*, translated into the English by Sudhakar Raje, Sahitya Sindhu Prakashana, Bengaluru, India, accessed online from www.golwalkarguruji.org, p. 34.
36. *The Hindu Nationalist Movement and Indian Politics: 1925-1994*, Christophe Jaffrelot, C. Hurst & Co., 1996, note 194, p. 55.
37. 'RSS officially disowns Golwalkar's book', *The Times of India*, 9 March 2006. https://timesofindia.indiatimes.com/india/RSS-officially-disowns-Golwalkars-book/articleshow/1443606.cms and A.G. Noorani in *Frontline*, vol. 15, no. 26, 19 December 1998-1 January 1999, https://www.frontline.in/static/html/fl1526/15261230.htm
38. Koenraad Elst, http://koenraadelst.bharatvani.org/articles/fascism/Nazi6GurujiWithdrawn.html
39. Quoted by Christophe Jaffrelot from the (original)*Rashtra Mimasa*, *The Hindu Nationalist Movement and Indian Politics: 1925-1994*, C. Hurst & Co., 1996, note 197, p. 55 and Martha Nussbaum, *The Clash Within: Democracy, Religious Violence, and India's Future*, Harvard University Press, 2007, p. 161.
40. C. P. Bhishikar in *Shri Guruji: Pioneer of A New Era*, translated into the English by Sudhakar Raje, Sahitya Sindhu Prakashana, Bengaluru, accessed online from www.golwalkarguruji.org, p. 36.
41. op. cit., p. 37.
42. *Lost Years of the RSS*, Sanjeev Kelkar, Sage Publications Pvt. Ltd., 2011, p. 11.
43. *The Brotherhood in Saffron*, Walter K. Andersen & Sridhar Damle, Vistaar, 1987, p. 63.

44. *Rashtriya Swayamsevak Sangh*, D.R. Goyal, Radha Krishna, 1979; revised edition, 2000, p. 89. He cited an unpublished dissertation by Surendra Bahadur Saxena, 'A Study of the Rashtriya Swayamsevak Sangh', submitted to Agra University, 1959.
45. *The Brotherhood in Saffron*, Walter K. Andersen & Sridhar Damle, Vistaar, 1987, p. 41.
46. *Organiser*, 14 July 1973.
47. *Lost Years of the RSS*, Sanjeev Kelkar, Sage Publications Pvt. Ltd., 2011, p. 41.
48. *The Brotherhood in Saffron*, Walter K. Andersen & Sridhar Damle, Vistaar, 1987, p. 63.
49. op. cit., p. 64.
50. ibid.
51. *The Brotherhood in Saffron*, Walter K. Andersen & Sridhar Damle, Vistaar, 1987, p. 43.
52. *Divine Enterprise: Gurus and the Hindu Nationalist Movement*, Lise McKean, University of Chicago Press, p. 92.
53. *The Brotherhood in Saffron*, Walter K. Andersen & Sridhar Damle, Vistaar, 1987, p. 44.
54. *Lost Years of the RSS*, Sanjeev Kelkar, Sage Publications Pvt. Ltd., 2011, p. 41.
55. *Rashtriya Swayamsevak Sangh*, D.R. Goyal, Radha Krishna, 1979; revised edition, 2000, p. 95.
56. See *Bunch of Thoughts*, chapter on 'Territorial Nationalism'; sub-section, 'Its Roots', p. 118. Also in the Introduction to the same volume, M. A. Venkata Rao writes – 'The national history of the Muslim period should be re-written giving the truth without varnish,' p. 9. Additionally read, Aakar Patel, https://scroll.in/article/669178/modis-biography-of-golwalkar-suggests-rss-leader-was-vital-influence. Also read, Danish Raza, 'Saffronising textbooks: Where Myth and Dogma Replace History', *Hindustan Times*, 8 December 2014, accessed online: https://www.hindustantimes.com/india/saffronising-textbooks-where-myth-and-dogma-

replace-history/story-CauM4dmmsPGrjZ3APAvNxO.html

57. *Lost Years of the RSS*, Sanjeev Kelkar, Sage Publications Pvt. Ltd., 2011, p. 42.

58. op. cit., p. 44.

59. op.cit., footnote 2, p. 95.

60. *The Brotherhood in Saffron*, Walter K. Andersen & Sridhar Damle, Vistaar, 1987, p. 44.

61. Rakesh Sinha in *The Times of India*, 9 August 2017, 'Hindu Mahasabha and many other Hindu organisations—which included Nathuram Godse's Hindu Rashtra Sena—viewed this as an opportunity to militarily train their cadres for waging war against the British at an opportune time...RSS, however, rejected this outlook outright.' https://timesofindia.indiatimes.com/blogs/toi-edit-page/this-day-75-years-ago-contrary-to-dogma-rss-did-take-part-in-the-freedom-movement-including-quit-india-movement/

62. Pavan Kulkarni, 'History Shows How Patriotic the RSS Really Is', *The Wire*, 17 April 2017. https://thewire.in/history/rss-hindutva-nationalism

63. *The Discovery of India*, Jawaharlal Nehru, Penguin Books, 2008, pp. 595-99.

64. *Lost Years of the RSS*, Sanjeev Kelkar, Sage Publications Pvt. Ltd., 2011, footnote 2, p. 67.

65. ibid.

66. ibid.

67. ibid.

68. C. P. Bhishikar in *Shri Guruji: Pioneer of A New Era,* translated into the English by Sudhakar Raje, Sahitya Sindhu Prakashana, Bengaluru, accessed online from www.golwalkarguruji.org, p. 43.

69. *The Brotherhood in Saffron*, Walter K. Andersen & Sridhar Damle, Vistaar, 1987, p. 45 & 65, note 101.

70. *The Hindu Nationalist Movement and Indian Politics: 1925-1994*, Christophe Jaffrelot, C. Hurst & Co., 1996, note 259, p. 68.

71. *Lost Years of the RSS*, Sanjeev Kelkar, Sage Publications Pvt. Ltd., 2011, p. 42, footnote 2, p. 71.
72. C. P. Bhishikar in *Shri Guruji: Pioneer of A New Era,* translated into the English by Sudhakar Raje, Sahitya Sindhu Prakashana, Bengaluru, accessed online from www.golwalkarguruji.org, p. 47.
73. K. S. Sudarshan, quoted by Sanjeev Kelkar, *Lost Years of the RSS*, Sage Publications Pvt. Ltd., 2011, p. 69.
74. http://www.milligazette.com/Archives/15-12-2000/Art6.htm
75. Mani Shanker Aiyar, NDTV Blog, 22 September 2015. https://www.ndtv.com/opinion/ram-madhav-gives-the-game-away-1220232. Also quoted by A.G. Noorani, *Frontline*, 1 December 1995.
76. C. P. Bhishikar in *Shri Guruji: Pioneer of A New Era,* translated into the English by Sudhakar Raje, Sahitya Sindhu Prakashana, Bengaluru, accessed online from www.golwalkarguruji.org, p. 50.
77. *Lost Years of the RSS*, Sanjeev Kelkar, Sage Publications Pvt. Ltd., 2011, p. 69.
78. ibid.
79. ibid.
80. C. P. Bhishikar in *Shri Guruji: Pioneer of A New Era,* translated into the English by Sudhakar Raje, Sahitya Sindhu Prakashana, Bengaluru, accessed online from www.golwalkarguruji.org, p. 48.
81. ibid.
82. *Terrifying Vision: M.S. Golwalkar, The RSS, and India*, Jyotirmaya Sharma, Penguin Books India, 2007, p. 87.
83. *Pt. Deendayal Upadhyay Ideology & Perception – Part 3: Political Thought,* B. K. Kelkar, Suruchi Prakashan, 2nd edition, 2014, p. 124.
84. Christophe Jaffrelot, *The Indian Express*, 12 January 2016.
85. Resolution dated 17 August 1965, Delhi AIGC, Bharatiya Jana Sangh, party documents, 1951-1972, vol. 4, pp. 78-79.
86. *The Hindu*, 26 December 2015; http://www.thehindu.com/news/national/akhand-bharat-india-pakistan-bangladesh-will-reunite-one-day-says-ram-madhav/article8031920.ece

87. *Rashtriya Swayamsevak Sangh*, D. R. Goyal, Radha Krishna, 1979; revised edition, 2000, p. 108.

88. op.cit., p. 109.

89. K. B. Jhari, 'I Was a Swayamsevak: Creating The Urge to Kill' in *Secular Democracy*, 3 July 1970, quoted in *The Brotherhood in Saffron*, by Walter K. Andersen & Sridhar Damle, Vistaar, 1987, note 114, p. 67.

90. *The Brotherhood in Saffron*, Walter K. Andersen & Sridhar Damle, Vistaar, 1987, p. 48.

91. *The Collected Works of Mahatma Gandhi*, vol. 96, pp. 380-81. He specifically also stated that 'it was for the Sangh to show by their uniform behaviour that the allegations were baseless' to establish that Gandhi actually said this; also see, *The Brotherhood in Saffron*, Walter Andersen & Sridhar Damle, Vistaar, 1987, p. 49 for Golwalkar distancing himself from the individual actions of his cadre.

92. *Rashtriya Swayamsevak Sangh*, D. R. Goyal, Radha Krishna, 1979; revised edition, 2000, p. 111

93. ibid.

94. Gopal Godse, the brother of Nathuram Godse, said that Gandhi's last fast had led the assassins and other accomplices to conclude that he was 'someone who had done and was doing great harm,' in an interview on 13 May 1969: http://www.sabrang.com/cc/comold/feb98/cover.htm

95. Cited by A.G. Noorani, *The RSS and the BJP: A Division of Labour*, Leftword, 2000, p. 27.

96. This has been taken from D.R. Goyal, *Rashtriya Swayamsevak Sangh*, Radha Krishna, p. 116 and Sanjeev Kelkar, *Lost Years of the RSS*, Sage, 2011, p. 79.

97. Statement of T. R. V. Sastri, *Justice On Trial, A Collection of the Historic Letters between Sri Guruji and the Government (1948-49)*, Prakashan Vibhag, Rashtriya Swayamsevak Sangh, Karnataka, first edition, December 1958; second edition, April 1959; third edition, December 1962; fourth edition, June 1968. Accessed online from the website of Hindu Vivek Kendra; url: http://www.hvk.org/specialarticles/justice/justice.html

98. Rakesh Ankit, *Economic & Political Weekly*, 21 April 2012.

99. Letter no. 28/23/48 POL. dated 3 May 1949 from H.V.R. Iyengar, I.C.S., Secretary to the Government of India to M.S. Golwalkar.

100. ibid.

101. Rakesh Ankit, *Economic & Political Weekly*, 21 April 2012.

102. Golwalkar's letter to Balasaheb Deoras. On 28 May 1949, he tried sending it through a prisoner deputed as his attendant, but it fell into the hands of the government of Madhya Pradesh.

103. *The Hindu Nationalist Movement and Indian Politics: 1925-1994*, Christophe Jaffrelot, C. Hurst & Co., 1996, p. 115.

104. *The Brotherhood in Saffron*, Walter K. Andersen & Sridhar Damle, Vistaar, 1987, p. 104; quotes in the preceding paragraph also from the same source.

105. *Khaki Shorts and Saffron Flags: A Critique of the Hindu Right*, Tapan Basu, Pradip Datta, Sumit Sarkar, Tanika Sarkar, Sambuddha Sen, Orient Longman, 1993, p. 32.

106. *The Brotherhood in Saffron*, Walter K. Andersen & Sridhar Damle, Vistaar, 1987, p. 56. 'Golwalkar, at the beginning of these negotiations, was ready to accept some kind of relationship between the RSS and the Congress in which the RSS would be entrusted with character building and the Congress with politics.'

107. Dr Ramachandra Guha in *Hindustan Times*, 17 June 2018. He referred to a headline in *Organiser* about the 30 August meeting – 'Two Men of Destiny Meet: A Happy Augury for the Future of Bharat'.

108. C. P. Bhishikar in *Shri Guruji: Pioneer of A New Era*, translated into the English by Sudhakar Raje, Sahitya Sindhu Prakashana, Bengaluru, accessed online from www.golwalkarguruji.org, p. 82.

109. ibid.

110. A.G. Noorani, *Frontline*, vol. 27, issue 1, 2-15 January 2010; url: https://www.frontline.in/static/html/fl2701/stories/19930326052.htm

111. C. P. Bhishikar in *Shri Guruji: Pioneer of A New Era*, translated into the English by Sudhakar Raje, Sahitya Sindhu Prakashana, Bengaluru, accessed online from www.golwalkarguruji.org, p. 82.

112. The elections were held in phases and the process was kicked off in two assembly seats—Chini and Pangi, Himachal Pradesh—which were soon to be snow-bound.
113. C. P. Bhishikar in *Shri Guruji: Pioneer of A New Era*, translated into the English by Sudhakar Raje, Sahitya Sindhu Prakashana, Bengaluru, accessed online from www.golwalkarguruji.org, p. 92.
114. op.cit., p. 96.
115. *The Hindu Nationalist Movement and Indian Politics: 1925-1994*, Christophe Jaffrelot, C. Hurst & Co., 1996, p. 113.
116. op.cit., p. 211.
117. op.cit., p. 196.
118. *Lost Years of the RSS*, Sanjeev Kelkar, Sage Publications Pvt Ltd., 2011, p. 94.

SYAMA PRASAD MOOKERJI

1. Nilanjan Mukhopadhyay, *The Economic Times*, 2 March 2015, https://blogs.economictimes.indiatimes.com/et-commentary/bjp-has-made-big-departure-from-shyama-prasad-mookerjee-and-modis-past-visions/. Additionally, the Akhil Bharatiya Hindu Mahasabha's all-India president, Chander Prakash Kaushik, argued in an interview that 'the BJP used Syama Prasad Mookerji as the party's slogan' although he doubted 'how many in the party know him or recognise his contribution.' https://www.firstpost.com/politics/hindu-mahasabha-head-speaks-to-firstpost-godse-was-a-martyr-and-patriot-1977649.html
2. *Political Mysteries*, K.R. Malkani, Ocean Books, 2006, p. 52. He wrote that the slogan was first coined by J&K Praja Parishad in 1953 to demand the state's 'complete integration' with the rest of India. Additionally, Kiren Rijiju, the current Union minister of State for Home, said in an interview, 'Our slogan has been "*Ek desh mein do vidhan, do Pradhan, aur do nishan, nahi challenge, nahi chalenge*" (In one country, there cannot be two constitutions, two heads and two flags).

That was Shyama Prasad Mukherjee's slogan and its spirit is being maintained by us.' https://www.outlookindia.com/magazine/story/we-cant-have-two-pms-two-constitutions-but-talks-with-the-nagas-are-still-going-/297431

3. *India's Struggle for Independence*, Bipan Chandra, Mridula Mukherjee, Aditya Mukherjee, Sucheta Mahajan, Penguin Books India, 1988, p. 107.
4. *The Life and Times of Shyama Prasad Mookerjee*, Tathagata Roy, Ocean Books, 2012, pp. 24-25.
5. op.cit., p. 29.
6. ibid. http://www.shyamaprasad.org/biography.htm—http://bit.ly/1OH7Qqp
7. *Portrait of a Martyr*, Balraj Madhok, Rupa Publications, 2003, pp. 16-17.
8. *Land of Two Rivers: A History of Bengal from the Mahabharata to Mujib*, Nitish Sengupta, Penguin Books, 2011, p. 393.
9. *Portrait of a Martyr*, Balraj Madhok, Rupa Publications, 2003, p. 20.
10. *The Life and Times of Shyama Prasad Mookerjee*, Tathagata Roy, Ocean Books, 2012, p. 51.
11. op.cit., p. 39.
12. Shoaib Daniyal, *Scroll.in*, 28 June 2015; url: http://scroll.in/article/736610/revisiting-syama-prasad-mookerjee-the-trinamools-latest-hero
13. *The Partition of Bengal and Assam, 1932-1947*, Bidyut Chakrabarty, Routledge, 2004; url: https://books.google.co.in/books?id=in1_AgAAQBAJ&pg=PT123&lpg=PT123&dq=too+technical+to+draw+the+sympathy+of+newly+enfranchised+individuals&source=bl&ots=9TQqlIR-A6&sig=ACfU3U1fiXc2ic1vcz01b3a33BkLK31ZjA&hl=en&sa=X&ved=2ahUKEwj-1OvP_JDgAhWI6Y8KHbWPC5AQ6AEwBXoECAgQAQ#v=onepage&q=too%20technical%20to%20draw%20the%20sympathy%20of%20newly%20enfranchised%20individuals&f=false or use the shorter url: https://bit.ly/2Rp4sHk

14. *Italian Fascist Regime and Nationalist India, 1921-45*, Mario Prayer, International Studies, 1991. Attention to this has been drawn by Christophe Jaffrelot and a few other academics.
15. *Road to Pakistan: The Life and Times of Mohammad Ali Jinnah*, B.R. Nanda, Routledge, 2010, p. 185. Also read, A.G. Noorani, *Frontline*, 23 August 2013.
16. *Eight Lives: A Study of the Hindu-Muslim Encounter*, Rajmohan Gandhi, Suny Press, 1986, p. 189.
17. *Portrait of a Martyr*, Balraj Madhok, Rupa Publications, 2003, p. 27.
18. *Eight Lives: A Study of the Hindu-Muslim Encounter*, Rajmohan Gandhi, Suny Press, 1986, p. 201.
19. *Veer Savarkar*, Dhananjay Keer, Popular Prakashan (first published in May 1950 as *Savarkar and His Times*); this taken from the third edition, 2012, pp. 241-243.
20. *Portrait of a Martyr*, Balraj Madhok, Rupa Publications, 2003, p. 30.
21. op. cit., p. 31.
22. *Veer Savarkar*, Dhananjay Keer, Popular Prakashan (first published in May 1950 as *Savarkar and His Times*); this taken from the third edition, 2012, p. 241.
23. op. cit., p. 249.
24. Marzia Casolari, *Economic and Political Weekly*, 22 January 2000.
25. *Bengal Divided: Hindu Communalism and Partition, 1932-1947*, Joya Chatterji, Cambridge University Press, 2002, p. 136.
26. *Portrait of a Martyr*, Balraj Madhok, Rupa Publications, 2003, p. 31.
27. *Understanding the Muslim Mind*, Rajmohan Gandhi, Penguin Books India, 2000, pp. 201-202.
28. *Eight Lives: A Study of the Hindu-Muslim Encounter*, Rajmohan Gandhi, Suny Press, 1986, p. 202.
29. *Understanding the Muslim Mind*, Rajmohan Gandhi, Penguin Books India, 2000, p. 205.
30. *Land of Two Rivers: A History of Bengal from the Mahabharata to Mujib*, Nitish Sengupta, Penguin Books, 2011, p. 408.

31. *Understanding the Muslim Mind*, Rajmohan Gandhi, Penguin Books India, 2000, p. 206.
32. Letter from Syama Prasad Mookerjee quoted by Balraj Madhok, *Portrait of a Martyr*, Rupa Publications, 2003, pp. 52-53.
33. *Land of Two Rivers: A History of Bengal from the Mahabharata to Mujib*, Nitish Sengupta, Penguin, 2011, p. 408.
34. Speeches of Syama Prasad Mookerjee cited in *Hindustan Standard*, Calcutta and quoted by several writers: Nitesh Sengupta, *Land of Two Rivers: A History of Bengal from the Mahabharata to Mujib*, Penguin Books, 2011, p. 422; S.C. Das, *Bharat Kesri Dr. Syama Prasad Mookerjee with Modern Implications*, Abhinav Publications, 2000, p. 65.
35. *Communalism in Bengal: From Famine to Noakhali 1943-47*, Rakesh Batabyal, Sage Publications, 2005, p. 145.
36. op. cit., Batabyal cites Ashutosh Lahiry, a prominent Hindu Mahasabha leader, p. 150.
37. Keith Meadowcroft, unpublished PhD thesis, Concordia University, Canada, p. 250.
38. *The Transfer of Power in India*, V.P. Menon, Orient Blackswan, 1957, p. 245.
39. *Communalism in Bengal: From Famine to Noakhali 1943-47*, Rakesh Batabyal, Sage Publications, 2005, p. 329.
40. *Veer Savarkar*, Dhananjay Keer, Popular Prakashan (first published in May 1950 as *Savarkar and His Times*); this taken from the third edition, 2012, p. 381.
41. ibid.
42. http://www.deccanherald.com/content/21777/content/215577/archives.php
43. Subrata Mukherjee, *The Statesman*, 26 September 2009.
44. https://www.livemint.com/Politics/xp1abW27kc6YJXWg9B6XVN/Pranab-slams-attempts-to-vilify-Nehru-on-Partition.html
45. Subrata Mukherjee, *The Statesman*, 26 September 2009.

46. *Jawaharlal Nehru, A Biography*, Sankar Ghose, Allied Publishers, 1993, p. 196.
47. *Patel a Life*, Rajmohan Gandhi, Navjivan Publishing House, 2011, p. 418.
48. *The Spoils of Partition: Bengal and India*, Joya Chatterji, Cambridge University Press, 2007, pp. 261-67.
49. *Portrait of a Martyr*, Balraj Madhok, Rupa Publications, 2003, p. 87.
50. Letter written to Ramlakhan Prasad Sinha, 15 December 1947, cited by Keith Meadowcroft, unpublished PhD thesis, Concordia University, p. 354.
51. op. cit., p. 380.
52. Party pamphlet, 1948.
53. *Portrait of a Martyr*, Balraj Madhok, Rupa Publications, 2003, p. 87.
54. Cited by B.D. Graham, *Soundings in Modern South Asian History*, University of California Press, 1968, ed. Donald Anthony Low, p. 345.
55. *The Hindu Nationalist Movement and Indian Politics: 1925-1994*, Christophe Jaffrelot, C. Hurst & Co., 1996, p. 91.
56. *Portrait of a Martyr*, Balraj Madhok, Rupa Publications, 2003, p. 116.
57. *Bengal Divided: Hindu Communalism and Partition, 1932-1947*, Joya Chatterji, Cambridge University Press, 2002, p. 189.
58. *Soundings in Modern South Asian History*, B.D. Graham, University of California Press, 1968, ed. Donald Anthony Low, p. 345.
59. *My Country My Life*, L. K. Advani, Rupa & Co, Delhi, 2008, p. 85.
60. *Portrait of a Martyr*, Balraj Madhok, Rupa Publications, 2003, p. 60.
61. op. cit., p. 61.
62. *The Hindu Nationalist Movement and Indian Politics: 1925-1994*, Christophe Jaffrelot, C. Hurst & Co., 1996, p. 117.
63. *The Brotherhood in Saffron*, Walter K. Andersen & Sridhar Damle, Vistaar, 1987, p. 125.

64. *The Demolition: India at the Crossroads,* Nilanjan Mukhopadhyay, HarperCollins, 1994, New Delhi, p. 163.
65. *Portrait of a Martyr*, Balraj Madhok, Rupa Publications, 2003, p. 123.
66. Quoted in *The Times of India* and *The Statesman* (various editions) November 1954.
67. *Portrait of a Martyr*, Balraj Madhok, Rupa Publications, 2003, p. 29.
68. http://www.kamalsandesh.org/why-jansangh/
69. Bharatiya Jana Sangh, party documents, 1951-1972, vol. I, pp. 55-56.
70. *Portrait of a Martyr*, Balraj Madhok, Rupa Publications, 2003, p. 70.
71. ibid.
72. Cited by Jagmohan in *My Frozen Turbulence in Kashmir*, Allied Publishers Pvt. Ltd., 2017 (revised and updated edition), p. 830.
73. ibid.
74. *Jawaharlal Nehru: A Biography 1947-1956*, vol.2, Sarvepalli Gopal, OUP India, 2003, p. 122.
75. Bharatiya Jana Sangh, party documents, 1951-1972, vol. IV, pp. 55-56.
76. *In Search of a Future: The Story of Kashmir*, David Devdas, Viking, Penguin Books, 2007, p. 85.

DEENDAYAL UPADHYAYA

1. Quoted by V.V. Nene, *Pt. Deendayal Upadhyaya: Ideology and Perception*, Part 2, Integral Humanism, p. 1.
2. *Pandit Deendayal Upadhyaya*, Mahesh Chandra Sharma, Prabhat Prakashan, 2016, pp. 11-12.
3. *Pandit Deendayal Upadhyaya*, Mahesh Chandra Sharma, Prabhat Prakashan, 2016, p. 12.
4. op. cit., p. 13.
5. Political adversaries and the media often accused Vidya Bharti of an ideological bias. For instance, in *India Today*, 3 January 2013, it was

stated that the 'subversion of the educational system by the RSS has the state BJP Government's backing. To give education a saffron hue, entire textbooks from nursery to the postgraduate level are being rewritten with a Hindu emphasis.' url:https://www.indiatoday.in/magazine/education/story/19920815-learning-acquires-saffron-hue-in-rss-run-schools-in-madhya-pradesh-766697-2013-01-03. Such examples abound in other states too and over a long period.

6. Deendayal Upadhyaya's words in the Manogat (Preface) of his book, cited by Mahesh Chandra Sharma, *Builders of Modern India, Pandit Deendayal Upadhyaya*, Publications Division, 2014, pp. 14-15
7. ibid.
8. op. cit., p. 16.
9. ibid.
10. op. cit., p. 21.
11. *Akhand Bharat Kyon?* 1952, cited by Mahesh Chandra Sharma Sharma, op. cit., p. 24.
12. ibid.
13. ibid.
14. *Akhand Bharat Kyon?* 1952, cited by Sharma, op. cit., p. 17.
15. Resolutions on Internal Affairs, party documents, Bharatiya Jana Sangh, vol. IV, pp. 24-25.
16. ibid.
17. ibid.
18. *My Country My Life*, L. K. Advani, Rupa & Co, Delhi, 2008, pp. 137-154. Also, http://lkadvani.in/excerpts-3.php
19. *Organiser*, July 1962.
20. *Builders of Modern India, Pandit Deendayal Upadhyaya*, Mahesh Chandra Sharma, Publications Division, 2014, quotes Upadhyaya's statement, p. 31.
21. *Seminar*, No. 29, January 1962.
22. *Organiser*, 17 February 1973.

23. *Pandit Deendayal Upadhyaya*, Mahesh Chandra Sharma, Publications Division, 2014, p. 138.
24. *The Jana Sangh: A Biography of an Indian Political Party*, Craig Baxter, Oxford University Press, 1971, p. 247.
25. *Builders of Modern India, Pandit Deendayal Upadhyaya*, Mahesh Chandra Sharma, Publications Division, 2014, p. 66.
26. http://deendayalupadhyay.org/democracy.html. The portal has been created by the Dr. Syama Prasad Mookerjee Research Foundation.
27. ibid.
28. *Builders of Modern India, Pandit Deendayal Upadhyaya*, Mahesh Chandra Sharma, Publications Division, 2014, pg. 91.
29. ibid.
30. http://deendayalupadhyay.org/democracy1.html
31. *Builders of Modern India, Pandit Deendayal Upadhyaya*, Mahesh Chandra Sharma, Publications Division, 2014, p. 74.
32. http://deendayalupadhyay.org/democracy2.html
33. The speech is available at multiple sources, including http://www.bjp.org/about-the-party/philosophy
34. *Pt. Deendayal Upadhyaya Ideology & Preception – Part 5: Concept of The Rashtra*, Suruchi Prakashna, C.P. Bhishikar, 1991, pp. 93-102.
35. ibid.
36. *Lost Years of the RSS*, Sanjeev Kelkar, Sage Publications Pvt Ltd., 2011, p. 90.
37. *Builders of Modern India, Pandit Deendayal Upadhyaya*, Mahesh Chandra Sharma, Publications Division, 2014, p. 86.
38. Bharatiya Jana Sangh, party documents, 1951-1972, vol. I, pp. 47-60.
39. The presidential speech, Calicut, https://deendayalupadhyay.org/leacture5.html
40. http://deendayalupadhyay.org/lecture5.html
41. *The Brotherhood in Saffron*, Walter K. Andersen & Sridhar Damle, Vistaar, 1987, p. 180, citing a report in *Northern Indian Patrika*, 1 March 1967.

42. *Lost Years of the RSS*, Sanjeev Kelkar, Sage Publications Pvt Ltd., 2011, p. 207.

BALASAHEB DEORAS

1. *The Aftermath of Partition in South Asia*, Tan Tai Yong and Gyanesh Kudaisya Routledge, 2000, p. 100.
2. *Lost Years of the RSS*, Sanjeev Kelkar, Sage Publications Pvt Ltd., 2011, p. 98.
3. *Rashtriya Swayamsevak Sangh*, D. R. Goyal, Radha Krishna, 1979; revised edition, 2000, p. 128.
4. op. cit., p.129.
5. M.K. Chauthaiwale, *Maine Dekhe Hue Balasaheb Deoras*, Shri Bharti Prakashan (an RSS Publication), 2014, p. 3.
6. Swapan Dasgupta, *India Today*, March 1999; url: http://indiatoday.intoday.in/story/positioning -for-life-after-vajpayee-and-advani/1/253104.html).
7. *Khaki Shorts and Saffron Flags: A Critique of the Hindu Right*, Tapan Basu, Pradip Datta, Sumit Sarkar, Tanika Sarkar, Sambuddha Sen, Orient Longman (now Orient Blackswan), 1993, p. 18.
8. *Outlook*, July 1996, url: http://www.outlookindia.com/magazine/story/a-seamless-hindu-vision/201628
9. Conversations with Dilip Deodhar and Rambhau Tupkari, April 2016.
10. *Rashtriya Swayamsevak Sangh*, D. R. Goyal, Radha Krishna, 1979; revised edition, 2000, p. 125.
11. ibid.
12. Interview with K. N. Govindacharya, March 2016.
13. *Maine Dekhe Hue Balasaheb Deoras*, M.K. Chauthaiwale, Shri Bharti Prakashan (an RSS Publication), 2014, pp. 11-12.
14. ibid.
15. ibid.
16. *Rashtriya Swayamsevak Sangh*, D. R. Goyal, Radha Krishna, 1979; revised edition, 2000, p. 127.

17. Conversations with Rambhau Tupkary, June 2016.
18. *The Brotherhood in Saffron*, Walter K. Andersen & Sridhar Damle, Vistaar, 1987, pp. 209-10.
19. *Lost Years of the RSS*, Sanjeev Kelkar, Sage Publications Pvt. Ltd., 2011, p. 110.
20. *The Hindu Nationalist Movement and Indian Politics: 1925-1994*, Christophe Jaffrelot, C. Hurst & Co., 1996, p. 235.
21. *Lost Years of the RSS*, Sanjeev Kelkar, Sage Publications Pvt. Ltd., 2011, p. 103.
22. *Maine Dekhe Hue Balasaheb Deoras*, M.K. Chauthaiwale, Shri Bharti Prakashan (an RSS Publication), 2014, p. 6.
23. Conversations with Dilip Deodhar, a well-known RSS thinker and author of several valuable tracts on the RSS, April 2016.
24. *Lost Years of the RSS*, Sanjeev Kelkar, Sage Publications Pvt. Ltd., 2011, p. 106.
25. ibid, p. 109.
26. *Maine Dekhe Hue Balasaheb Deoras*, M.K. Chauthaiwale, Shri Bharti Prakashan (an RSS Publication), 2014, p. 18.
27. op.cit., p. 22.
28. *Rashtriya Swayamsevak Sangh*, D. R. Goyal, Radha Krishna, 1979; revised edition, 2000, p. 108.
29. *Maine Dekhe Hue Balasaheb Deoras*, M.K. Chauthaiwale, Shri Bharti Prakashan (an RSS Publication), 2014, p. 26.
30. ibid, pp. 50-51. This instruction was also meant for Chauthaiwale who wrote the letter, but even in his memoirs, he mentions that he did not remember the contents of the letter.
31. Information on this entire episode is based on conversations with several RSS insiders including K.N. Govindacharya, Dilip Deodhar, Ravi Deshpande, and also from *Lost Years of the RSS*, Sanjeev Kelkar, Sage Publications Pvt. Ltd., 2011, pp. 99-100 & 102.
32. ibid.
33. op. cit., p. 102

34. op. cit., p. 103. Sanjeev Kelkar cites V.N. Deodhar, Hindutva Rajkiya Vyaspeeth Denera Drashta, *Tarun Bharat*, Nagpur, 5 July 1997.
35. *Maine Dekhe Hue Balasaheb Deoras*, M.K. Chauthaiwale, Shri Bharti Prakashan (an RSS Publication), 2014, pp. 24-25.
36. Ibid., pp. 25-16.
37. Conversations with Rambhau Tupkary, April 2016.
38. Deendayal Upadhyaya, Political Diary, 3 June 1963; url: http://deendayalupadhyay.org/lost.html
39. *Lost Years of the RSS*, Sanjeev Kelkar, Sage Publications Pvt Ltd., 2011, p. 101.
40. *Rashtriya Swayamsevak Sangh*, D. R. Goyal, Radha Krishna, 1979; revised edition, 2000, p. 128.
41. op.cit., p. 134.
42. *Organiser*, vol. 26, p. 38, 17 February 1973.
43. *The Hindu Nationalist Movement and Indian Politics: 1925-1994*, Christophe Jaffrelot, C. Hurst & Co., 1996, p. 257.
44. *Lost Years of the RSS*, Sanjeev Kelkar, Sage Publications Pvt. Ltd., 2011, p. 110.
45. Published by Suruchi Prakashan, the speeches are available in multiple sources. This is taken from https://groups.yahoo.com/neo/groups/rssdelhi/conversations/messages/4071 after verifying from other sources.
46. Subhash Gatade, *Mainstream*, vol. LII, No. 12, 15 March 2014; url: http://www.mainstreamweekly.net/article4794.html)
47. http://www.golwalkarguruji.org/shri-guruji/interviews/shri-gurujis-interviews/social-problems. Also in *Spotlights, Guruji Answers*, Sahitya Sindhu, Rashtrotthana Sahitya, 1974, p. 22.
48. *Lost Years of the RSS*, Sanjeev Kelkar, Sage Publications Pvt. Ltd., 2011, p. 126.
49. Conversations with Rambhau Tupkary, April 2016.
50. *The Brotherhood in Saffron*, Walter K. Andersen and Sridhar Damle, Vistaar, 1987, p. 186.

51. (http://www.livemint.com/Politics/dtQymwkmkAEaOOrDUJ6ASI/The-Emergency-started-long-before-25-June-1975.html).
52. 'RSS Resolves', Suruchi Prakashna, 2nd Edition, 2007, p. 74.
53. *Rashtriya Swayamsevak Sangh*, D. R. Goyal, Radha Krishna, 1979; revised edition, 2000, p. 136.
54. Nilanjan Mukhopadhyay, *The Demolition: India at the Crossroads*, HarperCollins, 1994, p. 181.
55. *Drishta Sanghatak: Balasaheb Deoras*, ed. Shrirang Godbole, p. 23.
56. *Maine Dekhe Hue Balasaheb Deoras*, M.K. Chauthaiwale, Shri Bharti Prakashan (an RSS Publication), 2014, p. 37.
57. *Rashtriya Swayamsevak Sangh*, D. R. Goyal, Radha Krishna, 1979; revised edition, 2000, p. 138.
58. ibid.
59. Baba Adhav (socialist leader from Maharashtra), *Secular Democracy*, August 1977.
60. *Rashtriya Swayamsevak Sangh*, D. R. Goyal, Radha Krishna, 1979; revised edition, 2000, p. 38.
61. ibid.
62. *The Brotherhood in Saffron*, Walter K. Andersen & Sridhar Damle, Vistaar, 1987, p. 222.
63. op.cit., p. 223.
64. *Lost Years of the RSS*, Sanjeev Kelkar, Sage Publications Pvt. Ltd., 2011, p. 141. He cites Rambhau Bondale's compilation of (unpublished) speeches by Deoras, 1977-1990, found in Dr Hedgewar Bhawan, Nagpur.
65. From the official RSS website; url: http://rss.org//Encyc/2017/5/20/Basic-FAQ-on-RSS.html.
66. *Lost Years of the RSS*, Sanjeev Kelkar, Sage Publications Pvt. Ltd., 2011, p. 155.
67. *Maine Dekhe Hue Balasaheb Deoras*, M.K. Chauthaiwale, Shri Bharti Prakashan (an RSS Publication), 2014, pp. 43-44.

68. *Rashtriya Swayamsevak Sangh*, D. R. Goyal, Radha Krishna, 1979; revised edition, 2000, p. 156.
69. http://vhp.org/conferences/world-hindu-conference/world-hindu-conference-2-whc-ii/
70. http://www.sevabharathitvm.com/about.php
71. https://positivebunch.wordpress.com/2014/05/22/sewa-bharati-delhi-35-years-of-social-change/
72. Malini Bhattacharjee, *Economic and Political Weekly*, 16 April 2016, vol. LI, Number 16.
73. Ajaz Ashraf, *Scroll.in*, 20 May 2016; url: https://scroll.in/article/808463/why-assam-is-likely-to-become-hindtuvas-new-laboratory
74. Malini Bhattacharjee, *Economic and Political Weekly*, 16 April 2016, vol. LI, Number 16; Shekhar Gupta, *Business Standard*, 8 April 2016.
75. *Maine Dekhe Hue Balasaheb Deoras*, M.K. Chauthaiwale, Shri Bharti Prakashan (an RSS Publication), 2014, p. 45.
76. *The Hindu Nationalist Movement and Indian Politics: 1925-1994*, Christophe Jaffrelot, C. Hurst & Co., 1996, p. 313.
77. http://vhp.org/featured-article/ashok-singhal-architect-of-hindu-awakening/
78. *The Hindu Nationalist Movement and Indian Politics: 1925-1994*, Christophe Jaffrelot, C. Hurst & Co., 1996, pp. 364-65.
79. ibid.
80. *Lost Years of the RSS*, Sanjeev Kelkar, Sage Publications Pvt. Ltd., 2011, p. 185.
81. 'RSS Resolves', p. 77.
82. *Lost Years of the RSS*, Sanjeev Kelkar, Sage Publications Pvt. Ltd., 2011, p. 191.
83. *Jyotipunj*, Narendra Modi, Prabhat Prakashan, 2008, translated from the Gujarati by A.K. Gandhi, p. 32.
84. *Lost Years of the RSS*, Sanjeev Kelkar, Sage Publications Pvt. Ltd., 2011, p. 192.

85. *The Demolition: India at the Crossroads,* Nilanjan Mukhopadhyay, HarperCollins, 1994, pp. 207-208, quoted from the BJP pamphlet for the media.

86. *Organiser*, 16 October 1988.

87. 'RSS Resolves', p. 200.

88. *My Country My Life*, L.K. Advani, Rupa & Co, Delhi, 2008, p. 397.

89. The Liberhan Commission Report, 'Conclusions', p. 939.

90. op. cit., p. 942. A few months after his report created a furore for naming the former and late Prime Minister Atal Bihari Vajpayee, Justice M.S. Liberhan told a journalist that there was nothing 'illegal' or 'improper' in the act of naming him, *The Hindu*, 29 November 2009. URL: https://www.thehindu.com/news/national/Liberhan-nothing-illegal-in-naming-Vajpayee-in-my-report/article16894837.ece

91. *Lost Years of the RSS*, Sanjeev Kelkar, Sage Publications Pvt. Ltd., 2011, p. 198

92. M.K. Chauthaiwale, *Maine Dekhe Hue Balasaheb Deoras*, Shri Bharti Prakashan (an RSS Publication), 2014, p. 32.

VIJAYA RAJE SCINDIA

1. *The Telegraph*, 7 February 2001; url: https://www.telegraphindia.com/india/rajmata-s-last-testament-portrays-a-palace-at-war-with-itself/cid/936233

2. *Princess: The Autobiography of the Dowager Maharani of Gwalior*, Manohar Malgonkar with Vijayaraje Scindia, Times Book International, 1988, p. 172.

3. op. cit., p. 174.

4. ibid.

5. op. cit., p. 184.

6. *The Post-Nehru Era: Political Memoirs*, Dwarka Prasad Mishra, Har Anand Publications, 1993, p. 63.

7. ibid.

8. *My Country My Life*, L. K. Advani, Rupa & Co, Delhi, 2008, p. 314.
9. *The Age of Kali: Indian Travels and Encounters*, William Dalrymple, Penguin Books India, 2004, p. 75.
10. op. cit., p. 77.

ATAL BIHARI VAJPAYEE

1. Dr Ramachandra Guha, *The Hindu*, 10 November 2002; url:https://www.thehindu.com/thehindu/mag/2002/11/10/stories/2002111000630300.htm
2. For a detailed reading about the controversy on the allegations of Vajpayee not having participated in the freedom movement, read Manini Chatterjee & V.K. Ramachandran, *Frontline*, vol. 15, No. 3, 7-20 February 1998; url:https://www.frontline.in/static/html/fl1503/15031150.htm
3. *My Country My Life*, L.K. Advani, Rupa & Co., Delhi, 2008, p.102.
4. Mani Shankar Aiyar, NDTV Blogs, 23 July 2018. https://www.ndtv.com/opinion/why-rahuls-hug-is-lost-on-modi-by-mani-shankar-aiyar-1887899
5. Lok Sabha Debates, vol. 28, col. 8511. Cited in 'Parliament and Foreign Policy Decision Making in India A Study on India's China Policy: 1959 to 75', Sibaram Badatya, Ph.D Thesis, Pondicherry University, url:http://shodhganga.inflibnet.ac.in/handle/10603/175801
6. Subramanian Swamy, *Frontline*, vol. 15, No. 22, 24 October-06 November, 1998.
7. C. Raja Mohan, *The Indian Express*, 30 December 2014.
8. *Poet Politician: Atal Bihari Vajpayee*, ed., Chandrika Prasad Sharma, Vikas Paperbacks, 2015, pp. 81-183.

LAL KRISHNA ADVANI

1. Available online: http://ia.rediff.com/news/1998/oct/02advani.htm

2. *A Time of Transition: Rajiv Gandhi to the 21st Century*, Mani Shankar Aiyar, Viking, Penguin Books India, 2009, p. 153. Accessed online: https://bit.ly/2BiM0ec.
3. *My Country My Life*, L.K. Advani, Rupa & Co., Delhi, 2008, pp. 406-409.

ASHOK SINGHAL

4. Rahul Pandita, *Open*, 1 December 2017, http://www.openthemagazine.com/article/ayodhya-25-years-later/kameshwar-chaupal-the-first-kar-sevak
5. Manjari Katju, *Scroll.in*, 22 November 2015, http://scroll.in/article/770912/soft-spoken-vhp-leader-ashok-singhal-created-indias-most-blistering-anti-minority-campaign
6. *The Hindu Nationalist Movement and Indian Politics: 1925-1994*, Christophe Jaffrelot, C. Hurst & Co., 1996, pp. 412-13. He cited a report published in *The Times of India*, 27 January 1990.
7. '*Modi, Shivaji ki tarah ajeya hain*' (Modi is invincible like Shivaji). He added that the 'authority of Hindutva that had ended with Prithviraj (Chauhan) has been reinstated with this victory (apropos Modi's win in 2014).' Later, the interviewer pointed out that there is a section within the religious minorities who resisted the construction of the Ram temple; abrogation of Article 370; and introduction of the Uniform Civil Code. Singhal responded to this question by asking, '*Kaun hai yeh tabka? Kahan hai yeh tabka and kitni taaqat hai iss tabke mein? Is tabke mein koi taaqat nahin rah gayi hai ab*' (Which section? Where is this section, and how much power do they wield? This section no longer has any power whatsoever). Interview with Rahul Kanwal 25 May 2014,httws://www.youtube.com/watch?v=hQCWgUqih9Q
8. *Vishva Hindu Parishad and Indian Politics*, Manjari Katju, Orient Blackswan, 2003, pp. 127-29.

BAL THACKERAY

1. *Maximum City: Bombay Lost & Found*, Suketu Mehta, Penguin Random HouseIndia,Delhi,p.64;https://www.npr.org/2012/11/19/165507971/indian-politician-was-popular-and-polarizing; and Soutik Biswas, BBC, 19 November 2012, https://www.bbc.com/news/world-asia-india-20389849
2. Jayadev Calamur, http://www.dnaindia.com/blogs/post-the-indian-who-admires-adolf-hitler-1766547; ibid., Soutik Biswas; *Fragile Democracies: Contested Power in the Era of Constitutional Courts*, Samuel Issacharoff, Cambridge University Press, 2015, p. 84, cites Larissa MacFarquhar, 'The Strongman: Where Is This Hindu-Nationalist Violence Leading?' *New Yorker*, 26 May 2003.
3. Sujata Anandan, http://blogs.hindustantimes.com/singly-political/2011/03/11/as-you-sow-so-you-reap/
4. *Mumbai Fables*, Gyan Prakash, Princeton University Press, 2010, p. 231.
5. ibid.
6. op. cit., p. 250.
7. *The Sena Story*, Vaibhav Purandare, Business Publications, 1999, p. 351. Shinde remained a Shiv Sena loyalist throughout his career except for crossing over to the Maharashtra Navnirman Sena for some years before joining back Shiv Sena in August 2018.
8. *Wages of Violence: Naming and Identity in Postcolonial Bombay*, Thomas Blom Hansen, Princeton University Press, 2001, pp. 121-122.
9. Shoaib Daniyal, *Scroll.in*, 27 July 2015; url: http://scroll.in/article/743554/yakub-memon-case-one-chart-that-shows-just-how-partisan-indias-criminal-justice-system-can-be
10. M. Rahman, *India Today*, 15 December 1995; url: https://www.indiatoday.in/magazine/special-report/story/19951215-remote-control-must-be-there-because-it-is-a-shiv-sena-and-bjp-government-bal-thackeray-808098-1995-12-15
11. *The Hindu*, 19 December 2005; url: https://www.thehindu.com/2005/12/19/stories/2005121906651200.htm

NATHURAM GODSE

1. https://www.deccanchronicle.com/141224/nation-current-affairs/article/hindu-mahasabha-announces-godse-temple. Accessed 1 March 2023.
2. She passed away in October 2015 at the age of sixty-eight. She was daughter of Gopal Godse, Nathuram's younger brother. She represented the joint legacy of Godse and Savarkar by marrying Savarkar's nephew.
3. https://www.thehindu.com/news/national/Uproar-in-RS-over-eulogising-Godse/article60443361.ece. Accessed 1 March 2023.
4. https://www.ndtv.com/india-news/bjp-condemns-mp-pragya-thakurs-remarks-on-nathuram-godse-in-parliament-drops-her-from-defence-panel-2139925. Accessed 1 March 2023.
5. Makarand R. Paranjape, *The Death and Afterlife of Mahatma Gandhi*, Random House India.
6. Dominique Lapierre and Larry Collins, *Freedom at Midnight*, p. 554.
7. Dominique Lapierre and Larry Collins; *Freedom at Midnight*, p. 426.
8. M.J. Akbar, *Nehru: The Making of India*, Viking, 1988, p. 428.
9. Koenraad Elst, *Gandhi and Godse: A Review and a Critique*, Voice of India, p. 26.
10. Dhirendra Jha, *Gandhi's Assassin: The Making of Nathuram Godse and His Idea of India*, Penguin, 2021, p. 11.
11. Manohar Malgonkar, *The Men Who Killed Gandhi*, Roli Books, 2018, p. 46.
12. Dhirendra Jha, *Gandhi's Assassins: The Making of Nathuram Godse and His Idea of India*, Penguin, pp. 39-40.
13. Dhirendra Jha, however, mentioned this in *Gandhi's Assassins: The Making of Nathuram Godse and His Idea of India*. Statement is referred to in multiple pages.
14. Dhirendra Jha, *The Apostle of Hate*, The Caravan, January 2020.
15. *The Hindu*, http://www.thehindu.com/2004/09/21/stories/2004092109381100.htm. Accessed 16 December 2016.

16. AG Noorani, *RSS & Gandhi's Murder*, Frontline, 28 September 2016, https://frontline.thehindu.com/the-nation/rss-amp-gandhis-murder/article23594989.ece. Accessed 16 March 2023 and Dhirendra Jha, op. cit., p. 68.
17. Dhirendra Jha, *Gandhi's Assassins: The Making of Nathuram Godse and His Idea of India*, Penguin, p. 72.
18. Manohar Malgonkar, *The Men Who Killed Gandhi*, Roli Books, 2008, pp. 60-61.
19. Dominique Lapierre and Larry Collins, *Freedom at Midnight*, p. 561.
20. Bhaganagar Unarmed Movement, https://savarkar.org/en/encyc/2017/5/23/Bhaganagar-Unarmed-Movement.html. Accessed 17 March 2023.
21. Kapur Commission Report, Vol I, p. 263.
22. Kapur Commission Report, Vol I, p. 332.
23. Nathuram Godse's statement at the trial court, 8 November 1948, p. 14.
24. Court order in Bombay High Court case: *Gajanan Vishwanath Ketkar vs The State*, 21 July 1965, https://indiankanoon.org/doc/383735/.
25. Ibid.
26. Ibid.
27. Sushila Nayar's deposition, Kapur Commission Report, p. 119.
28. JL Kapur Commission Report, p. 132.
29. Manohan Malgonkar, op. cit., p. 63.
30. Manohan Malgonkar, op. cit., pp. 76-77.
31. Ibid.
32. Ibid.
33. Malgonkar, p. 250.
34. Besides Malgonkar's *The Men Who Killed Gandhi*, others that are significant include J.C. Jain, *The Murder of Mahatma Gandhi: Prelude and Aftermath* and K.L. Gauba, *Assassination of Mahatma Gandhi*. Besides these older books, Dhirendra Jha's *Gandhi's Assassin* is a standout work.

35. Malgonkar, p. 186.
36. Kanika Sharma, *Spectacular Justice: Aesthetics and Power in the Gandhi Murder Trial*, https://eprints.soas.ac.uk/25458/1/sharma-spectacular-justice-aesthetics-power-in-the-gandhi-murder-trial.pdf. Accessed 18 March 2023.
37. G.D. Khosla, *The Murder of the Mahatma and Other Cases from a Judge's Note-book*, Chatto & Windus, London, 1963, p. 274.
38. Kanika Sharma, ibid.
39. Once unwisely proscribed the government, which only fuelled interest in it, Godse November 1948 defence statement is now available on numerous sites online and also several publications.
40. Kanika Sharma, op. cit.
41. Dhirendra Jha—his opinion that it was drafted by Savarkar.
42. Justice GD Khosla, *The Murder of the Mahatma*, originally published by University of Michigan (1963) and Jaico Publishing House (1965), p. 15. Also available online at https://www.mkgandhi.org/ebks/the-murder-of-the-mahatma.pdf.
43. Ibid, p. 18.
44. Ed. Rudrangshu Mukherjee, *The Great Speeches of Modern India*, Random House India, 2007.
45. AK Bhattacharya, *Business Standard*, 14 June 2013, http://www.business-standard.com/article/beyond-business/and-godse-may-not-have-been-convicted-107083101077_1.html.
46. Godse's statement.

INDEX

B

C

N

S